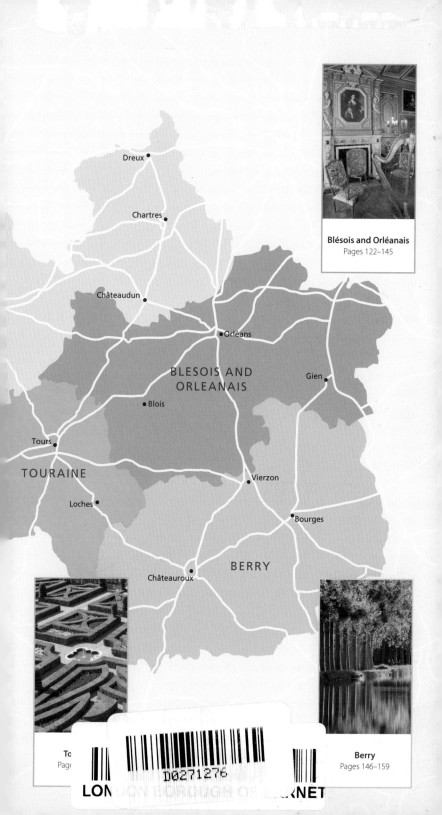

Dreux

Chartres

Châteaudun

Orléans

**BLESOIS AND ORLEANAIS**

Gien

Blois

Tours

**TOURAINE**

Vierzon

Loches

Bourges

**BERRY**

Châteauroux

**Blésois and Orléanais**
Pages 122–145

To
Page

**Berry**
Pages 146–159

EYEWITNESS TRAVEL

# LOIRE VALLEY

EYEWITNESS TRAVEL

# LOIRE VALLEY

Main Contributor **Jack Tresidder**

**DK**

LONDON, NEW YORK,
MELBOURNE, MUNICH AND DELHI
www.dk.com

**Produced by** Duncan Baird Publishers
London, England

**Project Editor** Stephanie Driver
**Editor** Slaney Begley
**Editorial Assistant** Joanne Levêque
**Designers** Paul Calver, Jill Mumford
**Design Assistant** Christine Keilty

**Photographers**
John Heseltine, Paul Kenward, Kim Sayer

**Illustrators**
Joanna Cameron, Roger Hutchins, Robbie Polley,
Pat Thorne, John Woodcock

Printed and bound in China

15 16 17 18 10 9 8 7 6 5 4 3 2 1

First published in Great Britain in 1996 by Dorling Kindersley Limited
80 Strand, London WC2R 0RL

**Reprinted with revisions 1997 (twice), 1999, 2000,
2001, 2003, 2004, 2007, 2010, 2013, 2015**

Copyright 1996, 2015 © Dorling Kindersley Limited, London
A Penguin Random House Company

All rights reserved. Without limiting the rights under copyright reserved above,
no part of this publication may be reproduced, stored in or introduced into
a retrieval system, or transmitted, in any form, or by any means (electronic,
mechanical, photocopying, recording or otherwise), without the prior written
permission of both the copyright owner and the above publisher of this book.

A CIP catalogue record for this book is available from the British Library.

ISBN 978-1-4093-7159-5

Floors are referred to throughout in accordance with European usage;
ie the "first floor" is the floor above ground level.

MIX
Paper from
responsible sources
FSC™ C018179
www.fsc.org

**The information in this DK Eyewitness Travel Guide is checked regularly.**
Every effort has been made to ensure that this book is as up-to-date as possible
at the time of going to press. Some details, however, such as telephone numbers,
opening hours, prices, gallery hanging arrangements and travel information are
liable to change. The publishers cannot accept responsibility for any consequences
arising from the use of this book, nor for any material on third party websites, and
cannot guarantee that any website address in this book will be a suitable source of
travel information. We value the views and suggestions of our readers very highly.
Please write to: Publisher, DK Eyewitness Travel Guides, Dorling Kindersley,
80 Strand, London, WC2R 0RL, UK, or email: travelguides@dk.com.

Front cover main image: Chateau Chambord, Loire Valley, France

◀ Aerial view over the River Loire at Amboise

# Contents

Joan of Arc

# Introducing the Loire Valley

A miniature from *Les Très Riches Heures
du Duc de Berry*

*The Entombment of Our Lord*, one of several groups of stone carvings in the church of the Abbaye de Solesmes, in the Sarthe region

North Rose Window, Chartres Cathedral

Art Nouveau decor in the dining room of the brasserie La Cigale, in Nantes

The small town of Montrichard, with the remains of its château

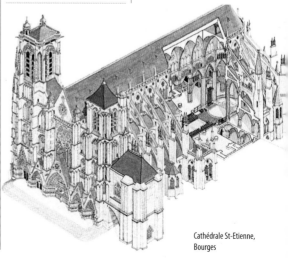

Cathédrale St-Etienne, Bourges

# HOW TO USE THIS GUIDE

This guide will help you get the most from your stay in the Loire Valley. It provides both expert recommendations and detailed practical information. *Introducing the Loire Valley* maps the region and sets it in its historical and cultural context. *The Loire Valley Area by Area* describes the important sights, with maps, photographs and illustrations. Suggestions for food, drink, accommodation, shopping and activities are in *Travellers' Needs*, and the *Survival Guide* has tips on everything from the French telephone system to getting to the Loire and travelling around the region.

## The Loire Valley Area by Area

In this guide, the Loire Valley has been divided into six regions, each of which has its own chapter. A map of these regions can be found inside the front cover of the book. The most interesting places to visit in each region have been numbered and plotted on a Regional Map.

**Each area** of the Loire Valley can be quickly identified by its colour coding.

**1 Introduction**
The landscape, history and character of each region is described here, showing how the area has developed over the centuries and what it has to offer the visitor today.

**A locator map** shows the region in relation to the whole of the Loire Valley.

### Exploring Touraine

**Getting Around**

**2 Regional Map**
This gives an illustrated overview of the whole region. All the sights are numbered, and there are also useful tips on getting around by car and public transport.

**Features and story boxes** highlight special or unique aspects of a particular sight.

**3 Detailed Information on each Sight**
All the important towns and other places to visit are described individually. They are listed in order, following the numbering on the Regional Map. Within each town or city, there is detailed information on important buildings and other major sights.

## 4 Major Towns

An introduction covers the history, character and geography of the town. The main sights are described individually and plotted on a Town Map.

**A Visitors' Checklist** gives contact points for tourist and transport information, plus details of market days and local festival dates.

**The Town Map** shows all major through-roads as well as minor streets of interest to visitors. All the sights are plotted, along with the bus and train stations, parking, tourist offices and churches.

## 5 Street-by-Street Map

Towns or districts of special interest to visitors are shown in detailed 3D, with photographs of the most important sights, giving a bird's-eye view of the area.

**A suggested route** for a walk covers the most interesting streets in the area.

**For all the top sights**, a Visitors' Checklist provides the practical information you will need to plan your visit.

## 6 Top Sights

These are given two or more pages. Important buildings are dissected to reveal their interiors.

**Stars** indicate the works of art or features that no visitor should miss.

# INTRODUCING THE LOIRE VALLEY

# DISCOVERING THE LOIRE VALLEY

These three itineraries taking in the Loire Valley's chief attractions have been designed to help you make the most of your time in the region. The Loire is known for its great châteaux, which were built here in the days when kings and dukes preferred this beautiful valley to Paris. These are covered in a week-long itinerary, beginning at the world-famous Chambord and ending with the wonderful châteaux near the coast that few visitors see. The Loire's fine wines are another big draw. These feature on the one-week tour down the river from Bourges to Nantes through the best AOC regions, combining some of the most important historical and artistic sites with wine tasting. Finally, there is a two-week tour of all the major sights, beginning in Nantes and ending near Tours. Pick a tour or combine elements of one or more of the routes to discover the most compelling sights in the Loire Valley.

## Tour of the Châteaux

- Start the tour by comparing two of the grandest châteaux, Renaissance **Chambord** and Classical **Cheverny**.

- Experience the royal splendour of Charles I's **Château de Blois**

- Fall in love with **Chenonceau** and the magnificent Renaissance gardens of **Villandry**.

- Experience **Chinon** and the magical château that inspired the tale of Sleeping Beauty, **Ussé**.

- Discover **Montsoreau**, the picturesque setting for a Dumas novel.

- Recapture a great change in French civilization, from the rugged medieval castle of **Angers** to the Renaissance **Château du Plessis-Bourré**.

- Admire the art and sumptuous tapestries of **Serrant**; carry on to **Goulaine** and its unique butterfly park.

**Château de Chambord**
The distinctive skyline of the central keep of the Château de Chambord combines turrets, cupolas and spires to create a dizzying effect.

◄ *Saumur, by the Loire Valley* by George Clarkson Stanfield

**Sancerre vineyards**
Many wineries in the hilly countryside around Sancerre, in Berry, open their doors to visitors for vineyard tours and tastings.

## A Wine and History Tour

- Explore the medieval alleys and the glorious cathedral of **Bourges**, then take a wine and cheese tour around **Sancerre**.

- Combine sampling the great wines of the **Touraine** with a visit to the spectacular royal **Château de Chambord**.

- Taste the delicate wines of **Saumur** before visiting fascinating **Chinon** and the historic **Abbaye de Fontevraud**.

- Go back in time at **Angers**, with its half-timbered houses and stout medieval castle; later, get to know the wines of **Quarts-de-Chaume** and **Savennières**.

- Discover the impressive museums and gardens at **Nantes**, then seek out the light, crisp wines of **Muscadet**.

Dreux

Chartres

Châteaudun

Orléans  *BLESOIS AND ORLEANAIS*

Gien    Briare-le-Canal

*OURAINE*  Blois  Chambord
Beauregard  Cheverny  La Sologne
urs  Amboise  Chaumont-sur-Loire
Montrichard  Sancerre
illandry  Chenonceau  St-Aignan-sur-Cher
ay-le-  Valençay  *BERRY*
eau  Reuilly  Bourges

Châteauroux

**Key**

— Tour of the Châteaux

— Two Weeks in the Loire Valley

— A Wine and History Tour

0 kilometres    50

0 miles    50

## Two Weeks in the Loire Valley

- Start with **Nantes** and its captivating Machines de l'Île; finish up on the beach at the **Guérandaise Peninsula**.

- Explore Angers and its rugged medieval castle; contrast it with the sophisticated **Château de Montgeoffroy**.

- Be charmed by the mellow old town of **Saumur**; visit the **Abbaye de Fontevraud** and take the **Troglodyte Tour** of the cave dwellings.

- Immerse yourself in the bustling street life of **Tours**, visit the great Romanesque cathedral and explore its museums.

- Devote a morning to the most exquisite of châteaux, **Chenonceau**, then visit nearby **Amboise**, once the home of Leonardo da Vinci.

- Walk the maze and admire the stunning stained glass and sculpture in **Chartres** cathedral.

- Spend an afternoon touring the pretty countryside and sleepy canals around **Gien** and **Briare-le-Canal**.

- Enjoy a delectable wine and cheese tour around **Sancerre** complete your day in **Bourges**, a city renowned for its fantastic art and culture.

- Spend a relaxing day along the River Cher for a swim or a boat ride at the charming villages of **Montrichard** and **St-Aignan**.

## Tour of the Châteaux

- **Airports** Arrive at Tours, return from Nantes-Atlantique.
- **Transport** A car is essential.

### Day 1: Chambord and Cheverny

Just an hour's drive from Tours is the grandest of all the Loire châteaux, **Chambord** (pp136–9). This graceful masterpiece of Renaissance architecture has a famous staircase that was supposedly designed by Leonardo da Vinci. Follow up with a tour of the nearby **Château de Cheverny** (p134), an imposing, richly furnished Classical palace that perfectly captures the spirit of the age of Louis XIII. Overnight in Blois.

### Day 2: Blois and its Château

The historic city of **Blois** (pp128–9) has witnessed many important events, ranging from the Hundred Years' War to the Wars of Religion. Start with a visit to its **Château Royal** (pp130–31), where three kings held court. Don't miss the famous staircase of François I and Catherine de Médici's room, full of secret cabinets. In the afternoon, visit the **Château de Beauregard** (pp134–5).

### Day 3: Chaumont, Chenonceau and Villandry

On the way west towards Tours, stop at the **Château de Chaumont** (p132), a

The delightful gardens of the Château d'Angers

Renaissance fantasy and once the home of Catherine de Médici. Next, head on to charming **Chenonceau** (pp110–13), perhaps the most delightful of the Loire châteaux, with its long wing extending across the River Cher. Inside, it is brimming with impressive art and fine furnishings. Finish the day just outside Tours with a visit to the **Château de Villandry** (pp98–9) and its Renaissance gardens. Spend the night in **Tours** (pp116–21).

### Day 4: Azay-le-Rideau, Chinon and Ussé

Continue westwards from Tours; the first stop is another turreted Renaissance fancy, the **Château d'Azay-le-Rideau** (pp100–1). From there, head for the **Château d'Ussé** (p105), a vision in stone that is said to have inspired the tale of Sleeping Beauty. Finally, end the day in **Chinon** (pp102–4),

an enchanting town with a château of its own behind stout medieval walls.

### Day 5: Montsoreau and Montgeoffroy

On the way to Angers, stop at the **Château de Montsoreau** (p89), the setting for the Alexandre Dumas novel La dame de Monsoreau. Next, visit the nearby **Abbaye de Fontevraud** (pp90–91), one of the Loire's great historic sites. Cross the river and head for the stately, Classical **Château de Montgeoffroy** (p75) before continuing on to **Angers** (pp76–7).

### Day 6: Angers and the Angevin Châteaux

Start the morning with a tour of the **Château d'Angers** (pp78–81), where medieval walls conceal charming gardens, courtyards and magnificent tapestries. Other fine châteaux in the Angers hinterlands include **Plessis-Bourré** (p74), with its lavish furnishings and mysterious alchemical paintings, and **Brissac** (p82), the tallest château in France.

### Day 7: Serrant and Goulaine

From Angers, follow the Loire to the moated **Château de Serrant** (p73), gorgeously appointed with French Classical decoration and furnishings. Just before Nantes, stop at the **Château de Goulaine** (p193), with its beautiful surroundings, grand salons and a glasshouse full of tropical butterflies.

View over the town of Chinon, with the River Vienne in the background

## A Wine and History Tour

- **Airports** Arrive at Tours, depart from Nantes-Atlantique.
- **Transport** A car is essential.

### Day 1: Bourges and Sancerre

Just over 90 minutes from Tours, travel to **Bourges** (pp154–7), for a visit to the classic High Gothic cathedral and the sumptuous Renaissance Palais Jacques-Coeur. In the afternoon, head eastwards for a **Wine and Cheese Tour** (p159). Learn about the wines at the Maison des Sancerre in **Sancerre** (p158) or at **Verdigny**'s Musée de la Vigne et du Vin (p159), then tour the vineyards and visit a traditional goat's cheese maker in Ménétréol-sous-Sancerre. Finish the day back at Bourges.

### Day 2: Bourges to Blois

Head towards the Blésois, through the vineyards of Reuilly, Valençay and Cheverny. Pay a visit to the **Château de Chambord** (pp136–9), the most spectacular of all the Loire châteaux. Later, there are opportunities for more wine touring in the Touraine around Blois, and a visit to another château, the stately **Cheverny** (p134).

### Day 3: Blois and Chenonceau

Spend the morning touring the lively streets of **Blois** (pp128–9), including a visit to the **Château Royal** (pp130–31), a treasure-trove of 15th- to 18th-century French architecture and art. In the afternoon, drive out to see the beautiful **Château de Chenonceau** (pp110–13), perched upon the River Cher, and sample sparkling Vouvray and other varieties of the Touraine along the way.

### Day 4: Tours, Touraine Wines and Châteaux

Start the day in **Tours** (pp116–21). Visit the Cathédrale St-Gatien, see the Renaissance paintings (and stuffed elephant) in the Musée des Beaux-Arts, and take a boat ride on the Loire.

Vineyards outside the walls of the majestic Château de Blois

After lunch, head out to the striking **Château d'Azay-le-Rideau** (pp100–1) and visit the enchanting medieval gardens of the **Château de Villandry** (pp98–9).

### Day 5: Medieval Heritage and Saumur Wines

Visit the pretty riverside town of **Chinon** (pp102–4) and its vineyards. Stop for a tour of the historic **Abbaye de Fontevraud** (pp90–91), where Eleanor of Aquitaine and Richard the Lionheart are buried. After lunch, explore **Saumur** (pp84–7) and the lush vineyards that surround it. While in this area, take the **Troglodyte Tour** (pp88–9) of fascinating cave dwellings.

### Day 6: Angers and Anjou Wines

Head towards Angers through the heartland of the wines of Anjou (Anjou, Quarts-de-Chaume and Savennières, among others). Tour **Angers** (pp76–81) and its famous château, ruggedly medieval from the outside but gracious and sophisticated within. Take the scenic **Corniche Angevine** (p72) westwards from Angers, and continue on to Nantes.

### Day 7: Nantes and Muscadet

One of France's most modern and bustling cities, **Nantes** (pp194–7) is home to a number of great museums: for fine arts, visit the **Musée Dobrée** (p195) and the **Musée des Beaux-Arts** (p196); and for something a little different, discover the museum dedicated to local writer Jules Verne (p197). Don't miss **Les Machines de l'Ile** (p197), where artist-engineers create incredible, handcrafted rides and installations. Later, tour the wine area of Muscadet, south and east of the city.

Visitors taking a ride on a mechanical elephant at Les Machines de l'Ile, Nantes

## Two Weeks in the Loire Valley

- **Airports** Arrive at Nantes-Atlantique, depart from Tours.
- **Transport** A car is essential.

### Day 1: Nantes

Spend the morning wandering the streets of **Nantes** *(pp194–7)*. This lively city was the ancient capital of the Dukes of Brittany. Its historic centre includes a Flamboyant Gothic **cathedral** *(p196)* and the moated **Château des Ducs de Bretagne** *(p196)*, now a museum of Breton history. Devote the afternoon to the giant, magical mechanical creatures and rides at **Les Machines de l'Île** *(p197)* or to Nantes' fine museums, the **Musée des Beaux-Arts** *(p196)* and the **Musée Jules Verne** *(p197)*.

---

**To extend your trip…**

Spend a day on the coast, relaxing on a sandy beach – either on the laid-back **Ile de Noirmoutier** *(pp184–5)* or at the busy resort of La Baule on the **Guérandaise Peninsula** *(p184)*. Or head south to take a boat trip through the waterways of the **Marais Poitevin** *(pp186–9)*.

---

### Day 2: Up the Loire to Angers

From Nantes, head inland for a long scenic drive, stopping to visit idyllic villages such as **St-Florent-le-Vieil** *(pp72–3)*. The highlight of the journey is the **Corniche Angevine** *(p72)*, which offers spectacular views over the Loire. Stay overnight in Angers.

### Day 3: Angers and Montgeoffroy

Start the day by exploring **Angers** *(pp76–7)*, a town of timber-framed medieval houses and lovely parks. Walk the old streets around the cathedral, and set aside a couple of hours for the **Château d'Angers** *(pp78–81)*, with its Renaissance courtyards, splendid views over the city, and the remarkable 14th-century Apocalypse Tapestries. In the afternoon, take a drive out to the imposing, Classical **Château de Montgeoffroy** *(p75)*, one of the few to have retained all of its original 18th-century furnishings.

### Day 4: Saumur and the Abbaye de Fontevraud

Leave Angers and head up the Loire, through **Gennes** *(pp82–3)* and **Cunault** *(p83)*, to the picturesque town of **Saumur** *(pp84–7)*. Tour its sights and museums (including one devoted to mushrooms), then continue on to the **Abbaye de Fontevraud** *(pp90–91)*, where Richard the Lionheart and 14 other notables from England's Plantagenet dynasty are buried. Afterwards, drive the fascinating **Troglodyte Tour** *(pp88–9)* of cave dwellings. Overnight in Fontevraud.

### Day 5: Chinon and the Touraine Châteaux

Three exquisite Renaissance châteaux provide this day's attractions. From Fontevraud,

Stained-glass windows in the Chapelle St-Hubert, in the Château d'Amboise

continue eastwards to the charming historic town of **Chinon** *(pp102–4)*, one of the most important in medieval France and the birthplace of the great satirical writer Rabelais. Back on the Loire, the next stop is the fairy-tale **Château d'Ussé** *(p105)*, followed by the beautiful **Château d'Azay-le-Rideau** *(pp100–1)*. Finally, there's the **Château de Villandry** *(pp98–9)*, with its unique Renaissance gardens and maze. Finish in Tours.

### Day 6: Tours

Spend the day in **Tours** *(pp116–21)*, the Loire Valley's major city. Enjoy the lively atmosphere of this university town: explore its medieval streets, see the Gothic cathedral, visit the **Musée des Beaux-Arts** *(p118)* and the master artisan works in the **Musée du Compagnonnage** *(p121)*.

The beautifully manicured gardens of the Château de Villandry

For practical information on travelling around the Loire Valley, see pp242–7

### Day 7: Chenonceau and Amboise

Continue eastwards from Tours. **Chenonceau** *(pp110–13)* is, for many, the perfect Loire château, with its wing spanning the river and its lovely gardens. From there, turn northwards, passing the **Pagode de Chanteloup** *(p115)*, an unusual 18th-century folly, before reaching **Amboise** *(pp114–15)*, with its timber housing and the château where King François I entertained his friend Leonardo da Vinci during the last years of his life.

### Day 8: Chartres

Head north for **Chartres** *(p175)*, maybe stopping at the pretty village of **Châteaudun** *(p174)* to visit its handsome Renaissance château. Exploring the **Cathédrale Notre-Dame** *(pp176–9)*, one of the world's greatest buildings, can fill most of a day. Don't miss the portals and other sculptures, the original stained-glass windows and the enigmatic maze built into the floor. For more fine art , head to Chartres' Musée des Beaux-Arts; to see stained glass, visit the Centre International du Vitrail.

### Day 9: Orléans and its Region

Drive south to **Orléans** *(pp142–3)*, a city rich in history where you can visit another great Gothic cathedral, excellent museums and the house where Joan of Arc lived. Devote the afternoon to touring the villages of the Orléanais south of the city: lovely **Gien** *(pp144–5)*, with its château on the Loire, and **Briare-le-Canal** *(p145)*, where you can take a boat ride on Europe's longest bridge-canal. Finish the day in Sancerre.

### Day 10: Wine, Cheese and Bourges

Start your day in **Sancerre** *(p158)* with a tour of the vineyards that produce its celebrated wines, passing through the sleepy villages of Chavignol and Ménétréol-sous-Sancerre, where the famous goat's cheeses are made. End up in **Bourges** *(pp154–7)*, one of France's premier art cities. It is home to one of the greatest

Crossing Gustave Eiffel's bridge-canal across the River Loire at Briare-le-Canal

Gothic cathedrals; its historic monuments house three important museums; and the Palais Jacques-Coeur provides a remarkable insight on late medieval life and economy.

### Day 11: Valençay and the Sologne

Head westwards to the **Château de Valençay** *(p150)*, a little-known palace that once belonged to Napoléon's brilliant minister Talleyrand. For car enthusiasts there are numerous vintage models in the Musée de l'Automobile nearby. To the north lies the **Sologne** *(p145)*, an unspoiled region of forests and small lakes. The Musée de Sologne in Romorantin-Lanthenay provides a great introduction to the area's attractions and wildlife and is a good place to spend the night.

### Day 12: Grand Châteaux and Gardens

Between St-Aignan and Blois lie some of the greatest of the

Period garments and art in a dressing room at the Château de Cheverny

Loire châteaux. First up is **Cheverny** *(p134)*, one of the first in the French Classical style, and housing an impressive collection of art. Next comes **Chambord** *(pp136–9)*, home of kings and the most opulent of them all. Finally, if there is time, tour the richly appointed **Château de Beauregard** *(pp134–5)*. Spend the night in Blois.

### Day 13: Blois and its Royal Château

Spend a day getting to know **Blois** *(pp128–9)*, an amiable town of old, winding streets, then head to the **Château Royal** *(pp130–31)*, scene of many important events in French history. It contains an impressive ensemble of Renaissance sculpture and architecture, and the scheming Catherine de Médicis' room full of secret compartments. In the afternoon there's another spectacular château to visit, **Chaumont** *(p132)*, just down the Loire.

### Day 14: Touring along the Cher

On the final day, relax along a delightful stretch of the River Cher, with opportunities for swimming and boating at **St-Aignan-sur-Cher** *(p133)*; just outside St-Aignan is one of France's biggest zoos, the Beauval Zoological Park. Other sights worth seeing are the Gallo-Roman relics at **Thésée** *(p133)* and charming villages such as **Montrichard** *(pp132–3)*. It's an hour's drive from here to Tours.

# Putting the Loire on the Map

The Loire Valley lies in central France, bordered by the regions of Brittany, Normandy and the Ile de France to the north, the Massif Central and Poitou to the south, Burgundy to the east and the Atlantic Ocean to the west. The river itself, the longest in France, flows for 1,020 km (634 miles) from its source in the Cévennes to the Atlantic Ocean just west of Nantes at St-Nazaire. The region covers an area of 71,228 sq km (27,500 sq miles) and has a population of about 6.1 million.

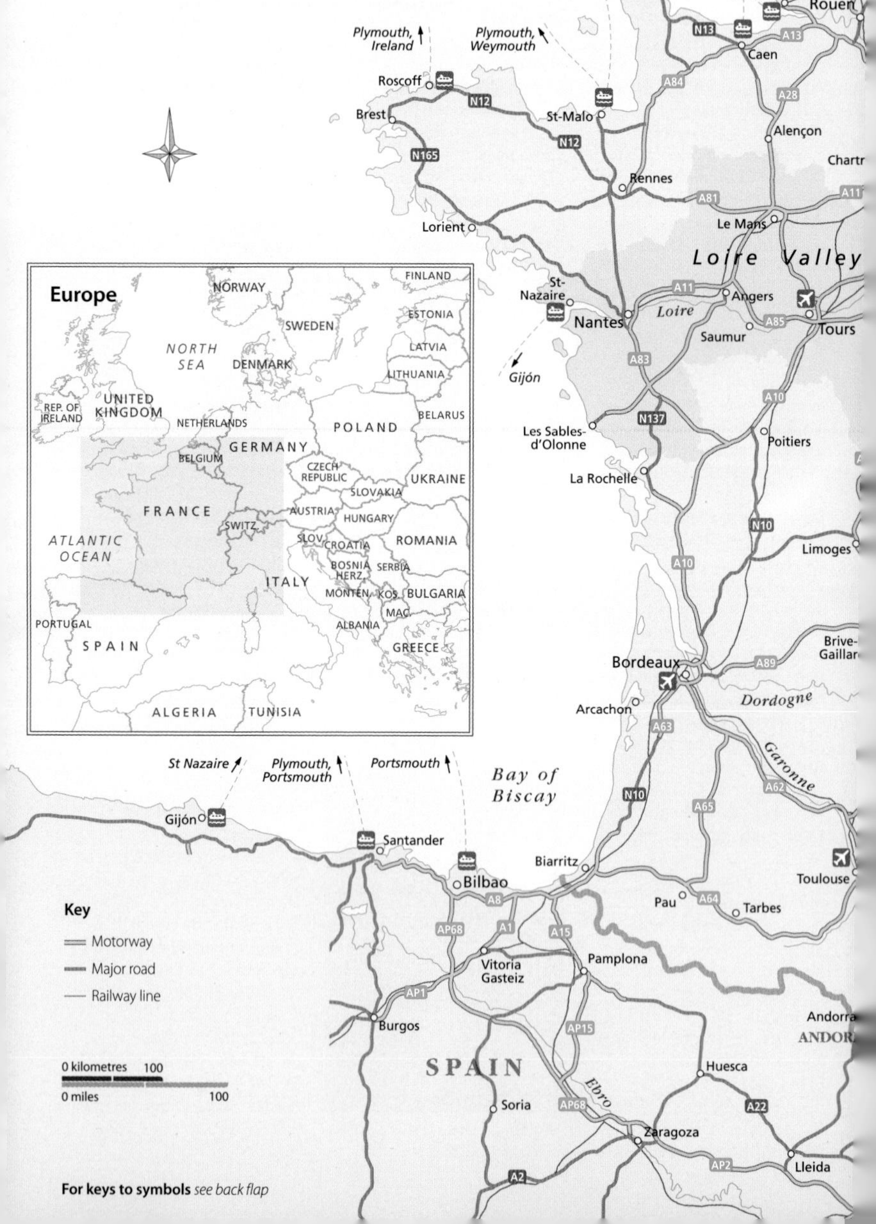

**Europe**

## Key

- ═══ Motorway
- ▬▬ Major road
- ── Railway line

0 kilometres 100
0 miles 100

**For keys to symbols** *see back flap*

# A PORTRAIT OF THE LOIRE VALLEY

The Loire Valley, world-famous for its beautiful châteaux, has long been described as exemplifying *la douceur de vivre*: it combines a leisurely pace of life, a mild climate, mellow wines and the gentle ways of its inhabitants. The overall impression conveyed by the region is one of an unostentatious taste for the good things in life.

What the world refers to as the Loire Valley is actually a conglomerate of 11 *départements*: Cher, Eure-et-Loir, Indre, Indre-et-Loire, Loir-et-Cher, Loire-Atlantique, Loiret, Maine-et-Loire, Mayenne, Sarthe and Vendée. In this central region of France, the people have neither the brisk, sometimes brusque, demeanour of their northern counterparts, nor the excitable nature of the southern provinces. They get on peacefully with their lives, benefiting from the prosperity generated not only by the region's centuries-old popularity with French and foreign visitors alike, but also by a fertile soil and a favourable climate, which rarely succumbs to extremes of heat or cold.

Outside of the main towns, the way of life remains in good part anchored to the traditional values of *la France profonde*, the country's conservative heartland – seeking to perpetuate a way of life that has proved its worth over the centuries. This is particularly true of the easternmost part of the region, near Bourges, where several communities can claim the honour of being "the geographical centre of France". It should come as no surprise to discover that a number of folk traditions, including witchcraft, are still recalled in some of these timeless villages, such as Bué, which holds a popular witches' festival, the Foire aux Sorcières, in August.

The bridge across the Loire at Blois, one of several historic bridges in the region

◄ The picturesque village of Chavignol, a hamlet of Sancerre, set deep in a valley and surrounded by vineyards

Folk dancers in costume at the Château de Blois

*champignons de Paris* (Paris mushrooms), grown in quarries near Saumur.

Although some local wines are reputed not to travel well, many of them do so very successfully, not only in France but also abroad, adding to the region's prosperity. In terms of the volume of production, the region ranks third in France, but the quality and popularity of Loire wines are both increasing. Bourgueil, Chinon, Muscadet, Sancerre, Saumur and Vouvray count among the best known, but there are many more good wines available.

## Local Strengths

The opportunity to stay in a private château is one of the many treats for visitors to the Loire Valley, where hospitality is a serious business. Even in Orléans, whose proximity to Paris has led to its reputation as a dormitory town, you can be assured of a warm welcome in hotels and restaurants. And throughout the towns and villages of Touraine and Anjou, conviviality is apparent. The many fairs, fêtes and festivals devoted to local wines and produce – garlic, apples, melons or even chitterling sausages – bear witness to the large part, even by French standards, that food and drink play in the social life of these old provinces.

Food and drink also play a major role in the region's economy: a reasonable percentage of the local population is involved in agriculture or the food industry in some way. Many a *primeur* (early fruit or vegetable) in the markets and restaurants of Paris has been transported from the fertile fields and orchards beside the Loire, and the region's melons and asparagus are sold all over the country. So are the button mushrooms, known as

Just as once the nobility of France established their châteaux and stately homes in the area, wealthy Parisians have flocked to the Loire Valley to buy *résidences secondaires*. The influx has swollen with the advent of the TGV rail service, which takes less than an hour to reach the region from Paris.

Colourful summer display

## Recent Developments

Since the 1990s, many of the cities along the Loire Valley have undergone spectacular transformations. Tours has

The Loire at Amboise, dotted with sandbanks

A walk along a river bank at Rochefort-sur-Loire, one of many country pursuits to enjoy

several modern developments; its cultural conference centre was designed by architect Jean Nouvel. The town continues to attract large numbers of foreign students who come to learn what's considered the "purest" French in France. By "pure", the experts mean well-modulated speech devoid of any strong accent.

Orléans, also on the Loire, has magnificently restored its historic quarter near the river, and has redesigned its broad cobbled quays. The latter had served for decades as makeshift car parks; now, they're the preserve of pedestrians and cyclists.

Angers, downstream from Tours, has also been changing on a grand scale. A contemporary quarter has emerged on the west bank of the Maine river, set around a revived port and new cultural centre.

Nearing the Atlantic, Nantes was once a massive industrial port but, as ships grew, maritime trade shifted nearer the Loire's estuary. The industrial space has now been reclaimed by the city, notably on the Ile de Nantes, a large island in the Loire just south of the centre. Here, you can admire the magical Machines de l'Ile, extraordinary outsized models of possible inventions inspired by Jules Verne.

Chinon, for several years, humorously proclaimed itself the largest medieval building site in Europe, as it embarked on the rebuilding of the huge Plantagenet fort dominating the old town. Interesting finds, unearthed during building work, are displayed in the restored fort.

Many stops along the Loire have revived their once bustling river quays, and now offer boat trips along the river, a wonderful way to see the region's stunning scenery.

Another major development for tourists has been the creation of the 800 km (500 mile) cycle path, La Loire à Vélo. The stretch from Sully-sur-Loire in the east to Chalonnes-sur-Loire was listed as a UNESCO World Heritage Site in 2000.

**VINS DE PROPRIETE**

Dégustation

Vente

Sign offering wine tastings

Locally grown asparagus

# From Defence to Decoration

Over the centuries, châteaux in the Loire Valley gradually developed from feudal castles, designed purely as defensive fortresses, into graceful pleasure palaces. Once the introduction of firearms put an end to the sieges that medieval castles were built to withstand, comfort and elegance became key status symbols. Many defensive elements evolved into decorative features: watchtowers became fairy-tale turrets, moats served as reflecting pools and crenellations were transformed into ornamental friezes. During the Renaissance, Italian crafts-men added features such as galleries and formal gardens, and carved decoration became increasingly intricate.

Château d'Angers in 1550, before its towers were lowered

Slate and stone walls

Fortifications with pepper-pot towers removed

**Angers** *(see pp76–81)* was built between 1228 and 1240 as a mighty clifftop fortress, towering over the River Maine. Along its curtain wall were spaced 17 massive round towers. These would originally have been 40 m (131 ft) high before their pepper-pot towers were removed in the 16th century.

Slate roof

Postern

**Ainay-le-Vieil** *(see p152)*, dating from the 12th century, contrasts two styles. An octagonal walled fortress, with nine massive towers topped by pepper-pot turrets and lit by arrow slits, was entered through a huge medieval postern gate across a drawbridge that crossed the moat. Inside, however, there is a charming, early 16th-century Renaissance home.

Ainay-le-Vieil's delightful living quarters, hidden inside an octagonal fortress

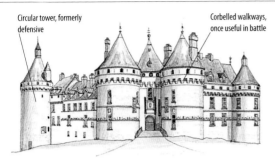

Circular tower, formerly defensive

Corbelled walkways, once useful in battle

**Chaumont** *(see p132)* stands on the site of a 12th-century fortress, destroyed in 1465 by Louis XI to punish its owners for disloyalty. The château was rebuilt from 1498 to 1510 in the Renaissance style. Although it has a defensive appearance, with circular towers, corbelled walkways and a gatehouse, these features have been lightened with Renaissance decoration.

**Chaumont's walls** are carved with the crossed Cs of Charles II d'Amboise, whose family rebuilt the château.

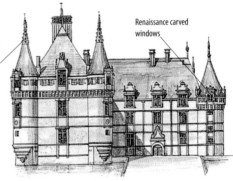

Decorated turret

Renaissance carved windows

Decoration on the north façade of Azay-le-Rideau

**Azay-le-Rideau** *(see pp100–101)*, its elegant turrets reflected in a peaceful lake, was built from 1518 to 1527 and is considered one of the best-designed Renaissance châteaux. Its main staircase, set behind an intricately decorated façade with three storeys of twin bays, is very striking.

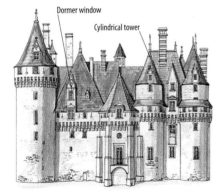

Dormer window

Cylindrical tower

**Ussé** *(see p105)* was built in 1462 as a battlemented fortress. Later, the walls overlooking the main courtyard were modified during the Renaissance, with dormer windows and pilasters. In the 17th century the north wing was replaced by terraced gardens.

Château d'Ussé, once a fortress, now an aristocratic château

# Inside the Châteaux

The typical Loire Valley château boasted several large, lavishly furnished reception rooms, adorned with luxurious tapestries and paintings and featuring decorative panelling and ceilings. The main rooms included the Grand Salon, often with an imposing fireplace, and an elegant dining room. The gallery was a focal point for host and guests to meet to discuss the events of the day and to admire the views over the grounds or the paintings displayed on the gallery walls. The châtelain's private rooms, and those reserved for honoured (particularly royal) guests, were grouped in a separate wing, while servants were housed in the attics.

**Apartments** in one wing were for private use.

**Grand Escalier** (Grand Staircase)

**Chairs** were often spindly – elegant but uncomfortable. The more comfortable models with armrests might be covered with precious tapestries, as with this one from Cheverny, upholstered in Aubusson.

**The Grand Salon**, mostly used for entertaining, had a majestic marble fireplace carved with the owner's coat of arms, emblem or intertwined initials.

**The Grand Escalier**, or *Escalier d'Honneur* (grand staircase), had richly carved balustrades and an elaborately decorated ceiling, such as this magnificent Renaissance staircase at Serrant *(see p73)*. The staircase led to the owner's private suites, as well as state guest bedrooms and rooms used on special occasions, such as the armoury.

Main entrance

**Galleries**, like this one at Beauregard *(see pp134–5)*, were where owners and guests met to converse or to be entertained. They were often hung with family and other portraits.

**State dining rooms**, for receiving important visitors, were as sumptuously furnished and decorated as the other main reception rooms. This one in Chaumont *(see p132)* features Renaissance furniture.

**Château rooms** were filled with costly tapestries, paintings and fine furniture, and attention was paid to detail. Decorative features, such as this French Limoges enamel plaque, or intricately carved wooden panelling were common. Even the tiles on stoves that heated the huge rooms were often painted.

**The Salle d'Armes**, or armoury, displayed suits of armour and weapons beside fine tapestries and furniture.

**The east wing** was reserved for important guests.

Dining Room

King's Bedroom

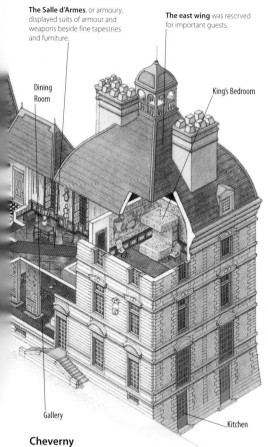

**The King's Bedroom** was kept permanently ready for a royal visit. Under the *droit de gîte* (right of lodging), château owners were bound to provide accommodation to the king in return for a building permit. This room, at Cheverny *(see p134)*, was used frequently.

Gallery

Kitchen

## Cheverny

*A dignified Classical building in white tufa, Cheverny (see p134) has scarcely been altered since it was built between 1620 and 1634. The central section, containing the staircase, is flanked by two symmetrical wings, each consisting of a steep-roofed section and a much larger pavilion with a domed roof. The interior is decorated in 17th-century style.*

**Kitchens** were in the cellars, or separately housed. Huge spits for roasting whole carcasses were worked by elaborate mechanisms. Though often dark, the kitchens gleamed with an array of copper pots and pans, like these at Montgeoffroy *(see p75)*.

# Churches and Abbeys

The Loire Valley has a fine array of medieval ecclesiastical architecture, ranging from tiny Romanesque village churches to major Gothic cathedrals like Chartres and Tours. In the early Middle Ages, the Romanesque style predominated, characterized by straightforward ground plans, round arches and relatively little decoration. By the 13th century, the rib vaulting and flying buttresses of Gothic architecture had emerged, enabling builders to create taller, lighter churches and cathedrals. The Late Gothic style in France, often referred to as Flamboyant Gothic, features window tracery with flowing lines licking upwards like flames.

**Locator Map**

① Romanesque architecture

⑨ Gothic architecture

## Romanesque Features

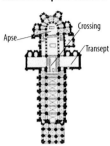

**The plan of St-Benoît-sur-Loire** is typical of Romanesque architecture, with its cross shape and rounded apse.

Apse, Crossing, Transept

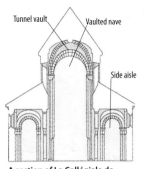

**A section of La Collégiale de St-Aignan-sur-Cher** shows Romanesque tunnel vaulting. The vaulted side aisles provide added support for the high nave.

Tunnel vault, Vaulted nave, Side aisle

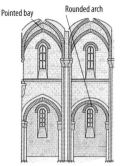

**The round arches of St-Aignan** are typically Romanesque, while the pointed nave bays predict the Gothic style.

Pointed bay, Rounded arch

## Gothic Features

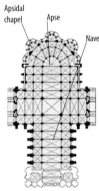

**The plan of Chartres Cathedral** shows its very wide nave, and its apse ringed with chapels.

Apsidal chapel, Apse, Nave

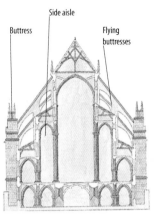

**A section of St-Etienne in Bourges** reveals its five divisions with two aisles on either side of the nave. The building also has five portals rather than the usual three.

Side aisle, Buttress, Flying buttresses

**Pointed arches** withstand greater stress and allow large windows, as in the nave at Bourges.

Pointed arch, Triforium

## Where to Find Romanesque Architecture

① St-Maurice, Angers *p76*
② L'Abbaye St-Vincent, Nieul-sur-l'Autise *pp186–7*
③ Notre-Dame, Cunault *p83*
④ L'Abbaye de Fontevraud *pp90–91*
⑤ St-Maurice, Chinon *p102*
⑥ La Collégiale, St-Aignan-sur-Cher *p133*
⑦ St-Eusice, Selles-sur-Cher *see below*
⑧ La Basilique de St-Benoît-sur-Loire *p144*

## Where to Find Gothic Architecture

⑨ St-Etienne, Bourges *pp156–7*
⑩ St-Louis, Blois *pp128–9*
⑪ St-Hubert, Amboise *p114*
⑫ St-Gatien, Tours *pp120–21*
⑬ La Trinité, Vendôme *pp126–7*
⑭ Notre-Dame, Chartres *pp176–9*
⑮ St-Julien, Le Mans *p170*
⑯ Asnières-sur-Vègre *p167*

## Terms Used in this Guide

**Basilica:** Early church with two aisles and nave lit from above by clerestory windows.

**Clerestory:** A row of windows illuminating the nave from above the aisle roof.

**Rose:** Circular window, often with stained glass.

**Buttress:** Mass of masonry built to support a wall.

**Flying buttress:** An arched support transmitting thrust of the weight downwards.

**Portal:** Monumental entrance to a building, often decorated.

**Tympanum:** Decorated space, often carved, over a door or window lintel.

**Vault:** Arched stone ceiling.

**Transepts:** Two wings of a cruciform church at right angles to the nave.

**Crossing:** Centre of cruciform church, where the transept crosses the nave.

**Lantern:** Turret with windows to illuminate interior, often with cupola (domed ceiling).

**Triforium:** Middle storey between arcades and the clerestory.

**Apse:** Termination of the church, often rounded.

**Ambulatory:** Aisle running round the east end.

**Arcade:** Set of arches and supporting columns.

**Rib vault:** Vault supported by projecting ribs of stone.

**Gargoyle:** Carved grotesque figure, often a water spout.

**Tracery:** Ornamental carved stone pattern within Gothic architecture.

**Flamboyant Gothic:** Style characterized by flame-like stone work.

**Capital:** Top of a column, usually carved.

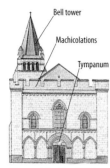
**The west façade of Notre-Dame at Cunault** is simply decorated. Its machicolations and lateral towers give it a fortified appearance.

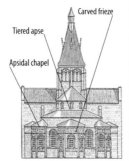
**The east end of St-Eusice in Selles-sur-Cher**, with its three apsidal chapels, is decorated with friezes of carved figures.

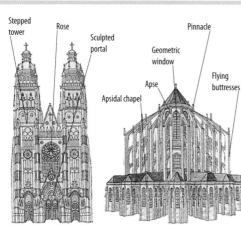
**The west façade of St-Gatien in Tours** has richly carved, Flamboyant Gothic portals.

**The east end of St-Julien cathedral, in Le Mans**, has a complex arrangement of paired flying buttresses, each topped by pinnacles.

# Writers and Artists of the Loire Valley

The valley of the River Loire is well known for its agricultural fertility, and it has also proved to be productive ground for literature, too. Over the centuries, internationally famous writers such as François Rabelais, the great lyrical poet Pierre de Ronsard and the novelists Honoré de Balzac and George Sand have lived close to the mighty river, often drawing inspiration from their native soil. Perhaps strangely, however, the pure light that so appeals to visitors to the region does not seem to have inspired as many of the country's greatest painters, although Claude Monet spent a fruitful period in the peaceful Creuse Valley.

Writer Marcel Proust, in a late 19th-century portrait by Jacques-Emile Blanche

## Writers

One of the earliest authors to write in the "vulgar", or native, French tongue was born in Meung-sur-Loire in the mid-13th century. Jean Chopinel, better known as Jean de Meung, produced the second part of the widely translated and influential *Roman de la rose*, a long, allegorical poem about courtly love. While the first half focuses delicately on two young lovers and their affair, Jean de Meung's sequel undermines the idealistic conventions of courtly love, taking a more cynical view of the world.

During the Hundred Years' War, a century and a half later, aristocratic poet Charles, Duc d'Orléans, was imprisoned by the English for 25 years. While in prison he was able to

Illumination from the *Roman de la rose*

develop his considerable poetic skills. On his return he made his court at Blois a key literary centre. He invited famous writers and poets, among them François Villon, a 15th-century poet as renowned for the skill of his writing as for his highly disreputable lifestyle. While he was in Blois, Villon won a poetry competition with his work, *"Je meurs de soif auprès de la fontaine"* ("I am Dying of Thirst by the Fountain").

François Rabelais, the racy 16th-century satirist and humanist, was born in 1483 near Chinon *(see pp102–4)* and educated at Angers. He became famous throughout Europe upon the publication of his *Pantagruel* (1532) and *Gargantua* (1535), huge, sprawling works full of bawdy humour and learned discourse in equal measure.

Pierre de Ronsard, born near Vendôme 30 years after Rabelais, was the leading French Renaissance poet, perhaps best known for his lyrical odes and sonnets to "Cassandre", "Hélène" and "Marie" (an Anjou peasant girl).

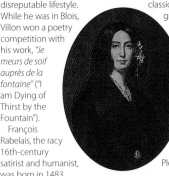

George Sand, the 19th-century novelist

Court poet to Charles IX and his sister Marguerite de Valois, he lived and died at St-Cosme Priory near Tours. Ronsard was also at the head of the Pléiade, a group of seven poets who were determined to revolutionize French poetry through the study of the classics. In the same group was Joachim du Bellay, an Anjou aristocrat and keen advocate of French literature. His *Defence and Illustration of the French Language* (1549) was a prose manifesto of the Pléiade doctrine. Another famous native of the Loire Valley spearheaded a 17th-century intellectual revolution. Mathematician and philosopher René Descartes, born in Touraine and educated at the Jesuit college in La Flèche *(see p171)*, developed a new method of philosophical inquiry involving the simultaneous study of all the sciences. Starting with the celebrated "I think, therefore I am", he developed the rationalist doctrine known as Cartesianism in his most famous work, the *Discourse on the Method*.

France's most prolific 19th-century novelist, Honoré de Balzac, often referred to his native Touraine as his favourite province. Tours, Saumur and the Indre Valley feature as settings for some of his best-known novels, all of which are keenly observant of 19th-century French mores. The work of Balzac's contemporary, George Sand (the masculine pen name of Aurore, Baroness Dudevant), is rooted in the landscapes of her native Berry, which also inspired Alain-Fournier's magical *Le grand meaulnes*, a romantic vision of his childhood in the region.

The hawthorn hedges and peaceful villages near Chartres provided the unforgettable setting for the early passages of Marcel Proust's impressive sequence of novels, *Remembrance of Things Past (see p174)*. At the mouth of the Loire, the city of Nantes saw the birth, in 1826, of the ever-popular Jules Verne *(see p197)*, whose pioneering works of science fiction have been enormously influential.

### Artists

Enchanting medieval wall paintings can be admired in a number of churches across the Loire Valley. In 1411 the three Limbourg brothers

Henri Rousseau, in a self-portrait that typifies his naive style

A miniature from *Les Très Riches Heures du Duc de Berry*

became court painters to the Duc de Berry in Bourges. He commissioned them to paint some 39 miniatures for *Les très riches heures du Duc de Berry*. This Book of Hours remains one of the finest achievements of the International Gothic style. Some of its intricate illustrations depict scenes from life in the Loire Valley.

Jehan Fouquet, born in Tours in about 1420, was officially appointed royal painter in 1474. His portraits include the famous image of the royal mistress Agnès Sorel *(see p108)* posing as the Virgin Mary.

A century after Fouquet's birth, François I persuaded the elderly Leonardo da Vinci to settle in the manor house of Cloux (now called Le Clos-Lucé, *see pp114–15)* near the royal château of Amboise. Aged 65, Leonardo was no longer actively painting, although he is known to have made some sketches of court life which have not survived. However, he was engaged in scientific investigations and inventions, the results of which can be seen in a museum in the basement of the château.

At about the time of Leonardo's death in 1519, François Clouet was born in Tours. He succeeded his father, Jean, as court painter

to François I and produced a string of truly outstanding portraits. His sitters included François I himself, Elizabeth of Austria and Mary, Queen of Scots. François Clouet's style, which was typical of the French Renaissance, was perpetuated by the artists and artisans in his workshop.

Anjou's most celebrated sculptor is David d'Angers, who was born in 1788. His works include busts and medallions of many of the major historical figures of his day, including a stirring memorial to the Marquis de Bonchamps, which can be found in the church at St-Florent-le-Vieil *(see pp72–3)*.

Exactly a century later, the Impressionist painter Claude Monet spent several weeks in the village of Fresselines in the Creuse Valley, painting the river as it passed through a narrow gorge *(see p151)*. One of these canvases, *Le pont de Vervit*, now hangs in the Musée Marmottan in Paris.

Henri Rousseau, the quintessential naive painter, was born in the town of Laval in 1844. Although he never left France, his best-known works are stylized depictions of lush jungles, home to all manner of wild animals. Part of the château in Laval has been converted into a Museum of Naive Art *(see p164)* in honour of the artist.

François Clouet's portrait of Mary, Queen of Scots

# Themed Tours of the Loire Valley

For those who wish to travel independently of tour companies, or who have a special interest in the region, self-guided themed tours provide an attractive alternative. Tourist offices produce information on routes visitors can travel in order to see the best sights on a given theme – including wine, churches, châteaux, historical buildings and beautiful botanical gardens and arboretums. Illustrated brochures and tourist maps describing each route, often in languages other than French, are available, and some of the routes are signposted along the way. Tourist office staff can assist in customizing a route for specific interests.

**A la Recherche des Plantagenêts** traces the lives of Henry Plantagenet, his wife, Eleanor of Aquitaine, and their sons *(see p54)*. The evidence of their remarkable lives, including this fortress in Loches, can be seen throughout the region.

**The Route Touristique du Vignoble** guides the traveller through some of the region's prettiest wine country, including the Coteaux de la Loire. Further information is available from the tourist offices in Angers, Nantes and Saumur.

**The Route de la Vallée des Rois** takes motorists to many former royal residences as well as to cathedrals and churches along the part of the Loire known as the Valley of the Kings. Information is available from tourist offices along the route.

**The Sentier Cyclable du Marais Poitevin** is a signposted cycle route which takes in the attractions of the south Vendée, including the Marais Poitevin, to give a selection of the varied sights in this area. The tourist office at La-Roche-sur-Yon provides details.

**The Route des Parcs et Jardins** takes visitors to Villandry and many other exquisite châteaux and manor house gardens, contemporary gardens, parks and arboretums in the region. Contact the tourist office in Tours for a brochure.

**The Route Jacques Cœur** leads motorists through some picturesque towns as well as to memorable châteaux, including the Château de Maupas and the Palais Jacques-Cœur in Bourges (see p155), the former home of the wealthy merchant who gives the tour its name. Some of the private châteaux along the route take paying guests (see pp204–5). The tourist office in Bourges provides details of the route.

| 0 kilometres | 50 |
| 0 miles | 50 |

**Key**

— Sentier Cyclable du Marais Poitevin

— Route des Parcs et Jardins

— A la Recherche des Plantagenêts

— Route François I en Val de Loire

— Route Jacques Cœur

— Route de la Vallée des Rois

— Route Touristique du Vignoble

**The Route François I en Val de Loire** explores the châteaux, such as Chambord. This magnificent château was originally constructed as a hunting lodge for François I (see p58), who held court in Blois and Chambord during the 16th century. Ask at Chambord tourist office for details.

# Walking in the Loire Valley

The best way to follow the "most sensual river in France", as Flaubert called the Loire, is on foot. The *Grande Randonnée 3* (GR 3) is one of the longest marked walks in France, accompanying the Loire from its source at Gerbier de Jonc to its mouth. There are many other walking routes throughout the region, some following beautiful rivers, others focusing on themes, for example, religious paths (one passes through a route to Santiago de Compostela, or there are tracks following in St Martin's footsteps – *see p34*). A Topo-Guide *(see p224)* is a useful companion for detailed information about your walk. The Fédération Française de la Randonnée Pédestre *(see p227)* offers more information on walking in the Loire Valley.

**Key**
— Recommended walk
— Grande Randonnée de Pays
— Grande Randonnée

**In the charming** Alpes Mancelles, on the edge of the Parc Régional Normandie-Maine, there is a variety of walks in the valleys of the Sarthe, the Mayenne and the Orne. *(IGN 1618 OT)*

**The Folies-Siffait**, hanging gardens close to Le Cellier, 15 km (9 miles) northeast of Nantes, offers a two-hour walk around a labyrinthine park. *(IGN 1323)*

0 kilometres 50

0 miles 50

**The Parc Naturel Régional de Brière** *(see p184)* is crisscrossed by paths that take walkers through the reeds where thousands of birds build their nests. *(IGN 83034)*

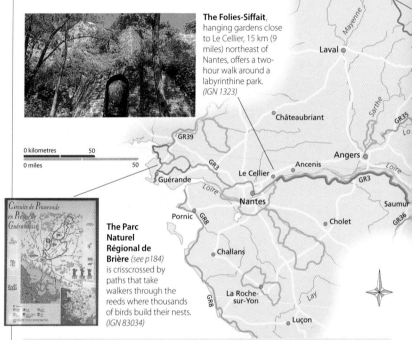

Laval

Châteaubriant

Angers

GR35
Lo

GR39

GR3

Le Cellier

Ancenis

Loire

GR3

Guérande

Loire

Saumur

Nantes

GR36

Pornic

GR8

Cholet

Challans

La Roche-sur-Yon

Lay

Luçon

GR8

Circuits de Promenade en Presqu'île Guérandaise

Mayenne

Sarthe

## Route Markers

All the walking routes are marked with symbols painted onto trees or rocks along the paths. The different colours of the symbols indicate which kind of route you are taking. A red and white mark denotes a *Grande Randonnée* (GR) route, yellow and red are used for a regional route *(Grande Randonnée de Pays)*, and local routes *(Promenade et Randonnée)* are marked in a single colour (usually yellow).

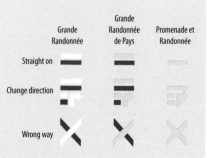

| | Grande Randonnée | Grande Randonnée de Pays | Promenade et Randonnée |
|---|---|---|---|
| Straight on | | | |
| Change direction | | | |
| Wrong way | | | |

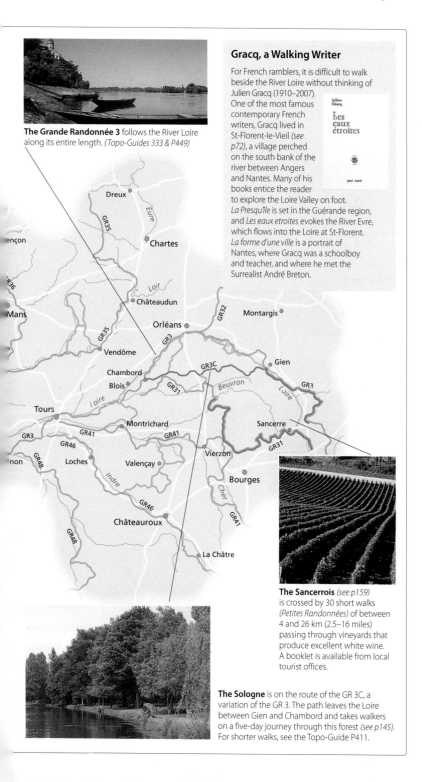

**The Grande Randonnée 3** follows the River Loire along its entire length. *(Topo-Guides 333 & P449)*

## Gracq, a Walking Writer

For French ramblers, it is difficult to walk beside the River Loire without thinking of Julien Gracq (1910–2007). One of the most famous contemporary French writers, Gracq lived in St-Florent-le-Vieil *(see p72)*, a village perched on the south bank of the river between Angers and Nantes. Many of his books entice the reader to explore the Loire Valley on foot. *La Presqu'île* is set in the Guérande region, and *Les eaux étroites* evokes the River Evre, which flows into the Loire at St-Florent. *La forme d'une ville* is a portrait of Nantes, where Gracq was a schoolboy and teacher, and where he met the Surrealist André Breton.

**The Sancerrois** *(see p159)* is crossed by 30 short walks *(Petites Randonnées)* of between 4 and 26 km (2.5–16 miles) passing through vineyards that produce excellent white wine. A booklet is available from local tourist offices.

**The Sologne** is on the route of the GR 3C, a variation of the GR 3. The path leaves the Loire between Gien and Chambord and takes walkers on a five-day journey through this forest *(see p145)*. For shorter walks, see the Topo-Guide P411.

# Winemaking and Vineyards

The importance of wine to life in the Loire Valley is immediately apparent. Fields of vines stretch along both banks of the river, and roadsides are lined with signs offering *dégustations*, or wine tastings *(see p220)*. Stretching 300 km (186 miles) from Nantes to Pouilly-sur-Loire, the Loire Valley is the third largest wine-producing area by volume in France and offers an unprecedented range of wine styles. The white Sancerres have an excellent reputation *(see p159)*, as do some of the rosé wines of Anjou, the sweet and sparkling Vouvrays, the full-bodied reds of Chinon and Bourgueil, and the dry *méthode champenoise* wines of Saumur. There are many more modest wines available, including Muscadet and its younger cousin Gros Plant, which are best served chilled.

Traditional vineyard cultivation

**The great sweet wine** of the Côteaux du Layon, Quarts de Chaume, is little known outside France.

**Muscadet** designated *sur lie* has greater flavour because of a special ageing process.

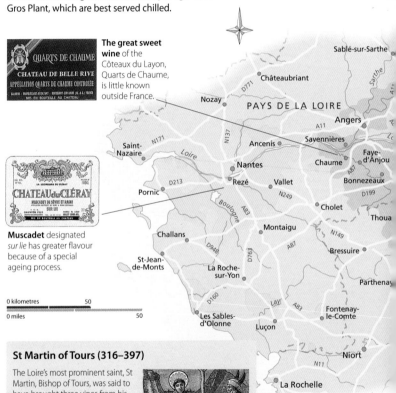

0 kilometres    50

0 miles    50

## Key

- Pays Nantais
- Anjou-Saumur
- Haut-Poitou
- Centre Loire Vineyards
- Touraine and Vallée du Loire

## St Martin of Tours (316–397)

The Loire's most prominent saint, St Martin, Bishop of Tours, was said to have brought three vines from his native Hungary and planted them in Touraine. But his donkey may have made a greater contribution when it stripped the leaves off vines near to where it had been tethered. Those vines later proved to be the most productive in the vineyard, and the now standard practice of pruning vines was born.

St Martin on his donkey

## Key Facts about Loire Wines

### Grape Varieties

The Muscadet grape makes simple, dry whites. The Sauvignon Blanc produces gooseberryish, flinty dry whites. Chenin Blanc is used for the dry and medium Anjou, Vouvrays, Savennières and Saumur, and the famous sweet whites, Vouvray, Quarts de Chaume and Bonnezeaux. Summery reds are made from the Gamay and the Cabernet Franc.

### Wine Touring and Festivals

Visiting the Loire Valley's vineyards is a very popular pursuit. The diversity of winemaking across the region is such that there are almost 70 *appellations d'orgine contrôlée (AOC)* wines, produced to strict standards in precisely laid-out territories. Routes and estates are generally well signposted. Tourist offices can supply details on local wineries open to

the public – quite a large number are in stunning underground caves or beside beautiful properties. In the major cities of Tours, Saumur, Angers and Nantes, the Maisons des Vins de Loire offer introductions to the whole range of regional wines, as well as more advanced themed tastings. Wine festivals are numerous throughout the year, and often very jolly, so look out for details on those at a local level.

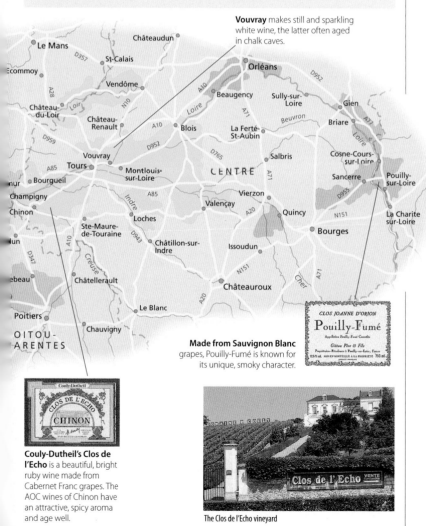

**Vouvray** makes still and sparkling white wine, the latter often aged in chalk caves.

**Made from Sauvignon Blanc** grapes, Pouilly-Fumé is known for its unique, smoky character.

**Couly-Dutheil's Clos de l'Echo** is a beautiful, bright ruby wine made from Cabernet Franc grapes. The AOC wines of Chinon have an attractive, spicy aroma and age well.

The Clos de l'Echo vineyard

# A VIEW OF THE RIVER LOIRE

A natural highway to the centre of France, the Loire was travelled from the earliest days. The remains of prehistoric canoes have been found along the river; later evidence shows that Celtic tribes and the Romans used the river extensively as a major trade route. In fact, until the development of the railway network during the 19th century, the river was a key transportation route. The growth of the French canal network from the 17th to 19th centuries, connecting the port of Nantes with Paris and the north, enhanced the Loire's importance. The River Loire can be unpredictable and sometimes dangerous, and it was one of the first rivers that man tried to control. There is evidence that embankments were being built as early as the 12th century – and work continues – but the river remains essentially wild and is still subject to floods, freezes, shifting sands and dangerous currents. Today, the river is no longer used for commerce, except by tour boats giving visitors a unique view of the surrounding landscape. This makes an exploration of the River Loire all the more pleasant.

See pages 38–9    See pages 40–41

**Sailing boats**, with their typical square sails, often travelled in groups of three or more.

**Steamers** would use powerful winches to dip their smokestacks, enabling them to pass under low bridges.

**Amboise's bridge** traverses the river and the Ile St-Jean.

**Château d'Amboise** is set on a promontory above the river, safe from possible flooding.

## Vue d'Amboise

*This painting by Justin Ouvrié, now kept in the vaults of the Musée de la Poste in Paris, was painted in 1847. The bustling river scene, which includes several types of vessel, gives an indication of the importance of the River Loire to life and trade in the region, before the railways came to dominate transportation later in the century.*

**Barges**, known in French as *chalands*, did not always have sails – sometimes they were rowed.

**Everyday objects** were often decorated with river scenes, such as this 19th-century plate from the Musée de la Marine de Loire in Châteauneuf-sur-Loire.

◄ View of the Château de Chinon, with the River Vienne in the foreground

# River View: St-Nazaire to Montsoreau

As the River Loire leaves Touraine and heads through Anjou and the Loire Atlantique, it widens and flows faster, as though rushing towards the Atlantic Ocean. Its waters are also swelled by many tributaries. Some flow alongside, creating a multitude of islands big and small; other tributaries flow north and south through the surrounding countryside. This land is rich in ancient monuments, including the Bagneux dolmen, the largest Neolithic construction of its kind, as well as fortresses built during the Middle Ages.

**St-Nazaire**
At the mouth of the River Loire, where it flows into the Atlantic Ocean, St-Nazaire *(see p194)* is renowned for ship-building. Its graceful bridge is the westernmost river crossing.

**Champtoceaux**
The village of Champtoceaux, on a cliff 80 m (260 ft) above the river, offers panoramic views. A private Renaissance château now occupies the lower part of the bluff, where a medieval citadel once stood.

**Nantes' Cathédrale**
St-Pierre et St-Paul is Gothic style.

**St-Nazaire** (map label)

St-Brévin-les-Pins

*Loire*

*Boulogne*

**LOIRE-ATLANTIQUE**

Nantes

Champtoce

Anc

*l'Erdre*

**Nantes**
Nantes was a prosperous port during the 18th and 19th centuries *(see pp 194–197),* the meeting point between the ocean and the inland river transportation channels.

```
0 kilometres        20
0 miles             20
```

**Péage Fortifié du Cul-du-Moulin**
This toll station was one of many constructed in the 13th century to collect revenue from passing vessels. It is one of the few still standing in France.

## The Bridges of the Loire

There have long been bridges across the River Loire – there was one at Orléans as early as AD 52, which was later destroyed by Julius Caesar's army. Now, with so many options for places to cross the river, it is difficult to imagine what it was like during the Middle Ages, when there were only five, or during the 15th century, when there were just 13. The bridges crossing the river today tell the story not only of the development of bridge building, but also of the region itself, its history and relationships.

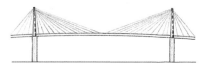

**St-Nazaire**
At 3,356 m (11,000 ft), St-Nazaire is one of the longest bridges in France. The central, suspended section is 404 m (1,300 ft) long. It opened for traffic in 1975. Before then, the estuary was crossed by ferry, and the nearest bridge was at Nantes.

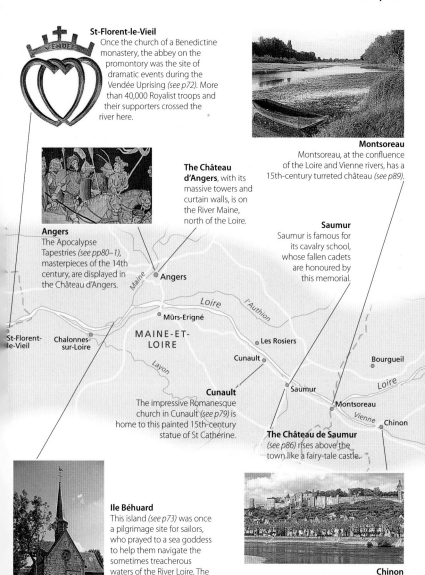

**St-Florent-le-Vieil**
Once the church of a Benedictine monastery, the abbey on the promontory was the site of dramatic events during the Vendée Uprising *(see p72)*. More than 40,000 Royalist troops and their supporters crossed the river here.

**Montsoreau**
Montsoreau, at the confluence of the Loire and Vienne rivers, has a 15th-century turreted château *(see p89)*.

**Angers**
The Apocalypse Tapestries *(see pp80–1)*, masterpieces of the 14th century, are displayed in the Château d'Angers.

**The Château d'Angers**, with its massive towers and curtain walls, is on the River Maine, north of the Loire.

**Saumur**
Saumur is famous for its cavalry school, whose fallen cadets are honoured by this memorial.

**Cunault**
The impressive Romanesque church in Cunault *(see p79)* is home to this painted 15th-century statue of St Catherine.

**The Château de Saumur**
*(see p86)* rises above the town like a fairy-tale castle.

**Ile Béhuard**
This island *(see p73)* was once a pilgrimage site for sailors, who prayed to a sea goddess to help them navigate the sometimes treacherous waters of the River Loire. The present church was built by Louis XI who had nearly drowned here.

**Chinon**
Above the River Vienne, Chinon *(see pp102–4)* was home to Henry Plantagenet in the 12th century.

**Ancenis**
The suspension bridge at Ancenis opened in 1953, replacing one destroyed in 1940. As the town is at the border of Brittany and Anjou, two coats of arms adorn either end of the bridge, one with the three lilies of Anjou and one with the ermine of Brittany.

**Les Rosiers**
The bridge at Les Rosiers is one of the two that cross the Loire at this point. The river is particularly wide here and has an island in the middle. The island is connected to the banks at the towns of Les Rosiers and Gennes by two bridges.

# River View: Tours to Nevers

This is truly the royal Loire Valley. As the river flows through the regions of Touraine, Blésois and Orléanais, it passes beside many Renaissance châteaux. Some, like Chaumont, Amboise and Gien, show their fortress-like exteriors to the river, often concealing courtyard gardens and highly decorated façades. Others, like Sully, glory in their luxury. Throughout Touraine, vineyards gently slope towards the river, while the lands behind are taken up by the forests that were once the hunting grounds of kings and courtiers.

**Beaugency's massive keep** *(see p140)* dates from the 11th century.

**Langeais**
In the town of Langeais, *(see p96)* high above the river, there is a massive 15th-century château, still furnished in keeping with its period.

**Château d'Amboise**
*(see p114)*, a Renaissance château, was built for a succession of kings.

**Pagode de Chanteloup**
All that remains of a once-lovely château, this strange pagoda *(see p115)* is 44 m (144 ft) tall.

**Blois**
On the north bank of the Loire, Blois *(see pp128–31)* was the seat of the counts of Blois, and then the residence of François I, whose salamander emblem decorates many parts.

**Tours**
In the heart of the Loire Valley region, Tours *(see pp116–21)* was always a significant crossing point on the river. The lively place Plumereau, lined with 15th-century buildings, is in the Old Town.

**Château de Chaumont**
The great fortress of Chaumont *(see p132)* is softened by Renaissance touches and offers impressive views from its terrace.

**Tours**
When Tours' original 18th-century bridge was built, the rue Nationale, which links it to the centre of the city, became the major thoroughfare, in place of the road between the cathedral and the Old Town.

**Blois**
The bridge at Blois was built between 1716 and 1724, replacing a medieval bridge destroyed when a ship crashed into it. It was built to a very high standard, enabling it to survive floods and freezes.

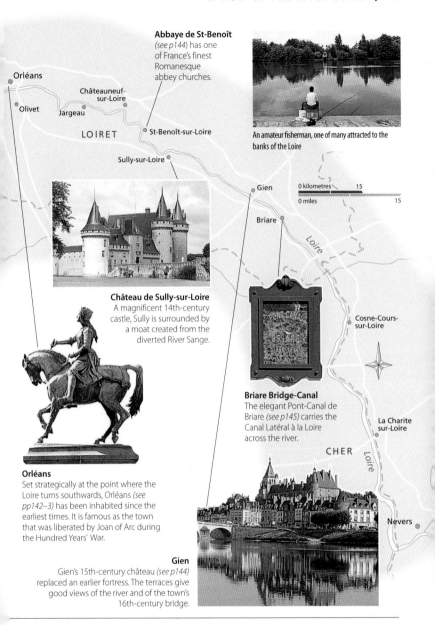

**Abbaye de St-Benoît**
(see p144) has one of France's finest Romanesque abbey churches.

An amateur fisherman, one of many attracted to the banks of the Loire

**Château de Sully-sur-Loire**
A magnificent 14th-century castle, Sully is surrounded by a moat created from the diverted River Sange.

**Briare Bridge-Canal**
The elegant Pont-Canal de Briare (see p145) carries the Canal Latéral à la Loire across the river.

**Orléans**
Set strategically at the point where the Loire turns southwards, Orléans (see pp142–3) has been inhabited since the earliest times. It is famous as the town that was liberated by Joan of Arc during the Hundred Years' War.

**Gien**
Gien's 15th-century château (see p144) replaced an earlier fortress. The terraces give good views of the river and of the town's 16th-century bridge.

**Beaugency**
Beaugency's bridge is built in several different styles, because sections of the original 12th-century wooden structure were gradually replaced with stone. The earliest date from the 14th century.

**Jargeau**
The original bridge was replaced by a wooden suspension bridge in the 19th century. A steel bridge, built in the 1920s, was hit in World War II. The current bridge dates from 1988.

# THE LOIRE VALLEY THROUGH THE YEAR

Spring and early summer are often particularly beautiful in the regions bordering the River Loire. But it should not be forgotten that this is the "Garden of France", and that successful gardens need plentiful watering in the main growing season, so be prepared for some showery days. In the sultry, humid heat of July and early August, the Loire is usually reduced to a modest trickle between glistening sandbanks. The châteaux can also become very crowded in the summer.

Perhaps the most pleasant season is autumn, when forests gleam red and gold in the mild sunshine, the restaurants serve succulent local game and wild mushrooms, and the grape harvest is celebrated in towns and villages with many colourful festivals. Music festivals are also very popular in the region. Concerts are staged all year round at countless venues across the region. For more information about the vast array of annual festivals, contact the local tourist offices.

## Spring

March sees the reopening of many châteaux after their winter closure, often on the Palm Sunday weekend that marks the beginning of the influx of visitors from the rest of France and abroad. The spring flowers and migrations of birds are particularly appreciated by nature lovers. Many special events, including numerous Easter egg hunts, are held on the Easter weekend.

### March
**Foire à l'Andouillette**
(*weekend before Easter*), Athée-sur-Cher (nr Chenonceau). One of the earliest traditional Loire Valley festivals, with a fairground, bands and craftspeople.
**Printemps Musical de St-Cosme** (*last week*), around Tours. A mainly classical music festival, held in numerous locations, notably St-Cosme priory.

### April
**Le Printemps de Bourges**
(*third week*), Bourges (pp154–5). This contemporary music festival starts off the long concert season.
**Carnaval de Cholet** (*end Apr*), Cholet (p73). Carnival ending in a fabulous night-time parade of multicoloured floats.

### May
**Fête de Jeanne d'Arc**
(*week of 8 May*), Orléans (pp142–3). One of France's oldest fêtes, begun in 1435 to celebrate the routing of the English in 1429, takes the form of a huge, colourful costume pageant.
**Europajazz** (*first week*), Le Mans. One of the longest-established jazz festivals in the Loire Valley.

Horse and rider from Saumur's Cadre Noir display team

**Concours Complet International** (*third weekend*), Saumur (pp84–7). This international horse-riding competition takes place at the famous Cadre Noir riding school, which also hosts tattoo and equestrian displays from April until September.
**Nuit Européenne des Musées** (*mid-May*), across the region. Many museums stay open late into the night and stage special events which are often free.
**Le Printemps des Arts** (*May and Jun*), Nantes (pp194–7) and surrounding area. A Baroque dance, theatre and music festival.
**Le Festival International des Jardins de Chaumont-sur-Loire** (*May–mid-Oct*), near Blois. A magnificent celebration of international horticultural innovation.

Farm workers in the fields around Bourgueil

## Average Daily Hours of Sunshine

Hours

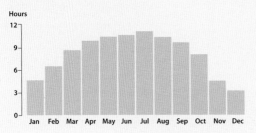

**Sunshine Chart**
The summer months are generally hot, with the hottest period in July. On the Atlantic coast, cool sea breezes often bring welcome relief from the heat but do not mean that sunbathers are less likely to burn. In the spring and autumn, river areas can be misty in the mornings.

## Summer

France's main summer celebrations include the Fête de la Musique on the longest night of the year, the Feast of John the Baptist on 24 June and Bastille Day, recalling the start of the French Revolution, on 14 July 1789. The Loire's famous son et lumière *(see pp46–7)* performances take place mainly at weekends on the long nights between mid-June and mid-August.

### June

**Vitiloire** *(first weekend)*, Tours. Touraine *vignerons* invade the town to lead the wine celebrations.

**Les 24 Heures du Mans** *(second or third weekend)*, Le Mans *(pp168–71)*. One of France's main events, this international 24-hour car race attracts enormous crowds.

**Sardinantes** *(second or third Sat)*, Nantes. Savour a plate of grilled sardines accompanied by Celtic music and dancing on the quay in old Nantes. A typical local festival.

**Festival d'Anjou** *(mid-Jun– mid-Jul)*. Major theatre festival held in historic sites throughout the *département*.

**Avanti la Musica** *(mid-Jun–mid-Aug)*, Amboise. Celebrating links between Amboise and Italy via music, theatre, cinema and more.

**Fêtes Musicales en Touraine** *(late Jun)*, Tours *(pp116–21)*. Started in 1964, this international festival of chamber music is held in a superb medieval tithe barn, at Parçay-Meslay, northeast of Tours.

The beach at the popular Atlantic resort, Les Sables d'Olonne

### July

**Des Lyres d'Eté** *(Jul & Aug)*, Blois. An exciting variety of theatre and music dominates the programme during this summer festival.

**Bastille Day** *(14 Jul)*. The celebrations for the Fête Nationale, commemorating the Storming of the Bastille in 1789, are the high point of the year in many small communities across the region. Visitors can join in the dancing and wine-quaffing, and enjoy the often very impressive firework displays.

**Foire à l'Ail et au Basilic** *(26 Jul)*, Tours. The headily scented garlic and basil fair is held every year on the Feast of St Anne *(p121)*.

**Festival International d'Orgue** *(Sun in Jul & Aug)*, Chartres Cathedral *(pp176–7)*. Internationally renowned organists from all over the world descend on Chartres to participate in this prestigious organ festival.

**Destination Moyen-Age** *(third weekend)*, Chinon. This takes shape as an impressive reconstruction of a medieval settlement, with festivities spread over two days. It includes acrobats, musicians and street theatre, which combine to fill the historic town of Chinon.

### August

**L'Epopée Médiévale** *(mid-Aug)*, Loches. Medieval mania takes over this fine old town.

**Foire aux Vins de Vouvray** *(around 15 Aug)*, Vouvray. The Feast of the Assumption is marked by numerous local festivities, with wine events predominating.

**Foire aux Sorcières** *(first Sun)*, Bué (nr Sancerre). The Berry was often said to be a centre of witchcraft and sorcery. On this occasion, children dressed as witches or ghosts parade through the village to a nearby field where crowds play games and watch folk groups performing.

**Festival de Sablé** *(last weekend)*, Sablé-sur-Sarthe *(p166)*. Over a period of five days, musicians perform in churches and manor houses around Sablé.

Folk dancers at a festival

**Les Rendez-Vous de l'Erdre** *(last weekend; first weekend in Sep)*, Nantes. Mixing jazz, boating and street festivities on Nantes' second river.

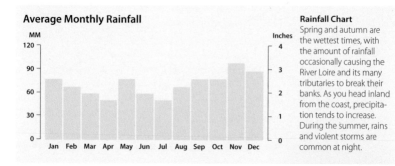

## Average Monthly Rainfall

## Autumn

The golden days of autumn attract large numbers of Parisians to the region for shooting weekends, especially to the forested eastern areas. This is also the season for the *vendanges*, or grape harvest, and the events and festivities associated with it, and for fairs celebrating the season's produce.

### September

**Les Accroche-Coeurs** *(second week)*, Angers *(pp76–7)*. During the course of three or four days, the streets of Angers are alive with open-air theatre, dance, circus, concerts and all manner of performance arts.
**Jazz en Touraine** *(mid-Sep)*, Montlouis-sur-Loire. One of the region's leading jazz festivals.
**Festival de Loire** *(mid-Sep)*, Orléans/Loiret. Joyous gathering of Loire boats and festivities along the river, held every second (odd-numbered) year.

**Journées du Patrimoine** *(third weekend)*. For one weekend a year, châteaux and other historic buildings that are usually closed to the public can be visited, and concerts, exhibitions and other cultural events are staged.
**Festival Européen de Musique Renaissance** *(last weekend)*, Clos Lucé, Amboise. This three-day festival, held in the Château du Clos Lucé, features musicians who specialize in Renaissance music.
**Entre Cours et Jardins** *(last weekend)*, Le Mans. A celebration of horticulture across the historic old town, with many private homes opening their gardens to the public.

### October

**Celtomania** *(first three weeks)*, Nantes. This lively celebration of Celtic culture includes music and theatre performances.
**Mondial du Lion** *(mid-Oct)*,

High-quality local produce on sale at the Saturday market in Saumur

Le Lion d'Angers. For horse lovers, this is a top-class international equestrian competition.
**Foire à la Bernache** *(last Sun Oct or first Sun Nov)*, Reugny (nr Tours). Although it may be an acquired taste, the *bernache* (unfermented new wine) is very popular with the locals.
**Foire aux Marrons** *(last Tue)*, Bourgueil (nr Chinon). Chestnuts are the traditional accompaniment to new wine, and for this reason they feature in many guises here.
**Rockomotives** *(last week; first week in Nov)*, Vendôme. The relaxed little town on the Loire hosts this popular rock festival.

### November

**Marché de Noël** *(last weekend)*, Château de Brissac *(p82)*. The Christmas market in the château, featuring local artisans and seasonal produce, marks the beginning of the Christmas season.

Wine tasting at Kerhinet in La Grande Brière

## Average Monthly Temperature

| | Jan | Feb | Mar | Apr | May | Jun | Jul | Aug | Sep | Oct | Nov | Dec |
|---|---|---|---|---|---|---|---|---|---|---|---|---|

**Key** ▢ Maximum ▢ Minimum

### Temperature Chart

It is rare for winter temperatures to fall below freezing in the Loire Valley. In the west, the sea moderates the climate, keeping it mild. Elsewhere, summer temperatures can reach over 30° C (86° F) in the middle of the day, but the evenings are usually cooler and perfect for eating outside on terraces by the river.

## Winter

Winter is the quiet season in the Loire Valley, when a damp chill rather than a frosty cold sets in, and many of the châteaux are closed. A few Christmas markets are held, and a film festival, but in general this is a time when local people prefer the pleasures of home.

### December

**Soleils d'Hiver** *(through Dec)*, Angers. One of the best programmes of seasonal entertainments along the Loire, as well as a traditional Christmas market and fair-trade craft stalls.

**Marché de Noël et Crèche Vivante** *(through Dec)*, Cholet. A living Nativity scene, festive market and Christmas lights competition.

**Noël au Fil des Siècles** *(Dec– 6 Jan)*, Château d'Amboise. An interesting trawl through the history of Christmas.

**Foire de Noël** *(first weekend)*, Richelieu *(pp106–7)*. This is a traditional Christmas market

An old windmill in the Anjou countryside

selling gifts, decorations and a variety of seasonal food.

### January

**La Folle Journée** *(last week)*, Nantes and various other towns around the region. As many as 400 classical music concerts take place in 12 different towns, all focusing on a theme that changes every year.

### February

**Fêtes des Vins d'Anjou** *(last weekend)*, Chalonnes-sur Loire. The winter period is enlivened with wine fairs, such as this gathering of producers of the Saumur and Anjou *appellations*.

### Public Holidays

**New Year's Day** (1 Jan)

**Easter Monday**

**Ascension** (sixth Thursday after Easter)

**Labour Day** (1 May)

**VE Day** (8 May)

**Bastille Day** (14 Jul)

**Feast of the Assumption** (15 Aug)

**All Saints' Day** (1 Nov)

**Remembrance Day** (11 Nov)

**Christmas Day** (25 Dec)

A concert at the Abbaye de Fontevraud

# Son et Lumière in the Loire

"I love with a passion things that mix sound with light", wrote the poet Charles Baudelaire in 1857, anticipating the great sound-and-light shows for which the Loire Valley would become famous. The idea of combining sound (chiefly music) and light in a night-time spectacle dates back to the era of Louis XIV, when outdoor entertainment consisted of musicians and flaming torches. The modern form of son et lumière, exploiting the powers of electric light and recorded sound to enhance the grandeur of a historic building, was born at the Château de Chambord in 1952. The concept has since spread around the world, but the Loire Valley remains the heart of son et lumière. Today, many of the shows use lasers, fireworks and a cast of hundreds to create a spectacular pageant. Advances in digital technology have given designers even greater scope for their creativity. Most shows take place in the summer, but there are also light shows and festivals around Christmas, often accompanied by outdoor markets. Check performance times online and book tickets well in advance. The following list includes the main regular shows, but keep an eye open for one-off events, too.

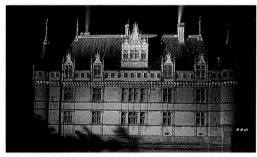

Lighting effects bringing drama to the Château d'Azay-le-Rideau

## Touraine

**Amboise**
**At the Court of King François**
**Tel** 02 47 57 14 47.
**W** renaissance-amboise.com

This show, a celebration of the life of François I, takes place at his favourite château *(see p114)*. Enacted by local residents, it re-creates the court, with sumptuous costumes, thrilling hunts and elaborate festivities.

**Azay-le-Rideau**
**The Enchanted Mirror**
**Tel** 02 47 45 42 04.
**W** azay-le-rideau.monuments-nationaux.fr

This son et lumière show is actually a fascinating promenade production, where all the spectators are invited to walk around the grounds of this elegant château *(see pp100–101)*, as they admire a succession of stage, sound and lighting effects.

**Chenonceau**
**Night-time Promenade**
**Tel** 02 47 23 90 07.

This beautiful royal residence *(see pp110–13)* puts on a play of light and shadow orchestrated by Pierre Bideau, the designer of the Eiffel Tower illuminations. The promenade leads through the gardens designed by Diane de Poitiers and Catherine de Médicis. Corelli's music adds to the romantic atmosphere.

## Blésois and Orléanais

**Blois**
**The Story of Blois**
**Tel** 02 54 90 33 32.
**W** chateaudeblois.fr

Images of key moments in the history of the Château Royal de Blois *(see pp130–31)* are projected on to the building's façade during this sound-and-light show. The loves, dramas and mysteries portrayed include the visit of Joan of Arc in 1429, the poetry contest between Charles of Orléans and François Villon in 1457, and the assassination of the Duc de Guise in 1563. Enjoy the show from the château's courtyard.

**Cléry-Saint-André**
**La Révolution Française**
**Tel** 02 38 45 94 06.
**W** cleryraconte.com

A cast of hundreds recreates the uprising, struggles and other key events of the French Revolution. These include the storming of the Bastille and

Faces from the past projected on to the walls of the Château de Blois

Fireworks and lighting effects illuminate the Château du Puy-du-Fou

the battle of Valmy. Before the show, spectators can sit down to a Republican banquet (starting at 7pm; advanced reservation advised), during which more entertainment is provided.

## Berry

### Valençay
**Tel** 02 51 00 01 12.
**W** spectacle-valencay.fr

The dramatically lit grounds of this château *(see p150)* are the ideal setting for a retelling of classic fairy tales such as *Cinderella* and *Beauty and the Beast*. There are 10 enchanting performances by the 100-strong cast, complete with elaborate period costumes and a musical score.

## Loire Atlantique and the Vendée

### Le Puy-du-Fou Cinéscénie
**Tel** 02 51 64 11 11.
**W** puydufou.com

The Château du Puy-du-Fou *(see p192)* hosts the Cinéscénie, which bills itself as the world's largest permanent son et lumière spectacle. More than 1,000 actors, 250 horses, countless volunteers and various spectacular high-tech effects combine to trace the turbulent history of the Vendée from the Middle Ages to the end of World War II.

## Medieval Illuminations

Digital technology enables images to be projected onto monuments, turning them into giant screens. One of the best shows is in Chartres *(see p175)*. From mid-April to mid-October, 29 historic buildings in the city are spectacularly illuminated – some with moving images projected onto them. The lights are on from nightfall until 1am nightly. It takes 2.5 hours to complete the route, which is available online, or from hotels or the tourist office. In September, Chartres also celebrates a Festival of Light, with concerts and street performances to complement the projections (Tel: 03 27 23 40 00; www.chartresenlumieres.com).

Two other cities put on similar spectacles. The lights of Les Nuits Lumières in Bourges *(see pp154–5)* are switched on at nightfall (Thu–Sat in May, June & September; daily in July & August). The 2.5 km (1.5 mile) route starts at the Jardin de l'Archevêché in rue des Hémerettes and finishes at the cathedral (Tel: 02 48 23 02 60 www.bourges-tourisme.com/pages/bourges-les-nuits-lumiere/). In Le Mans *(see pp168–70)*, the Nuit des Chimères consists of projections on historic buildings such as the cathedral, the Musée de la Reine-Bérengère and the city walls (Tel: 02 43 28 17 22; www.nuitdeschimeres.com).

The history of the Vendée re-enacted in the Cinéscénie at the Château du Puy-du-Fou

# THE HISTORY OF THE LOIRE VALLEY

The Loire's central role in French history is splendidly displayed in the breadth of its architectural styles, ranging from megalithic structures to royal and ducal châteaux.

Imposing prehistoric monuments testify to the existence of thriving Neolithic cultures as early as the third millennium BC. By the 1st century BC, the conquering Romans found sophisticated Celtic communities already established. Later, as Christianity spread, the ancient Celtic towns at Angers, Bourges, Chartres, Orléans and Tours became well known as centres of learning.

A long period of territorial conflict began in the 9th century, first among local warlords and later between France and England, when Henry Plantagenet, count of Anjou and duke of Normandy and Aquitaine, inherited the English crown in 1154. In the 15th century, major battles between the two countries were fought in the region during the Hundred Years' War,

with Joan of Arc spurring on French victories. A series of French kings made the Loire Valley their home, ruling from the magnificent châteaux. The fierce 16th-century Wars of Religion between Catholics and Protestant Huguenots brought yet more bloodshed to the area.

By the 17th century, France's political focus had shifted to Paris, although the River Loire remained a key transportation route until the advent of the railway. Later, the Vendée Uprising of 1793 was the most serious civil threat to the French republic after the 1789 Revolution.

In the 20th and 21st centuries, the architectural evidence of the Loire's rich history has led to the growth of the region's tourist industry. This balances with a diverse and well-established industrial base, as well as thriving agriculture, to make the valley one of the most economically stable regions of France.

Sixteenth-century views of Tours, with its cathedral, and Angers, with its slate quarries

◀ A portrait of François I, the Renaissance king (reigned 1515–47), attributed to Jean Clouet

# Rulers of the Loire

In the course of the Loire's history, the power of the local nobility often rivalled that of the French throne. The dukedoms of Anjou and Blois were established when Charlemagne's territory was divided among his sons upon his death in 814. Henry Plantagenet, count of Anjou, duke of Normandy and king of England, could trace his lineage to Charlemagne. The French monarchy did not consolidate its authority until Charles VII moved from the Loire back to Paris in 1436. Another local family, the royal house of Orléans, saw two of its sons become kings.

**1151–89** Henry Plantagenet

**1180–** Philipp Augus

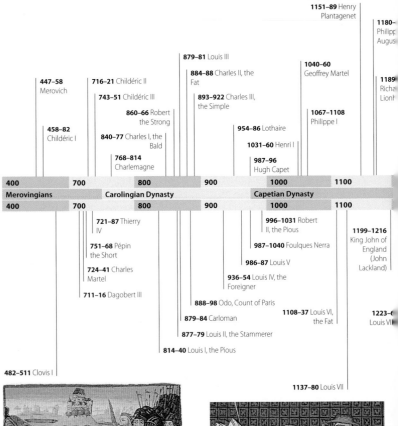

**879–81** Louis III

**884–88** Charles II, the Fat

**893–922** Charles III, the Simple

**1040–60** Geoffrey Martel

**1189** Richa Lionh

**447–58** Merovich

**716–21** Childéric II

**743–51** Childéric III

**860–66** Robert the Strong

**954–86** Lothaire

**1067–1108** Philippe I

**458–82** Childéric I

**840–77** Charles I, the Bald

**1031–60** Henri I

**768–814** Charlemagne

**987–96** Hugh Capet

| 400 | 700 | 800 | 900 | 1000 | 1100 |
|---|---|---|---|---|---|
| Merovingians | | Carolingian Dynasty | | Capetian Dynasty | |
| 400 | 700 | 800 | 900 | 1000 | 1100 |

**721–87** Thierry IV

**996–1031** Robert II, the Pious

**1199–1216** King John of England (John Lackland)

**751–68** Pépin the Short

**987–1040** Foulques Nerra

**724–41** Charles Martel

**986–87** Louis V

**711–16** Dagobert III

**936–54** Louis IV, the Foreigner

**1108–37** Louis VI, the Fat

**1223–** Louis VI

**888–98** Odo, Count of Paris

**879–84** Carloman

**877–79** Louis II, the Stammerer

**814–40** Louis I, the Pious

**482–511** Clovis I

**1137–80** Louis VII

**1422–61** Charles VII, the Victorious

**1270–85** Philippe III

**1285–1314** Philippe IV, the Fair

**1314–16** Louis X

**1316–22** Philippe V, the Tall

**1322–28** Charles IV, the Fair

**1328–50** Philippe VI

**1483–98** Charles VIII, the Affable

**1498–1515** Louis XII, Father of the People

**1515–47** François I

**1547–59** Henri II

**1559–60** François II

**1643–1715** Louis XIV, the Sun King

**1774–92** Louis XVI

**1804–14** Napoléon I

| 1300 | 1400 | 1500 | 1600 | 1700 | 1800 |

Valois Dynasty — Bourbon Dynasty

| 1300 | 1400 | 1500 | 1600 | 1700 | 1800 |

**1350–64** Jean II, the Good

**1430–80** René I of Anjou

**1560–74** Charles IX

**1574–89** Henri III

**1461–83** Louis XI, the Spider

**1814–24** Louis XVIII

**1824–30** Charles X

**1830–48** Louis-Philippe I, Duc d'Orléans, King of the French

**1226–70** Louis IX (St Louis)

**1364–80** Charles V, the Wise

**1380–1422** Charles VI, the Fool

**1715–74** Louis XV

**1610–43** Louis XIII

**1852–70** Napoléon III

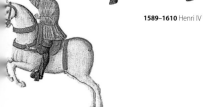

**1589–1610** Henri IV

# Neolithic and Roman Loire

Neolithic culture produced some of France's largest prehistoric tombs and sacred sites. Their builders had Central European roots, as did the Celts who established cities along the Loire in the Bronze and Iron Ages. Julius Caesar's conquest of the valley in 51 BC left the Celtic tribes under a light Roman rule, the basis of relative prosperity for the next 300 years. The spread of Christianity coincided with Rome's military decline and the rise of kingdoms ruled by Visigoths to the south and Germanic Franks to the north. The Frankish king Clovis I converted to Christianity and took power in 507 by routing the Visigoths.

**Baptism of Clovis**
Frankish chieftain Clovis converted to Christianity at the end of the 5th century to legitimize his rule.

**The entrance porch** is a distinctive feature of Angevin dolmens.

**Palaeolithic Remains**
Flint tools made in the Loire basin were traded by Palaeolithic tribes at least 50,000 years ago.

**Celtic Art**
Celtic art was not dominated by the naturalistic ideals of the occupying Romans. This bronze statuette of a young woman dates from the 1st–2nd century AD.

**Bagneux Dolmen**
*This 5,000-year-old chamber tomb in Saumur is 21 by 7 m (69 by 23 ft). The nine massive uprights were levered onto loose stones, dragged to the site, tilted and sunk into ditches 3 m (10 ft) deep.*

**c.2500** Loire dolmens with porches set new style of Neolithic burial chamber

**c.800** Celtic Carnutes found settlements at Blois, Chartres and Orléans

**57–56** Romans conquer western Loire tribes

**51** Julius Caesar ends Gaulish uprising that began in Orléans

*Julius Caesar, first to unite Gaul*

| 2500 BC | | 100 BC | AD 1 | AD 100 |
|---|---|---|---|---|

**c.1200** Loire region exports bronze weapons made using local tin resources.

**31** Roman emperor Augustus sets framework for 300 years of Pax Romana (peace and prosperity) in the Loire

**50** Loire Valley flourishes as border link between two Gallo-Roman provinces, Lugdenunsis and Aquitania

*Celtic helmet*

**Celtic Armour**
The warlike Celts were skilled armourers, as this bronze breastplate of 750–475 BC shows. The Romans found them formidable opponents.

**An inner pillar,** perhaps part of a wall, helps support a 40 tonne capstone.

## Where to See Neolithic and Roman Loire

Anjou is rich in Neolithic sights, mostly on the south bank of the Loire. The largest are at Saumur *(see pp84–7)* and Gennes *(p82)*. Gennes' amphitheatre and the walls at Thésée *(p133)* are two of the few surviving Gallo-Roman monuments. Museums at Orléans *(pp142–3)* and Tours *(pp118–19)* have major Gallo-Roman collections.

**Gennes Amphitheatre**
Roman gladiatorial combats were held in the amphitheatre at Gennes.

**Orthostats** (upright stones) were sunk in holes 3 m (10 ft) deep and filled with sand, which was then dug out.

**Gallo-Roman Art**
This beaten bronze stallion, displayed in the archeology museum in Orléans, was dedicated to Mars, god of war and guardian of agriculture.

**Fresh Water by Aqueduct**
Roman pillars near Luynes supported a 2nd-century aqueduct which carried spring water to baths in Caesarodunum (Tours).

**250** Gatien, Bishop of Tours, among the first Christian evangelists in the Loire

**313** Emperor Constantine makes Christianity official Roman religion

**372** Martin, Bishop of Tours, leads monastic growth

**507** After converting to Christianity, Clovis defeats Visigoths near Poitiers

**498** Clovis I takes Orléans

**511** Clovis I dies; his sons divide his lands

**200**  **300**  **400**  **500**

**50** Romans build amphitheatre at Gennes

**275** Emperor Aurelian gives Orléans independent status

*St Martin, Bishop of Tours*

**451** Visigoth kingdom of Toulouse helps repel Attila the Hun at Orléans

**473** Visigoths capture Tours

*Wine: an early Loire export*

**c.550** First record of wine production in the Loire region

# The Early Middle Ages

In raising the massive keep at Loches, Foulques Nerra of Anjou was typical of the warlords who took power in the Loire after the 9th century. The chains of citadels they built laid the foundations for the later châteaux. The Plantagenets, who followed Nerra as rulers of Anjou, also claimed territory from Normandy to Aquitaine and then inherited the English throne. It was not until the 13th century that the French King Louis IX brought Anjou back under direct control of the crown. Throughout this period the Church was a more cohesive power than the French crown. Its cathedrals and monastic orders established schools and *scriptoria* (where manuscripts were copied and illuminated), and it was to the Church rather than the throne that feudal warlords turned to mediate their brutal disputes.

**The Loire Around 1180**
- Other fiefs
- French royal domain

**Gregory I** codified the liturgical music sung during his reign as pope (590–604).

**St Louis**
Popularly called St Louis for his piety, Louis IX (1214–70) was the first Capetian monarch to inherit a relatively stable kingdom. A brave crusading knight and just ruler, he forced England to abandon claims to the Loire.

**687** Pépin II establishes the power of the "mayors" of the Carolingian dynasty, ancestors of Charlemagne, over Merovingian kings

**732** Charles Martel drives Moors back from the Loire in decisive battle south of Tours

**850** Normans lay waste to Loire Valley

**866** Robert the Strong, ancestor of Capetian king killed by Normans in Anj

**911** Chartres repe Norman

| 600 | 700 | 800 | 90 |
|---|---|---|---|

*Charlemagne, the Frankish king*

**768–84** Charlemagne conquers Brittany and all Loire

**796** Charlemagne's mentor, Alcuin, makes Tours a centre of Carolingian art

*Coinage of Charles the Bold*

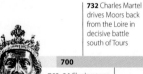

### Carolingian Ivory

Ivory plaques, reliquaries and book covers are among the most beautiful Frankish decorative objects to survive Norman destructions of the 10th century. Carolingian art usually served a religious or utilitarian purpose.

### Where to See Early Medieval Loire

Early churches such as the one at Cunault *(see p83)* are charged with medieval atmosphere, as are abbeys such as Noirlac *(p153)* or at Solesmes *(p166)* and Fontgombault *(p151)*, where you can hear Gregorian chant. Fortress châteaux such as the one at Loches *(p108)* and ruined towers at Lavardin *(p126)* or Montrichard *(p132)* tell grimmer feudal stories.

**Medieval musical notation** showed variations in pitch (high and low notes). The length of each note depended on the natural rhythm of the text.

### Monastic Arts

The development of the Caroline Minuscule style of calligraphy was led by the monks of Tours' Basilique St-Martin in the 9th century.

### Romanesque Capitals

This Romanesque sculpture is on a capital in Cunault church.

### Fine Craftsmanship

Many of the finest surviving pieces of medieval craftsmanship are worked in metal. This 13th-century funerary mask was cast in copper from the effigy of a woman and then gilded.

### Illuminated Manuscript

*This manuscript is the first page of a 13th-century gradual, a book of plainsong sung during mass. It is typical of the style of illuminated manuscripts that were produced by the abbeys of the Loire Valley. This collection of Gregorian chant was compiled by monks of the strict Cistercian Order (see p153).*

### Hugh Capet of Orléans

Hugh, depicted here being handed the keys to Laon, was elected king in 987, ending the Carolingian dynasty. He set a precedent for kings to seek refuge in the Loire in troubled times.

**1101** Founding of Abbaye de Fontevraud

**1096** First Crusade launched

Hugh Capet of Orléans becomes first Capetian king of France

**1128** Marriage in Le Mans of Geoffrey Plantagenet and Matilda, daughter of Henry I of England

**1189** Henry II's death leaves his son, Richard the Lionheart, as the Angevin rival to the French king

| **1000** | **1100** | **1200** |

*Foulques Nerra*

**992** Bretons driven out of Anjou by Foulques Nerra

**1154** Henry Plantagenet accedes to the English throne as Henry II

**1125** Thibaut IV of Blois and Champagne rivals Capetian power

**1214** Angevin empire ends with defeat of King John at Angers

# The Hundred Years' War

The destructive climax of the Middle Ages was war between the French and English crowns, flaring intermittently from 1337 to 1453. When the English besieged Orléans in 1428, the Loire region became the focus for a struggle that seemed likely to leave France partitioned between England and its powerful ally, Burgundy. Instead, the teenage heroine, Joan of Arc, inspired Orléans to fight off the English and brought the dauphin Charles VII out of hiding in Chinon. Her martyrdom in 1431 helped to inspire a French recovery. In spite of marauding soldiery and the more widespread disaster of the plague known as the Black Death, the Loire knew periods of peace and prosperity, during which medieval court life flourished.

**The Loire in 1429**
French territory in the Loire
English possessions

**The English longbow** was a powerful weapon, requiring strong, skilled archers.

**Charles VII**
Joan of Arc's dauphin, often portrayed as a weakling, was in fact a crafty man in a difficult situation. Disinherited by the French royal family in 1420, he used Joan's charisma to rally support. However, he distrusted her political judgement.

**Cannons** could fire stone balls that weighed as much as 200 kg (440 lb).

**Jousting Tournament**
The sumptuous trappings of their warlike recreations display the wealth of the ruling class in the early 15th century. Jousting was dangerous – Henri II died from a lance blow.

**1341** English support John of Montfort against Charles of Blois in War of Breton Succession

**1346** English longbows defeat French knights at Crécy

**1352** Loire begins recovery from four years of plague

*Black Death depicted in a 15th-century illuminated manuscript*

**1325**

**1350**

**1375**

**1337** Philippe VI, the first elected Valois king, confiscates English lands in Guyenne, starting Hundred Years' War

*Portrait of Philippe VI*

**1360** Anjou becomes a duchy

### Apocalypse

War and the plague made the end of the world a preoccupation of 15th-century art. In this tapestry from Angers (see pp80–81), St John hears the clap of doom.

## Where to See the Loire of the 14th and 15th Centuries

Guérande (p184) is a well-preserved, 15th-century walled town. Many others, such as Chinon (pp102–4), have half-timbered houses. Orléans (pp142–3) has a replica of the house in which Joan of Arc lodged. Le Plessis-Bourré (p74) exemplifies the shift towards more graceful lifestyles after the end of the Hundred Years' War.

### Château de Chinon

This château is strategically positioned on a cliff above the River Vienne.

**The halberd** was a typical infantryman's weapon.

### Joan of Arc

Although shown here in feminine attire, the real Joan (see p141) wore men's dress into battle

**Siege tower**

### René, Duke of Anjou

René I (1409–80) loved tournaments but was also a painter, scholar and poet. To some, he represented the ideal 15th-century ruler.

## The Siege of Orléans

*The English first besieged Orléans in November 1428, and they quickly established their position and built major siegeworks. In February 1429, a French attempt to cut English supply lines was defeated, and it was not until 30 April that Joan of Arc's troops were able to enter the city. Within a week the English were forced to abandon the siege.*

**1409** Birth of René I, Duke of Anjou

**1417–32** English occupy Chartres

**1418** Charles VI burns Azay-le-Rideau

**1429** Joan of Arc visits the dauphin Charles at Chinon, ends English siege of Orléans and crowns him King Charles VII at Reims

**1453** War ends without a treaty, with English retaining only Calais

**1461** Louis XI begins his reign

**1400**

**1425**

**1450**

**92** Louis, Duke [Or]léans, [ac]quires Blois

**1415** Crushing English victory at Agincourt leads to alliance between England and Burgundy

**1428** English besiege Orléans

**1435** Charles VII makes peace with Burgundy. Army reforms lead to French victories

**1438** Jacques Cœur of Bourges becomes court banker and reorganizes France's tax system

*15th-century sporting crossbow*

**1470** Silk weaving in Tours begins

# Renaissance Loire

The Italian wars of Charles VIII, Louis XII and François I between 1494 and 1525 gave all three kings a taste for Italian art and architecture. At Amboise and Blois they made the Loire a centre of court life, establishing the culture of the French Renaissance. François I patronized countless artists and craftsmen who worked in the Italian style, setting an example for the aristocracy throughout France. The Loire suffered 40 years of warfare when his son's widow, Catherine de Médicis, could not persuade Catholics, led by the Guise family, to live in peace with Protestants during the reigns of her sons, Charles IX and Henri III.

**Fortress of Faith**
The pope is besieged by Protestants in this portrayal of the Wars of Religion.

**François I**
France's strongest Renaissance king made the Loire his hunting playground. His great confidence is captured here by François Clouet of Tours *(see p29)*.

**Colonnades** were a feature of the Classical Renaissance style.

**An arcaded** central courtyard formed the basis of 15th-century palaces in the Italian style.

**The First Tank Design**
Da Vinci spent his last years at Le Clos-Lucé *(see p115)*. This tank is a model of one of the inventions he worked on there.

### The Ideal Château
*From Charles VIII (1483–98) onwards, French Renaissance kings dreamed of creating the ideal château. The symmetrical vistas of this plan by Androuet du Cerceau display a late-Renaissance stylistic move towards Classical grandeur.*

**1484** Etats Généraux, a national assembly, meets at Tours

**1493** Charles VIII redesigns his birthplace, the Château d'Amboise, in Italian style

**1498** Duke of Orléans is crowned Louis XII and marries Anne of Brittany

**1515** François I conquers Milan and invites Italian artists to the Loire

**1532** Treaty binds Brittany and Nantes to France

**1475**

**1500**

**1525**

*Charles VIII, France's first Renaissance king*

**1508** Louis XII remodels Blois as Renaissance royal capital

*Cellini's salt cellar for François I (1515–47)*

**1491** Marriage of Charles VIII to Anne of Brittany links autonomous Brittany to French crown

**1519** François I begins building Chambord. Leonardo da Vinci dies at Le Clos-Lucé *(see p115)*

### Henri IV

Brave, astute and likeable, Henri IV of Vendôme and Navarre, France's first Bourbon king, reasserted the authority of the crown over a disintegrating kingdom within 10 years of his accession in 1589. Rubens (1577–1640) shows him receiving a betrothal portrait of Marie de Médicis.

## Where to See Renaissance Loire

Fine Renaissance buildings can be seen throughout the region. Older châteaux that reflect the Italian influence include Amboise (p114) and Blois (pp130–31). The most delightful achievements of the French Renaissance are Chenonceau (pp110–13) and Azay-le-Rideau (pp100–101). Smaller examples, such as Beauregard (pp134–5), are widespread. Undoubtedly the most spectacular is Chambord (pp136–9).

**Château de Chambord**
This impressive château sits on the banks of the River Cosson.

**High roofs** and dormers show the persisting French influence.

**Anne of Brittany's Reliquary**
By marrying successively Charles VIII and Louis XII, Anne of Brittany, whose reliquary is in Nantes (see p195), welded her fiercely independent duchy to France.

**Diane de Poitiers**
The mistress of Henri II was flatteringly portrayed as Diana, the Roman goddess of the hunt.

---

**1559** Death of Henri II begins power struggle between his widow, Catherine de Médicis, and anti-Protestant followers of the Duc de Guise

**1547** Henri II begins reign and gives Chenonceau to his mistress, Diane de Poitiers

**1550**

**1562** Wars of Religion start with major battles and massacres along the Loire

**1572** Court moves to Fontainebleau after St Bartholomew's Day massacre of Protestants

**1576** Henri, Duc de Guise, founds pro-Catholic Holy League. Meeting of Etats Généraux at Blois fails to find a peace formula

**1575**

**1588** Holy League virtually takes over government. Henri III has Duc de Guise and his brother murdered at Blois

*Coin of Henri IV "the Great"*

**1598** Edict of Nantes establishes Protestant rights of worship

**1594** Protestant Henri IV crowned at Chartres after becoming Catholic to end the Wars of Religion

# Growth and Prosperity

The Loire lost its central role in French politics when the focus of court life moved to the Paris region at the end of the 16th century. The Vendée, however, was the centre during the French Revolution of a violent popular uprising against Republican excesses, including rising taxes, the persecution of priests and conscription. River trade remained important, especially for the increasingly wealthy port of Nantes. As early as the 17th century, work had begun on canals to connect Nantes and the Loire directly with Paris, of which Eiffel's 19th-century bridge-canal at Briare was the aesthetic high point. Although industry grew slowly, the region remained predominantly agricultural.

**19th-Century Waterways**
— Rivers
— Canals built before 1900

**Cardinal Richelieu**
As Louis XIII's chief minister between 1624 and 1642, Cardinal Richelieu helped to establish orderly government in France.

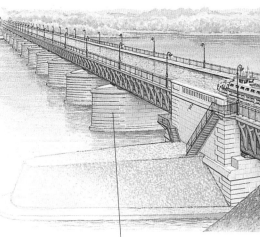

**The 15 granite piers** supporting the structure were bedded using early compressed-air techniques.

**Winemaking in the Loire**
Winemaking in the 18th century remained a pastime for the idle rich, who used badly paid peasants to harvest and press the grapes.

**1610–16** Regency of Henri IV's widow, Marie de Médicis, over Louis XIII

**1617** Louis XIII banishes his mother to Blois. They are reconciled by Richelieu in 1620

**1631** Richelieu starts building planned town and château on the Touraine border

**1720s** Loire again becomes a centre of country life for the nobility

**1600**

**1650**

**1700**

*Louis XIII*

**1648–53** La Fronde: a series of French civil wars

*17th-century watch made in Blois*

**1685** Saumur and other cities lose Huguenot population as these terrorized Protestants flee after Louis XIV's revocation of the Edict of Nantes

**Vendée Hero**
Bonchamps' plea to spare Republican prisoners *(see p191)* was depicted in stone by David d'Angers.

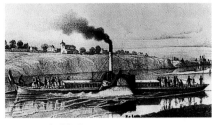

**Loire "Inexplosibles"**
Faced by competition from the railways, 19th-century steamboats were a last attempt to maintain the Loire's role as a great French trade route.

**Graceful lamps** above the wide pavements provide a Parisian boulevard touch.

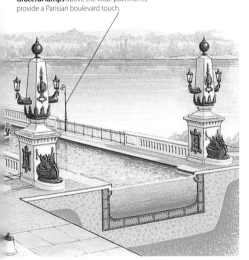

**Passage Pommeraye**
The elegance of this 19th-century shopping arcade reflected the wealth of Nantes.

**Briare Bridge-Canal**
*Gustave Eiffel designed this 662 m bridge to carry canal traffic safely across the Loire. Opened in 1896, it completed a grand waterway system begun in the 17th century linking the Loire, Seine and Rhône rivers. The metal structure used new steel technology.*

**Steam Omnibus**
In 1873, Amédée Bollée's *L'Obéissante* was the first car to be built in Le Mans.

**1756** Royal College of Surgeons founded at Tours

**1789** French Revolution

**1793–4** Vendée Uprising

**1846** Paris railway reaches Tours

**1896** Opening of Eiffel's bridge-canal spanning the Loire at Briare

**1852** Napoléon III crowned emperor

**1856** Great flood of the Loire

'50

**1800**

**1850**

**1770–90** Nantes reaches peak of mercantile wealth

**1804** Napoléon makes La Roche-sur-Yon the capital of pacified Vendée and funds drainage of the eastern Marais Poitevin

*The Vendée heart emblem*

**1829** First Loire steamboat, *Le Loire*, travels from Nantes to Angers in 16 hours

**1863** Last Loire steamboat company closes

**1870** Franco-Prussian War drives Napoléon III into exile

**1873** Amédée Bollée begins manufacturing steam-driven cars at Le Mans

# The Modern Era

Although ship-building reached a peak at Nantes and St-Nazaire in the 1920s, and light industry expanded steadily around Orléans, Le Mans and Angers, the region did not become prosperous until after World War II. Its larger cities were occupied by the Germans in 1940 and many were bombed in 1944. Since the 1960s, when the recovery gathered momentum, tourism has supplemented the Loire's traditional strength as the "Garden of France". Private châteaux have been opened to the public, and the state has funded major restoration schemes, as at the Abbaye de Fontevraud.

**Wilbur Wright**
The pioneer US flying ace galvanized European aviation when he demonstrated this commercial prototype near Le Mans in 1908.

**Dramatic fireworks** light up the night sky.

**TGV Links**
With stops at Vendôme, Tours, Angers and Nantes, the Loire is well served by France's TGV (Train à Grande Vitesse) network.

**Son et Lumiere**
Puy-du-Fou's Cinéscénie laser spectacle updates a tradition begun at Chambord in 1952 by Robert Houdin, son of a famous Blois magician. Evening performances draw thousands to Amboise, Blois, Chenonceau and other great châteaux (see pp46–7).

**Orléans, 1944**
Bridges across the River Loire were prime bombing targets at both the beginning and the end of World War II.

| | | | | | |
|---|---|---|---|---|---|
| **1905** Loire farming in decline as falling wheat prices follow damage to vines from phylloxera | **1908** Wilbur Wright stages test flights at Auvours near Le Mans | **1936** Renault opens Le Mans factory | **1944** Liberation of Loire cities ends four-year German occupation | | **1959** André Malraux ma Minister of Cultural Affa He speeds up restorat work on Loire monume |
| | **1920** Cheverny opens to the public | **1923** First 24-hour race at Le Mans | | | |

| **1900** | **1910** | **1920** | **1930** | **1940** | **1950** |
|---|---|---|---|---|---|

| | **1914** World War I begins. Among the first dead is the writer Alain-Fournier (see p29) | **1929** Town of La Baule builds promenade and becomes one of France's top beach resorts | **1940** German advance forces temporary government to move from Paris to Tours | **1952** First son et lumi ère perfor- mance at Chambord |
|---|---|---|---|---|

*Alain-Fournier (1886–1914)*

**Earth Day Ecology Protests on the Loire**
Environmentally aware locals are committed to preserving the rich natural resources of the great river.

**Nuclear Power**
The Loire was an early resource for cooling nuclear reactors. Avoine, near Chinon, opened in 1963.

**Computer-controlled** lighting effects, lasers and water jets add a modern twist.

**More than 2,000** local residents volunteer as performers, security patrols and guides at each Cinéscénie evening.

**Le Vinci**
The sensitive modernization of Tours city centre shows how old and new architectural styles can be combined.

**Le Mans**
The renowned 24-hour race at Le Mans attracts motor enthusiasts from around the world.

**1963** First French nuclear power station starts operating at Avoine

**1970s** Loire wine exports, especially of Muscadet, soar

**1989–90** Inauguration of TGV Atlantique high-speed services brings Angers within a mere 90 minutes of Paris

**2007** Nicolas Sarkozy wins the presidential election. He appoints François Fillon from the Sarthe as Prime Minister

**2014** Manuel Valls is appointed Prime Minister

| 1970 | 1980 | 1990 | 2000 | 2010 | 2020 |
|------|------|------|------|------|------|

*Muscadet, produced east of Nantes*

**1994** Government dismantles dam at Maisons Rouges to allow salmon to reach spawning grounds

**2000** The Loire Valley from Chalonnes-sur-Loire to Sully-sur-Loire is inscribed on UNESCO's World Heritage list

**2002** The euro replaces the Franc as France's currency

**2012** Socialist François Hollande becomes French President. Jean-Marc Ayrault, mayor of Nantes, becomes French Prime Minister

# THE LOIRE VALLEY AREA BY AREA

# The Loire Valley at a Glance

Rich in history and architecture, the Loire Valley is best known for its sumptuous Renaissance châteaux, such as Chambord and Chenonceau. But the region has also retained the wealth of earlier ages, from Bronze Age dolmens to medieval keeps, such as the Château d'Angers, and an impressive heritage of religious architecture, including the Gothic marvels of Chartres and Bourges cathedrals. Visitors who desire a break from the past can revel in the beauty of the landscape, which contains natural surprises such as the lush Marais Poitevin. In a region packed with delights, those shown here are among the very best.

The Gothic spires of **Chartres Cathedral**, which tower over an attractive town (see pp176–9)

The **Château d'Angers**, protected by its formidable curtain walls (see pp78–81)

**Abbaye de Fontevraud**, the largest medieval abbey complex in France (see pp90–91)

Mayenne

Laval

NORTH OF
THE LOIRE
(see pp160–179)

Le Mans

Sergé

Blain

Angers

Loire

ANJOU
(see pp68–91)

Nantes

Cholet

LOIRE-ATLANTIQUE
AND THE VENDÉE
(see pp180–197)

La Roche-
sur-Yon

Les Sables-
d'Olonne

0 kilometres        50

0 miles             50

The **Marais Poitevin**, a labyrinth of shady canals contrasting with rich fields of painstakingly reclaimed land (see pp186–9)

◀ Pretty half-timbered houses in Le Mans' Old Town

**Chambord**, the largest royal residence in the Loire *(see pp136–9)*

The memorable François I Renaissance staircase of the **Château de Blois** *(see pp130–31)*

Chartres Cathedral

**Bourges Cathedral**, a Gothic masterpiece *(see pp156–7)*

Chartres

Châteaudun

Pithiviers

Calais

Orléans

**BLESOIS AND ORLEANAIS** *(see pp122–145)*

Loire

URAINE
*pp92–121)*

Loire

Blois

Tours

**Chenonceau**, stretching languidly across the River Cher *(see pp110–13)*

Vierzon

Bourges

Issoudun

Châteauroux

**BERRY** *(see pp146–159)*

Argenton-sur-Creuse

The graceful symmetry of **Azay-le-Rideau** *(see pp100–1)*

Villandry's spectacular reconstructed **Renaissance gardens** *(see pp98–9)*

# ANJOU

The landscape of Anjou is as gentle and pleasant as its climate and its people. The region's rolling plains are intersected by a network of rivers, which help to irrigate the already fertile land. North of the city of Angers, the confluence of the Sarthe, Mayenne and Loir rivers forms a great flood-plain in the winter months and is a regular port of call for thousands of migrating birds.

The creamy limestone, or tufa, used to build the great châteaux of Anjou combines with black roof slates to give Angevin architecture its distinctive look. Tufa quarrying has created hundreds of caves. Many are now used for growing mushrooms, and others have been transformed into troglodyte dwellings, some of which are open to visitors.

Some of the Loire Valley's finest fruits and vegetables are grown here. Trees and flowers also flourish; the rose gardens of Doué are legendary. The region's vines produce not just white, red and rosé wines, but also the sparkling wines of Saumur and St-Cyr-en-Bourg. Visitors can see the complicated process of the *méthode champenoise* first-hand by visiting the major wine houses around Saumur.

Anjou is steeped in the history of the powerful rival dynasties of medieval France. Then, as now, Angers, dominated by its barrel-chested fortress, was the centre of the region. The city was a feudal centre of the Plantagenets, among them Henry of Anjou, who became Henry II of England. Fifteen of the family, including Henry II, his wife, Eleanor of Aquitaine, and their famous son, Richard the Lionheart, are buried at Fontevraud Abbey. Nearby, Saumur's château formed the fairy-tale backdrop to the "September" miniature in the 15th-century masterpiece, *Les Très Riches Heures du Duc de Berry*. Other impressive châteaux in this region include Brissac, the tallest château in the Loire, and Le Plessis-Bourré, a charming pre-Renaissance château.

Château de Saumur, towering above the town and the River Loire

◀ Detail of the Apocalypse Tapestries on display at the Château d'Angers

# Exploring Anjou

Northern Anjou is crossed by the Mayenne, Sarthe and Loir rivers, flowing southwards to their convergence in the River Maine. Angers, the geographical and administrative centre of the region, straddles the Maine 8 km (5 miles) before it flows into the Loire. Anjou's most famous châteaux, antiquities and troglodyte sites are located around Angers and Saumur, 50 km (30 miles) up the Loire. But there are also dozens of lesser-known châteaux, clustered around Segré in the northwest and Baugé in the northeast.

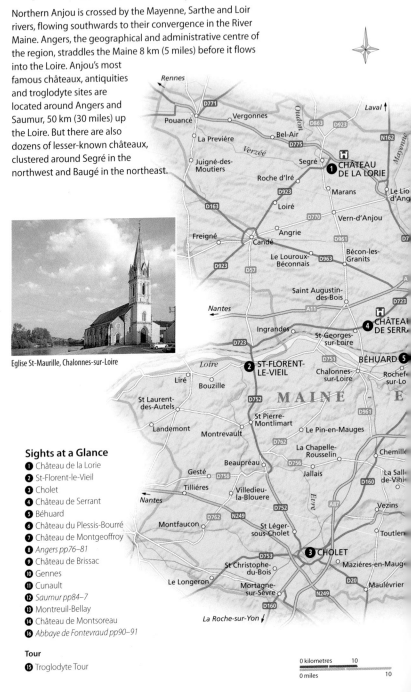

Eglise St-Maurille, Chalonnes-sur-Loire

## Sights at a Glance

0 kilometres    10

0 miles    10

The Loire in full flood in Anjou

## Getting Around

Angers is 90 minutes' drive from Paris by TGV. *L'Océane* autoroute (A11) via Le Mans is the fastest road access from Paris. Tours and Angers are linked by the A85 motorway. The D751 from Saumur follows the south bank of the Loire and is the most pleasant drive towards Angers. It continues as the Corniche Angevine, providing splendid views of the Loire on the road to Champtoceaux. Leisurely boat cruises are available on the Sarthe and Mayenne tributaries.

## Key

- ▬ Motorway
- ▬ Major road
- ▬ Secondary road
- ⋯ Minor road
- ⋯ Main railway
- — Minor railway
- ▬ Regional border

One of Angers' lively pavement cafés

**For keys to symbols** *see back flap*

St-Florent-le-Vieil's 18th-century church, on a hill above the old town

put an end to these types of extravagant shows of wealth and personal power.

## ❷ St-Florent-le-Vieil

Road map B3. 🏘 2,700. 🚃 Varades, then taxi. 🚌 ℹ 4 pl de la Févrière (02 41 72 62 32). 🎵 Festival de Musique, Les Orientales (mid-Jun–mid-Jul). 🌐 ville-saintflorentlevieil.fr

A walk through the narrow streets of the old town, lined with buildings dating from the 16th to the 18th centuries, ends atop a hill with magnificent views over the Loire Valley. Here stands a large 18th-century church, the scene of dramatic events during the Vendée Uprising. The Uprising began in March 1793, with a mass revolt against conscription into the Republican army.

Seven months later, the Royalist army, beaten at Cholet, crossed the Loire here with 40,000 troops and at least as many supporters. They planned to kill more than 4,000 Republicans held in the church, but were stopped by one of their leaders, the Marquis de Bonchamps, who cried "Spare the prisoners" as he lay dying. Among those saved was the father of the sculptor David

## ❶ Château de la Lorie

Road map B3. 🚃 Segré, then taxi. Tel 02 41 92 10 04. Open Jul–mid-Sep: Wed–Mon; groups by appt. 🅿 ♿ 🌐 chateaudelalorie.fr

Elegant gardens in the 18th-century French style introduce this dry-moated château, 2 km (1 mile) southeast of the old town of Segré on the River Oudon. The original building, which is embellished by a statue of the Roman goddess Minerva over the central door, was built during the 17th century by René le Pelletier, provost-general of Anjou.

A century later, two wings were added to form a courtyard, together with an ornate marble ballroom. This *pièce de résistance* is crowned with a musicians' gallery located in an overhead rotunda. It was completed by Italian craftsmen in 1779, only a few short years before the French Revolution

## The Corniche Angevine

One of the most scenic routes in the region, the Corniche Angevine (D751) curves along the cliffs above the south side of the Loire through western Anjou, offering lovely views of the islands that break up the river in this area, and of the opposite bank, with its fertile vineyards and beautiful manor houses. The road is never more than hilly and has a pleasantly rural feel as it runs alongside the Louet (a tributary of the Loire), flanked by vineyards and fields.

Chalonnes-sur-Loire, at the western end, is an ancient village with a graceful church, the Eglise St-Maurille, parts of which date back to the 12th century. The quay beside the church is a good place to stop for a picnic. Further along, La Haie Longue has particularly pretty views across the river. At the eastern end of the Corniche Angevine, the town of Rochefort-sur-Loire has a 15th-century bell tower and a square of old turreted houses. Powerful fortresses once stood on outcrops of rock below the village, and the ruins of some of them can be explored.

The view across the river at La Haie Longue

d'Angers, whose marble statue of Bonchamps was placed in the church in 1825 *(see p61)*. Stained-glass windows in the chancel recount the story, as does the **Musée d'Histoire Locale et des Guerres de Vendée**.

🏛 **Musée d'Histoire Locale et des Guerres de Vendée**
pl J et M Source. **Tel** 02 41 72 62 32. **Open** May–Jun: Sat & Sun pm only; Jul–mid-Sep: daily pm. ⚲

Emile Boutigny's 1899 depiction of the Vendée Uprising in Cholet

## ❸ Cholet

**Road map** B4. 🗻 57,000. 🚊 🚌
ℹ 14 av Maudet (02 41 49 80 00). 🗓 Sat. 🎭 Carnaval de Cholet (Apr); Festival des Arlequins (Apr–May); L'Eté Cigale (Jun–mid-Sep). 🌐 ot-cholet.fr

Capital of the Mauges region and second city of Anjou, Cholet was a thriving town until 1793 when it lost half of its population in the Vendée Uprising *(see p191)*. Its revival was testimony to the strength of the area's textile industry.

The tomb of the Marquis de Vaubrun in Serrant's chapel

Cholet's red handkerchiefs with white borders are souvenirs of a crucial battle. The Vendée Uprising is commemorated in the city's **Musée d'Art et d'Histoire**.

🏛 **Musée d'Art et d'Histoire**
27 av de l'Abreuvoir. **Tel** 02 72 77 23 20. **Open** Wed–Sun (Jul & Aug: Wed–Mon). **Closed** 1 Jan, 1 May, 25 Dec. ♿ 🚻

## ❹ Château de Serrant

**Road map** B3. 🚊 Angers, then taxi. **Tel** 02 41 39 13 01. **Open** Feb–Jun: Wed–Sun; Jul & Aug: daily, Sep–mid-Nov: Wed–Mon. ⚲ 📷
🌐 chateau-serrant.net

The most westerly of the great Loire châteaux, the privately owned Serrant was begun in 1546 and developed in an entirely harmonious style over the next three centuries. Its pale tufa and dark schist façades, with massive corner towers topped by cupolas, create an air of dignity. Inside, the central pavilion contains one of the most beautiful Renaissance staircases in the region. The château also has 18th-century furniture, Flemish

tapestries, and a library of some 12,000 books. Serrant's most famous owner was the Marquis de Vaubrun, whose death in battle (1675) is commemorated by a magnificent tomb in the chapel, sculpted by Antoine Coysevox. The Irish Jacobite family of Walsh, shipowners at Nantes, owned Serrant in the 18th century, and the château displays a painting of Bonnie Prince Charlie bidding farewell to Anthony Walsh, whose ship took the prince to Scotland.

In 1830 Serrant passed to the Duc de la Trémoille. His descendants still own it today.

A statue of the Madonna, set in the church wall at Béhuard

## ❺ Béhuard

**Road map** C3. 🗻 110. 🚌 Baiche Maine, then taxi. ℹ Angers tourist office (02 41 23 50 00).
🌐 behuard.mairie49.fr

The narrow lanes of the medieval village on this delightful island in the Loire were made for pilgrims visiting a tiny church fitted into an outcrop of rock. It is dedicated to the safety of sailors navigating the often treacherous river.

The lovely wine village of Savenniéres, on the north bank of the Loire opposite Béhuard, is also worth a visit. Its vineyards produce delicious Chenin Blanc white wines that are sold at some of the gorgeous, walled properties in the area.

The south façade of Château de Serrant, with huge corner towers

## ❻ Château du Plessis-Bourré

**Road map** C3. 🚉 Angers, then taxi.
**Tel** 02 41 32 06 72. **Open** mid-Feb–
Mar & Oct–mid-Nov: Thu–Tue pm
only; Apr–13 Jul & Sep: Fri–Tue, pm
Thu; 14 Jul–Aug: daily; 14–30 Nov: Fri–
Sun pm only. **Closed** Dec–mid-Feb.
🅿️ 🅵 🅦 plessis-bourre.com

Set in a moat so wide it looks
more like a lake, Château du
Plessis-Bourré, with its silvery-
white walls and dark slate roofs,
seems to float on the water.
Built in five years from 1468, it is
the least altered and perhaps
even the most perfect example
of the work of Jean Bourré,
whose home it was. As advisor

and treasurer to the king of
France, Bourré also oversaw the
creation of Langeais *(see p96)*
and Jarzé and was influential
in the transformation of Loire
castles from fortresses into
pleasure palaces. The Château
du Plessis-Bourré itself is well
defended, but its fortifications
do not interfere with a design
that is orientated towards
gracious living. Its wonderful
condition stands as a testament
to the quality of the materials
used in its construction and to
the skills of the craftsmen who
created it.

After crossing a long, seven-
arched bridge, visitors enter the
château's arcaded courtyard by

Ceiling of the Salle des Gardes

one of four working draw-
bridges. The state rooms are
surprisingly light and airy, with
finely carved stone decoration.
An astounding painted ceiling
in the Salle des Gardes depicts
many allegorical and alchemical
scenes, including a lively
representation of the demon-
wolf Chicheface, emaciated
because she could eat only
wives who always obeyed
their husbands.

Some furniture, mainly dating
from the 18th century, is
displayed. During the French
Revolution, coats of arms on the
library fireplace were defaced,
and graffiti can still be seen.

Château du Plessis-Bourré, set in its wide moat

### Bird-Watching in the Basses Vallées Angevines

At the confluence of the Sarthe, Loir and
Mayenne rivers, some 4,500 ha (11,100 acres)
of land, the Basses Vallées Angevines, are
flooded between October and May each year.
Thousands of migrating birds visit the area,
making it an exceptional bird-watching site.

Perhaps the rarest visitor is the elusive
corncrake, which arrives in the grasslands
during April. There are more than 300 breeding

pairs in the area, making it one of the best sites in
Western Europe. Protection of this species is aided
by enlightened local farming methods, such as
late hay harvests.

Insects in the meadows, ditches and rivers attract
swifts, hobbys, whinchats and yellow wagtails.
In early summer the Basses Vallées resound with
birdsong and in the evenings the strange call of
the corncrake can be heard.

The floodplains of Anjou at twilight

# ❼ Château de Montgeoffroy

**Road map** C3. 🚃 Angers or Saumur, then taxi. ☎ **Tel** 02 41 80 60 02. **Open** mid-Mar–mid-Nov: daily. 🅿 ✔ 🆆 **chateaudemont geoffroy.com**

Montgeoffroy is a masterpiece of late 18th-century style, built for the Maréchal de Contades by the architect Nicolas Barré between 1773 and 1775, and beautifully preserved by his descendants. The château is a model of balance, with subtle blue and grey harmonies of stone and paintwork, tall French windows and a lovely park.

The central building is flanked by flat-roofed pavilions, which connect two side wings to the main house. The wings are both rounded off with towers built in the 16th century. One tower houses a harness room smelling of fresh Norwegian spruce, leading to

The symmetrical façade of the Château de Montgeoffroy

Hérault de Séchelles by Hubert Drouais

magnificent stables and a fine display of carriages. The chapel in the opposite wing is also 16th-century. Next to the main house, the kitchen has a collection of 260 copper and pewter pots.

The charming principal rooms are alive with pictures, tapestries and furniture made especially for the château. An innovation in the dining room is a porcelain stove fashioned in the shape of a palm tree, brought from

Strasbourg where the *maréchal* (marshal) was governor. His crossed batons are used as a decorative motif in the superbly positioned Grand Salon. The marshal's "friend", Madame Hérault, had her own rooms, where a portrait of their "natural" grandson, Marie-Jean Hérault de Séchelles, can be seen.

Montgeoffroy's stables, where the collection of carriages is housed

## BIRD-WATCHERS CHECKLIST

**Practical Information**
**Road map** C3. **Tel** 02 41 44 44 22. Ligue pour la Protection des Oiseaux (LPO), Maison de la Confluence, 10 rue du Port-Boulet, Bouchemaine. Day, night and weekend outings.
🅿 By reservation for LPO programmes. 🆆 **lpo-anjou.org**

**Transport**
🚃 Angers, then taxi.
Best viewing area (Feb–late Jul): confluence of Loir and Sarthe rivers, southwest of Briollay. Take the D107 from Angers to Cantenay-Epinard. Turn right just before the village and follow signs for Le Vieux Cantenay. Return to the D107 via Vaux. Continue north to Noyant, where all of the little roads across the meadows lead to the River Sarthe. Return to Noyant and head for Les Chapelles and Soulaire-et-Bourg. Then take the D109 to Briollay if the road is passable.

Snipe

Lapwing

## Bird Species

*In winter, resident ducks, coots and cormorants are joined by geese and swans at the margins and golden plovers in the fields. February sees the arrival of the black-tailed godwits. Pintail ducks, greylag geese, lapwings and black-headed gulls also appear for a time, as do waders such as ruff, snipe, redshank and dunlin. In summer, the meadows dry out, and things are quieter.*

Golden plover

# ❽ Angers

Situated on the River Maine, only 8 km (5 miles) before it joins the Loire, Angers was once the power base for Foulques Nerra *(see pp54–5)* and the other notorious medieval counts of Anjou. By the 12th century, under the rule of the Plantagenets, Angers became a key stronghold of an empire stretching as far as Scotland. Today, it is a thriving university town, with wide boulevards, beautiful public gardens and narrow older streets evocative of its long history.

### Exploring Angers

Angers is divided into two sections by the River Maine. The oldest part is on the east bank of the river, guarded by the fortress-like 13th-century **Château d'Angers** *(see pp78–9)*. Shielded inside the château's massive walls are the Apocalypse Tapestries, the oldest and largest of France's tapestries, dating from the 14th century *(see pp80–81)*. Nearby is the Maison des Vins de Loire, which offers an introduction to the region's wines, and the **Cathédrale St-Maurice**.

Angers has 46 timber-framed houses, most of them near the cathedral. The best is the **Maison d'Adam**, on place Ste-Croix. This 15th-century merchant's house is decorated with carved wooden figures of sirens, musicians and lovers.

On the right bank of the River Maine, the old quarter of **La Doutre** (*"d'outre Maine"*, or "the other side of the Maine") is well worth a visit. Its most famous building is the medieval hospital, now home to a collection of modern tapestries.

A rewarding stroll from rue Gay-Lussac to place de la Laiterie passes many of La Doutre's historic buildings. Included among them are the elegant **Hôtel des Pénitentes** (once a refuge for reformed prostitutes), a 12th-century **apothecary's house** and the restored church of **La Trinité**, which adjoins the ruins of Foulques Nerra's Romanesque **Abbaye du Ronceray** – a Benedictine abbey reserved for daughters of the nobility. A little way south down the Maine is Angers' old port. It has been revived and an attractive area has grown up around it, full of restaurants, and cafés. Le Quai, a major arts complex with an impressive theatre can also be found here.

### ⛪ Cathédrale St-Maurice

pl Freppel. **Tel** 02 41 87 58 45.
**Open** daily.

This striking cathedral was built at the end of the 12th century, although the central lantern tower was added during the Renaissance period. The façade's Gothic sculptures are impressive.

The elegant Angevin vaulting in the nave and the transept is one of the best, and earliest,

Maison d'Adam, the best of Angers' timber-framed houses

examples of its kind, and gives a dome-like shape to the high ceiling. The cathedral's interior is lit through glowing stained glass, which includes a stunningly beautiful rose window in the northern transept that dates from the 15th century.

### ▥ Musée des Beaux Arts

14 rue du Musée. **Tel** 02 41 05 38 00.
**Open** mid-May–mid-Sep: 10am–6:30pm daily; mid-Sep–mid-May: 10am–noon & 2–6pm Tue–Sun.
**Closed** pub hols. ⬚ ♿
**W** musees.angers.fr

The museum is arranged according to two themes: the history of Angers told through works of art from Neolithic to modern times; and fine arts from the 14th century. Don't miss the intriguing display of religious antiquities on the first floor, including a lapidary Cross of Anjou and a beautiful 13th-century copper-gilt mask of a woman.

### ⛪ Collégiale St-Martin

23 rue St-Martin. **Tel** 02 41 81 16 00.
**Open** Jun–Sep: 10am–7pm daily; Oct–May: 1–6pm Tue–Sun. ⬚ ♿
**W** collegiale-saint-martin.fr

This 9th-century church was reopened in 2006 after 20 years of restoration. It now houses a superb collection of religious statues dating from the 14th century, including a delightful representation of the Virgin preparing to suckle the infant Jesus.

One of the many beautiful public gardens in Angers

## Cointreau

Angers, the city of Cointreau, produces some 15 million litres of the famous liqueur every year. The distillery was founded in 1849 by the Cointreau brothers, local confectioners well known around Angers for their exotic, curative tonics. But it was Edouard, the son of one of them, who created the original recipe. The flavour of this unique colourless liqueur is artfully based on sweet and bitter orange peels.

### VISITORS' CHECKLIST

**Practical Information**
Road map C3. **Tel** 02 41 23 50 00.
157,000. pl Kennedy.
Wed & Sat. Spring Organ
Festival (Mar–Jun); Festival
d'Anjou (Jul); Les Accroche-
Coeurs (Sep); Soleils d'Hiver (Dec).
**w** angersloiretourisme.com

**Transport**
pl de la Gare.

### 🏛 Galerie David d'Angers

33 bis, rue Toussaint. **Tel** 02 41 05 38 90. **Open** May–mid-Sep: 10am–6:30pm daily; mid-Sep–Apr: 10am–noon, 2–6pm Tue–Sun. **Closed** public hols. 🗗 ♿ **w** musees.angers.fr

The glassed-over ruins of the 13th-century abbey church of Toussaint are filled with plaster casts of the work of local sculptor Pierre-Jean David (1788–1856), known as David d'Angers. His idealized busts and figures were much in demand as memorials for people such as the Marquis de Bonchamps (see p61). They are forceful examples of Academic art.

**Sculpture by David d'Angers**

### 🏛 Musée Jean Lurçat et de la Tapisserie Contemporaine

4 blvd Arago. **Tel** 02 41 24 18 45. **Open** May–mid-Sep: 10am–6:30pm daily; mid-Sep–Apr: 10am–noon, 2–6pm Tue–Sun. **Closed** public hols. 🗗 ♿

A Gothic masterpiece in La Doutre, this graceful building functioned as a hospital until 1875, the oldest surviving in France. It was founded in 1175 by Henry II of England, and the Plantagenet coat of arms is displayed with the Anjou heraldry inside the entrance to the grounds.

A reconstruction of the dispensary occupies one corner of the Salle des Malades, and a chapel and 12th-century cloisters can also be visited. The Hôpital St-Jean houses Le Chant du Monde, a

set of extraordinary tapestries by artist Jean Lurçat (see p81).

### 🏛 Musée Cointreau

Bd des Brétonnières, St. Barthélémy d'Anjou. **Tel** 02 41 31 50 50. **Open** by appointment. **Closed** Jan, 25 Dec. 🗗 🗗 (in English at 1pm Jul & Aug).

From a walkway high above the alambics and bottling machines, visitors can observe the production processes involved in the creation of Cointreau here. The 90-minute tour takes you round the distillery, in the St. Barthélémy district of Angers, ending up with a dégustation of the famous orange-flavoured liqueur. Thousands of objects, documents, photos, publicity posters and films illustrate the long history of the company and its famous square bottle.

## Angers Town Centre

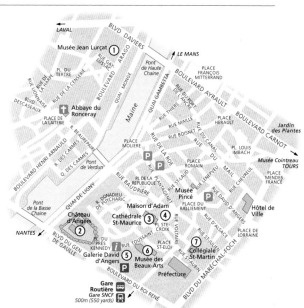

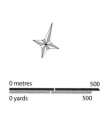

0 metres 500
0 yards 500

**For keys to symbols** see back flap

# Château d'Angers

The huge drum towers and curtain walls of this powerful feudal fortress were built on the site of Count Foulques Nerra's stronghold from around 1230. The work was begun at the behest of Blanche of Castille, the mother of Louis IX and regent during his youth. Within the 650 m (2,100 ft) perimeter, later nobles developed a château lifestyle in almost playful contrast to the forbidding outer towers. The last duke of Anjou, King René I, added charming buildings, gardens, aviaries and a menagerie. After several centuries as a prison, the citadel-château now houses France's most famous tapestries.

**★ Moat Gardens**
The dry moat, which is a remarkable 11 m (36 ft) deep and 30 m (98 ft) wide, is now filled with a series of geometric flower beds.

**Fortress Towers**
The 17 towers rise up to 40 m (131 ft) in height. They lost their pepper-pot roofs and were shortened during the 16th century to adapt them for the use of artillery.

**From 1230** Fortress built on a rocky spur, where counts of Anjou had built older castles

**1410** Louis II and Yolande of Aragon reconstruct chapel and Logis Royal

*Henry III*

**1945** Allied bombers damage fortress, in use as a German munitions base

**1648–52** Louis XIV turns fortress into a prison

| 1200 | 1300 | 1400 | 1500 | 1600 | 1700 | 1800 | 1900 |
|---|---|---|---|---|---|---|---|

**1360** Louis I of Anjou cuts doors and windows to relieve the grimness of the walls

**1435–50** René I renovates interior, adding gardens and new buildings

**1585** Fortress taken by Huguenots. Henri III wants towers demolished but governor merely lowers them

**1875** Declared a historic monument

**1952–54** Bernard Vitry builds gallery to house Apocalypse Tapestries

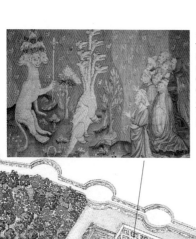

★ **Apocalypse Tapestries**
Bernard Vitry's modern Galerie de l'Apocalypse displays the Apocalypse Tapestries *(see pp80–81)*.

★ **Châtelet**
Built in 1450 by René I, the gatehouse still retains its charming pepper-pot roofs.

## KEY

① **The drawbridge** leading to the Porte de la Ville (Town Gate) is the entrance to the château.

② **Formal gardens** have been planted in the great courtyard.

③ **The Logis du Gouverneur** was built in the 15th century and modified in the 18th century. It now houses a restaurant and reception areas.

④ **The King's Window** depicts René I, king of Naples, and his wife, Jeanne de Laval, kneeling on either side of the Virgin.

⑤ **The Logis Royal** was built for King René between 1435 and 1440.

⑥ **Walkways along the wide walls** stretch for more than a kilometre (¾ mile). There are fine views of the town, as well as some beautiful gardens.

⑦ **The towers** are ascended by spiral staircases.

★ **Ducal Oratory**
The ducal oratory opens on to the Chapelle Saint-Jean-Baptiste. Equipped with a fireplace, it was used by the duke and members of his family.

# The Tapestries at Angers

The Apocalypse Tapestries depict the dramatic visions of the end of the world, as recounted by the Book of Revelation, the closing book of the Bible. They were designed by Hennequin de Bruges and woven in Parisian workshops in 1375–82 for Duke Louis I of Anjou. Around 1760, however, the tapestries were thrown out, cut up and used as bed canopies and horse blankets before being restored in the 19th century. In its graphic portrayal of war, plague and famine, this masterpiece of medieval art evokes not only the original text but also the hardships of the 14th century.

**Detailed Work**
Each of the devils devouring Babylon has a distinct character. The tapestries were woven so skilfully that the front and the back are almost mirror images.

**St John** appears as the narrator of each version.

**An angel dictates to St John** in one of the best-preserved scenes. Elsewhere, the green textiles have faded to beige.

## The Fall of Babylon

*The tapestries stretch for 103 m (338 ft) along a specially built gallery. They are divided into six chapters, each with an introductory panel and 14 scenes. One of the most animated panels, showing the fall of Babylon, comes near the end of the series, before the coming of the New Jerusalem: "Babylon the Great is fallen, is fallen, and is become the habitation of devils" (Rev. 18:2). Earlier scenes show the breaking of the seven seals and the unleashing of the four horsemen of the apocalypse.*

**Water is changed** to poisonous wormwood in this cataclysmic scene.

**Vibrantly Coloured Tapestries**
These panels show St John, the worship of the beast in the presence of Christ, and the angel announcing the fall of Babylon.

**The tumbling towers** of Babylon reveal a nest of demons.

**Blue backgrounds** alternate with red, providing continuity through the series.

## Le Chant du Monde

The vast, vaulted medieval interior of the Musée Jean Lurçat *(see p77)* provides a stunning background to *The Song of the World*. This piece, which stretches for 79 m (260 ft) around three sides of the hall, was Lurçat's response to the Apocalypse Tapestries, which he saw for the first time in 1937. The ten panels are 4 m (13 ft) high and were woven at workshops in Aubusson between 1957 and 1963. Thematically, the images move from the horrors of Nazi genocide and the bombing of Hiroshima to the conquest of space, conceived as the dawning of a new age.

Jean Lurçat (1892–1966)

"Ornamentos Sagrados" from Lurçat's *Le Chant du Monde* tapestry

## The Art of Tapestry

In medieval times, tapestries were a symbol of luxury, commissioned by royal and noble families to adorn châteaux and churches. Hung on the thick stone walls, they helped to keep the vast rooms warm by preventing drafts.

Paris and Flanders were the centres of tapestry work in the 14th century, where highly skilled

Medieval tapestry weaver

weavers followed an artist's full-size drawing, called a "cartoon". Threads were stretched vertically (the warp) on a loom to the length of the finished piece, then coloured threads (the weft) were woven horizontally across them.

Tapestry-making declined from the 16th century, but the 20th century saw a revival, with artists such as Pablo Picasso and Henri Matisse experimenting in the medium.

Coloured tapestry threads at the Manufacture St-Jean in Aubusson

Brissac's wine cellars

## ❾ Château de Brissac

Brissac-Quincé. **Road map** C3.
🚊 Angers, then taxi or bus. 🚌
**Tel** 02 41 91 22 21. **Open** Apr–Jun &
Sep–Oct: Wed–Mon; Jul & Aug: daily;
Nov–Mar: Wed–Mon during school
hols. **Closed** Jan, 25 & 31 Dec. 🎟 📷
♿ 📷 **w** brissac.net

The château of the dukes of
Brissac, towering above the
River Aubance 18 km (11 miles)
southeast of Angers, is the
tallest along the Loire, and is
perhaps the grandest still in
private hands. Ownership has
passed down a long family line.

Charles de Cossé, governor
of Paris and marshal of France,
ordered the building of a vast
palace on top of an earlier
fortress, but its completion was
halted by his death in 1621.

On the entrance façade, an
ornate, 17th-century, domed
pavilion soars to 37 m (120 ft)
between two 15th-century
towers. Fifteen of the 204 rooms
are open to the public and are
filled with furniture, paintings
and tapestries. Among the most
striking is the Salle des Gardes,
which is decorated with
Aubusson tapestries and gilded
ceilings. The room is lit through
the distinctive paned windows
that are a feature of architect
Jacques Corbineau's work.

Other memorable rooms are
Louis XIII's bedroom and an
1883 opera theatre, still used
for concerts. In the château's
picture gallery hangs a
19th-century portrait of

Madame Clicquot, matriarch of
the famous champagne house
and a distant ancestor of the
present duke. The castle's fine
grounds can be explored, and
its wines tasted in cellars dating
from the 11th century.

## ❿ Gennes

**Road map** C3. 🔼 2,000. 🚊 Saumur
or Les Rosiers-sur-Loire. 🛈 square de
l'Europe (02 41 51 84 14). 🛒 Tue.
**w** cc-gennois.fr

During the Gallo-Roman
period (see pp52–3) Gennes,
on the south bank of the
River Loire, was an important
religious and commercial
centre. The largest **amphitheatre** in western France
was built on a hillside here
more than 1,800 years ago and
was used from the 1st to the
3rd centuries for gladiatorial
contests. A restoration project
in the 1980s revealed the
sandstone walls and brick tiers
of a stadium that seated at least
5,000 spectators and included
changing rooms and an
efficient drainage system.
In front of the arena, which
measures 2,160 sq m (2,600 sq
yds), marshlands on the Avort
river were probably flooded for
aquatic combats and displays.

The area around Gennes is
also very rich in Neolithic sites.
Among the 20 ancient burial
chambers and menhirs nearby
is the **Dolmen de la Madeleine**,
one of the largest in France.
Formerly used as a bakery, it

The medieval Eglise St-Vétérin in the town
of Gennes

can be found 1 km (1,100 yds)
east, past Gennes' medieval
**Eglise St-Vétérin** on the D69.

There is a lovely panoramic
view over the Loire from
**St-Eusèbe**, a ruined church
dating from the 11th to the
15th centuries, sited on a knoll
above the village. Beside the
old nave is a moving memorial
to cadets of the Saumur cavalry
school (see p87) who died trying
to prevent the German army
crossing the Loire in June 1940.

A bronze statue of Mercury
has been discovered on the hill,
and this seems to suggest that
a temple to the Roman god
may have stood here in the
Gallo-Roman period.

🏛 **Amphithéâtre**
**Tel** 02 41 51 94 70. **Open** May & Jun:
Sat & Sun; Jul & Aug: Wed–Sun; rest of
the year: by appt. 📷

🏛 **Dolmen de la Madeleine**
**Open** daily. ♿ restricted.

The Neolithic Dolmen de la Madeleine, near Gennes

## Environs

At L'Orbière, 4 km (2½ miles) from Gennes, the late sculptor Jacques Warminsky created a monumental underground work, named *L'Hélice Terrestre* (*The Earth's Helix*), consisting of intriguing, interlinking carved galleries that represent the universal philosophy of the artist.

To the west, in the village of Coutures, another extraordinary underground gallery is to be found at the **Manoir de la Cailliére**. Here, the artist Richard Rak has been creating other worlds and paintings from gathered objects.

### 🏛 L'Hélice Terrestre
L'Orbière, St-Georges-des-Sept-Voies. **Road map** C3. 🚃 Saumur, then taxi. **Tel** 02 41 57 95 92. **Open** daily (Oct–Apr: pm only, by appt). 🅿
🌐 heliceterrestre.canalblog.com

### 🏛 Manoir de la Cailléře
Coutures. **Tel** 02 41 57 97 97. **Open** May–Sep: Tue–Sun; Oct–Apr: Sat, Sun & public hols, or by reservation.

## ⑪ Cunault

**Road map** C3. 🔼 1,000. 🚃 Saumur. 🅸 Gennes (02 41 51 84 14). 🎵 Mois de L'Orgue (May); Les Heures Musicales (Jul & Aug).

Cunault's pale limestone priory church, the **Eglise Notre-Dame**, has rightly been called the most majestic of all the Romanesque churches in Anjou, if not the whole of the Loire Valley. In the 12th century, Benedictine monks from Tournus in Burgundy built the church in this small village on

Artist Jacques Warminsky at work on *L'Hélice Terrestre*

the south bank of the Loire. They incorporated the bell tower, dating from the 11th century, from an earlier building. A short spire was added in the 15th century.

Cunault is the longest Romanesque church without a transept in France. Inside, the first impression is of simplicity and elegance. The height of the pillars is impressive; they are topped with 223 carved capitals, decorated with fabulous beasts, demons and religious motifs, and are placed high enough so as not to interfere with the pure architectural lines. Binoculars are needed to see details.

Three aisles of equal width were made to accommodate the crowds of pilgrims who travelled to the church to see its relics, which included one revered as the wedding ring of the Virgin Mary, and the floor is deeply worn beside a 12th-century marble stoup at the foot of the entrance steps.

Towards the chancel, the ambulatory is floored with scalloped terracotta tiles. Traces of 15th-century frescoes remain, including a figure of St Christopher.

Other treasures include some impressive furniture in oak and ash, a 13th-century carved wooden reliquary and a painted 15th-century statue representing St Catherine.

The central aisle of Cunault's majestic 12th-century church

## Cultivated Mushrooms

Around 75 per cent of French cultivated mushrooms come from Anjou. The damp, dark caves in the tufa cliffs along the Loire are the perfect environment for the *champignons de Paris*, so called because they were first cultivated in disused quarries in the Paris region before production began in the Loire Valley in the late 19th century. Today, mushroom cultivation is a thriving business, employing thousands of people in the region. Growers have been diversifying in recent years, cultivating more exotic mushrooms such as *pleurottes* and *shiitake*, in response to demand from food-lovers.

Oyster mushrooms, known as *pleurottes*

# ⑫ Street-by-Street: Saumur

The storybook château is set on a hill high above the town, making it easy for visitors to locate Saumur's old quarter, which lies mainly between the château, the river and the main street running straight ahead from the central bridge over the Loire. The twisting streets that wind up and down the hill on which the château is built merit exploration. Saumur's modest size, which suits sightseeing on foot, is only one of the many charms of this friendly town.

**Theatre**
Saumur's theatre, which opened in the late 19th century, was modelled on the Odéon in Paris.

**Rue St-Jean** is the heart of Saumur's main shopping area.

**The Hôtel des Abbesses de Fontevraud**, at No. 6 rue de l'Ancienne-Messagerie, was built in the 17th century and has a marvellous spiral staircase.

**Maison du Roi**
This pretty Renaissance building at No. 33 rue Dacier once housed royalty but is now the headquarters of the Saumur Red Cross. In the courtyard is a plaque to the cultured duke, René I of Anjou, who often held court at Saumur.

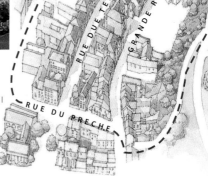

0 metres    50
0 yards     50

### Hôtel de Ville
The town hall was originally a manor house forming part of the city's fortified river wall. Built in 1508, with subsequent restorations and additions that have been in keeping with its Gothic style.

### Place St-Pierre
Saumur's oldest half-timbered houses, dating from the 15th century, are situated in place St-Pierre (Nos. 3, 5 and 6).

### ★ Eglise St-Pierre
First erected in the 12th and 13th centuries, and completed during the 15th and 16th centuries, this church has a fascinating collection of tapestries.

### Maison des Compagnons is a
15th-century building at the top of La Montée du Fort, which has been restored by a guild of stonemasons whose apprentices can be seen at work.

### ★ Château de Saumur
Saumur's château is situated next to the Butte des Moulins, a small hill that was once covered with windmills, and has great views of the surroundings, including a picturesque vineyard to one side.

**Key**

— Suggested route

# Exploring Saumur

Today, Saumur is best known for its wines, mushrooms and fine horse riders. It was a major power base for the medieval counts and dukes of Anjou, then a refuge for French Protestants in the 16th and 17th centuries, until the revocation of the Edict of Nantes in 1685 forced many Protestants to leave. Saumur has a rich legacy and is a vibrant town today. An excellent self-guided walking tour is available from the tourist office.

Skyline of the Château de Saumur

Panel from the 15th-century choir stalls in the Eglise St-Pierre

### The Old Quarter

At the heart of Saumur's old quarter stands the **Eglise St-Pierre**, which was built in the late 12th century. Its treasures include the beautifully carved 15th-century wooden stalls in the choir, and the magnificent 16th-century tapestries of the lives of Sts Peter and Florent. The latter was an influential figure in the monastic history of the region. He is depicted being rescued from Roman persecution, slaying a dragon and founding a monastery.

Nearby, the **Grande Rue**'s limestone and slate houses reflect Saumur's prosperity in the late 16th century under Protestant rule. The "Huguenot Pope", Philippe Duplessis Mornay, who governed the town between 1589 and 1621, owned the house at No. 45.

The oldest church in Saumur, **Notre-Dame de Nantilly**, was the town's principal place of worship for centuries. It too has a fine collection of 16th- and 17th-century tapestries, as well as carved capitals and an epitaph composed by the poet-king René I (see p57) to his childhood nurse inscribed on the third pillar on the nave's south side.

### 🏛 La Distillerie Combier

48 rue Beaurepaire.
**Tel** 02 41 40 23 00. **Open** Apr, May & Oct: Wed–Sun; Jun–Sep: daily; Nov–Mar: by appt. 🅿 🚭 ♿
**W** combier.fr

Since 1834 this distillery has been producing liqueurs according to traditional methods. The recipes remain a well-kept secret, but you can see the process and then have a tasting.

### 🏰 Château de Saumur

**Tel** 02 41 40 24 40. **Open** Tue–Sun.
🅿 🚭

The famous miniature of this château in *Les Très Riches Heures du Duc de Berry (see p97)* shows a white fairy-tale palace. The château was built for Louis I, Duke of Anjou, in the second half of the 14th century. It was constructed on the base of an earlier fortification. The glittering mass of chimney stacks and pinnacles was later simplified to a more sturdy skyline of shortened pencil towers, but the shape of the château remains graceful. The powerful-looking outbuildings that surround the château recall its later, although less pleasant, roles as a Protestant bastion, state prison and finally army barracks.

The château has undergone extensive renovations, following the collapse of part of the ramparts in 2001. The first floor houses the **Musée des Arts Décoratifs** which comprises a collection formed by Count Charles Lair, a native of Saumur, who left it to the château in 1919. It includes paintings, many fine tapestries, furniture, statuettes and ceramics that date from the 13th up to the 19th century.

Statuette from the Musée des Arts Décoratifs

### 🏛 Musée de la Cavalerie

pl Charles de Foucauld.
**Tel** 02 41 83 69 23. **Open** Wed–Mon (Sat–Mon: pm only).
**W** musee cavalerie.free.fr

Saumur's great horse-riding traditions stem from the training of cavalry elites for the French military. In the Ancien Régime, Saumur became one of the most specialized training centres in France. This museum starts the story in the 15th century, when the first royal military riding corps was created under Charles VII, to help end the Hundred Years' War.

The façade of the Eglise Notre-Dame de Nantilly

### ⚏ Musée des Blindés

1043 rte de Fontevraud. **Tel** 02 41 83 69 95. **Open** daily. **Closed** 1 Jan, 25 Dec. ⚏ ⚏ ⚏ **museedesblindes.fr**

Owned by the Cavalry and Armoured Vehicles School, this barn-like museum has on display more historic tanks and armoured personnel carriers in working order than any other international military collection.

Beginning with a FT 17 Renault dating from 1917 and moving through the German World War II panzers to the monsters produced today, the museum offers a chance to see at close quarters these veterans of many conflicts.

### ⚏ Dolmen de Bagneux

56 rue du Dolmen, Bagneux. **Tel** 02 41 50 23 02. ⚏ Saumur. ⚏ **Open** Sep–Jun: Thu–Tue; Jul & Aug: daily. ⚏ ⚏ ⚏ **ledolmendebagneux.com**

Saumur's main street leads to the suburb of Bagneux. Here, in a local bar's garden, one unexpectedly finds one of the most impressive Neolithic burial chambers in Europe. Visitors can sip drinks in the garden, absorb the impact of the dolmen and marvel at the massive sandstone slabs, some weighing 40 tonnes, that were dragged, tilted and wedged into position 5,000 years ago *(see pp52–3)*.

A signpost for the Bagneux dolmen

**Environs** The village of St-Hilaire-St-Florent, 2 km (1½ miles) northwest of Saumur on the D751, is well worth a visit for its museums and the famous Cadre Noir riding school. It also

A 1917 Renault tank in the collection of the Musée des Blindés

has a number of wine cellars where visitors can taste and buy the famous Saumur Brut, a sparkling wine that is produced by the *méthode champenoise*. The Maison des Vins de Loire de Saumur, next to the tourist office, provides information on local wines, vineyards and tourist routes.

### ⚏ Musée du Champignon

rte de Gennes, St-Hilaire- St-Florent. **Tel** 02 41 50 31 55. **Open** mid-Feb–mid-Nov: daily. ⚏ ⚏ ⚏ **musee-du-champignon.com**

This unique museum takes visitors through a network of limestone caves. Displays show how mushrooms that are grown from spores in bagged or boxed compost thrive in the high humidity and constant temperature of this environment *(see p83)*. The museum has an excellent collection of live mushroom species, as well as of fossils found during quarrying. On sale, and worth tasting, is a local speciality, *gallipettes farcies*, large mushrooms stuffed with a variety of fillings.

### ⚏ Parc Miniature Pierre et Lumière

rte de Gennes, St-Hilaire- St-Florent. **Tel** 02 41 50 70 04. **Open** Feb–mid-Nov: 10am–7pm daily. **Closed** mid-Nov–Jan. ⚏ ⚏ ⚏ **pierre-et-lumiere.com**

The gallery of a former underground quarry is now the setting for 20 scale models carved from the tufa rock. They represent some of the most famous – and a few less well-known – monuments, towns and villages of the Loire Valley. Among the highlights are Fontevraud Abbey, Tours Cathedral and the Château d'Amboise. The models are the work of self-taught sculptor Philippe Cormand.

### ⚏ Ecole Nationale d'Equitation

Terrefort, St-Hilaire-St-Florent. **Tel** 02 41 53 50 60. **Open** mid-Feb–early Nov: Mon pm–Sat am, visits at fixed times. **Closed** Sun and public hols. ⚏ ⚏ ⚏ **cadrenoir.fr**

The National Riding School, founded in 1814, is world famous for its team, known as the Cadre Noir because of the riders' elegant black and gold ceremonial uniforms. The team of riders is generally restricted to just 22 elite horsemen. The Cadre Noir's horses are trained in a distinctive style of dressage, which was first practised in the 19th century. They are taught perfect balance and control and learn choreographed movements that show their natural grace. During the summer months, visitors can enter the academy team's quarters and watch a morning training session. There are also regular performances of the spectacular summer gala.

The 5,000-year-old Bagneux dolmen near Saumur

## ⓮ Montreuil-Bellay

**Road map** C4. 🏘 4,500. 🚉 Saumur.
🚌 **ℹ** pl du Concorde (02 41 52 32
39). 🛒 Tue am, Sun (May–Sep).
**w** ville-montreuil-bellay.com

Combining an ancient village
and a fascinating feudal
château, Montreuil-Bellay,
18 km (11 miles) south of
Saumur, is one of the most
attractive towns in Anjou. The
château complex occupies a
site which was first fortified in
the 11th century by Foulques
Nerra and besieged by Geoffrey Plantagenet during the
following century. In the 13th
century it was surrounded by
strong walls, with a grand
towered entrance (known
as the Château-Vieux) and
11 other towers. Inside the
ramparts is a collection of
mainly late 15th-century

Frescoes in the oratory of the Château de
Montreuil-Bellay

buildings, looking over
landscaped terraces falling
to the pretty River Thouet.
  The Château-Neuf is an
elegant Renaissance-fronted
building, begun in the late

15th century. The turret was
made famous by the infamous
French noblewoman, Anne
de Longueville (1619–79),
who rode her horse to the
top of its spiral staircase.
  The château's interior is
superbly furnished and has a
number of fireplaces in the
Flamboyant style as well as
splendid painted and carved
ceilings. The 15th-century
frescoes adorning the oratory
are currently under restoration,
but the guided tour still takes
in the medieval kitchens, which
are said to be modelled on
those of the earlier Fontevraud
Abbey (see pp90–91).

🏠 **Château de Montreuil-Bellay**
**Tel** 02 41 52 33 06. **Open** Apr–Jun &
Sep–Nov: Wed–Mon; Jul & Aug: daily.
🌐 📷 **w** chateau-de-montreuil-
bellay.fr

## ⓯ Troglodyte Tour

Caves, cut into the tufa cliffs beside the
Loire and other limestone-rich areas in
Anjou, are used as dovecotes, chapels,
farms, wine cellars and even homes.
These so-called "troglodyte" dwellings,
some of which date back to the 12th
century and have hardly changed over
the centuries, are fashionable again as
artists' studios or holiday homes.
Life in and among these caves
is the subject of this
fascinating tour.

**⑥ Dénézé-sous-Doué**
In these underground
caves, carved by
Protestant stonemasons
during the 16th-century
Wars of Religion, more
than 400 figures are
chiselled into the walls,
floors and ceilings.

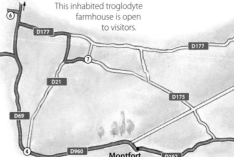
Carved figures at Dénézé-sous-Doué

**⑦ La Fosse**
This inhabited troglodyte
farmhouse is open
to visitors.

Troglodyte houses at Rochemenier

**⑤ Rochemenier**
This former troglodyte
farming community
has been turned into
a museum displaying
underground farmyards,
barns, houses and a simple
rock chapel.

**④ Doué-la-Fontaine**
The rue des Perrières was excavated
from a stratum of shell marl (faluns);
its "cathedral" vaults were dug
vertically from the top. The town
also has an amphitheatre cut from
the rock and an outstanding zoo
set in old quarries.

# ⑭ Château de Montsoreau

**Road map** C3. 🚂 Saumur, then taxi.
🚌 **Tel** 02 41 67 12 60. **Open** Apr:
daily pm; May–Sep: daily; Oct–
mid-Nov: daily pm. ♿ &
**w** chateau-montsoreau.com

This picturesque late-medieval château stands in the midst of a beautiful village. The castle was built for its lords to control the port and river toll.

In Alexandre Dumas' novel *La dame de Monsoreau*, the jealous count, Charles de Chambes, forces his wife to lure her lover to the château, where he is murdered. This story is true, in part, and one of the exhibitions inside retells this violent tale. The focus of the other displays is the Loire, covering nature along the river, as well as the people who have transformed it over the years.

Château de Montsoreau on the River Loire

Also in Montsoreau is the Parc Naturel Régional Loire-Anjou-Touraine, a nature reserve that is home to 329 species of butterfly and 52 kinds of dragonfly. Visit the ecologically built visitors centre (**Maison du Parc**) to learn more.

🏢 **Maison du Parc Régional Loire-Anjou-Touraine**
15 av de la Loire, Montsoreau.
**Tel** 02 41 53 66 00. **Open** Mar:
Sat & Sun; Apr, Oct & Nov:
Tue–Sun; May–Sep: daily. &
**w** parc-loire-anjou-touraine.fr

---

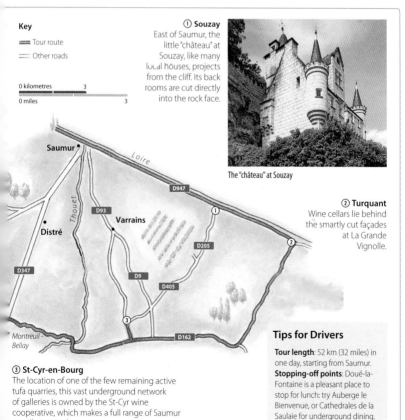

### Key

🚌🚌 Tour route
═══ Other roads

0 kilometres    3
0 miles    3

① **Souzay**
East of Saumur, the little "château" at Souzay, like many local houses, projects from the cliff. Its back rooms are cut directly into the rock face.

The "château" at Souzay

② **Turquant**
Wine cellars lie behind the smartly cut façades at La Grande Vignolle.

Saumur
Loire
D947
Thouet
D93
**Varrains**
①
• **Distré**
D205
②
D347
D9
D405
*Montreuil Bellay*
③
D162

③ **St-Cyr-en-Bourg**
The location of one of the few remaining active tufa quarries, this vast underground network of galleries is owned by the St-Cyr wine cooperative, which makes a full range of Saumur *appellations* in these caves.

### Tips for Drivers

**Tour length**: 52 km (32 miles) in one day, starting from Saumur.
**Stopping-off points**: Doué-la-Fontaine is a pleasant place to stop for lunch: try Auberge le Bienvenue, or Cathedrales de la Saulaie for underground dining.

# ⑯ Abbaye de Fontevraud

Fontevraud Abbey, founded in 1101 by the hermit Robert d'Arbrissel for both women and men, is the largest and most extraordinary of its kind in France. It was run for nearly 700 years by aristocratic abbesses, almost half of them royal-born. They governed a monks' priory outside the main walls, and three distinct communities of nuns and lay sisters, ranging from rich widows to repentant prostitutes, as well as a leper colony and an infirmary. Restoration work has removed traces of the 150 years after the Revolution when the abbey served as a prison. Now it is fully open to tourists and hosts many cultural events.

**★ Chapter House Paintings**
The paintings in the Chapter House date from the 16th century. However, some figures were added later.

**★ Plantagenet Effigies**
These four effigies (*gisants*), each a realistic portrait, are displayed in the nave of the abbey church.

## KEY

① **Nursing sisters** of the St Benoît order cared for invalids in this section of the abbey.

② **The grand refectory**, with its Renaissance ribbed vaulting, is 60 m (200 ft) long.

③ **Former orangery in a wing** of the Abbess's Palace

④ **Reception and information centre**

⑤ **Grand-Moûtier**, the cloisters of the main convent are the largest, and possibly the finest, in France. They have Gothic and Renaissance vaulting and upper galleries built in the 19th century.

## The Resting Place of the Plantagenets

The medieval painted effigy of Henry Plantagenet, count of Anjou and king of England (1133–1189), lies beside that of his wife, Eleanor of Aquitaine, who died in Poitiers in 1204. With them are the effigies of their son, King Richard the Lionheart (1157–1199), and Isabelle, wife of his brother, King John. In all, around 10 of the family are buried here.

Effigies of Eleanor of Aquitaine and Henry II

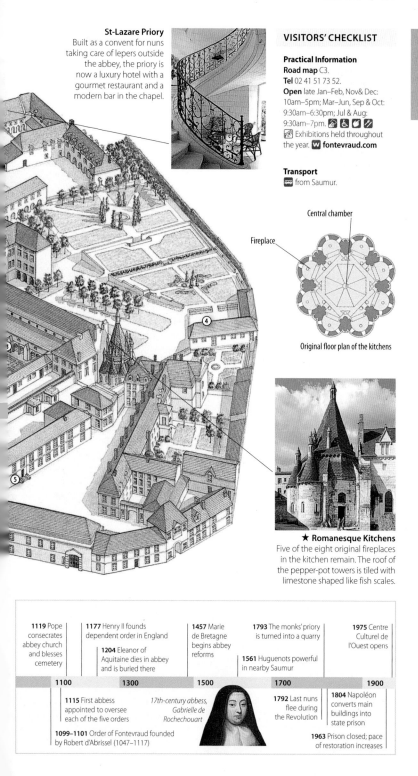

**St-Lazare Priory**
Built as a convent for nuns taking care of lepers outside the abbey, the priory is now a luxury hotel with a gourmet restaurant and a modern bar in the chapel.

### VISITORS' CHECKLIST

#### Practical Information
Road map C3.
**Tel** 02 41 51 73 52.
**Open** late Jan–Feb, Nov & Dec: 10am–5pm; Mar–Jun, Sep & Oct: 9:30am–6:30pm; Jul & Aug: 9:30am–7pm. Exhibitions held throughout the year. **fontevraud.com**

#### Transport
from Saumur.

Central chamber

Fireplace

Original floor plan of the kitchens

**★ Romanesque Kitchens**
Five of the eight original fireplaces in the kitchen remain. The roof of the pepper-pot towers is tiled with limestone shaped like fish scales.

**1119** Pope consecrates abbey church and blesses cemetery

**1177** Henry II founds dependent order in England

**1204** Eleanor of Aquitaine dies in abbey and is buried there

**1457** Marie de Bretagne begins abbey reforms

**1793** The monks' priory is turned into a quarry

**1561** Huguenots powerful in nearby Saumur

**1975** Centre Culturel de l'Ouest opens

**1100**  **1300**  **1500**  **1700**  **1900**

**1115** First abbess appointed to oversee each of the five orders

*17th-century abbess, Gabrielle de Rochechouart*

**1792** Last nuns flee during the Revolution

**1804** Napoléon converts main buildings into state prison

**1099–1101** Order of Fontevraud founded by Robert d'Abrissel (1047–1117)

**1963** Prison closed; pace of restoration increases

# TOURAINE

Touraine is known chiefly for the magnificent white châteaux strung out along the broad Loire and its tributaries. Added to these are its rich history and fertile landscape, making it the archetypal Loire Valley region. The rolling terrain and lush forests that once attracted the kings and queens of France continue to work their charm over visitors from all around the world today.

The feudal castles that still exist, at Loches and Chinon for example, remind visitors that this now tranquil region was once a battleground for the warring counts of Blois and Anjou. It was also here, at Chinon, that the Anglo-French Plantagenet monarch, Henry II of England, held court and where, later, Joan of Arc managed to bully the future Charles VII of France into raising the army that she would lead to victory over the English.

Charles VIII, Louis XII and François I brought the influence of the Italian Renaissance to France and set a fashion in architecture that produced the unforgettable châteaux of this region. The most magical – the delicate Azay-le-Rideau, the majestic Chenonceau and Villandry with its extraordinary formal gardens – were built during this period. However, at the end of the 16th century, Touraine ceased to be a playground for the court.

Tours, at the heart of the region, makes a natural base for visitors, who can enjoy its sensitively restored, medieval old town.

The rolling terrain and gentle climate of Touraine encourage outdoor pursuits, including hiking, boating and fishing. The area is also famous for its *primeurs*, early fruit and vegetables, such as white asparagus, grown on its low-lying, fertile soils. Its many wines, including the well-known *appellations* of Bourgueil, Chinon and Vouvray, are the perfect accompaniment to the region's excellent cuisine.

A view of the Château de Chinon, on a cliff above the River Vienne

◄ The impeccably manicured Garden of Love at the Château de Villandry

# Exploring Touraine

Crisscrossed by rivers great and small, Touraine sits regally at the heart of the Loire Valley. Châteaux are distributed along the paths of the rivers: Langeais and Amboise by the Loire itself; Ussé, Azay-le-Rideau and Loches by the gentle Indre; and Chenonceau gracefully straddling the Cher. Tours, the main town in the region, is also on the Loire. The Gâtine Tourangelle to the north of the river was once a magnificent forest but was felled progressively from the 11th century by local people in search of wood and arable land. However, small pockets of woodland remain, delightful for walking and picnicking.

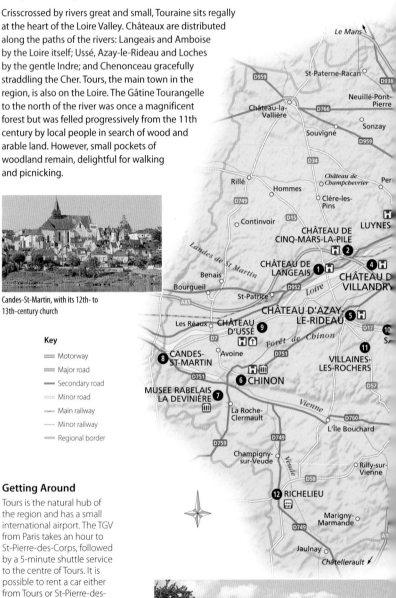

Candes-St-Martin, with its 12th- to 13th-century church

## Key

=== Motorway
=== Major road
— Secondary road
···· Minor road
⌐⌐⌐ Main railway
— Minor railway
=== Regional border

## Getting Around

Tours is the natural hub of the region and has a small international airport. The TGV from Paris takes an hour to St-Pierre-des-Corps, followed by a 5-minute shuttle service to the centre of Tours. It is possible to rent a car either from Tours or St-Pierre-des-Corps. The A10 is the fastest route from Paris by car. The A85 is the easiest way to get across the region. The D952 and D751 hug the Loire and pass through attractive countryside. The prettiest drives, however, include those along the rivers Cher, Indre and Vienne.

Le Mans

St-Paterne-Racan

Neuillé-Pont-Pierre

Château-la-Vallière

Souvigné

Sonzay

Rillé

Château de Champchevrier

Per

Hommes

Clére-les-Pins

Continvoir

**LUYNES**

**CHÂTEAU DE CINQ-MARS-LA-PILE** ❷

Benais

**CHÂTEAU DE LANGEAIS** ❶

**CHÂTEAU D VILLANDR** ❹

Bourgueil

St-Patrice

Loire

**CHÂTEAU D'AZAY-LE-RIDEAU** ❺

Les Réaux

**CHÂTEAU D'USSÉ** ❾

Forêt de Chinon

❿

Avoine

**VILLAINES-LES-ROCHERS** ⓫

**CANDES-ST-MARTIN** ❽

**CHINON** ❻

**MUSÉE RABELAIS LA DEVINIÈRE** ❼

La Roche-Clermault

Vienne

L'Île Bouchard

Champigny-sur-Veude

Rilly-sur-Vienne

**RICHELIEU** ⓬

Marigny-Marmande

Jaulnay

Châtellerault

One of Touraine's renowned vineyards

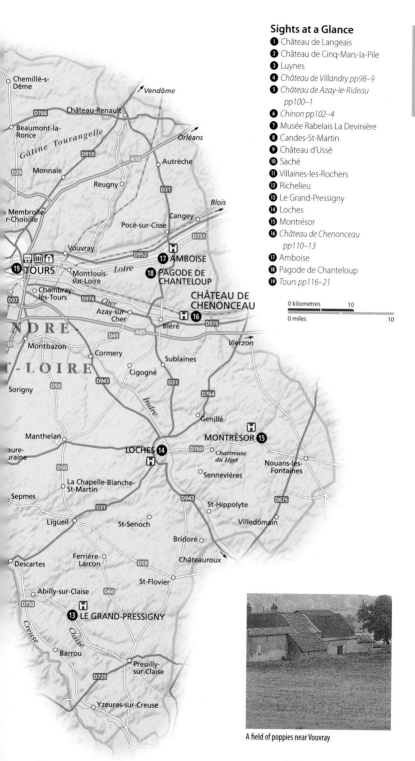

0 kilometres    10
0 miles    10

A field of poppies near Vouvray

Chapel of the Château de Langeais, with its curved, wood ceiling

# ❶ Château de Langeais

**Road map** D3. 🚉 **Tel** 02 47 96 72 60.
**Open** daily. 🅿️ 📷 **W** chateau-de-langeais.com

The feudal Château de Langeais, looming up in the centre of the small town, was built for King Louis XI between 1465 and 1490 by his treasurer, Jean Bourré. It stands on the site of an earlier fortress built by the fearsome Foulques Nerra (*see p54*), of which only the rectangular keep remains – this can now be climbed up and it serves as a backdrop for historical re-enactments.

Langeais' forbidding outer walls, towers, drawbridge and heavily machicolated sentry walk contrast strongly with its elegant interiors, unaltered over the centuries. Its collection of beautifully displayed 15th- and 16th-century furniture, paintings and tapestries was amassed in the late 19th century by its last private owner, the well-known Alsace banker and philanthropist, Jacques Siegfried.

Among the treasures in the castle is the wedding chest brought by the 14-year-old Duchess Anne of Brittany when she married the tiny, hunchbacked Charles VIII here in the early hours of 6 December 1491. A waxwork tableau re-creates this clandestine event – both were already betrothed to others – and includes a copy of Anne's cloth-of-gold wedding gown, lined with 160 sable skins.

From the castle's parapets visitors can view the handsome town below, which has a good Sunday morning food market. The remodelled castle grounds, which include a remarkable treehouse, are also worth exploring.

The Gallo-Roman tower near Cinq-Mars-la-Pile

# ❷ Château de Cinq-Mars-la-Pile

**Road map** D3. 🚉 **Tel** 02 47 96 40 49.
**Open** Apr–Jun & 16 Sep–Oct: Sat & Sun; Jul–15 Sep: Wed–Mon.
**Closed** Nov–Mar. 🅿️ **W** chateau-cinq-mars.com

The most famous inhabitant of the castle of Cinq-Mars was Henri Ruzé d'Effiat, Marquis de Cinq-Mars, and the eponymous hero of a novel by the Touraine writer Alfred de Vigny. The marquis, a favourite of King Louis XIII, rashly became involved in a plot against Louis' minister, Cardinal Richelieu, and was beheaded in 1642, aged 22. Richelieu ordered the castle at Cinq-Mars to be truncated – it is said that even the trees had their crowns chopped off. A pair of towers remain, each with three vaulted chambers, surrounded by an extremely wide moat. The château's fragrant, romantic gardens are adorned with topiary.

The *Pile* in the town's name refers to a strange Gallo-Roman brick tower, more than 30 m (98 ft) high, on a ridge just east

Towers of the Château de Cinq-Mars-la-Pile

Luynes' imposing château, dominating the village below

The present Renaissance manor house, with various 18th-century additions, is set in a lush forest. Its elegant rooms are beautifully furnished, with particularly fine family portraits and Beauvais tapestries. A pack of hounds is kept at the château.

🏠 **Château de Champchevrier**
Cléré-les-Pins. **Tel** 02 47 24 93 93.
**Open** Mid-Jun–mid-Sep: Mon–Sat, Sun pm only; mid-Sep–mid-Jun: groups by appt. 🖼 🎥
🌐 **champchevrier.com**

The Chambre du Roi in the Château de Champchevrier

of the village. The south side of the tower, whose purpose and precise date are a mystery, was decorated with 12 multi-coloured brick panels, laid out in a geometric design, four of which are still intact today.

## ❸ Luynes

**Road map** D3. 🔼 5,000. 🚍 Tours, then bus 🚌 🛈 9 rue Alfred Baugé (02 47 55 77 14). 🛒 Sat. Château: **Tel** 02 47 55 67 55. **Open** Apr–mid-Sep: daily. 🖼 🎥 🌐 **luynes.fr**

Brooding over this pretty little town is an imposing château, originally called Maillé after the noble owners who rebuilt it in the early 13th century. It is still inhabited by descendants of the first Duc de Luynes, who bought it in 1619, and furnished with Renaissance and17th-century pieces. The old town developed to the south of the château, and its 15th-century wooden market hall remains.

The remaining 44 arches of a **Gallo-Roman aqueduct** can be seen 1.5 km (1 mile) northeast of Luynes. Standing in isolation amid fields, they are a striking sight.

The wealthy Maillé family also owned a feudal castle on the site of the **Château de Champchevrier**, 10 km (6 miles) northwest of Luynes.

## Life in a Medieval Château

During times of peace, life in a medieval château took on a pleasant routine. To fill the long winter days, nobles played board games, such as chess and draughts, or cards. Ladies, when they were not playing music or embroidering, had dwarves to entertain them, while the court jester kept banquet guests amused by making fun of everyone, even the king. Mystery plays (dramas based on the life of Christ) were very popular and cycles of these plays often lasted for several weeks. Outdoor pursuits enjoyed during the summer included bowling, archery and ball games, but it was the tournaments, with jousting and swordplay, that provoked the most excitement. Hunting was also favoured by kings and nobles and much practised in the woods and forests of the Loire Valley.

The illumination for August from *Les Très Riches Heures du Duc de Berry*

# ❹ Château de Villandry

The Château de Villandry, dating from the late Renaissance (1536), has an almost Classical elegance. But it is most famous for its superb gardens, restored since the estate was bought in 1906 by the Spanish Carvallo family. Working from 16th-century designs, skilful gardeners mixed flowers and vegetables in fascinating geometric patterns. The garden is spread between three levels: you will find the sun garden and the water garden on the highest level; a flower garden on the same level as the château; and below it, the world's largest ornamental kitchen garden *(below)*. Also explore the delightful smaller plots, such as the cross garden.

**★ Garden of Love**
Flower designs here symbolize four types of love: tragic, adulterous, tender and passionate.

**Shaped Pear Trees**
In Villandry's gardens, nature is completely controlled. The pear trees are carefully pruned to form neat oval shapes.

**Gardeners**
Nine full-time gardeners look after the 60,000 vegetables and 45,000 bedding plants in the kitchen garden and the ornamental flower garden, using organic methods.

**★ Ornamental Kitchen Garden**
The current state of the garden can be studied in the plan pinned up near the moat. The plant and vegetable names for each square are listed and the colours shown.

## Renaissance Kitchen and Herb Gardens

A 16th-century French treatise on diet reveals that the melons, artichokes, asparagus and cauliflower that fill Villandry's kitchen gardens today all also commonly appeared on Renaissance dinner tables. Herbs were widely used both for their medicinal and culinary applications. They formed the borders in the kitchen gardens of monasteries, such as that at Solesmes (*see p166*), which were the first to feature geometric planting. Villandry has a *jardin des simples* (herb garden) on its middle level.

*Knautia dipsacifolia,* from a 16th-century manual on plants

### VISITORS' CHECKLIST

**Practical Information**
Road map D3.
**Tel** 02 47 50 02 09.
**Open** from 9am daily. Closing times vary throughout the year; for details, see the website. Last adm: 30 mins before closing time.
**Closed** early Jan–mid-Feb & mid-Nov–mid-Dec; check the website for full details. 🅿 🚻 ♿ 🚫
🅦 **chateauvillandry.com**

**Transport**
🚌 Savonnières, then taxi. Daily shuttle bus service from Tours (Jul & Aug). **Tel** 02 47 66 70 70. 🅦 **filbleu.fr**
By bike: follow the Loire à Vélo route (14.5 km/9 miles). Cycle routes can be downloaded from 🅦 **loireavelo.fr**

**Decorative Cabbage**
Ornamental Japanese cabbages were introduced by the mother of the present owner to provide year-round colour in the kitchen garden.

### KEY

① **Jardin du Soleil**

② **Maze**

③ **Herb garden**

④ **A collection of Spanish paintings** is housed in the château.

⑤ **The elegant stone balustrades** above the kitchen garden have been restored.

⑥ **The pool** for irrigating the gardens is shaped like a gilt-framed mirror.

The flower gardens, including the garden of love, level with the south façade of the château

# ❺ Château d'Azay-le-Rideau

Memorably described by Honoré de Balzac as a "faceted diamond set in the Indre", Azay-le-Rideau is one of the most popular châteaux in the Loire. Its graceful silhouette and richly decorated façades are mirrored in the peaceful waters of its lake, once a medieval moat. Azay was built from about 1518 by Gilles Berthelot, only to be confiscated by François I in 1527. The unknown architect, influenced by Italian design and innovative in his use of a straight staircase, took the defensive elements of an earlier, more warlike age and transformed them into charming ornamental features. Furnished in 16th- to 19th-century styles, the château has some notable tapestries and a famous portrait said to be of Henri IV's mistress, Gabrielle d'Estrées.

**Kitchen**
The kitchen, situated in the west wing, has rib vaulting and a huge open fireplace.

**Renaissance Room**
With plaited bulrush on the walls, this room looks just as it would have in the 1500s.

**La Dame au Bain**
Henri IV's haughty mistress Gabrielle d'Estrées is said to feature in the château's finest painting, done in the style of François Clouet.

## Azay's Creators

Treasurer to François I and mayor of Tours, Gilles Berthelot bought Azay-le-Rideau in 1510. With the help of his wife, he soon began transforming the medieval castle here into a Renaissance palace befitting his station. The emblems of François I and Claude de France were sculpted in stone above various doors in the château in an attempt to flatter the sovereigns. But flattery did not save Berthelot's career – about to be accused of embezzlement, he was forced to flee Azay before the building was completed.

François I's salamander emblem

**Entrance Façade**
The entrance façade is dominated by the galleried stairwell topped by a tall gable. Its decoration, full of shells, medallions and candelabras, was influenced by Italian Renaissance artists.

**VISITORS' CHECKLIST**

**Practical Information**
Road map D3.
**Tel** 02 47 45 42 04.
**Open** Apr–Jun & Sep: 9:30am–6pm daily; Jul & Aug: 9:30am–7pm daily; Oct–Mar: 10am–5:15pm daily.
**Closed** 1 Jan, 1 May, 25 Dec.
🅿 📷 🆆 azay-le-rideau. monuments-nationaux.fr

**Transport**
🚉 Azay-le-Rideau.

**★ Central Staircase**
Azay's most significant design feature is its central staircase, consisting of six straight flights with landings, rather than the spiral staircase that was usual for the period.

**KEY**

① **The elegant turrets** adorn the château's façade rather than protect it, as the sturdy towers of medieval fortresses had done in the past.

② **The Antechamber** to the *Chambre du Roi* (the King's Bedroom) houses a portrait gallery of kings. The walls are hung with portraits of, among others, François I, Henri II and Henri III.

③ **Ballroom with Flemish tapestries**

**★ South Façade**
Symmetry is the underlying motif of the exterior design, with its matching turrets and its stripe of decoration imitating machicolations.

# ❻ Street-by-Street: Chinon

The Château de Chinon stands on a golden-coloured cliff above the River Vienne. Below it, Chinon's old crooked streets resonate with history. The travel-weary Joan of Arc *(see p141)* arrived in the town on 6 March 1429. It was here that she began her transformation from peasant girl to the warrior-saint – the saint is shown sitting astride a charger in a statue in the marketplace. In the nearby Maison des Etats-Généraux, now the Musée d'Art et d'Histoire, Richard the Lionheart lay in state in 1199. His father, Henry Plantagenet, had died a few years earlier in the château, one of the main bases from which he had ruled England as well as much of the Loire Valley.

**Tour de l'Horloge**
This 14th-century clock tower stands out from the other towers along the ramparts.

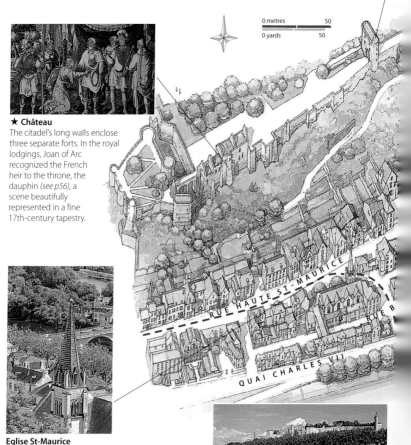

0 metres 50
0 yards 50

★ **Château**
The citadel's long walls enclose three separate forts. In the royal lodgings, Joan of Arc recognized the French heir to the throne, the dauphin *(see p56)*, a scene beautifully represented in a fine 17th-century tapestry.

RUE HAUTE ST-MAURICE

RUE B

QUAI CHARLES VII

**Eglise St-Maurice**
Henry II rebuilt this church with Angevin vaults, retaining the Romanesque lower part of what is now the steeple.

**Ramparts**
The château's ramparts are an impressive sight from the opposite bank of the River Vienne.

★ **Musée d'Art et d'Histoire**
Now a museum of local history, this building was once the scene of France's first attempt at a parliament. It met to fund the war against the English in 1428.

**Hôtel Torterue de Langardière**'s Classical façade is ornamented with wrought-iron balconies.

**Caves Painctes**
were originally dug under the château in the 15th century.

**Musée Animé du Vin**
Animated figures show 19th-century winemaking and coopering techniques.

**Maison Rouge**, a superbly restored medieval house, has sculpted beams across its red-brick façade.

**François Rabelais**
A bronze statue, made in 1882 by Emile Hébert, celebrates the famous satirist.

**Grand Carroi**
This crossroads, at the heart of the old fortified town, is where Joan of Arc is said to have dismounted at a well.

**Key**

— Suggested route

**VISITORS' CHECKLIST**

**Practical Information**
Road map D3.
9,000. pl Hofheim.
Thu. **Tel** 02 47 93 17 85.
chinon-valdeloire.com

**Transport**
blvd Gambetta. blvd Gambetta.

# Exploring Chinon

A walk through the narrow streets to the east of the château shows how much Chinon has to offer. High above the place Jeanne d'Arc is the remarkable Chapelle de Ste-Radegonde, carved into the limestone cliff. Behind this 12th-century frescoed chapel are ancient hermit caves and dizzying steps to an underground well. For a leisurely tour of the town, opt for a horse-drawn carriage, or board a traditional riverboat from the southbank to enjoy a different perspective from the Vienne. Heading east out of town leads to enchanting vineyards and villages, with many wineries open to visitors.

### 🏰 Forteresse Royale de Chinon

**Tel** 02 47 93 13 45. **Open** daily all year. **Closed** 1 Jan, 25 Dec. 🗟
🖥 **w** forteressechinon.fr

This magnificent fortress, running along the hill above the Vienne river, is closely associated with the Plantagenet kings of England, and with Joan of Arc, who helped boot the dynasty out of France at the end of the Hundred Years' War.

The huge citadel, built for King Henry II in the 12th century, fell into ruin during the Ancien Régime *(see pp58–61)*. However, it has since been stunningly restored and its fascinating history is brought to life using imaginative methods, including a series of short films designed to evoke key moments in the building's history. The citadel's western section has large towers that you can climb up and down. The views across the Vienne Valley are beautiful.

Statue of Joan of Arc by Jules Roulleau

### 🏛 Le Carroi, Musée d'Art et d'Histoire

44 rue Haute St-Maurice. **Tel** 02 47 93 18 12. **Open** pm only. Wed–Sat (mid-Nov–mid-Feb: Fri–Mon). 🗟

The treasures in this museum of local history include a portrait of Rabelais by Eugène Delacroix (1798–1863), and the "Cope of St Mexme", the first large Arab tapestry brought to France.

### 🏛 Caves Painctes

Impasse des Caves Painctes. **Tel** 02 47 93 30 44. 🗒 only. Jul & Aug: 11am, 3pm, 4:30pm, 6pm Tue–Sun. 🗟

Oenology and literature come together in these wine cellars, which occupy a subterranean quarry dug under the château in the 15th century. They are the headquarters of the *Confrérie des Bons Entonneurs Rabelaisiens*, a brotherhood of wine growers who meet four times a year to celebrate Chinon wine and commemorate Rabelais' humanism and *joie de vivre*. The caves are allegedly inspired by the author's description of the Temple of the Divine Bottle. The price of a visit includes a wine tasting session.

### 🏛 Musée Animé du Vin et de la Tonnellerie

12 rue Voltaire. **Tel** 02 47 93 25 63. **Open** 15 Mar–15 Nov: daily; 16 Nov –14 Mar: groups by appt. **Closed** 1 Jan, 25 Dec. 🗟

Here you can taste sharp, dry, strawberry-like Chinon red wine, while watching automated models demonstrate the various stages in wine- and barrel-making (both are important Chinon industries) using some of the museum's 19th-century implements.

The Tour de l'Horloge, leading to the middle castle

---

### François Rabelais (1483–1553)

Priest, doctor, humanist and supreme *farceur* of French literature, François Rabelais is everywhere present in "Rabelaisie", as the area around La Devinière has become known. Rabelais enthusiasts will recognize in the old farmhouse the castle of Grandgousier, besieged by the hordes of King Picrochole, but saved by the arrival of giant Gargantua on his mare, who drowns most of them by creating a flood with his prodigious urination. Rabelais' thirst for knowledge imbued his *Gargantua* and *Pantagruel* (see p28) with a wealth of learning that sits surprisingly easily alongside a ribald *joie de vivre*.

The infant Gargantua

View of the Château d'Ussé from the bridge crossing the River Indre

## ❼ Musée Rabelais La Devinière

**Road map** D3. 🚆 Chinon, then taxi. **Tel** 02 47 95 91 18. **Open** Wed–Mon (Apr–Sep: daily). **Closed** 1 Jan, 25 Dec. **W** **musee-rabelais.fr**

The 16th-century writer François Rabelais was probably born in this modest farmhouse, 2 km (1½ miles) southwest of Chinon. It is now a museum devoted to the man and his contemporaries. Brought up in Chinon, Rabelais became an eminent monk, doctor and scholar, as well as the most brilliant satirist in French Renaissance literature.

La Devinière, the birthplace of Rabelais and now a museum devoted to him

## ❽ Candes-St-Martin

**Road map** C3. 230. 🚆 Chinon or Port Boulet, then taxi. **i** Chinon (02 47 93 17 85).

Beautifully situated overlooking the shimmering waters where the Loire and Vienne rivers converge, picturesque Candes is famous as the place where St Martin died in 397. Stained glass in the 12th-century church depicts the saint's body being secretly rowed to Tours for burial. The porch of the church was fortified in the 15th century and is adorned with carved heads. Inside, the ceiling is a fine example of Angevin vaulting. You can embark on a Loire boat trip from Candes.

## ❾ Château d'Ussé

**Road map** D3. 🚆 Chinon, then taxi (15 km/9 miles). **Tel** 02 47 95 54 05. **Open** mid-Feb–mid-Nov: daily. park & grd flr only. **W** **chateaudusse.fr**

With its countless pointed turrets gleaming white against the sombre trees of the Forêt de Chinon, the gorgeous Château d'Ussé is said to have inspired 17th-century French author Charles Perrault to write the fairy tale *The Sleeping Beauty*. The fortified château was begun in 1462 for the powerful courtier Jean de Bueil on the foundations of a medieval castle. In 1485 it was sold to the Espinay family, chamberlains to both Louis XI and Charles VII, who softened the courtyard façades with Renaissance features.

In the 17th century the north wing was demolished, opening up the main courtyard to views of the River Indre. Formal gardens designed by the landscape architect André Le Nôtre were planted in terraces to the river and an orangery was added, completing the transformation from fortress to aristocratic country house.

The interior of the château, which is still lived in, is also decorated in a variety of styles. In one tower, visitors can see a waxwork tableau of *The Sleeping Beauty*. The chapel, stables and wine cellar are also worth a visit.

The Late Gothic exterior of Ussé's chapel

Mobile by Alexander Calder (1898–1976) in Saché

## ⑩ Saché

**Road map** D3. 🔢 1,200. 🚌 Jul–Sep. 🚆 Azay-le-Rideau, then taxi. *i* Azay-le-Rideau (02 47 45 44 40). 🌐 **sache.fr**

The pretty village of Saché is notable for having been second home to both a writer and an artist of world renown: the 19th-century novelist Honoré de Balzac and the 20th-century American sculptor Alexander Calder, one of whose mobiles adorns the main square.

Admirers of Balzac make pilgrimages to the **Musée Balzac** in the Château de Saché. The plain but comfortable manor house, built in the 16th and 18th centuries, was a quiet place to work and a source of inspiration for many of the writer's best-known novels. The house has been well restored – one of the reception rooms has even been redecorated with a copy of the

bright green wallpaper with a Pompeiian frieze that was there in Balzac's day.

It is full of busts, sketches and memorabilia of the great man, including the coffee pot that kept him going during his long stints of writing. There are manuscripts and letters, as well as portraits of the women in Balzac's life: his mother; his first love, Madame de Berny; and his loyal friend, Madame Hanska, whom he finally married shortly before his death in 1850.

### 🏛 Museé Balzac
Château de Saché. **Tel** 02 47 26 86 50. **Open** daily. **Closed** Tue (Oct–Mar); 1 Jan, 25 Dec. 🅿️ 🌐 **musee-balzac.fr**

## ⑪ Villaines-les-Rochers

**Road map** D3. 🔢 930. 🚆 Azay-le-Rideau, then taxi. *i* Azay-le-Rideau (02 47 45 44 40).

Since the Middle Ages, willows from the local river valleys have been made into baskets in this peaceful village. Production has been on a more substantial scale since the mid-19th century, when the local priest organized the craftsmen into one of France's first cooperatives. Everything is still hand made by the many wickerworkers (*vanniers*) in the town. This explains the relatively high prices of the attractive furniture and baskets on sale in the **cooperative**'s shop. Craftsmen and women can be watched at work in the adjoining studio.

In the summer, you can also visit a small museum with displays on the subject of basket-making, the **Musée de l'Osier et de la Vannerie**.

### 🏛 Coopérative de Vannerie de Villaines
1 rue de la Cheneillère. **Tel** 02 47 45 43 03. **Open** daily (Sat, Sun: no work in progress). **Closed** 1 Jan, 25 Dec. ♿ 🌐 **vannerie.com**

### 🏛 Musée de l'Osier et de la Vannerie
7 pl de la Mairie. **Tel** 02 47 45 23 19. **Open** last fortnight Apr & Oct: Wed–Sat; May, Jun & Sep: Tue–Sun; Jul & Aug: daily. 🅿️ 🌐 **musee-vannerie.fr**

A wickerworker in Villaines

## ⑫ Richelieu

**Road map** D4. 🔢 2,000. 🚆 Chinon, then bus. *i* pl du Marché (02 47 58 13 62). 🛒 Mon, Fri. 🌐 **office. tourisme-richelieu.fr**

It would be difficult to find a better example of 17th-century urban planning than the town of Richelieu, on the border between Touraine and Poitou. Its rigid design was the brainchild of Armand Jean du Plessis who, as Cardinal Richelieu and chief minister, was the most powerful man in the kingdom, not excepting his monarch, Louis XIII.

The Cardinal was determined to build a huge palace near his modest family estate of Richelieu. In 1625 he commissioned the architect Jacques Lemercier to draw up the plans and, in 1631, he received permission from the king to proceed, not only

The Château de Saché, often visited by Honoré de Balzac

with the palace, but also with the creation of a new walled town. Lemercier had already designed the Palais Royal and the Church of the Sorbonne in Paris, and would later be appointed chief royal architect. His brothers, Pierre and Nicolas, were put in charge of the building work, which lasted more than a decade.

The resulting town is a huge rectangle, surrounded by walls and moats (mostly taken up with gardens today) and entered through three monumental gates. The Grande Rue, running from north to south through the centre of the town and linking two large squares, is lined with identical Classical mansions. In the south square, place du Marché, the buildings include the Classical **Eglise Notre-Dame**, the market building with its superb timber framework, and the former law courts, in which the **Hôtel de Ville** (town hall) and a small **history museum** are now housed. In the north square, the place des Religieuses, stands a convent and the Royal Academy, which was founded by Richelieu in 1640.

Richelieu clearly intended that his palace should be incomparably luxurious, and that vision was impressively realized. It was filled with priceless furniture and works

Richelieu's timber-framed market hall

of art, including paintings by Caravaggio and Andrea Mantegna. Michelangelo's *Dying Slaves*, statues that were originally designed for the tomb of Pope Julius II (now housed in the Louvre museum in Paris), adorned one of the palace's inner courtyard façades.

Extremely fearful of competition, Richelieu ordered many of the châteaux in the area to be razed to the ground. While his town managed to survive the ravages of the French Revolution intact, the sumptuous palace, ironically, was confiscated, damaged and then dismantled.

By visiting the beautiful **Parc de Richelieu**, visitors can get an inkling of its former glory. There is also an interesting virtual presentation,

**Cardinal Richelieu**
**(1585–1642)**

L'Espace Richelieu, which tells the history of the Cardinal, his city and his castle through interactive 3D at 28 Grande Rue.

**▥ Musée de l'Hôtel de Ville**
pl du Marché. **Tel** 02 47 58 10 13.
**Open** Wed–Mon (Sep–mid-Apr: Mon–Fri). **Closed** public holidays. ▨

**▧ Parc de Richelieu**
5 pl du Cardinal. **Open** daily.
▧ restricted. Visitors Centre:
**Open** mid-Apr–Sep: Wed–Mon. ▨

**Environs**
Champigny-sur-Veude, 6 km (4 miles) to the north of Richelieu, boasts another stunning castle. It is not open to the public, but visitors can see the splendid Renaissance **Ste-Chapelle**, with its superb stained glass.

**▧ Ste-Chapelle**
Champigny-sur-Veude. **Tel** 02 47 95 73 48. **Open** May–Jun: Thu–Sun pm; Jul & Aug: daily pm; Sep: Wed–Mon pm. ▨

## Balzac at Saché

Honoré de Balzac's (1799–1850) regular stays at the Château de Saché between 1829 and 1837 coincided with the most productive period in his highly industrious career as a writer. Here, hidden well away from his creditors, he would work at least 12 hours a day. Despite starting in the early hours of the morning, he remained able to entertain his hosts, Monsieur and Madame de Margonne, and their guests in the evenings by reading aloud the latest chunk of text from his novels, acting out all the characters as he did so.

Two of Balzac's major novels, *Le Père Goriot* (*Father Goriot*) and *Le Lys dans la Vallée* (*The Lily of the Valley*), were written at Saché. The latter is set in the Indre Valley, which can be seen from the house and does indeed have something of that "intangibly mysterious quality" to which Balzac refers with typical eloquence.

Balzac's bedroom at Saché

### ⓲ Le Grand-Pressigny

**Road map** D4. 🏰 1,100. 🚉
Châtellerault, then taxi. 🚌 Tours.
ℹ️ pl de Savoire Villars (02 47 94 96
82). 🛒 Thu. 🌐 **tourainedusud.fr**

Perched high above the town,
the **Château du Grand-Pressigny**
has lovely views over the Claise
and Aigronne valleys. The
château is part medieval ruins,
part 15th-century castle and
part Renaissance residence.
The rectangular, 12th-century
ruined keep contrasts
dramatically with the elegant
16th-century Italianate wing.

Important prehistoric finds
have been made around here,
and various excavations have
revealed that the area was a
key centre for the large-scale
production of flint implements,
such as blades produced from
blocks known as "pounds of
butter", which were exported
as far afield as Switzerland and
Great Britain.

Many of these finds are
displayed at the **Musée de la
Préhistoire**, which has been
rebuilt, partly in startling
contemporary style, within the
ruins of the castle. The collection
includes examples of tools and
other objects from all the
prehistoric eras, along with rock
flints, large blocks of obsidian
and multicoloured jasper. The
museum is also home to an
important collection of plant
and animal fossils, some of
which date back 60 million
years. The museum also has a
room dedicated to temporary

exhibitions and an educational
workshop on the ground floor.

On summer afternoons you
can visit the **Archéolab**, 6 km
(4 miles) northwest at Abilly-sur-
Claise, where a transparent
dome covers a site that was
inhabited by stone cutters
between 2800 and 2400 BC.

🏛 **Château du Grand-Pressigny:
Musée de la Préhistoire**
**Tel** 02 47 94 90 20. **Open** Apr–Sep:
daily; Oct–Mar: Wed–Mon. **Closed** 1
Jan, 25 Dec. 🅿️ 👨‍🦽 🌐 prehistoire
grandpressigny.fr

🏛 **Archéolab**
Abilly-sur-Claise. **Tel** 02 47 91 07 48.
**Open** Jul & Aug: Tue–Sun pm. 🅿️ 📷

Neolithic tool from the Musée de la
Préhistoire

### ⓴ Loches

**Road map** D3. 🏰 7,000. 🚉 🚌 ℹ️ pl
de la Marne (02 47 91 82 82). 🛒 Wed,
Sat. 🎭 Epopée Medievale Fair (Aug).
🌐 **loches-tourainecotesud.com**

Its medieval streets lined with
picturesque houses, the
peaceful town of Loches lies
beside the River Indre on the
edge of the Forêt de Loches.
Thanks to its strategic location,
it became an important citadel
in the Middle Ages, with an

Agnès Sorel as the Virgin, painted by
Jehan Fouquet

11th-century keep begun by
Foulques Nerra (see p54). The
château (now part of the **Cité
Royale de Loches**) remained
in the hands of the counts of
Anjou until 1194, when John
Lackland ceded it to King
Philippe Augustus. John's
brother, Richard the Lionheart,
recaptured Loches in a surprise
attack in 1195. It took Philippe
Augustus nearly ten years to
retake the castle by force, and
eventually it became a French
royal residence. It was in the
15th-century Logis Royal that
Joan of Arc persuaded the
dauphin to travel to Rheims
and be crowned king of France
as Charles VII. This event is
commemorated in the tapestry-
hung Salle Jeanne d'Arc.

Also in the Logis Royal is the
tiny, Late Gothic private chapel
of twice-queen Anne of Brittany
whose ermine tail emblem
recurs in the decoration. On
show in the château are a fine
Crucifixion triptych by Tours
painter Jehan Fouquet (c.1420–
80) or one of his pupils, and a
copy of his colourful Virgin with
Child, which was modelled on
Agnès Sorel, another woman
of influence in Charles VII's life.

The massive donjon (keep)
with its surrounding towers is
famous for its torture chambers.
One of the most famous
prisoners here was Lodovico
Sforza, the duke of Milan, who
died in the Tour Martelet, where
the tempera wall paintings
he made can still be seen.

Beside the château is the
Collégiale St-Ours, a church

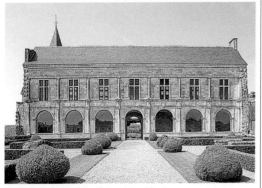

Renaissance façade of the Gallery, Château de Grand-Pressigny with four pyramid-like spires and a Romanesque portal. Inside is the Gothic marble tomb of Agnès Sorel.

Near the Porte Royale lies the **Maison Lansyer**, birthplace of the 19th-century painter Emmanuel Lansyer. Some of his canvases are on display, along with his collection of Japanese armour and prints.

Underground, below the citadel, lie the extensive former quarries of the **Carrière Troglodytique de Vignemont**, which are best explored with a tour guide.

**🏠 Cité Royale de Loches**
7 mail du Donjon. **Tel** 02 47 59 01 32. **Open** daily. **Closed** 1 Jan, 25 Dec. ♿ 📷 Spectacle Nocturne (Aug). 🌐 **chateau-loches.fr**

**🏛 Maison Lansyer**
1 rue Lansyer. **Tel** 02 47 59 05 45. **Open** Apr–Oct: hours vary; call to check.

**🏠 Carrière Troglodytique de Vignemont**
52ter, rue des Roches. **Tel** 02 47 91 54 54. **Open** Easter–Nov & school hols: daily. 📷 📷 🌐 **carriere-de-vignemont.fr**

## ⑮ Montrésor

**Road map** E3. 🚗 415. 🚌 Loches, then taxi. 🛈 Maison du Pays (02 47 92 70 71).

The turreted **Château de Montrésor**, largely built in the 15th and 16th centuries, stands above this lovely village, on the site of medieval fortifications built by Count Foulques Nerra (*see p54*). It was bought in the mid-19th century by Count Branicki, an émigré Polish financier linked to the future Napoléon III. Still owned by Branicki's descendants, the château's Second Empire decor remains virtually unaltered.

As well as a fine collection of early Italian paintings and some elegant portraits, there are many gold and silver pieces. The rooms, with their mounted stags' and wolves' heads and dark panelling, retain a somewhat Central European feel. The château terrace and informal gardens offer fine views of the river.

An estate building, which used to house the château's wine press, has been converted into the Maison du Pays, an information centre and showcase for the Indrois Valley and its products.

The village's small Gothic and Renaissance church was built by Imbert de Bastarnay, lord of Montrésor, adviser to François I and grandfather of Diane de Poitiers (*see p112*). On the beautiful marble Bastarnay tomb lie *gisants* (effigies) of the lord, his lady and their son, guarded by angels and with their feet resting on grey-hounds. The tomb, believed to be the work of the Renaissance sculptor Jean Goujon (c.1510–68), is decorated with statues of the apostles. There are also some wonderful Flemish and Italian paintings in the church, and a 17th-century *Annunciation* by Philippe de Champaigne (1602–74), the Baroque painter who worked on the Luxembourg palace in Paris with Nicolas Poussin.

In a lovely forest setting, to the east of the village of Montrésor, are the ruins of the **Chartreuse du Liget**, a Carthusian monastery founded

Farm buildings and poppy fields near the village of Montrésor

by the Plantagenet king Henry II of England in expiation for the murder of Archbishop Thomas à Becket. The nearby Chapel of **St-Jean-du-Liget** is decorated with 12th-century frescoes.

**🏠 Château de Montrésor**
**Tel** 02 47 92 60 04. **Open** Castle: Apr–Oct: daily; Nov–Mar: Sat & Sun; grounds: daily. 📷 📷 🌐 **chateaudemontresor.fr**

**🏠 Chapelle St-Jean-du-Liget**
Pick up the key from the tourist office in Loches (pl de la Marne, Tel: 02 47 91 82 82). ♿

Château de Montrésor, built on medieval fortifications

# ⑯ Château de Chenonceau

Stretching across the River Cher, Chenonceau is thought of as the loveliest of the Loire châteaux. Surrounded by formal gardens, over the centuries this Renaissance building was transformed from a manor built on the plans of a Venetian palace into a château by the addition of two galleries. The château holds a fantastic collection of furniture and artworks, including a rare depiction of Henri III by the great French Renaissance painter François Clouet. Other spaces are the Médicis Gallery, on the first floor, the Dômes Gallery, in the old stables, and the Carriage Gallery, in the old farm courtyard. There is also a restaurant in the old stables.

**★ Cabinet Vert**
The walls of Catherine de Médicis' study were originally covered with green velvet.

**Chapelle**
The chapel has a vaulted ceiling and pilasters sculpted with acanthus leaves and cockle shells. The stained glass, ruined by a bomb in 1944, was replaced in 1953.

**KEY**

① **The Tour des Marques** survives from the 15th-century castle of the Marques family.

② **Louise de Lorraine's room** was painted black and decorated with monograms, tears and knots in white after the death of her husband, Henri III.

**The Three Graces**
Painted by Charles-André Van Loo (1705–65), *The Three Graces* depicts the pretty Mailly-Nesle sisters, all royal mistresses.

**Tapestries**
As was the practice in the 16th century, Chenonceau is hung with Flemish tapestries that both warm and decorate its well-furnished rooms.

## Château Guide

Ground floor

First floor

1 Vestibule
2 Salle des Gardes
3 Chapelle
4 Terrasse
5 Librairie de Catherine de Médicis
6 Cabinet Vert
7 Chambre de Diane de Poitiers
8 Grande Galerie
9 Chambre de François I
10 Salon Louis XIV
11 Chambre des Cinq Reines
12 Cabinet des Estampes
13 Chambre de Catherine de Médicis
14 Chambre de Vendôme
15 Chambre de Gabrielle d'Estrées

**★ Grande Galerie**
Catherine de Médicis added this elegant gallery to the bridge designed by Philibert de l'Orme in 1556–9 for Diane de Poitiers.

Chenonceau's Florentine-style gallery, which stretches across the River Cher for 60 m (197 ft)

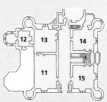

# The Creation of Chenonceau

Chenonceau reflects the combined influence of five women, who brought a feminine touch to this graceful building. First came Catherine Briçonnet, wife of the royal chamberlain, who supervised the construction of the château. Later, Diane de Poitiers, Henri II's mistress, created a formal garden and built a bridge over the Cher. After Henri's death, his widow, Catherine de Médicis, reclaimed the château and topped the bridge with a gallery. Chenonceau survived the 1789 Revolution – because of local respect for Louise Dupin, wife of a tax collector – to be restored by Madame Pelouze in the 19th century.

**Sphinxes**
Inscrutable stone sphinxes guarding the entrance to the gardens came from the Château de Chanteloup, which was destroyed in the 19th century *(see p115)*.

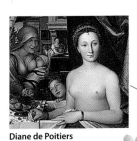

**Diane de Poitiers**
Henri II's mistress, here painted by François Clouet, created a large, formal garden, as well as the bridge across the Cher.

**★ Formal Gardens**
The current designs of the formal gardens of Diane de Poitiers and Catherine de Médicis date from the 19th century.

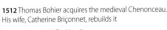

---

**1512** Thomas Bohier acquires the medieval Chenonceau. His wife, Catherine Briçonnet, rebuilds it

**1559** On Henri's death, Catherine forces Diane to leave

**1913** The château is bought by the Menier family, the *chocolatiers* who still own it today

**1789** Chenonceau is spared in the French Revolution, thanks to Louise Dupin

*Henri II*

| 1500 | 1600 | 1700 | 1800 | 1900 |
|------|------|------|------|------|

**1575** Louise de Lorraine (1554–1601) marries Henri III, Catherine's son

**1547** Henri II gives Chenonceau to Diane de Poitiers, his lifelong mistress

**1533** Marriage of Catherine de Médicis (1519–89) to Henri II (1519–59). Chenonceau becomes a Loire royal palace

**1730–99** Louise Dupin creates a salon for intellectuals at Chenonceau

**1863** Madame Pelouze restores the château to its original state

**1944** Chenonceau chapel is damaged in a bombing raid

**Louise Dupin**
A well-read beauty with huge brown eyes, Louise Dupin entertained all the literary lions of her day, including Montesquieu and Voltaire. One guest, Jean-Jacques Rousseau, stayed on to tutor her children and famously praised Chenonceau's cuisine, claiming he had become "as plump as a monk".

**Catherine de Médicis**
After ousting Diane de Poitiers, Catherine de Médicis made her own mark on Chenonceau's design. She built the Grande Galerie over the Cher and added a formal garden to rival Diane's.

Catherine de Médicis' emblem

**Court Festivities**
Catherine de Médicis staged lavish balls and festivities at Chenonceau, some featuring plaster triumphal arches and statues designed by Francesco Primaticcio, others with living "nymphs" leaping out of the bushes chased by "satyrs".

**KEY**

① **Madame Pelouze** bought Chenonceau in 1863 and restored it to Catherine Briçonnet's original design. Fortunately, she stopped short of taking down the Grande Galerie.

② **Catherine Briçonnet** supervised the creation of an innovative château design, with rooms leading off a central vestibule on each floor.

**Louise de Lorraine**
Catherine de Médicis left Chenonceau to her daughter-in-law, Louise de Lorraine. Louise had her room redecorated in black upon the death of her husband, Henri III.

The Château d'Amboise, high above the town and the River Loire

# ⑰ Amboise

**Road map** D3. 🖼 13,000. 🚆
ℹ quai du Général de Gaulle (02 47
57 09 28). 🚌 Fri, Sun. 🌐 **amboise-valdeloire.com**

The bustling little town of
Amboise is famed for its château,
and for being Leonardo da Vinci's
final home.

## 🏠 Château Royal d'Amboise
**Tel** 02 47 57 00 98. **Open** daily.
**Closed** 1 Jan, 25 Dec. 🚫 📷 🗺
Avanti la Musica (Jun–Aug); A la Cour
du Roy François (Jul & Aug): Wed & Sat).
🌐 **chateau-amboise.com**

The Late Gothic Chapelle St-Hubert, with its highly ornate
roof and spire

While much of the château has
been destroyed, it is still
possible to see the
splendour that
prevailed when
first Charles VIII, then
François I and, later,
Henri II and Catherine
de Médicis
brought the
Italian love of
luxury and
elegance to the
French court.

Sculpted detail from
the Logis du Roi

Amboise has also played a
tragic part in history. In 1560 a
Protestant plot to gain religious
concessions from the
young King François II
was uncovered, 1,200
conspirators were
slaughtered and
some of their bodies
strung up from the
castle and town walls.

This horrifying
episode was to spell
the end of Amboise's
glory, and the château
was gradually
dismantled. The
enchanting, Late
Gothic **Chapelle
St-Hubert**, where a
plaque recalls that
Leonardo da Vinci
was buried at the
castle, has fortunately
survived, perched on
the ramparts of the
château. Carvings on
the exterior lintel of

the chapel depict St Hubert and
St Christopher. The guard rooms
and state rooms in the part-
Gothic, part-Renaissance
**Logis du Roi** are open to
visitors, along with fascinating 19th-century
apartments once
occupied by King
Louis-Philippe.
Flanking the Logis
du Roi is the **Tour
des Minimes**, one
of the original
entrances to the château, with
its impressive spiral inner ramp,
up which horsemen could ride.

## 🏠 Château du Clos-Lucé
2 rue du Clos-Lucé. **Tel** 02 47 57 00 73.
**Open** daily. **Closed** 1 Jan, 25 Dec.
🚫 ♿ restricted. 📷 🌐 **vinci-closluce.com**

This graceful Renaissance
manor house on the outskirts
of Amboise was Leonardo da
Vinci's last home. In 1516
François I enticed Leonardo
to the royal court at Amboise
and settled him at Le Clos-
Lucé, where he lived until
his death in 1519.

Inside the house, da Vinci's
bedroom, reception room,
study, kitchen and a small
chapel built for Anne of Brittany
by Charles VIII are open to
visitors. There are models made
from Leonardo's astonishing
technical drawings in the
basement. More information
on Leonardo's life is displayed

in the outbuildings, while out in the gardens are larger models showing how some of his inventions worked.

### 🐟 Aquarium du Val de Loire

Lussault-sur-Loire. **Tel** 02 47 23 44 57. **Open** daily. **Closed** 2 wks Jan & 2 wks Nov. 🖟 🕭 🖤 decouvrez-levaldeloire.com

With thousands of freshwater fish on display, the Aquarium du Val de Loire is the largest such collection in Europe.

### Environs

Behind the Renaissance Château de la Bourdaisière, now also a hotel, hides a *potager* with 500 varieties of tomato, 150 kinds of lettuce and over 200 different herbs. Sample its produce at the Tomato Festival (mid-Sep).

### 🏠 Château et Jardins de la Bourdaisière

Montlouis-sur-Loire. **Tel** 02 47 45 16 31. **Open** Apr–Oct: daily. 🖟 🖤 🖿 🖤 labourdaisiere.com

Leonardo da Vinci's bedroom at the Château du Clos-Lucé

### ⑱ Pagode de Chanteloup

Route de Bléré. **Tel** 02 47 57 20 97. **Open** Feb–Mar: school hols; Apr–mid-Nov: daily. 🖟 🕭 park only. 🖤 pagode-chanteloup.com

In the forest of Amboise, southwest of Amboise itself, stands this Chinese-style pagoda, more than 44 m (144 ft) high and built in seven storeys, linked by steep spiral staircases. Each layer is smaller than the preceding one and contains an airy, octagonal

### Leonardo da Vinci (1452–1519)

François I, who developed a love of Italian Renaissance art during his military campaigns there, persuaded Leonardo to join his court at Amboise, offering him an annual allowance and free use of the manor house at Clos-Lucé. The great Italian polymath arrived in Amboise in 1516 with some precious items in his luggage – three major paintings, in leather bags tied to a mule. One of them was the *Mona Lisa*, which François was to buy and place in the royal collection (hence its presence today in the Louvre in Paris). Leonardo spent the last three years of his life at Le Clos-Lucé as the *Premier Peintre, Architecte, et Mécanicien du Roi* (first painter, architect and engineer to the king), mainly writing and drawing. As he was left-handed, the paralysis that affected his right hand was not a major handicap. Fascinated by hydrology, he produced plans to link the royal residences of the Loire Valley via waterways and even proposed rerouting the river. He also organized a series of elaborate court festivities, planning them down to the last detail with the same meticulous care he lavished on his scientific designs.

Engraving of Leonardo da Vinci

A model of Leonardo's prototype for a "car"

room with a domed ceiling. Seven avenues lead into the forest from the pagoda, which is reflected in a large lake.

This is all that is left of a splendid château built by Louis XV's minister, the Duc de Choiseul (1719–85). In the 1770s, Choiseul fell out with the king's mistress, Madame du Barry – he had been a protégé of her predecessor Madame de Pompadour – and was exiled from Versailles. He retreated to the château he had bought at Chanteloup in 1761 and rebuilt it. He spent his time entertaining on a large scale and dabbling in farming. After his death, the château was abandoned and then pulled down in 1823.

An exhibition in the pavilion explains the history of the once magnificent château and, for those brave enough to climb, there are impressive views of the Loire Valley from the top of the tower.

The Pagode de Chanteloup, in the heart of the forest of Amboise

# ⑲ Street-by-Street: Tours

The medieval old town, Le Vieux Tours, is full of narrow streets lined with beautiful half-timbered houses. Now sensitively restored, it is a lively area crammed with little cafés, bars and restaurants that attract locals as well as tourists. There are also numerous chic fashion boutiques and small shops devoted particularly to craft work and to stylish kitchen equipment. At its heart is the attractive place Plumereau, which in fine weather is filled with parasol-shaded café tables.

| 0 metres | | 50 |
| 0 yards | | 50 |

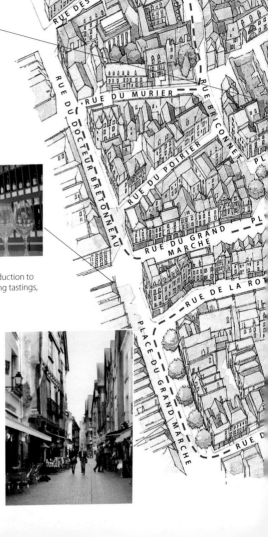

**Place Pierre-le-Puellier**
Medieval buildings surround this bustling square, which once formed part of a Renaissance cloister.

**Maison des Vins de Loire**
The *maison* offers a wonderful introduction to the wines of the Loire Valley, including tastings, for a small fee.

**★ Place du Grand Marché**
This street has undergone an exciting makeover, turning it into a very popular spot, with lovely café and restaurant terraces extending along it in warmer weather.

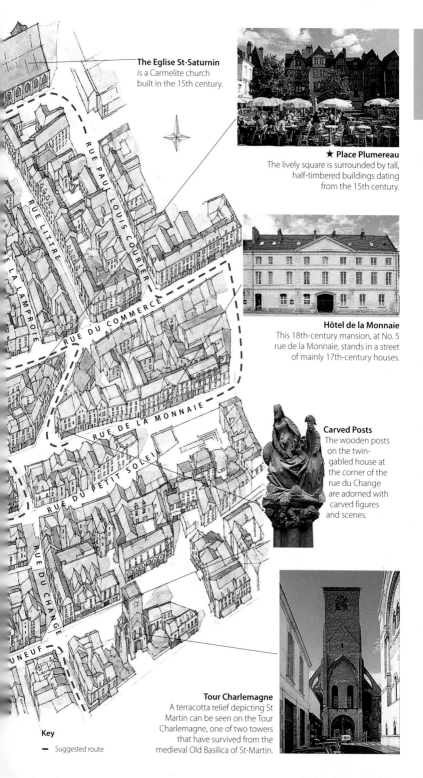

**The Eglise St-Saturnin**
is a Carmelite church
built in the 15th century.

**★ Place Plumereau**
The lively square is surrounded by tall,
half-timbered buildings dating
from the 15th century.

**Hôtel de la Monnaie**
This 18th-century mansion, at No. 5
rue de la Monnaie, stands in a street
of mainly 17th-century houses.

**Carved Posts**
The wooden posts
on the twin-
gabled house at
the corner of the
rue du Change
are adorned with
carved figures
and scenes.

**Tour Charlemagne**
A terracotta relief depicting St
Martin can be seen on the Tour
Charlemagne, one of two towers
that have survived from the
medieval Old Basilica of St-Martin.

**Key**
— Suggested route

# Exploring Tours

The pleasant cathedral city of Tours, popular with foreign students eager to learn the country's purest French, is a perfect base for exploring Touraine. But Tours itself, its medieval heart imaginatively restored, repays exploration too. Once a major Gallo-Roman centre, then filled with pilgrims flocking to St Martin's tomb, it became a wealthy courtly town from the mid-15th century, when the kings of France moved to the Loire. It has remained prosperous over the centuries, yet despite rapid expansion, it has managed to retain its provincial charm.

Tours' Pont Wilson, recently rebuilt, spanning the Loire

### Tours Town Centre

The area of the town close to the magnificent **Cathédrale St-Gatien** *(see pp120–21)* was part of the original Roman settlement. In the 3rd century AD, it was enclosed by a wall, the shape of which can still be seen in the rue des Ursulines, circling the cathedral and the Musée des Beaux Arts. The rue du Général-Meunier, a curving cobbled street of elegant houses once occupied by the clergy, follows the line of a Roman amphitheatre.

On the west side of Tours, a religious community grew up around the sepulchre of St Martin. The saint's tomb now lies in the crypt of the late 19th-century New Basilica, which was built on the site of the considerably larger, medieval Old Basilica. Two stone towers – the **Tour Charlemagne** and the **Tour de l'Horloge** – on either side of the rue des Halles, survive from the earlier building. Not far from the towers, the **place Plumereau**, with its charming medieval houses and tempting cafés, attracts locals, foreign students and tourists in large numbers. Close to the cathedral, the half-timbered house at No. 39 rue Colbert bears a wrought-iron sign dedicated to the *Pucelle Armée* (the armed maid), recalling that Joan of Arc *(see p141)* bought her suit of armour here, before setting out to liberate Orléans in 1429. Nearby is the **place Foire-le-Roi**, a square where, thanks to a permit granted by the king in 1545, regular fairs were once held. The main merchandise was the silk that had been a key factor in the town's economy since the middle of the previous century. Of the gabled houses that line the square, the finest is the Renaissance Hôtel Babou de la Bourdaisière, named after the finance minister to François I, who lived there. Slightly to the west, the 13th-century **Eglise St-Julien** stands on the site of an abbey founded in the 6th century.

The central bridge crossing the Loire, the **Pont Wilson**, is known locally as the *pont de pierre* (stone bridge). It is an exact replica of the town's original 18th-century bridge, which collapsed suddenly in 1978, making national headlines. One delight in central Tours is walking along the south quays of the Loire.

### Musée des Beaux-Arts

18 pl François-Sicard. **Tel** 02 47 05 68 82. **Open** Wed–Mon. **Closed** 1 Jan, 1 May, 14 Jul, 1 & 11 Nov, 25 Dec.
**mba.tours.fr**

The Museum of Fine Arts, conveniently situated next to the Cathédrale St-Gatien, is shaded by a cedar of Lebanon nearly two centuries old and fronted by attractive formal gardens. Once the Archbishop's Palace, the building dates mainly from the 17th and 18th centuries.

Its collections of paintings range from the Middle Ages to contemporary artists and include two celebrated altarpiece panels by Andrea Mantegna, *The Resurrection* and *Christ in the Olive Grove*, which were painted between 1456 and 1460 for the church of San Zeno in Verona.

To the right of the entrance courtyard is an outbuilding housing a huge stuffed circus elephant that died in Tours in the early 20th century.

*Christ in the Olive Grove* (1456–60) by Andrea Mantegna

Tour's neo-Byzantine Basilique St-Martin

### 🔼 Basilique St-Martin
rue des Halles. **Tel** 02 47 05 63 87.
**Open** daily. Musée St-Martin: 3 rue
Rapin. **Tel** 02 47 64 48 87. **Open** mid-
Mar–mid Nov. Wed–Sun.

One of the greatest religious figures in French history, St Martin, was born in the 4th century in what is now Hungary. Joining the Roman army, he travelled to northern France. Moved by a naked beggar's plight there, he famously used his sword to cut his cloak in half to help the pauper. He went on to found one of France's first monasteries and become a bishop of Tours. After his death, his tomb became one of Europe's most important pilgrimage sites. This led to the building of one of the largest of all medieval churches, dedicated to him. Just two staggering towers remain from that edifice and in the late 19th century, a glittering new basilica went up in his honour. The great dome is topped by a statue of St Martin and the interior is richly styled with grand arches. Today, many Catholic pilgrims still come to pay homage to him at his tomb in the crypt. Nearby, a small museum in a Gothic chapel is dedicated to St Martin's memory and to the previous church.

## Tours Town Centre
① Tour Charlemagne
② Basilique St-Martin
③ Château Royal
④ Cathédrale St-Gatien
⑤ Musée des Beaux-Arts

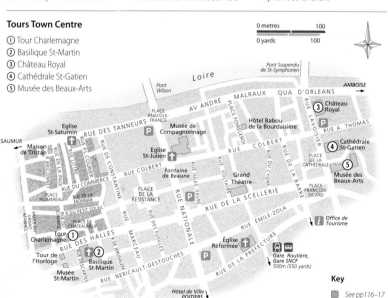

Key
See pp116–17

*For keys to symbols see back flap*

# Tours: Cathédrale St-Gatien

The foundation stone of Tours' Gothic cathedral, named after St Gatien, a 3rd-century bishop, was laid in the early 13th century. Because building work continued until the mid-16th century, the cathedral provides an illustration of how the Gothic style developed over the centuries. The Early Gothic chancel was the first area to be completed, while the nave and transept represent the Middle or High Gothic period and the highly decorated west façade is Flamboyant (or Late) Gothic.

**★ West Façade**
The richly carved Flamboyant west façade has three portals surmounted by a fine rose window.

**Cloître de la Psalette**
The cloisters, which lead off the north aisle, are made up of three galleries dating from the mid-15th and early 16th centuries.

**★ Colombe Tomb** (1499)
The marble tomb of Charles VIII's and Anne of Brittany's infant sons features lifelike effigies by Michel Colombe or one of his pupils.

**Fresco**
This 14th-century fresco, restored in 1993, shows St Martin giving half his cloak to a beggar.

## VISITORS' CHECKLIST

**Practical Information**
pl de la Cathédrale.
**Tel** 02 47 70 21 00.
**Open** 9am–8pm daily (to 7pm in winter). 🕇 11am, 6:30pm Sun.
♿ ✿

**Colombe Statue**
This statue of Tours' famous sculptor, Michel Colombe, stands in a square near the cathedral.

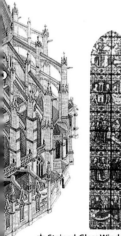

**★ Stained-Glass Windows**
The stained glass is notable for its rich, strong colours and for the paler stained panels, or *grisailles,* which let in more light than ordinary stained glass.

## KEY

① **Colombe tomb**

② **The narrow nave** has a vaulted ceiling, dating from the late 15th century.

③ **Inside the North Tower** is the elegant 16th-century "royal staircase".

④ **In the chancel**, the stained-glass windows, depicting Christ's Passion and the legends of St Martin and other saints, date from around 1265.

### 🏰 Château Royal de Tours
25 av André Malraux. **Tel** 02 47 70 88 46. **Open** Tue–Sun.
Atelier Histoire de Tours: (entry from church square). **Tel** 02 47 70 88 46. **Open** Wed & Sat. **Closed** public hols. ♿

The château, which served as a royal residence in the 13th and 15th centuries, was erected on top of the ancient Gallo-Roman walls, parts of which are still visible.

The Tour de Guise tower is named after the Duc de Guise, who made a daring escape while being held as a prisoner here following the assassination of his father at the Château de Blois in 1588.

In the Renaissance Logis des Gouverneurs, the exhibitions of the **Atelier Histoire de Tours** explain the city's long urban history using 3D models and plans.

### 🏛 Centre de Création Contemporaine
53 rue Marcel Tribut. **Tel** 02 47 66 50 00. **Open** during exhibitions; Wed–Sun, pm only. ♿ 🌐 ccc-art.com
Occupying a modern building just a short walk southeast of the fine 19th-century railway station, this venue regularly stages shows by both internationally established contemporary artists and fresh names to the scene.

### 🏛 Musée du Compagnonnage
8 rue Nationale. **Tel** 02 47 21 62 20. **Open** mid-Sep–mid-Jun: Wed–Mon; mid-Jun–mid-Sep: daily. **Closed** public hols. 📷 ♿
🌐 museecompagnonnage.fr

Housed in part of the abbey once attached to the medieval **Eglise St-Julien**, this unusual museum is devoted to craftsmanship. It has a fascinating collection of "masterpieces" made by members of a guild of itinerant *compagnons* (journeymen) who applied to be awarded the prestigious title of Master Craftsman. Displays cover many trades, ranging from the work of stonemasons to that of clog makers, and even include some extraordinary spun-sugar creations.

A barrel on display in the Musée du Compagnonnage

## Garlic and Basil Fair

On 26 July, the Feast of St Anne, the place du Grand-Marché in the Old Town, near the colourful covered market (*Les Halles*), is the scene of the traditional Garlic and Basil Fair (*Foire à l'Ail et au Basilic*). Pots of basil form a green carpet, and stalls are garlanded with strings of garlic heads, purple onions and grey or golden shallots.

Stalls laden with garlic and basil in the place du Grand-Marché

# BLESOIS AND ORLEANAIS

These two closely linked regions are excellent starting points for an exploration of the central Loire Valley. The area's forests and marshlands have attracted nature lovers for centuries. During the Renaissance, magnificent hunting lodges were built by kings and nobles throughout the area, including the great Chambord, the sumptuously furnished Cheverny and the charming Beauregard.

Blésois and Orléanais remain richly forested, with abundant game, including rabbits and hares, deer and wild boar. The great forest of Orléans, still magnificent, contrasts with the heaths and marshy lakes of the Sologne, a secretive region of small, quiet villages and low, half-timbered brick farmhouses. Although a paradise for hunters and fishermen, other visitors rarely venture into the depths of this area.

The northern stretch of the Loire flows through towns whose names resound throughout the history of France. Bridges and castles at Gien, Orléans, Beaugency and Blois all assumed strategic significance during wars from the Middle Ages to the 20th century.

It was at Orléans in 1429 that Joan of Arc, lifting the English siege of the town, galvanized the spirit of the French army engaged in the Hundred Years' War.

The modern city's proximity to Paris has led to its growth as a commercial centre, but careful reconstruction after the devastation of World War II has meant that a sense of the past survives in the old *quartier*.

During the Wars of Religion, the château at Blois was sunk in political intrigue. Now restored, its walls still echo with the events of 1588, when the Duc de Guise was assassinated on the orders of the king, Henri III.

To the west of the region, the River Loir, smaller than its majestic soundalike, flows through the countryside of the Vendômois and also through Vendôme itself, one of the most attractive towns in the region. Vendôme's cathedral, La Trinité, is only one of the memorable churches in Blésois and Orléanais, many of them decorated with early frescoes and mosaics.

Anglers taking part in a competition on a local canal

◀ The Grand Salon at the Château de Cheverny

# Exploring Blésois and Orléanais

Orléans, the largest city in Blésois and Orléanais, lies at the northernmost point of the River Loire. To the west is the Petite Beauce, fertile, wheat-growing land, while to the east is the great forest of Orléans, dense and teeming with wildlife. Blois, downstream from Orléans, is also surrounded by forests. To the south, the Sologne is a land of woods and marshes, scattered with small lakes, or *étangs*. The River Cher marks its southern border, as it flows through charming villages.

One of the region's stone farmhouses

## Key

▬▬ Motorway
▬▬ Major road
▬▬ Secondary road
▬▬ Minor road
▬▬ Scenic route
▬▬ Main railway
▬▬ Minor railway
▬▬ Regional border

## Sights at a Glance

1. Trôo
2. Lavardin
3. Vendôme
4. Château de Talcy
5. *Blois pp128–31*
6. Château de Chaumont-sur-Loire
7. Montrichard
8. St-Aignan-sur-Cher
9. Thésée
10. Château de Cheverny
11. Château de Beauregard
12. Château de Villesavin
13. *Château de Chambord pp136–9*
14. Beaugency
15. Meung-sur-Loire
16. Château de Chamerolles
17. *Orléans pp142–3*
18. St-Benoît-sur-Loire
19. Gien
20. Briare-le-Canal
21. Sologne

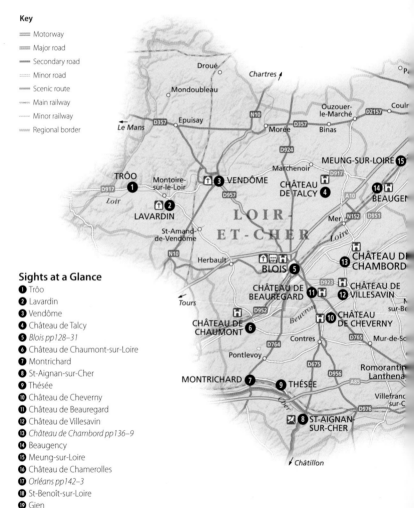

## Getting Around

The fastest route by car from Paris is *L'Aquitaine* autoroute (A10), which passes through Orléans and Blois. Some Paris-to-Tours TGVs stop at Vendôme, only a 45-minute journey. The Corail express train from Paris takes one hour to Les Aubrais (a suburb of Orléans with a connecting train to the city centre) and a further 30 minutes to Meung-sur-Loire and Blois via Beaugency. From Tours, a local line follows the Cher, stopping at Montrichard, Thésée and St-Aignan. Bus services between towns are extremely limited, especially during the school holidays. The drive along the D976, which parallels the River Cher, is very scenic, and the roads through the cool, forested areas of the region are tranquil and pleasant.

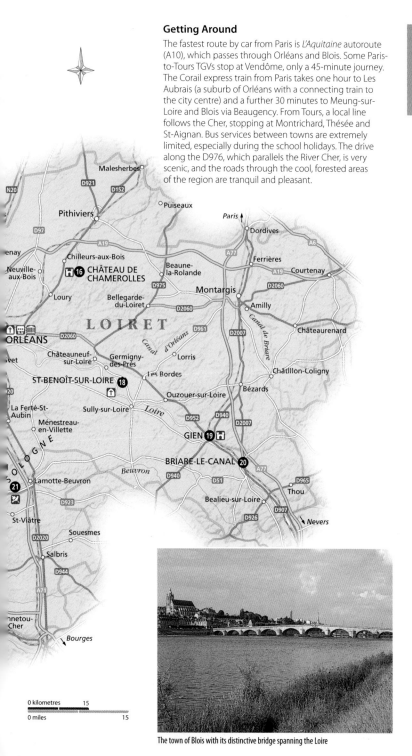

The town of Blois with its distinctive bridge spanning the Loire

**For keys to symbols** *see back flap*

Trôo's "speaking well"

# ❶ Trôo

**Road map** D3. 🗺 320. 🚌 Vendôme, then taxi. 🛈 02 54 72 87 50.
🖥 troo.fr

On a cliff above the Loir, this village should be entered from the top through its ruined medieval gate. To the left of the gate is a covered "speaking well" with a very clear echo. During the Middle Ages, a massive fortress stood here. All that remains today is a mound, or *motte*, from the top of which there is a good view of the valley below. Parts of the **Eglise St-Martin**, nearby, date from the 11th century.

Steep paths wind down the hill, passing on the way the pretty flower gardens of a group of troglodyte dwellings, some of which are open to visitors. At the bottom of the hill is the **Grotte Pétrifiante**, a cave full of stalactites that have been developing for more than 4,000 years. The **Cave Yuccas** offers visitors the chance to explore a typical subterranean house with rooms dug out of the rock.

Across the river, the little church at **St-Jacques-des-Guérets**, built in the 12th century, is justly famous for its 13 murals, painted in a distinctive Byzantine style. They were rediscovered in 1890 during restoration work. The *Christ in Majesty* in the apse is a particularly beautiful example.

**St-Gilles** chapel in nearby Montoire-sur-le-Loir is also worth a visit. It has some even finer 12th-century murals, remarkable for the range of colours used. A dark day in French history, when Hitler met the collaborationist French leader, Marshal Pétain, at the former railway station is recalled at the **Gare Historique**. World music is celebrated with an annual festival in August, and at the **Musikenfête** museum.

🚶 **Grotte Pétrifiante**
39 rue Arnault (Trôo). **Tel** 02 54 72 87 50. **Open** Apr–Oct: daily. 🔲

🚶 **Cave Yuccas**
12 rue Gouffier (Trôo). **Tel** 02 54 85 30 45. **Open** Apr–Oct: daily. 🔲

🏛 **Gare Historique**
av de la République (Montoire-sur-le-Loir). **Tel** 02 54 85 33 42. **Open** Apr–Jun & Sep: Tue, Thu, Sat & Sun; Jul & Aug: Tue–Sun. 🔲

🏛 **Musikenfête**
Espace de l'Europe (Montoire-sur-le-Loir). **Tel** 02 54 85 28 95. **Open** Mar–Dec: Tue–Sun. 🔲 🖥 musikenfete.fr

# ❷ Lavardin

**Road map** D3. 🗺 250. 🚉 Vendôme, then taxi. 🚌 🛈 Montoire-sur-le-Loir (02 54 85 23 30). 🖥 **lavardin.net**

The fortifications of Lavardin's ruined **château** tower above the medieval bridge leading to the village. On the boundary between the Capetian and Angevin kingdoms, the fortress was a key stronghold for centuries in battles between the French crown and the Plantagenet dynasty.

Lavardin's finest treasure is the Romanesque **Eglise St-Genest** with its fragile murals from the 12th–16th centuries.

🏰 **Château de Lavardin**
**Tel** 02 54 85 07 74 (Mairie). **Open** May, Jun & Sep: Sat & Sun; Jul & Aug: Tue–Sun. 🔲 📷

# ❸ Vendôme

**Road map** D3. 🗺 18,000. 🚉 🚌
🛈 47–49 rue Poterie (02 54 77 05 07). 🖥 Fri & Sun. 🖥 **vendome-tourisme.fr**

One of the region's most scenic towns, Vendôme is built over a group of islands in the Loir, its bridges, water gates and old stone buildings forming a delightful tableau.

Situated on the border between French and English feudal territories, the town changed hands many times throughout its history. It passed to the Bourbons in 1371, eventually becoming a duchy in 1515. Later, held by the Holy League during the Wars of Religion, it was recaptured by Henri IV in 1589; the skulls of his leading Catholic opponents are a grisly exhibit in the **Musée de Vendôme**. Set by an old abbey's cloisters, the museum also has a harp said to have been played by the ill-fated Marie-Antoinette, and some frescoes in the adjoining chapter house.

Vendôme's undisputed jewel is the abbey church of **La Trinité**, which was founded in 1034 by Geoffroy Martel, son of Foulques Nerra. It stands beside a

Delicate murals in Lavardin's Eglise St-Genest

Ornate façade of Abbaye de la Trinité in Vendôme

12th-century Romanesque bell tower, with a spire reaching more than 80 m (260 ft). The church's bold, ornate façade was created by Jean de Beauce, who also designed the Old Bell Tower of Notre-Dame de Chartres. Its flame-like tracery is a typically virtuoso statement of the Flamboyant Gothic style.

Inside, beyond the transept, which dates from the 11th century, are choir stalls carved with amusing figures. To the left of the altar, a pretty latticework base with tear-drop motifs once held a cabinet displaying a famous relic, which was said to be the tear supposedly shed by Jesus on the grave of Lazarus.

Wooden carving from La Trinité

Shopping is centred around the place St-Martin, with its 15th-century clock tower and carillon, and a statue of the local count of Rochambeau, who commanded the French forces during the American Revolution. There is also a graceful, *fin-de-siècle* covered market just off rue Saulnerie.

The best views of the town's old fortifications are from the square Belot. Also visible from here is the Porte d'Eau, a water gate built during the 13th and 14th centuries, which once controlled the water for the town's mills and tanneries. At certain times, you can take a boat trip on the Loire through town.

In the centre of town is the Parc Ronsard, with its 15th-century wash house, the Lavoir des Cordeliers, and the Old Oratorians College, which dates from the 17th and 18th centuries. Vendôme's ruined château stands on a bluff above the town, with the 12th-century Tour de Poitiers at one corner. The extensive garden offers some delightful panoramic views of the town.

**🏛 Musée de Vendôme**

Cloître de la Trinité.
**Tel** 02 54 89 44 50.
**Open** Wed–Mon (Nov–Mar: Mon & Wed–Sat). **Closed** 1 Jan, 1 May, 25 Dec.

The Lavoir des Cordeliers in Vendôme's Parc Ronsard

Talcy's over 300-year-old wine press, still in working order

## ❹ Château de Talcy

**Road map** E3. 🚉 Mer, then taxi. **Tel** 02 54 81 03 01. **Open** Apr–Sep: daily; Oct–Mar: Wed–Mon. **Closed** 1 Jan, 1 May, 25 Dec. 🚗 🚫 also night tours Jul–Aug. 🎨 exhibition every summer.
**w** talcy.monuments-nationaux.fr

After the grander châteaux of the Loire Valley, Talcy comes as a delightful surprise: a fascinating, human-scale home, hiding behind a stern façade. The original building, a keep, dates from the 15th century. It was transformed by Bernardo Salviati, a Florentine banker and cousin of Catherine de Médicis, who bought it in 1517 and added to the building significantly.

In 1545, the poet Pierre de Ronsard *(see p28)* fell in love with Salviati's 15-year-old daughter, Cassandre. Over the following decade, his love for her inspired the sonnets of his famous collection, known as *Amours de Cassandre*.

Bernardo Salviati gave Talcy its feudal look, adding the crenellated sentry walk and fake machicolations to the gatehouse. In the first courtyard, with its arcaded gallery, is an elegant domed well. A 3,000-bird dovecote in the second courtyard, dating from the 16th century, is the best-preserved in the Loire.

A huge wooden wine press, over 300 years old but still in working order, is worth a look. The château's vineyards are no longer productive, but an orchard preserves old varieties of fruit trees.

Inside the château, the charming rooms have retained their original 17th- and 18th-century furnishings.

# ❺ Street-by-Street: Blois

A powerful feudal stronghold for several centuries, Blois became a royal city under Louis XII, who established his court here in 1498. The town remained at the centre of French royal and political life for much of the next century. Now an important commercial centre for the agricultural districts of the Beauce and Sologne, Blois, with its harmonious combination of white walls, slate roofs and redbrick chimneys, is the quintessential Loire town. The hilly, partly pedestrianized old quarter, bordered by the river, the château and the cathedral, is full of architectural interest.

**Hôtel d'Alluye**
Blois' outstanding Renaissance mansion was built in 1508 by Florimond Robertet, treasurer to three kings.

| 0 metres | 100 |
| 0 yards | 100 |

**Façade des Loges**, the château's most theatrical side, has Renaissance window bays rising in tiers to a gallery.

★ **Château Royal de Blois**
The rich history of the Château de Blois is reflected in its varied architectural styles.

Blois as seen from the Loire, with the three spires of the Eglise St-Nicolas in the centre

★ **Eglise St-Nicolas**
This striking, three-spired church once belonged to a 12th-century Benedictine abbey. Its high, narrow Gothic nave leads to an apse of magical beauty, sheltered by elegant Corinthian columns and lit through lovely blue glass.

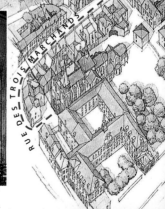

**Key**

— Suggested route

**Escalier Denis-Papin**
Named after the native son (1647–1714) who invented the pressure cooker, these stairs provide a remarkable view over the town and the river.

## VISITORS' CHECKLIST

**Practical Information**
**Road map** E3.
**Tel** 02 54 90 41 41, 02 54 90 21 00.
🚇 51,000. 🅸 23 pl du Château.
🗓 Tue & Sat. 🎭 Son et Lumière: Château de Blois (mid-Apr–mid-Sep: daily); Tous sur le Pont (music and theatre; early Jul). Musée d'Histoire Naturelle & Musée d'Art Religieux: Couvent des Jacobins. **Open** Tue–Sun pm. **Closed** 1 Jan, 1 May, 1 Nov, 25 Dec. 🅿 ♿
🆆 bloischambord.com

**Transport**
🚊 🚌 pl de la Gare.

**Cathédrale St-Louis**
Most of the original building was destroyed by a hurricane in 1678. The present cathedral was erected during the reign of Louis XIV.

**Maison des Acrobates**, in the place St-Louis, has carvings of medieval characters on its posts.

**Maison de la Magie** is a museum about magic with interactive displays and daily shows.

**Couvent des Jacobins** now houses museums of religious art and natural history.

**★ Quartier Vieux Blois**
This well-preserved area of Blois has some marvellous 16th-century buildings. This galleried town house is at the top of rue Pierre de Blois.

# Château Royal de Blois

Home to kings Louis XII, François I and Henri III, no other Loire château has such a sensational history of skulduggery at court. It culminated with the stabbing, on the order of Henri III, of the ambitious Duc de Guise, leader of the formidable Catholic Holy League *(see pp58–9)*. This macabre event, which took place in the king's own bedroom, marked the end of the château's political importance. The building itself juxtaposes four distinct architectural styles, dating from the 13th century through the Gothic and Renaissance periods to the Classical. The château has benefited from major restorations, which began in 1989.

**Gaston d'Orléans Wing**
Of striking Classical design, as shown in the ceiling of the entrance hall, the Gaston d'Orléans wing hosts major temporary exhibitions.

**King Louis XII**
A statue of Louis XII (1462–1515) is the centrepiece of the entrance archway. Known as "Father of the People", he was popular for his benevolent domestic policies.

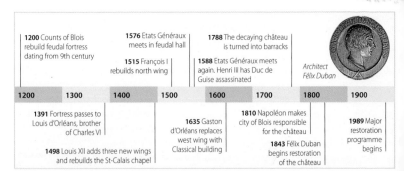

| | | | | | | | |
|---|---|---|---|---|---|---|---|
| **1200** Counts of Blois rebuild feudal fortress dating from 9th century | | **1576** Etats Généraux meets in feudal hall | | **1788** The decaying château is turned into barracks | | *Architect Félix Duban* | |
| | | **1515** François I rebuilds north wing | | **1588** Etats Généraux meets again. Henri III has Duc de Guise assassinated | | | |
| **1200** | **1300** | **1400** | **1500** | **1600** | **1700** | **1800** | **1900** |
| **1391** Fortress passes to Louis d'Orléans, brother of Charles VI | | | **1635** Gaston d'Orléans replaces west wing with Classical building | **1810** Napoléon makes city of Blois responsible for the château | | **1989** Major restoration programme begins | |
| **1498** Louis XII adds three new wings and rebuilds the St-Calais chapel | | | | **1843** Félix Duban begins restoration of the château | | | |

★ **Cabinet de Catherine de Médicis**
The queen's room has 237 carved panels, four with secret cupboards for her jewels, works of art or, some believed, poisons.

## VISITORS' CHECKLIST

**Practical Information**
pl du Château. **Tel** 02 54 90 33 32.
**Open** daily, opening times vary; check the website for details. **Closed** 1 Jan, 25 Dec.
🖼 📷 📹 The Story of Blois *(see p46).*
**W** chateaudeblois.**fr**

★ **Salle des Etats Généraux**
Used for royal receptions and Etats Généraux meetings *(see pp58–9),* this vast 13th-century room survives from the original fortress.

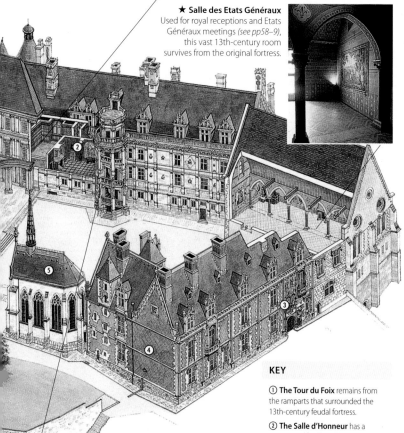

## KEY

① **The Tour du Foix** remains from the ramparts that surrounded the 13th-century feudal fortress.

② **The Salle d'Honneur** has a sumptuous fireplace bearing the salamander and ermine emblems of François I and his wife, Claude. It is one of a string of royal apartments that have Renaissance features.

③ **Statue of Louis XII**

④ **The Gothic Louis XII wing** has intricate, decorative exterior brickwork.

⑤ **The nave of the St-Calais chapel** was pulled down during the 17th century to make way for Gaston d'Orléans' wing, leaving only the chancel standing today.

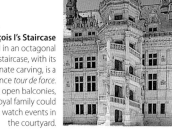

★ **François I's Staircase**
Enclosed in an octagonal well, the staircase, with its highly ornate carving, is a Renaissance *tour de force.* From its open balconies, the royal family could watch events in the courtyard.

Château de Chaumont, towering above the town

## ❻ Château de Chaumont

Chaumont-sur-Loire. **Road map** D3.
🚉 Onzain, then taxi. **Tel** 02 54 20 99
22. **Open** daily. **Closed** 1 Jan, 1 May,
1 & 11 Nov, 25 Dec. 🅿️ ♿ 🎫 Festival
International des Jardins (May–mid-
Oct). **W domaine-chaumont.fr**

Chaumont, set on a wooded hill above the Loire, appears like a fantasy of a feudal castle. Its tall, white towers, built between 1466 and 1510, were never tested in battle and have remained in immaculate condition. Emblems carved on the towers include the crossed Cs of Charles II d'Amboise.

When Charles inherited Chaumont in 1481, he made major alterations to the pre-existing castle, bringing the Renaissance architectural style to France.

Catherine de Médicis, wife of Henri II, acquired the château in 1560. Legend has it that Catherine's astrologer, Ruggieri, revealed to the queen the tragic fate of her three royal sons in a magic mirror. Catherine's chamber also has a balcony adjoining the attractive chapel, which was restored towards the end of the 19th century. In 1562 Catherine gave Chaumont to Diane de Poitiers, mistress of the late Henri II, after forcing her out of Chenonceau (see pp112–13). Diane's entwined Ds and hunting motifs are carved on the machicolations of the entrance and on the east wing.

Subsequent owners either neglected the chateau or altered it to their own purposes. One 18th-century owner, abandoning the fortress design, demolished the north wing so that the whole courtyard was opened up to the river views. The sculptor Nini also worked here during the period and Benjamin Franklin was one famous visitor he depicted. Sweeping improvements began in 1875 when Prince Amédée de Broglie came to live in the château with his wife Marie, a sugar heiress. Their lavish lifestyle can be sensed not just in the castle, but also in the handsome stables, which once housed an elephant, given to them on a visit to the Maharajah of Kapurtala in India.

The council room has tapestries by Reymbouts and majolica floor tiles, brought from a 17th-century Palermo palace, while the library has medallions made in the château by Jean-Baptiste Nini in the 1700s.

Stained glass from the dining room at Chaumont

The château's park was landscaped in 1884 by Achille Duchêne and follows the lines of an English country garden.

Each summer, the park hosts an extraordinarily detailed array of miniature gardens by leading designers. These predominantly cutting-edge designs are for the prestigious Festival International des Jardins. Chaumont has also become the Centre d'Arts et de Nature, commissioning major works by contemporary artists in its grounds. Several exciting restaurants set up on the estate cater to the crowds that come for these events.

## ❼ Montrichard

**Road map** D3. 🏰 3,500. 🚉 🚌
ℹ️ 1 rue du Pont (02 54 32 05 10).
🅰️ Mon pm, Fri am. **W office
tourisme-montrichard.com**

This small town is dominated by the remnants of its **château**. The 11th-century drawbridge,

Montrichard, seen from across the River Cher

archers' tower and the remains of its Renaissance apartments remain, and the keep houses the small **Musée du Donjon** on local life.

Adjoining the château is the **Eglise Ste-Croix**. Here, in 1476, the future Louis XII reluctantly wed Jeanne, the tragically deformed daughter of Louis XI. The marriage was later annulled so Louis could marry Anne of Brittany.

**Château de Montrichard & Musée du Donjon**
**Tel** 02 54 32 57 15. **Open** Apr–Sep: Tue–Sun. Spectacle du Donjon (a show with stuntmen on horseback, twice daily; mid-Jun–mid-Aug).

White tiger from Beauval Zoological Park

### ❽ St-Aignan-sur-Cher

**Road map** E3. 3,700. St-Aignan-Noyers-sur-Cher. 02 54 75 22 85. Sat. **W** tourisme-valdecher-staignan.com

Once a river port, St-Aignan is now an engaging summer resort for boating, swimming and fishing. The town is dominated by the Renaissance château of the dukes of Beauvillier and the collegiate church of St-Aignan, a marvel of Romanesque art.

The château interior is not open to the public, but visitors can climb 19th-century stairs to look at its two elegant wings and enjoy the views from its courtyard terrace as a reward for their exertions. Ruined towers and walls remain from a feudal fortress built by the counts of Blois. In rue Constant-Ragot, leading to the château and

church, there is a fine half-timbered Renaissance house on the corner with rue du Four.

The **Collégiale de St-Aignan**, with its two impressive bell towers, was begun around 1080. Its majestic chancel and sanctuary are built over an earlier Romanesque church, which now forms the crypt. Once used as a cowshed, the crypt still retains its Romanesque feel. Among the important frescoes to survive here are a portrayal of the miracles of St Gilles in the southern chapel and a rare 11th-century *Christ in Majesty* on the chancel vault.

Some of the 250 sculpted capitals in the main church are carved with scenes from the Old and New Testaments as well as allegories of sin and punishment. Others are worked with decorative motifs. In the Chapel of Our Lady of Miracles, the 15th-century ceiling paintings are equally fascinating.

The **Beauval Zoological Park**, 2 km (1¼ miles) south of the town, contains some 4,000 animals, a superb jungle house, a lagoon of piranhas and impressive landscaped

St-Aignan's Chapel of Our Lady of Miracles

enclosures for big cats, including several magnificent prowling white tigers.

**Beauval Zoological Park**
**Tel** 02 54 75 50 00. **Open** daily. **W** zoobeauval.com

### ❾ Thésée

**Road map** E3. 1,300. St Aignan (02 54 75 22 85). Thu.

Just outside the charming little wine village of Thésée is the most important Gallo-Roman site in the Loire-et-Cher *département*, Les Maselles (or Tasciaca). Impressive ruined walls with brick courses testify to the skills of stonemasons who built it in the 2nd century AD. This settlement was a major staging post and ceramic-making centre on the road between Bourges and Tours. The **Musée Archéologique** within the town hall displays a quite dazzling and instructive array of jewels, coins, pottery and other interesting artifacts from this little-known site.

**Musée Archéologique**
Hôtel de Ville. **Tel** 02 54 71 40 20. **Open** Apr–Sep: Sat & Sun (Jul & Aug: Wed–Mon). 11:15am & 4pm. Les Maselles: **Open** same as the museum. 10am & 2:30pm. **W** tasciaca.com

Fresco of *Christ in Majesty*, from the Collégiale de St-Aignan

Classical façade of the Château de Cheverny

# ⑩ Château de Cheverny

**Road map** E3. 🚌 **Tel** 02 54 79 96 29. **Open** daily. 🅿 ♿ grnd floor & park only. 🆆 **chateau-cheverny.fr**

The elegance of Cheverny's white stone façade, with its pure Louis XIII lines, was achieved in a single phase of construction between 1620 and 1634, with all the finishing touches completed by 1648 (*see pp24–5*).

Initiating a new architectural style for the châteaux of the Loire Valley, Cheverny has no defensive elements, such as large turreted towers or formidable entrances. Instead, its Classical façade is striking in its simplicity. The

château stands on the site of a previous castle and is owned by the illustrious Hurault family. Henri Hurault, with his wife, Marguerite, led the château's reconstruction, and the family has retained its ownership.

Jean Mosnier worked on the interior for 10 years, using gilded beams, panels and ceilings. His finest work is in the dining room, with its scenes from Don Quixote's travels, and in the king's bedroom, where the combined effect of wall-hangings, painted ceilings and a bed canopied in Persian silk is stunning. The château's largest room, the Salle d'Armes, displays a collection of arms and armour and is adorned with Mosnier's paintings.

Famous paintings in the château include a portrait of Cosimo de' Médici by Titian, Pierre Mignard's striking portrait of the Countess of Cheverny above the fireplace in the Grand Salon, and a collection of fine portraits by Jean Clouet and Hyacinthe Rigaud in the adjoining gallery.

The Cheverny hunt, which rides twice a week in winter, is famous throughout the Sologne. A visit to the kennels (open Apr–mid-Sep) is a highlight of the château, especially in the late afternoon,

when 70 hungry hounds wait their turn to be fed.

The gardens can be explored by visitors, including an ornate kitchen garden and elegant English-style park. You can even hire electric buggies or an electric boat to discover more of the grounds and canals.

Fans of *Tintin* will recognize that the lovely Cheverny features as the Château de Moulinsart (or Marlinspike Hall in English) in his adventures. A special permanent exhibition reveals more.

The Grand Salon at Cheverny

# ⑪ Château de Beauregard

Cellettes. **Road map** E3. 🚉 Blois, then taxi. **Tel** 02 54 70 41 65. **Open** mid-Feb–mid-Nov: daily. **Closed** mid-Nov–mid-Feb. 🅿 ♿ 🆆 **beauregard-loire.com**

Beauregard stands in a well-tended park on the edge of the Russy forest. A manor here was used as a hunting lodge for François I, but this was transformed into a graceful château in the mid-16th century for Jean du Thier, scholarly secretary of state to Henri II. It was du Thier who commissioned the king's Italian cabinet-maker, Scibec de Carpi, to make him an exquisite study panelled in gilded oak, the Cabinet des Grelots. This little room is decorated with the bells, or *grelots*, found on du Thier's crest, and has some charming

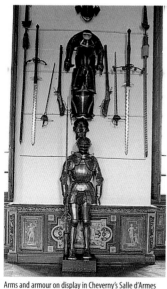

Arms and armour on display in Cheverny's Salle d'Armes

Detail from Beauregard's portrait gallery

paintings from the studio of Niccolo dell'Abate.

The portrait gallery, the château's most spectacular feature, was added in the 17th century by Henry IV's former treasurer, Paul Ardier. A catalogue of famous European faces from 1328 to 1643 – kings, queens, saints, explorers – is arranged in three rows around the gallery. Adding to the impact of these 327 portraits are beautiful beams and panels painted by Jean Mosnier and the largest Delft-tiled floor in Europe, which depicts an army on the move in Louis XIII costume.

Other delights include the southern gallery, with its rich Brussels tapestry and carved furniture, and the kitchen, with its flagstone floors and a table built around the central column. Above the ratchet-operated spit, a motto on the chimney breast advises that those who keep promises have no enemies.

## ⑫ Château de Villesavin

Villesavin. **Road map** E3. 🚉 Blois, then taxi. **Tel** 02 54 46 42 88. **Open** Mar: Fri–Wed; Apr–mid-Nov: daily. **Closed** mid-Nov–Feb. 🅿️ ♿ grd flr only. 📷
W **chateau-de-villesavin-41.com**

Renaissance Villesavin, built between 1527 and 1537 by Jean Breton, was his home while he supervised works at Chambord *(see pp136–9)* nearby. Stone carvers from the royal château ornamented Villesavin and presented Breton with the beautiful Florentine basin in the entrance courtyard.

This is one of the least altered of the many late-Renaissance châteaux in the Loire Valley. Villesavin, with its low walls and unusually high roofs, was built around three very spacious court-yards. The elegant southern façade ends with a large dovecote, which has 1,500 pigeonholes and a revolving ladder.

One of Villesavin's antique carriages

The château's essentially domestic spirit is also evident in the service court, overlooked by a spacious kitchen with a working spit. The interesting collection of old carriages on display here includes an 18 m- (59 ft)- long *voiture de chasse* with four rows of seats, from which ladies could watch the hunt.

### Environs
Situated on the southern banks of the Beuvron river, Bracieux is worth a visit for its grand covered market, which was built during the reign of the Renaissance king François I (1515–47). At that time, the town acted as an important staging post on the routes between the towns of Tours, Chartres and Bourges.

The market is built of brick, stone and wood, with an upper tithe barn. Its original oak posts were strengthened during the 19th century. There are also 17th- and 18th-century houses here.

Garden façade of the Château de Villesavin

# ⓭ Château de Chambord

Henry James once said: "Chambord is truly royal – royal in its great scale, its grand air, and its indifference to common considerations." The brainchild of the extravagant François I, the château began as a fortress on the edge of a well-stocked hunting forest. In 1519 the original building was razed and Chambord begun, to a design probably initiated by an unknown architect inspired by traditional French medieval architecture combined with elements borrowed from the Italian Renaissance. By 1539 the keep, with its towers and terraces, had been completed. François I made further additions, including a private royal pavilion on the northeast corner and a chapel, and Louis XIV completed the edifice in 1685.

The Château de Chambord with the Cosson, a tributary of the Loire, in the foreground

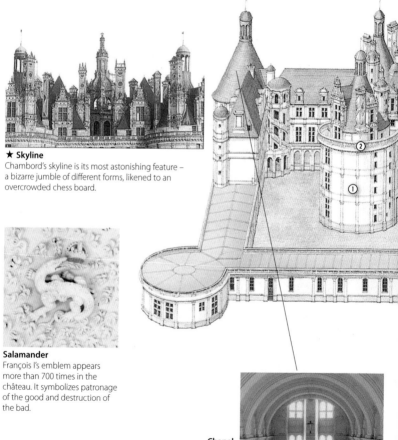

**★ Skyline**
Chambord's skyline is its most astonishing feature – a bizarre jumble of different forms, likened to an overcrowded chess board.

**Salamander**
François I's emblem appears more than 700 times in the château. It symbolizes patronage of the good and destruction of the bad.

**Chapel**
Begun by François I shortly before his death in 1547, the chapel was given a second storey by Henri II. Later, Louis XIV finished the roof.

**François I Staircase**
The external spiral staircase located in the northeastern courtyard was added at the same time as the galleries, starting in 1545.

**Oratory of François I**
The king's barrel-vaulted private chapel in the outer north tower was annexed to the Royal Wing in 1540. It retains its original wooden door and a beautiful vaulted roof adorned with royal emblems.

**VISITORS' CHECKLIST**

**Practical Information**
**Road map** E3.
**Tel** 02 54 50 40 00, 02 54 20 31 01.
**Open** Apr–Sep: 9am–6pm daily; Oct–Mar: 10am–5pm daily.
**Closed** 1 & 31 Jan, 1 May & 25 Dec. ♿ 🅿 📷 🎭 Spectacle d'Art Equestre (May–Sep daily). 🎫 Various exhibitions, concerts and events are held throughout the year.
**w** chambord.org

**Transport**
🚌 Blois, then bus or taxi.

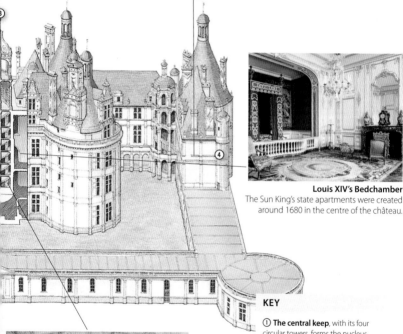

**Louis XIV's Bedchamber**
The Sun King's state apartments were created around 1680 in the centre of the château.

**KEY**

① **The central keep**, with its four circular towers, forms the nucleus of the château.

② **The roof terraces** include chimney stacks, stair turrets, sculpted dormer windows and cupolas.

③ **The lantern tower**, 32 m (105 ft) high, is supported by flying buttresses.

④ **François I's bedchamber** in the east wing, as it was at his death in 1547.

⑤ **The guardrooms**, which were once the setting for royal balls and plays, have ornate, vaulted ceilings.

**★ Grand Staircase**
Seen here from the guardrooms, this innovative double staircase was supposedly designed by Leonardo da Vinci. Two flights of stairs spiral around each other.

# The History of Chambord

Chambord, the largest château in the Loire, was a *folie de grandeur* of the young François I, whose passions included not only politics and the arts but also hunting and flirting. "He is forever chasing, now stags, now women," the Venetian ambassador once said of him. The king supervised the enclosure of the game park surrounding Chambord with the most extensive wall in France – nearly 32 km (20 miles) long. At one point, he even suggested diverting the Loire to flow in front of his château, but settled for redirecting the nearer Cosson to fill his moat.

Louis XIV portrayed as Jupiter, conquering La Fronde

François I as a young man, with various symbols of his kingship

### After François I
On his father's death, Henri II took charge of François I's ambitious project. The subsequent owner, Gaston d'Orléans, brother of Louis XIII, continued to modify the château. By the 17th century, Chambord comprised 440 rooms and had more than 300 chimneys and dozens of staircases.

Louis XIV, whose chief amusement was hunting, took Chambord very seriously.

His full court retinue visited the château numerous times. Louis XV used Chambord to accommodate first his father-in-law, the exiled king of Poland, Stanislas Leszczynski (from 1725 to 1733), and then the Marshal of Saxony, to reward him for his victory against the English at the battle of Fontenoy in 1745.

The need for heating and a greater degree of comfort encouraged the various occupants of the château to furnish it in a more permanent manner. They also carried out works around the château, including channeling the river, to make the surroundings more salubrious.

Chambord then fell into neglect. Stripped during the French Revolution, the château was hardly used by the Bourbon pretender, Henri, Duc de Bordeaux, to whom it was given by public subscription in 1821. It was bought by the state in 1930, and a restoration programme was begun after World War II. The castle now contains thousands of objects, including portraits, tapestries and furniture. It also hosts many temporary exhibitions and visitors can enjoy varied activities, including boating and cycling.

A view of Chambord (detail) by P D Martin (1663–1742)

Marshal of Saxony

**1547–59** Henri II adds the west wing and second storey of the chapel

**1560–74** Charles IX continues tradition of royal hunting at Chambord and writes *Traité de la Chasse Royale*

**1840** Chambord declared a *Monument Historique*

| 1500 | 1600 | 1700 | 1800 | 1900 |
|------|------|------|------|------|

**1670** Molière's *Le Bourgeois Gentilhomme* staged at Chambord

**1519–47** The Count of Blois' fortress is demolished by François I and the château created

**1745** Given to the Marshal of Saxony by Louis XV. On his death the château falls into decline

**1725–33** Inhabited by exiled king of Poland

**1685** Louis XIV completes the building

**1981** UNESCO declares the estate of Chambord a World Heritage Site

# Royal Hunting at Chambord

Under the influence of François I and his heirs, hunting and hawking were the foremost pastimes of the court during the 16th century. A Tuscan nobleman complained that the king only stayed in a place "as long as the herons last". They were quick prey for the 500 falcons that travelled with the rest of the royal retinue.

Within his vast oak forests, the king rode out at dawn to a prepared picnicking spot, there to feast and await the selection of a red deer tracked by his beaters. The quarry flushed, he would ride at full tilt in pursuit, sometimes for hours. For ladies of the court, Chambord's roof terraces offered matchless views of these exertions. François' son Henri II and grandson Charles IX were also keen and practised hunters, sometimes pursuing quarry on foot. Louis XIV favoured the English sport of following packs of hounds, but falconry was preferred by Louis XV.

Hunting was regarded as an art by the court, and for centuries it was also a favourite subject for painters and tapestry designers. A legacy of Chambord's hunting past is the location of the château, which stands in the largest enclosed forest in Europe, a domain equivalent to the surface area of the city of Paris.

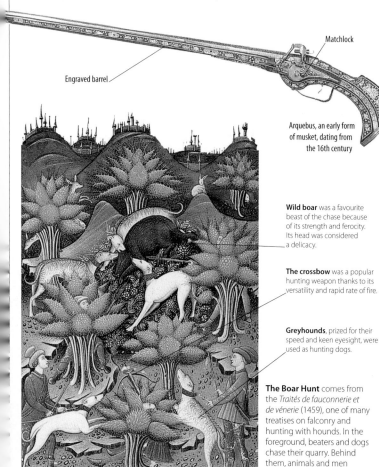

**Matchlock**

**Engraved barrel**

**Arquebus**, an early form of musket, dating from the 16th century

**Wild boar** was a favourite beast of the chase because of its strength and ferocity. Its head was considered a delicacy.

**The crossbow** was a popular hunting weapon thanks to its versatility and rapid rate of fire.

**Greyhounds**, prized for their speed and keen eyesight, were used as hunting dogs.

**The Boar Hunt** comes from the *Traités de fauconnerie et de vénerie* (1459), one of many treatises on falconry and hunting with hounds. In the foreground, beaters and dogs chase their quarry. Behind them, animals and men witness the end of the hunt.

## ⑭ Beaugency

**Road map** E3. ⚄ 8,000. 🚗 🚌
ℹ 3 pl du Docteur Hyvernaud (02
38 44 54 42). 🕐 Sat. 🎪 Festival de
Beaugency (first & second w/end Jul).
🅦 beaugency.fr

With the Loire racing beneath
its famous 23-arch bridge, the
medieval town of Beaugency
makes a delightful base for
exploring the Orléanais area.
The town is surprisingly well
preserved, although its bridge,
the best on the Loire between
Orléans and Blois, has attracted
the attentions of a number of
armies over the centuries.
Restored in the 16th century,
the bridge was damaged
again in 1940 when the Allied
army blew up its southern end
to prevent the Nazis from
crossing the river.

On the place Dunois at the
top of rue de l'Abbaye stands
a massive 11th-century keep.
Opposite is the Romanesque
abbey church of **Notre-Dame**,
where Eleanor of Aquitaine's
marriage to Louis VII was
annulled in 1152, leaving
her free to marry the future
Henry II of England.

Higher up is the 16th-century
Tour St-Firmin, near an
equestrian statue of Joan of
Arc. Her companion-in-arms,
Jean Dunois, Bastard of Orléans
and Lord of Beaugency,
built the **Château Dunois**,
which is undergoing restoration.
Nearby, in rue des Trois

Beaugency's 11th-century clock tower,
once gateway to the town

Marchands, is a medieval
clock tower and the Renaissance façade of the Hôtel de
Ville. Inside is a collection of
elaborate embroideries.

## ⑮ Meung-sur-Loire

**Road map** E3. ⚄ 6,300. 🚗 🚌
ℹ 1 rue Emmanuel Troulet (02 38
44 32 28). 🕐 Sun am, Thu pm.
🅦 tourisme-valdesmauves.fr

This pretty town, sloping
down to the Loire, was the
birthplace of Jean de Meung
*(see p28)*, one of the authors
of the 13th-century
masterpiece *Roman de
la rose*. There has been a
town on this site since Gallo-
Roman times, when it was
known as Magdunum.

Close to the impressive
Romanesque church of
**St-Liphard**, built from the
11th to the 13th century,
rise the feudal towers of the
**Château de Meung**. Frequently
altered from the 12th century to
the 18th century, the château
was built in a variety of styles.
The 18th-century wing has an
interesting collection of furniture, paintings and tapestries.

More intriguing are the
underground passages and
dungeons of the older castle,
dating from the 12th to 13th
centuries and used for 500 years
by the bishops of Orléans as a
prison. It is said that in 1461 the
poet François Villon *(see p28)*,
renowned for his life of disrepute
as well as his fine writing, spent
five months fighting with the
other condemned criminals on
a ledge above a cesspool in
the château's claustrophobic
oubliette. Thanks to a royal
pardon from Louis XI, he was
the only prisoner ever to
emerge alive from there.

Nearby, two gardens worth
seeing are open in summer
months. The Arboretum des
Prés de Culands lies to the
north of the centre; the Jardins
de Roqulin just south across
the Loire.

🏠 **Château de Meung**
**Tel** 02 38 44 36 47. **Open** Mar–Oct:
Tue–Sun; times vary during Easter
week. ♿ 🅶 grd flr only.
🅦 chateau-de-meung.com

Beaugency's medieval bridge, the Tour St-Firmin and the keep rising above the trees

The entrance to the Château de Chamerolles

## ⓰ Château de Chamerolles

Chilleurs-aux-Bois. **Road map** E2. 🚗
Orléans, then taxi. **Tel** 02 38 39 84 66.
**Open** Wed–Mon. **Closed** Jan, 25 Dec.
🅰 🆆 chateauchamerolles.fr

On the edge of the huge forest of Orléans, this Renaissance château was built between 1500 and 1530 by Lancelot du Lac, Governor of Orléans (who was named after the legendary Arthurian knight). Although it was built in the form of a fortress, with a drawbridge crossing a moat and a courtyard enclosed by turreted wings, Chamerolles was designed as a pleasant personal residence.

Baccarat perfume bottle in Chamerolles' museum

Pretty Renaissance gardens, accurately reconstructed, extend to a gazebo offering views back to the château across a "mirror" lake. There is an area of rare aromatic plants, many of which were used during the 1500s for making medicines and perfumes.

A museum in the château traces the development of perfumery through the centuries, covering the variety of uses for perfumes as well as the refinement of the science of making them. This includes the laboratories of perfumers and naturalists and glittering displays of bottles, as well as a charming gift shop.

## Joan of Arc

Joan of Arc is France's supreme national heroine, a virgin-warrior, patriot and martyr whose self-belief turned the tide of the Hundred Years' War against the English. Nowhere is she more honoured than in the Loire Valley, scene of her greatest triumphs.

Responding to heavenly voices telling her to "drive the English out of France", Joan left her home soon after her 17th birthday in 1429 and travelled via Gien to Chinon to see the dauphin, the as yet uncrowned Charles VII. He faced an Anglo-Burgundian alliance on the verge of capturing Orléans. Joan convinced him she could save the city, armed herself in Tours, had her standard

Joan of Arc, pictured in a medieval tapestry

blessed in Blois and entered Orléans with a small force on 29 April. Galvanized by her leadership, the French drove the English off on 7 May. The people of Orléans have celebrated 8 May as a day of thanksgiving almost ever since. Joan returned to Gien to urge Charles forward to Reims for his coronation in July. In 1430 she was captured and accused of witchcraft. Handed over to the English, she was burned at the stake at the age of 19.

Stained-glass portrait of Charles VII from Loches

Joan's piety, patriotism and tragic martyrdom led to her canonization almost 500 years later, in 1920.

*Joan of Arc Entering Orléans* by Jean-Jacques Scherrer (1855–1916)

# ⑰ Orléans

Orléans was the capital of medieval France and a royal duchy until the 18th-century French Revolution, when it became staunchly Republican. Its historical fame might, at first glance, seem submerged by its contemporary role as a rail junction, food processing and business centre, especially as the old quarter of the city was badly damaged during World War II. However, an area of the old town and the Loire-side quays have been attractively restored, and there are many beautiful gardens in this "city of roses".

## Exploring Orléans

A sense of grandeur lingers in Vieil Orléans, the old quarter bounded by the cathedral, the River Loire and the **place du Martroi**. Dominating this square is Denis Foyatier's statue of the city's heroine, Joan of Arc *(see p141)*, whose festival on 8 May is a highlight of the year. The plinth of the statue, which was erected in 1855, is beautifully sculpted with the events of her life. Two splendid Classical buildings, the Chancellery and the Chamber of Commerce, are also found in the square.

A few medieval buildings have survived in the narrower streets around rue de Bour-gogne, a partly pedestrianized shopping street with an astonishing range of ethnic restaurants. Other delightful and often inexpensive restaurants can also be found close to the **Nouvelles Halles**, the city's covered market. The most sophisticated shopping street is the rue Royale, which leads to the 18th-century bridge, the Pont George V.

### 🏛 Maison de Jeanne d'Arc
3 pl de Gaulle. **Tel** 02 38 68 32 63. **Open** Tue–Sun (Oct–Mar: pm only). **Closed** public hols. 🅿 🆆 **jeanne darc.com.fr/maison/maison.htm**

A reconstruction of the half-timbered house that lodged the warrior-saint for 10 days in 1429, the Maison de Jeanne d'Arc has been completely modernized. The museum now presents the life of Joan of Arc in striking contemporary fashion, with evocative audiovisual dioramas.

Orléans' Renaissance Hôtel Groslot, once a private residence

### 🏨 Hôtel Groslot
pl de l'Etape. **Tel** 02 38 79 22 22. **Open** Sun–Fri. **Closed** Sat & public hols. 🅿

The most handsome of the many Renaissance buildings in the city, the Hôtel Groslot, built between 1549 and 1555, served until recently as the town hall.

Built out of red brick crossed with black, this was a grand residence, with scrolled staircase pillars, caryatids and an ornately tooled interior. It was once considered fine enough to lodge the kings of France. Here, in 1560, the sickly young François II died after attending a meeting of the Etats Généraux with his child bride, Mary, later Queen of Scots. The beautiful statue of Joan of Arc guarding the steps

was sculpted by Princess Marie d'Orléans in 1840. Walk through the building to visit a charming little park, backed by the re-erected façade of the 15th-century Flamboyant Gothic chapel of St Jacques.

### ⛪ Cathédrale Ste-Croix
pl Ste-Croix. **Tel** 02 38 24 05 05 (tourist office). **Open** daily. 🅿 🆑

The cathedral, set on a spacious esplanade, was begun in the 13th century. The original building was badly damaged by Huguenots in the 16th century and then restored in Gothic style between the 17th and 19th centuries. Behind the ornate façade, the towering nave is lit by the radiating spokes of the rose window dedicated to the "Sun King", Louis XIV. The chapel of Joan of Arc, whose martyrdom is portrayed in the stained glass, features a kneeling sculpture of Cardinal Touchet, who fought for Joan of Arc's canonization. The cathedral's most famous painting, a masterly rendition of *Christ Bearing the Cross*, by the Spanish religious painter Francisco de Zurbarán (1598–1664), has temporarily been removed for restoration.

The nave of the Cathédrale Ste-Croix

The peaceful Parc Floral in Orléans-la-Source

## Musée des Beaux-Arts

pl Ste Croix. **Tel** 02 38 79 21 55.
**Open** Tue–Sun. **Closed** public hols.

The high standard of
the collection, which
includes a self-portrait by
Jean-Baptiste-Siméon Chardin
(1699–1779) and *St Thomas*
by the young Diego Velázquez
(1599–1660), represents the
strength of European painting
from the 14th to the early
20th century. There is a
charming collection of
miniature enamelled
statuettes on the second
floor, a delightful contrast to
the heavier richness of the
19th-century paintings.

## Musée Historique et Archéologique

square de l'Abbé Desnoyers. **Tel** 02 38
79 25 60. **Open** Tue–Sun (Sun pm
only). **Closed** public hols.

The chief treasures of this
museum are the Celtic statues
discovered at nearby Neuvy-
en-Sullias in 1861, which
include a fine horse from the
2nd century AD *(see p53)*. The
museum also has interesting
pieces on Joan of Arc and a
pleasing variety of arts and
crafts from the Middle
Ages onwards.

### Environs

The suburbs of Orléans are
pleasant places to relax after
a day spent sightseeing in
the city centre. In Olivet,
for example, it is possible
to go boating on the River
Loiret. This river also provides
opportunities for pretty walks.
A tributary of the Loire, the
Loiret flows underground
from near the town of
St-Benoît-sur-Loire *(see p144)*
and rises in the grand **Parc
Floral** of Orléans-la-Source.
A nature reserve, the park
is a mass of blooms from
April. Adjoining the park
is the 17th-century Château
de la Source.

## Parc Floral

Orléans-la-Source. **Tel** 02 38 49
30 00. **Open** Apr–Oct: daily;
Nov–Mar: daily, pm only.
**Closed** 1 Jan, 25 Dec.
**w** parcfloraldelasource.com

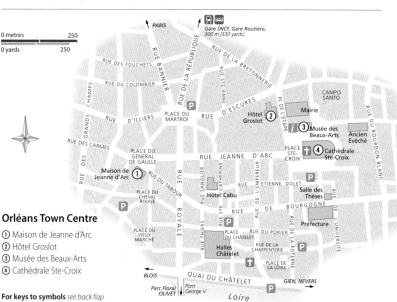

## Orléans Town Centre

① Maison de Jeanne d'Arc
② Hôtel Groslot
③ Musée des Beaux-Arts
④ Cathédrale Ste-Croix

**For keys to symbols** *see back flap*

The Romanesque façade of the abbey church of St-Benoît

### ⓲ St-Benoît-sur-Loire

**Road map** F3. ⓜ 2,800. 🚌
ⓘ 44 rue Orléanaise (02 38 35 79 00).
ⓦ abbaye-fleury.com

This quiet town has one of the finest Romanesque abbey churches in France, constructed between 1067 and 1108. The most appealing feature of the façade is the belfry porch, probably built early in the 11th century by Abbot Gauzlin, son of the first Capetian king, Hugh. On the capitals of its 50 golden pillars are carved figures, including beasts and goblins.

Inside, thickset columns separate the side aisles from the rib-vaulted Gothic nave. The chancel, dating from the earlier Romanesque period, has blind arcades and a mosaic floor brought from Rome. The bas-relief head of a Norman raider is carved on the wall of the north transept. Its cheeks are pierced to expel its pagan spirit.

In the crypt, a lamplit casket contains the relics of St Benedict, the 6th-century father of Western monasticism. They were spirited here in 672 from Benedict's own monastery of Monte Cassino in Italy. By the 11th century, when the present building was begun, the Benedictine order was rich and St-Benoît-sur-Loire was renowned for its scholarship as well as its purloined relics. St-Benoît is a living monastery, and one of the best ways to experience the spirit of the

place is to attend midday mass sung in Gregorian chant.

The 9th-century church of **St Germigny-des-Prés** lies 5 km (3 miles) along the D60 from St-Benoît-sur-Loire. The small cupola of the east apse has an enchanting mosaic of angels bending over the Ark of the Covenant – a composition made up of 130,000 coloured glass cubes probably assembled during the 6th century.

### ⓳ Gien

**Road map** F3. ⓜ 16,000. 🚌 🚍
ⓘ pl Jean-Jaurès (02 38 67 25 28).
🚩 Wed, Sat. ⓦ gien.fr

Sensitively restored after being devastated during World War II, Gien is considered one of the Loire's prettiest towns. From its handsome quays and 16th-century bridge, houses of brick, slate and pale stone rise steeply to a château. It was built for Anne de Beaujeu, who acted as regent for her brother Charles XIII at the end of the 15th century.

Only the steeple tower of the **Eglise Ste-Jeanne d'Arc**, next to the château, survived the destruction of the war, but a remarkable

Max Ingrand's stained glass

church replaced it in the 1950s. Warm facings, composed of bricks made in Gien's famous pottery kilns, blend with the patterned red and black brickwork of the château. The interior glows with stained glass by Max Ingrand and the faïence that is a speciality of the area. A museum of fine china and earthenware is open daily (except Sundays and public holidays) at the factory, which was founded in 1821 (see p221).

The **château** of Anne de Beaujeu, built between 1484 and 1500 on the site of one of the Loire's oldest castles, sheltered the young Louis XIV and the Queen Mother during the Fronde civil war (1648–53). Its grand beamed halls and galleries now house a superb museum of hunting, tracing the sport's development since prehistoric times. The collection covers the weaponry, costumery, techniques and related artistry of almost every associated activity, from falconry to the royal chase. The memorable entrance hall of the château features a 17th-century painting of St Hubert, the patron saint of hunting, depicting his conversion by the vision of a

Gien's château and its 16th-century bridge across the Loire

resurrected stag carrying a crucifix between its horns. An Italian crossbow and a powder horn decorated with images of the mythical and tragic encounter between Diana and Actaeon are beautiful examples of 17th-century carving. Other prominent artists on display here include the 20th-century sculptor Florentin Brigaud, the Flemish etcher, Stradanus, and François Desportes, whose fine paintings dominate the spectacular trophy hall.

🏛 **Château et Musée International de la Chasse**
**Tel** 02 38 67 69 69. **Closed** for renovation until the end of 2015. 🖼

A pleasure boat crossing Briare's elegant bridge-canal

## ⑳ **Briare-le-Canal**

**Road map** F3. 🏔 6,000. 🚉 🚌 𝒊 pl Charles-de-Gaulle (02 38 31 24 51). 🛍 Fri. 🖥 **briare-le-canal.com**

This small town, with its attractive marina, is the setting for a sophisticated engineering masterpiece – the longest bridge-canal in Europe *(see pp60–61)*. With stonework and wrought-iron flourishes designed by Gustave Eiffel (1832–1923), the structure crosses the Loire, linking the Briare-Loing canal with the Canal Latéral. These waterways in turn join the Seine and the Rhône rivers respectively. Visitors can stroll its length, lined in the style of a Parisian boulevard with elegant lampposts, or cruise across the 662 m (2,170 ft) bridge in a *bateau-mouche*.

Fishing on one of the peaceful *étangs* of the Sologne

## ㉑ **The Sologne**

**Road map** E3. 🚉 🚌 Romorantin-Lanthenay. 𝒊 02 54 76 43 89. 🖥 **tourisme-romorantin.com**

Between Gien and Blois, the Loire forms the northern boundary of the Sologne, a vast area of flat heathland, marshes and forests covering nearly 5,000 sq km (1,930 sq miles). The area is dotted with *étangs*, broad lakes teeming with fish, which are magnets for migratory birds and waterfowl. The forests are just as attractive to hunters and nature lovers now as they were during the Renaissance, when members of royalty chose to build their grand hunting lodges here. Much of the land is privately owned, although there are some public paths.

Romorantin-Lanthenay is the "capital" of the Sologne, which boasts 17th- to 19th-century buildings and a medieval quarter. The town is proud of its associations with racing car manufacturers Matra; it is also home to the **Musée de Sologne**,

whose exhibits explain the local economy and wildlife.

The **Maison des Etangs** at St-Viâtre gives information on the Sologne lakes. This is one of several small tourist maisons on specific local themes dotted around the area. Closer to Chambord's great park *(see pp138–9)* is the Maison du Cerf, where deer can often be seen, especially in autumn.

Another public nature reserve is the **Domaine du Ciran**, 25 km (15 miles) south of Orléans, near Ménestreau-en-Villette.

🏛 **Musée de Sologne**
**Tel** 02 54 95 33 66. **Open** Wed–Mon. **Closed** 1 Jan, 1 May, 25 Dec. 🖼 🖼 🖥 **museedesologne.com**

🦌 **Maison des Etangs**
**Tel** 02 54 88 23 00. **Open** daily (Nov–Mar: Wed, Sat, Sun & pub hols, pm only). **Closed** 1 Jan, 25 Dec. 🖼 🖥 **maison-des-etangs.com**

🦌 **Domaine du Ciran**
Ménestreau-en-Villette. 🚉 La Ferté-St-Aubin, then taxi. 𝒊 02 38 76 90 93. **Open** daily (Oct–Mar: Wed–Mon). 🖼 🖥 **domaineduciran.com**

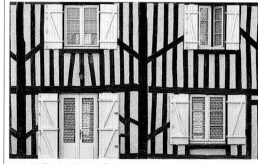

A typical, half-timbered building of La Sologne

# BERRY

Berry lies in the very centre of France, south of the Paris Basin and just north of the Massif Central. It is a varied land of wheat fields, pastures and vineyards, ancient forests, rolling hills and lakes, peaceful villages and elegant manor houses. Mainly off the beaten tourist track, the region gives visitors an opportunity to experience the rural heart of France.

Bourges, the principal town of Berry, was one of the capitals of Aquitaine in the Gallo-Roman period. It then enjoyed another moment of glory in the 14th century, with the administration of Jean, Duc de Berry. This warmongering patron of the arts built a splendid palace in the city (now destroyed) and collected paintings, tapestries, jewellery and illuminated manuscripts.

In the 1420s, when Charles VII was fighting for the French crown (*see pp56–7*), Bourges was his campaign base. Afterwards, his treasurer Jacques Cœur did much to make the kingdom financially secure. The Palais Jacques-Cœur in Bourges competes with the city's magnificent cathedral in drawing crowds of admiring visitors.

Berry is ideal for those who love the outdoors, whether walking in the many well-tended forests, fishing or bird-watching in La Brenne, or sailing and canoeing on its rivers and lakes. Among the region's literary associations are George Sand's novels (*see p28*) and Alain-Fournier's evocative tale *Le Grand Meaulnes* (1913), which combines his childhood memories of the Sologne in the north and the rolling country of the south.

The culinary highlights of Berry include dishes made from local game and wild mushrooms. To the northeast, the renowned Sancerre wine district (*see p159*) is also known for its excellent goat's cheeses, such as the famous Crottin de Chavignol.

A river view by the village of Argenton-sur-Creuse

◄ The bucolic landscape of Mehun-sur-Yèvre

# Exploring Berry

Bourges is the natural starting point for exploring
the heart of France. From here it is only a short drive
to the edge of the Sologne *(see p145)* in the north or
La Brenne in the southwest, both havens for wildlife.
Below Bourges is the Champagne Berrichonne, a
vast agricultural region producing wheat, barley
and oil-rich crops such as rape and sunflowers. The
River Loire forms the ancient border between Berry
and Burgundy to the east as it flows through the
vineyards of the Sancerrois hills.

The Palais Jacques-Cœur in Bourges

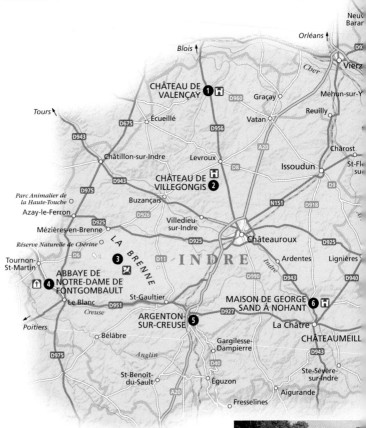

## Getting Around

The A71 autoroute from Orléans passes through Vierzon,
Bourges and St-Amand-Montrond and is an excellent route
from north to south. The A20 serves western Berry. The
TGV doesn't stop in the region, but Corail trains from Gare
d'Austerlitz in Paris take around two hours to either Bourges
or Châteauroux. There are also frequent trains between
Bourges and Tours. Public transport to the more isolated sights
is limited and a car is a great advantage, especially when
touring the Sancerre wine estates or La Brenne nature reserves.

A riverside scene, typical of the Berry region's
gentle landscape

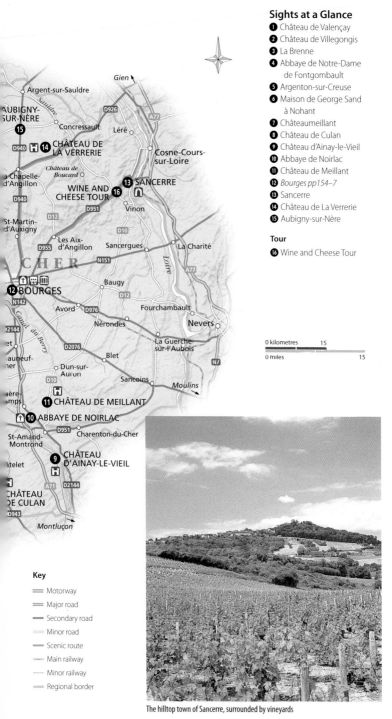

## Sights at a Glance

1. Château de Valençay
2. Château de Villegongis
3. La Brenne
4. Abbaye de Notre-Dame de Fontgombault
5. Argenton-sur-Creuse
6. Maison de George Sand à Nohant
7. Châteaumeillant
8. Château de Culan
9. Château d'Ainay-le-Vieil
10. Abbaye de Noirlac
11. Château de Meillant
12. *Bourges pp154–7*
13. Sancerre
14. Château de La Verrerie
15. Aubigny-sur-Nère

## Tour

16. Wine and Cheese Tour

0 kilometres 15

0 miles 15

## Key

▬▬ Motorway
▬▬ Major road
▬ Secondary road
∷∷ Minor road
▬ Scenic route
┄┄ Main railway
── Minor railway
▬▬ Regional border

The hilltop town of Sancerre, surrounded by vineyards

A resident peacock in front of the Château de Valençay

# ❶ Valençay

**Road map** E4. 🏔 2,800. 🚆
🚌 Valençay. 🛈 2 av de la
Résistance (02 54 00 04 42). 🛍 Tue.
Ⓦ **paysdevalencayenberry.fr**
Château & Park: **Tel** 02 54 00 15 69.
**Open** mid-Mar–mid-Nov: daily.
🎭 🚹 restricted. 🚗 🎥 There
are plays at the château in
summer; themes and dates vary.
Son et Lumière (Jul & Aug).
Ⓦ **chateau-valencay.com** Musée
de l'Automobile: **Tel** 02 54 00 07 74.
**Open** mid-Mar–mid-Nov: daily. 🎭
🚹 Ⓦ **musee-auto-valencay.fr**

From its tree-lined approach,
the Château de Valençay is a
fine sight. Started in 1510, it
took more than 300 years to
complete, but its Renaissance
and Classical elements are
convincingly blended. In 1803,
it was bought by Bonaparte's
foreign minister, Charles-
Maurice de Talleyrand Périgord.
Until his death in 1838,
the famous statesman
entertained many of Europe's
dignitaries here.

Valençay's rooms are richly
furnished, mostly in the Empire
style, and they display many
*objets d'art* connected with
Talleyrand. Entertaining tours
guide you through the château,
and provide details about the
statesman's beautiful mistress,
his famous visitors and his
illustrious chef. Formal gardens
extend in front of the château,
while the park itself houses an
enormous labyrinth.

Next to the château, the
**Musée de l'Automobile** has a
private collection of motoring
memorabilia and vintage cars.

# ❷ Château de Villegongis

**Road map** E4. 🚆 Châteauroux,
then taxi. **Tel** 02 54 36 63 50 (Mairie).
**Open** closed to public.

Elegant and moated, the
Château de Villegongis was
probably built by Pierre
Nepveu, one of the master
masons for Chambord (see
pp136–9). Since the 15th
century, ownership has stayed
in the same family. Barely
touched since that time, it is
one of the purest examples of
the French Renaissance style.

The château's most striking
features are its richly decorated
chimneys, which suggest the
link with Chambord, and its
cylindrical towers at either
end of the main building.

The interior is exceptionally
well furnished, with some fine
17th- and 18th-century pieces.
There is also a remarkable
carved stone staircase.

# ❸ La Brenne

**Road map** E4. 🚆 Mézières-en-
Brenne, then taxi. 🛈 Maison du
Parc, Rosnay (02 54 28 12 13);
Mézières-en-Brenne (02 54 38 12 24).
Ⓦ **parc-naturel-brenne.fr**

The Parc Naturel Régional de la
Brenne, covering 1,650 sq km
(640 sq miles), is known as the
*Pays des Mille Etangs* (The Land
of a Thousand Meres). La Brenne
is a paradise for nature lovers –
more than 260 bird species
can be seen here.

Other specialist reserves in
this area include the **Réserve
Naturelle de Chérine**, good
for spotting European pond
tortoises, and the **Réserve de
la Haute-Touche**, home to
many endangered species and
also close to the fine **Château
d'Azay-le-Ferron**. The aquaria of
the **Maison de la Pisciculture**
display local fish species.

🐾 **Réserve Naturelle de Chérine**
St-Michel-en-Brenne. **Tel** 02 54 28 11
02. Reserve: **Open** daily. Visitors'
Centre: **Open** Wed–Mon (Oct–Mar:
Sat & Sun). Ⓦ **reserve-cherine.fr**

🐾 **Réserve de la Haute-Touche**
Obterre. **Tel** 02 54 02 20 40. **Open**
Apr–Sep: daily; Oct–mid-Nov: Wed,
Sat, Sun & pub hols.
Ⓦ **haute-touche.mnhn.fr**

🏰 **Château d'Azay-le-Ferron**
Azay-le-Ferron. **Tel** 02 54 39 20 06.
**Open** Apr–mid-Nov: daily. 🎭
Ⓦ **chateau-azay-le-ferron.com**

🐾 **Maison de la Pisciculture**
Mézières-en-Brenne. **Tel** 02 54 38 12
24. **Open** mid-Mar–Oct: Mon & Wed–
Sat, pm only. 🎭 🚹 grd flr only.

One of the many idyllic lakes in La Brenne

## ❹ Abbaye de Notre-Dame de Fontgombault

**Road map** E4. **Tel** 02 54 37 12 03. **Open** daily. 🕀 Mass: 10am daily; Vespers: 6pm Mon–Sat, 5pm Sun. ♿

This beautiful Benedictine abbey, famous for its Gregorian chant, was founded in 1091 but, by 1741, when the number of monks had dwindled to just five, it was abandoned. Restored by a local priest in the 19th century, it now houses monks from Solesmes *(see p166)*.

The church, with its five radiating chapels, has a richly decorated doorway, carved capitals and a much-venerated 12th-century statue known as Notre-Dame du Bien-Mourir, believed to comfort the dying. Gregorian chant is still sung during services and is more prominent in the morning service. The monks run a pottery, whose products can be bought. Accommodation is available for those in search of a spiritual retreat.

The radiating chapels of the Abbaye de Notre-Dame de Fontgombault

Old houses overhanging the river in Argenton-sur-Creuse

## ❺ Argenton-sur-Creuse

**Road map** E4. 🚉 5,500. 🚌 🚋 👥 pl de la République (02 54 24 05 30). 🛒 Thu & Sat. 🎭 International Folklore Festival, biennial (Jul). 🌐 ot-argenton-sur-creuse.fr

This is a pretty town along the Creuse river, which winds from Fresselines to Argenton, passing through deep gorges. Streets of picturesque houses climb up to the chapel of Notre-Dame-des-Bancs, dominated by its gilded statue of the Virgin Mary.

In the 19th century, the town became an important centre for the clothing industry. The informative collections of the **Musée de la Chemiserie et de l'Elégance Masculine** honour this heritage. The **Musée Archéologique**

d'Argentomagus, just outside town, recalls Argenton's Gallo-Roman predecessor.

🏛 **Musée de la Chemiserie et de l'Elégance Masculine**
**Tel** 02 54 24 34 69. **Open** mid-Feb–Dec: Tue–Sun. 🎟 ♿ 🌐 cc-argenton.fr/chemiserie.htm

🏛 **Musée Archéologique d'Argentomagus**
**Tel** 02 54 24 47 31. **Open** Wed–Mon (Jul & Aug: daily). **Closed** mid-Dec–Jan. 🎟 ♿ 🌐 argentomagus.fr

## ❻ Maison de George Sand à Nohant

**Road map** E4. **Tel** 02 54 31 06 04. 🚌 🚋 Châteauroux. **Open** daily. **Closed** pub hols. 🎟 🎭 Fêtes Romantiques de Nohant (Jun); Rencontres Internationales Frédéric Chopin (Jul). 🌐 maison-george-sand.monuments-nationaux.fr

George Sand, the *nom de plume* of the novelist Baroness Aurore Dudevant (1804–76), was largely brought up in this manor house. She frequently returned here during her unconventional life, to enjoy the calm beauty of her beloved Berry countryside.

Many of George Sand's novels, including *La mare au diable* (*The Devil's Pool*) and *La petite fadette* (*The Little Fairy*), are set here *(see p28)*. Sand's admirers can view the boudoir where she first wrote; the stage on which she acted out her plays; the puppets made by her son, Maurice; the bedroom used by her lover, Frédéric Chopin; and the room in which she died in 1876.

### Monet at Fresselines

In 1889 the Impressionist painter Claude Monet travelled to the village of Fresselines, perched high above the Creuse. He visited a local beauty spot, with views plunging down into the river gorge, was captivated, and painted a series of canvases showing the scene in different lights. In February, bad weather forced him to stop painting and wait for spring. He then found that new growth had changed the view and had to pay the owner of an oak featured in five of his paintings to strip the tree of its new leaves.

*Valley of the Petite Creuse* by Claude Monet

### ❼ Châteaumeillant

**Road map** F4. 🗺 2,150. 🚌
Chateauroux, then bus. 🚌 ℹ 69 rue
de la Libération (02 48 61 39 89). 🗓
Fri. **w** chateaumeillant-tourisme.fr

The chief glory of this town
is the Romanesque **Eglise
St-Genès**, built between 1125
and 1150, with its elegant pink
and grey west façade. The
interior is exceptionally airy, due
not only to its great height, but
also to its very wide chancel
with six apsidal chapels and
side passages that are separated by graceful double bays to
create a cloisters effect.

Châteaumeillant was once an
important Gallo-Roman centre.
The **Musée Emile-Chenon**,
based in a 15th-century manor
house, contains Roman artifacts and local medieval finds.

🏛 **Musée Emile-Chenon**
ℹ rue de la Victoire (02 48 61 49 24).
**Open** Mon pm, Wed am,
Thu–Sat (Jun–Sep: daily).
**Closed** pub hols. 🐾 📷
**w** museechenon.e-monsite.com

### ❽ Château de Culan

**Road map** F4. **Tel** 02 48 56 66 66.
**Open** Apr–Sep: daily. 🐾 📷
**w** culan.fr

Strategically positioned on an
escarpment above the River
Arnon, this medieval fortress
dates from the 13th and 14th
centuries. Its three conical
towers are topped by wooden
siege hoardings. A series of
furnished rooms relate the
castle's long history, recalling
famous visitors who have

The interior courtyard of the Château d'Ainay-le-Vieil

stayed here, including the
Admiral of Culan, who was a
comrade-in-arms of Joan of
Arc (who also stayed here in
1430), and the writers George
Sand *(see p28)* and Madame
de Sévigné, and telling of an
attack during the 17th-century
Fronde uprising.

Lovely views over Culan's
replanted gardens and the pastoral Arnon Valley can be enjoyed from the château's terrace.

### ❾ Château d'Ainay-le-Vieil

**Road map** F4. 🚉 St-Amand-Montrond, then taxi. **Tel** 02 48 63 50 03.
**Open** Mar, Oct & Nov: Wed–Mon;
Apr–Sep: daily. 🐾 📷
**w** chateau-ainaylevieil.fr

From the outside, Ainay-le-Vieil
has the appearance of a fortress,
with formidable walls and its
nine massive towers lit only by
thin arrow slits. The octagonal
enclosure, surrounded by a
moat, is entered through a
huge, 13th-century postern

gate. The exterior belies the fact
that hidden inside is a graceful
Renaissance château designed
for an elegant lifestyle, with its
richly decorated façade
enlivened by sunny loggias.

The castle changed hands
many times during its early
history. In the 15th century,
it belonged briefly to Charles
VII's treasurer Jacques Cœur
*(see p155)*, but in 1467 it was
bought by the Seigneurs de
Bigny whose descendants still
live here today.

The Grand Salon was
decorated in honour of a
visit by Louis XII and Anne
of Brittany around 1500. It
has a painted ceiling and a
monumental fireplace, which
is said to be one of the most
attractive in the Loire Valley.
On display is a portrait of Louis
XIV's chief minister Jean-
Baptiste Colbert and portraits
of other family members, as
well as an amber pendant
that belonged to Queen
Marie-Antoinette and several
*objets de vertu*, friendship gifts
given by Napoléon to General
Auguste Colbert.

The tiny Renaissance chapel
has some beautiful, late 16th-
century wall paintings, which
were discovered under 19th-
century decoration. Its stained-
glass windows were made by
an artist who also worked on
the Cathédrale St-Etienne in
Bourges *(see pp156–7)*.

In the park is a delightful and
sweet-smelling rose garden.
Some of the varieties of roses
which are grown here date
back to the 15th century.

The Château de Culan, set high above the River Arnon

# ⓾ Abbaye de Noirlac

**Road map** F4. St-Amand-Montrond, then taxi. **Tel** 02 48 62 01 01. **Open** daily. **Closed** 23 Dec–Jan. Les Traversées (music festival Jun & Jul). abbaye denoirlac.com

The Cistercian Abbaye de Noirlac, founded in 1136, is a fine example of medieval monastic architecture. The Cistercian Order's austerity is reflected in the pure lines of the partly 12th-century church and visually echoed in its sober, modern stained glass.

The chapter house, where the monks' daily assemblies were held, and the *cellier*, where the lay brothers were in charge of the food, wine and grain stores, were also built in this plain but elegant style. The cloisters, with their graceful arches and decorated capitals, date from the 13th and 14th centuries, which was a less severe period.

At **Bruère-Allichamps**, 4 km (2½ miles) northwest of the abbey, a Gallo-Roman milestone marks the alleged exact central point of France.

# ⓫ Château de Meillant

**Road map** F4. St-Amand-Montrond, then taxi. **Tel** 02 48 63 32 05. **Open** Mar–mid-Nov: daily. grd flr only. **chateau-de-meillant.com**

Sumptuously furnished rooms and elaborate carved ceilings complement the

The austere lines of the Abbaye de Noirlac

rather exuberantly decorated façade of this well-preserved Berry château. Built for Charles d'Amboise in 1510 by skilful Italian craftsmen, the Château de Meillant represents a fine combination of Late Gothic and early Renaissance architecture. It is dominated by the *Tour du Lion* (Lion's Tower), an octagonal three-storey staircase tower. The plainer west façade,

*A small grotesque carving in Meillant*

mirrored in a moat, dates from the early 1300s.

Other highlights of a visit include the château's graceful chapel and its surrounding grounds in which peacocks strut. On the estate, you'll also find old horse-drawn carriages and vintage cars; the Parcours de Miniatures, featuring small-scale models illustrating ways of living through different historic periods, and a collection of dolls' houses.

## Life in a Cistercian Abbey

The rules of the Cistercian Order were based on the principles of austerity and simplicity. Abbeys were divided into two communities, which did not mix. Lay brothers, not bound by holy vows, ensured the self-sufficiency of the abbey by managing the barns, tilling the fields, milling corn and welcoming guests. The full, or choir, monks were the only ones allowed into the cloister, at the heart of the complex, and could not leave the abbey without the permission of the abbot.

The monks' days started at 2am and ended at 7pm and were regularly punctuated by religious devotions, which included prayers, confession, meditation and mass. The strict rule of silence was broken only to read from the Bible or from the Rules of the Order. Many monks were literate, and monasteries played a leading role in copying manuscripts.

A Cistercian monk labouring in the fields

# ⑫ Bourges

The heart of modern Bourges, once the Roman city of Avaricum, is the network of ancient streets around its magnificent cathedral. The city was an important religious, courtly and arts centre in the Middle Ages. In the late 19th century, it became a prosperous industrial town. Today Bourges has a relaxed atmosphere that complements its excellent museums, housed in superb old buildings. The town is known for its music festivals including *Le Printemps de Bourges*, and *Un Eté à Bourges*, a programme of free events held during the summer.

The 16th-century *Concert champêtre*, displayed in the Hôtel Lallemant

### 🏛 Hôtel des Echevins & Musée Estève

13 rue Edouard Branly. **Tel** 02 48 24 75 38. **Open** Wed–Mon. **Closed** 1 Jan, 1 May, 1 & 11 Nov & 25 Dec. &

The Hôtel des Echevins (the house of the aldermen) is remarkable for its intricately carved octagonal tower and fireplaces. Built in 1489, it served as the seat of the city council that governed Bourges for more than three centuries.

The building was classified an historic monument in 1886. In 1985 work to renovate the building began, and in 1987 it became the Musée Estève, displaying paintings by the self-taught artist Maurice Estève, who was born in Culan in the south of Berry *(see p152)*. The collection is mainly made up of Estève's powerful, brightly coloured canvases. However, this permanent display is augmented by temporary exhibitions of his watercolours, collages and line drawings. The collection is arranged in chronological order on three levels, connected by elegant stone spiral staircases. This modern work seems surprisingly at home in the spacious Gothic rooms.

*Samsâra* by Maurice Estève (1977)

### 🏛 Hôtel Lallemant & Musée des Arts Décoratifs

6 rue Bourbonnoux. **Tel** 02 48 57 81 17. **Open** Tue–Sun. **Closed** 1 Jan, 1 May, 1 & 11 Nov & 25 Dec.

This Renaissance mansion, which was built for a rich merchant family originally from Germany, houses the city's decorative arts museum. It still has the little chapel used by the Lallemant family, its coffered ceiling carved with alchemical symbols, and an elegant, restored courtyard. On display is a fine collection of tapestries from the 16th and 17th centuries, clocks, ceramics, glassware, miniatures and 15th- and 17th-century paintings and furniture, including a beautiful 17th-century ebony inlaid cabinet.

### 🏛 Musée du Berry

4–6 rue des Arènes. **Tel** 02 48 70 41 92. **Open** Wed–Mon. **Closed** 1 Jan, 1 May, 1 & 11 Nov & 25 Dec. & grd flr only.

The Musée du Berry, housed in the Renaissance Hôtel Cujas, concentrates on local history. The collections include a large display of Gallo-Roman artifacts, many of which were unearthed in the area. There is some wonderful Gothic sculpture, especially Jean de Cambrai's weeping figures from the base of the tomb of Jean, Duc de Berry, the upper section of which can be seen in the crypt of the Cathédrale St-Etienne *(see pp156–7)*.

On the upper floor of the museum is a permanent exhibition of Berry's rural arts, crafts and everyday objects, including the distinctive stoneware made in La Borne near Sancerre.

Jehan Fouquet's Angel Ceiling in the Palais Jacques-Cœur

## Jacques Cœur

The son of a Bourges furrier, Jacques Cœur (c.1400–56) became one of the richest and most powerful men in medieval France. With his merchant fleet he sailed to the eastern Mediterranean and Far East, bringing back luxury goods such as silks, spices and precious metals, until Charles VII appointed him head of the Paris Mint, then treasurer of the Royal Household. In 1451 he was accused of fraud and falsely implicated in the death of the king's mistress, Agnès Sorel. He was arrested, tortured and imprisoned, but escaped to Rome. There he took part in the pope's naval expedition against the Turks and died on the Greek island of Chios.

The merchant Jacques Cœur

### 🏛 Palais Jacques-Cœur

rue Jacques-Cœur. **Tel** 02 48 24 79 42. **Open** daily. **Closed** 1 Jan, 1 May, 1 & 11 Nov, 25 Dec. 🏛 📷 **w** palais-jacques-coeur.monuments-nationaux.fr

Built on the remains of the city's Gallo-Roman walls, this house is among the finest secular Gothic edifices in Europe. It was built at great expense between 1443 and 1451 for Jacques Cœur, one of the most fascinating men in medieval France.

The palace has a number of innovations remarkable for their period. Rooms open off corridors instead of leading into each other. Appealingly, each room is "labelled" over the doorway with carved scenes illustrating its function.

From *trompe l'oeil* figures peeping out from the turreted façade to the mysterious, possibly alchemical, symbols carved everywhere, the palace offers a feast of interesting details. Hearts are a common motif – the newly ennobled Jacques Cœur naturally had hearts, *cœurs* in French, on his coat of arms.

Other features are a large courtyard, majestic wooden

The fireplace in the south gallery of the Palais Jacques-Cœur

vaulting in the galleries, and the beautiful ceiling in the chapel, painted by the 15th-century artist, Jehan Fouquet (*see p29*). Temporary exhibitions are held here annually.

## Bourges Town Centre

① Musée du Berry
② Palais Jacques-Cœur
③ Hôtel des Echevins (Musée Estève)
④ Hôtel Lallemant (Musée des Arts Décoratifs)
⑤ Cathédrale St-Etienne

0 metres 350
0 yards 350

**For keys to symbols** *see back flap*

# Bourges: Cathédrale St-Etienne

St-Etienne, one of France's finest Gothic cathedrals, was built mainly between 1195 and 1260. The unknown architect designed St-Etienne without transepts, which, combined with the interior's unusual height and width, makes it seem much lighter than most Gothic cathedrals. This effect is beautifully enhanced by the brilliant hues of the medieval stained glass. Also unusual are the asymmetrical west front; the double row of flying buttresses rising in pyramid-shaped tiers; and a "crypt", a lower, window-lit church, created because the ground is 6 m (20 ft) lower at the east end.

**Vast Interior**
The interior is 124 m (400 ft) long and 37 m (120 ft) high.

★ **Astrological Clock**
Dating from the 1420s, this fascinating clock was designed by Canon Jean Fusoris, a mathematician.

Entrance

## The Last Judgement

The tympanum on the central portal of the west façade depicts Archangel Michael weighing souls. Those found wanting are hustled by devils into the mouth of Hell, while the elect are gathered into the bosom of Abraham. The youthful, naked dead lift up their tombstones in a dramatic Resurrection scene.

*The Last Judgement portal of the Cathédrale St-Etienne*

★ **Stained-Glass Windows**
The medieval stained glass in the choir was sponsored by local guilds, whose members are depicted practising their crafts at the bottom of each window.

## VISITORS' CHECKLIST

**Practical Information**
pl Etienne Dolet. **Tel** 02 48 23 02 60. **Open** 8:30am–7:15pm daily (Oct–Mar: 9am–5:45pm). 🕮 🕇 6:30pm Sat, 11am Sun; Jul & Aug 6:30pm daily. 🅿 🕮 **w** **cathedrale-bourges. monuments-nationaux.fr**

**Praying Figures**
In the crypt are statues of the Duc and Duchesse de Berry. During the Revolution the statues were decapitated and the existing heads are copies.

★ **St Sépulcre**
This dramatic sculpture of the *Entombment of Christ* was placed at the far end of the lower church in 1540.

## KEY

① **The five portals** of the west front are surrounded by carved scenes. The doorways vary in size and shape, adding to the asymmetry of the façade.

② **The Grand Housteau** is a striking rose window, donated by the renowned patron of the arts Jean, Duc de Berry.

③ **The Tour Sourde** (Deaf Tower) is so called because it has no bell.

④ **The Chapelle Jacques-Coeur** has a glorious Annunciation window.

⑤ **The crypt**, or lower church, was built in the earlier Gallo-Roman moat.

⑥ **The Romanesque portal** on the cathedral's south side is decorated with a *Christ in Majesty* and the 12 apostles.

**Jean, Duc de Berry**
The recumbent marble effigy of Jean, Duc de Berry, his feet resting on a bear, was originally part of his tomb.

A Sancerre vineyard

## ⑬ Sancerre

**Road map** F3. 🚗 1,800. 🚌
ℹ️ esplanade Porte-César (02 48 54
08 21). 🛒 Tue & Sat. 🎪 Foire aux
Crottins (goat's cheese fair, May);
Foire aux Vins (wine fair, Whitsun);
Foire aux Vins de France (French
wine fair, Aug). **w tourisme-sancerre.com**

The ancient Berry town of
Sancerre is perched on a
domed hill, a rare sight in the
flat landscape of the Loire
Valley. Its narrow streets
boast interesting 15th- and
16th-century houses. All that
remains of the medieval castle
that once dominated the town
is the **Tour des Fiefs**, which
gives a superb view of the
River Loire. The town and
surrounding area are famous
for their dry white wines.

To learn of the wine-making
traditions, visit the **Maison des
Sancerre**, which also hosts
cultural events. You can enjoy
a tasting here and at other
wineries in the area.

🏠 **Tour des Fiefs**
Parc du Château de Sancerre.
**Open** daily in summer. 🎟️

🏛️ **Maison des Sancerre**
3 rue du Meridian. **Tel** 02 48 54 11 35.
**Open** Apr–mid-Nov: daily. 🎟️
**w maison-des-sancerre.com**

## ⑭ Château de la Verrerie

**Road map** F3. 🚉 Gien, then taxi.
**Tel** 02 48 81 51 60. **Open** Easter–Oct:
Wed–Sun (Jul & Aug: daily). 🎟️🚗🎟️

This fine, early Renaissance
château is on the edge of the
Forêt d'Ivoy. The land was

given to the Scot Sir John
Stewart of Darnley by Charles
VII. It was a gift of thanks for
defeating the English at the
battle of Baugé in Anjou in
1421. John's son, Béraud
Stewart, began to build on
the land several decades
later, and the Château de
la Verrerie was eventually
completed by Béraud's
nephew, Robert Stewart.

La Verrerie reverted to the
French crown in 1670. Three
years later Louis XIV gave the
château to Louise de Kéroualle.
She lived here until her death
in 1734 at the age of 85.

La Verrerie has a lovely
Renaissance gallery adorned
with beautiful 16th-century
frescoes. The chapel also boasts
some fine frescoes. In the
19th-century wing are four
beautiful alabaster statuettes
from the tomb of the Duc de
Berry (see p157).

Alabaster statuettes in the Château de la
Verrerie's 19th-century wing

## ⑮ Aubigny-sur-Nère

**Road map** F3. 🚗 6,000. 🚌 ℹ️ rue
de l'Eglise (02 48 58 40 20). 🛒 Sat.
🎪 Fête Franco-Ecossaise (mid-Jul).
**w tourisme-sauldre-sologne.com**

Attractive Aubigny is proud of
its association with the
Scottish Stewart clan.
In 1423 the town was
given by Charles VII to
Sir John Stewart of
Darnley, along with
nearby La Verrerie. After
a major fire in 1512, the
Stewarts rebuilt Aubigny
in the Renaissance style
and also constructed a
new château.

In 1673 Louis XIV gave
the duchy of Aubigny
to Louise de Kéroualle.
Although she spent most

of her time at La Verrerie, Louise
had a large garden created at
the Château d'Aubigny. The
Aubusson tapestries presented
to her by the king are displayed
in the château, which now
serves as the town hall.

The 13th-century **Eglise
St-Martin**, in transitional Gothic
style, was largely rebuilt by the
Stewarts. It has a beautiful
wooden Pietà and a moving
16th-century Entombment.

Berry has a reputation for
sorcery, a tradition well illustrated in Concressault's lively
**Musée de la Sorcellerie**, 10 km
(6 miles) east of Aubigny. Here
waxworks bring to life the
history of herbalism, healing
and magic, and portray the
gruesome fate of those
accused of witchcraft during
the Inquisition.

The **Château de la Chapelle
d'Angillon**, between Aubigny
and Bourges, houses a museum
devoted to Alain Fournier
(1886–1914), author of the
novel *Le grande meaulnes*,
who was killed in action two
months into World War I.

🏛️ **Musée de la Sorcellerie**
La Jonchère, Concressault. **Tel** 02 48
73 86 11. **Open** Apr–Nov: daily.
🚫 ♿ **w musee-sorcellerie.fr**

🏛️ **Château de la Chapelle
d'Angillon (Musée Fournier)**
18380 La Chapelle d'Angillon. **Tel** 02
48 73 41 10. **Open** daily (except Sun
am). 🚫 **w chateau-angillon.com**

The Maison de François I, one of the many old houses in
Aubigny-sur-Nère

# ⑯ Wine and Cheese Tour

The Sancerrois in eastern Berry is renowned for its wines and goat's cheese. Gourmets can visit the top-class Sancerre cellars and taste the fresh and fragrant white wines made from the Sauvignon grape, or charming light reds and rosés made from the Pinot Noir. The flavours combine beautifully with the sharp little goat's cheeses called Crottins de Chavignol, which are also produced locally. This rural route passes by gently hilly vineyards and fields of grazing red goats. The tour takes in many of the major producers, as well as a few local museums that explain the long history of both wine and cheese.

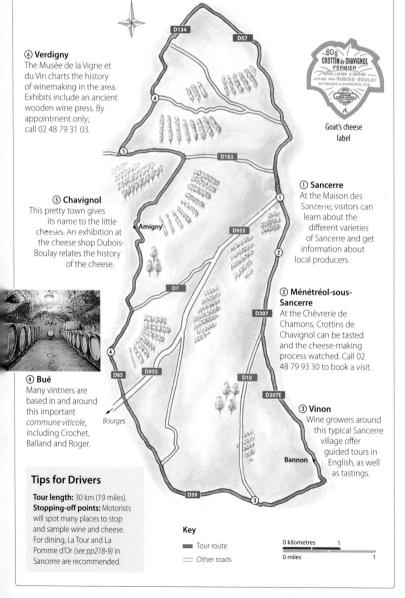

**⑥ Verdigny**
The Musée de la Vigne et du Vin charts the history of winemaking in the area. Exhibits include an ancient wooden wine press. By appointment only; call 02 48 79 31 03.

Goat's cheese label

**⑤ Chavignol**
This pretty town gives its name to the little cheeses. An exhibition at the cheese shop Dubois-Boulay relates the history of the cheese.

**① Sancerre**
At the Maison des Sancerre, visitors can learn about the different varieties of Sancerre and get information about local producers.

**② Ménétréol-sous-Sancerre**
At the Chèvrerie de Chamons, Crottins de Chavignol can be tasted and the cheese-making process watched. Call 02 48 79 93 30 to book a visit.

**④ Bué**
Many vintners are based in and around this important *commune viticole*, including Crochet, Balland and Roger.

Bourges

**③ Vinon**
Wine growers around this typical Sancerre village offer guided tours in English, as well as tastings.

Bannon

## Tips for Drivers

**Tour length:** 30 km (19 miles).
**Stopping-off points:** Motorists will spot many places to stop and sample wine and cheese. For dining, La Tour and La Pomme d'Or (*see pp218–9*) in Sancerre are recommended.

### Key

▬ Tour route
— Other roads

0 kilometres 1
0 miles 1

# NORTH OF THE LOIRE

The peaceful Mayenne and Sarthe regions seem worlds away from the tourist-frequented château country of the central Loire Valley. A grouping of districts with little common history, the area north of the Loire has very different attractions from the former royal domains to the south. The rivers, hills, forests and plains abound with opportunities for fishing, boating and country walks.

The more dramatic scenery of the Mayenne Valley, from Laval southwards, with steep cliffs and villages perched on wooded hills, makes a pleasant spot for a restful break from château-visiting. The river, studded with locks, runs into the Maine and then into the Loire, a pattern also followed by the Loir (Le Loir, which is not to be confused with La Loire).

The valley of the Loir is also very pretty, the slow-moving river flowing through peaceful villages. It is a perfect place for relaxing and enjoying the countryside. The valley also offers a few spectacular sights of its own, including the château at Le Lude, with its four imposing corner towers, and the stern-faced château of Châteaudun further upstream, which was once a stronghold of the counts of Blois. Le Mans, world famous for its 24-hour car race, also has an attractive old centre. East of Le Mans, gentle scenery gives way first to the wooded hills of the Perche and then to the vast wheat-fields on the plain of the Beauce, which is dominated by the magnificent cathedral at Chartres. Two lovely châteaux, Anet and Maintenon, were homes to royal mistresses: Diane de Poitiers *(see p59)*, mistress of Henri II, retreated to Anet, and Madame de Maintenon was the mistress of Louis XIV. Like Chartres Cathedral, these great houses stand on the edge of the Ile de France, the region around Paris, so they attract many day visitors from the country's capital.

Clog-making at the woodwork centre in Jupilles in the Forêt de Bercé

◀ Splendid stained-glass window in the Cathédrale Notre-Dame, in Chartres

# Exploring North of the Loire

Consisting of the *départements* of Mayenne, Sarthe and
Eure-et-Loire, the region north of the Loire borders Brittany,
Normandy and the Ile de France. It combines characteristics
of all these regions with those of the central Loire Valley.
In the north, the hills of the Alpes Mancelles have more in
common with the landscapes of Normandy than they do
with the rolling fields further south. The rivers traversing
the region – the Loir, Sarthe and Mayenne – are smaller
and gentler than the mighty Loire but still very scenic.
The largest towns in the region are Chartres, Le Mans
and Laval, all of them worth a visit.

One of Chartres' winding, cobbled streets

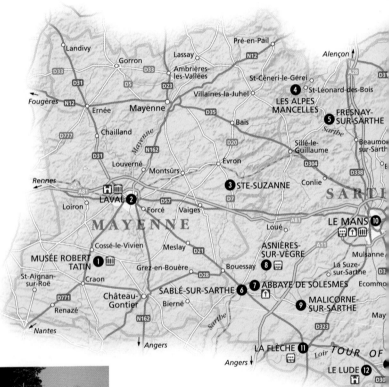

Cruising on the River Sarthe, upstream
from Sablé

## Getting Around

Chartres and Le Mans are both reached from Paris by the A11
autoroute (*L'Océane*), which continues to Angers. The A81
crosses the region from Le Mans to Laval, while the A28 cuts
north–south from Alençon to Tours. Trains from Paris are
frequent: the TGV takes 55 minutes to Le Mans, and regional
express trains take 60 minutes to Chartres. From Chartres to
Le Mans is about 90 minutes. Buses link most of the main
towns in the region but are less regular during school holidays.
Boating is one of the best ways of seeing the countryside.

**Key**

- Motorway
- Major road
- Secondary road
- Minor road
- Scenic route
- Main railway
- Minor railway
- Regional border

The waterfront at Malicorne-sur-Sarthe

Ivry-la-Bataille

CHÂTEAU D'ANET **17**

Nonancourt

Dreux

Brezolles

Le Boullay-Mivoye

La Ferté-Vidame

Nogent-le-Roi

Senonches

Châteauneuf-en-Thymerais

Maintenon

*Paris*

La Loupe

Courville-sur-Eure

CHARTRES **18**

Auneau

EURE-ET-LOIR

Thiron-Gardais

Allonnes

Nogent-le-Rotrou

**16** ILLIERS-COMBRAY

Beaumont-les-Autels

Voves

La Ferté-Bernard

Brou

Allaines-Mervilliers

etable

Authon-du-Perche

Bonneval

Orgères-en-Beauce

Janville

Montmirail

Courtalain

**15** CHÂTEAUDUN

Connerré

Vibraye

*Orléans*

Bouloire

Cloyes-sur-le-Loir

St-Calais

*Tours*

Grand-Lucé

CHÂTEAU DE COURTANVAUX **14**

Lhomme

La Chartre-sur-le-Loir

hâteau-du-Loir

*rs*

View of the old town in Le Mans from the river

0 kilometres 15
0 miles 15

## Sights at a Glance

1. Musée Robert Tatin
2. Laval
3. Ste-Suzanne
4. Les Alpes Mancelles
5. Fresnay-sur-Sarthe
6. Sablé-sur-Sarthe
7. Abbaye de Solesmes
8. Asnières-sur-Vègre
9. Malicorne-sur-Sarthe
10. *Le Mans pp168–71*
11. La Flèche
12. Le Lude
14. Courtanvaux
15. Châteaudun
16. Illiers-Combray
17. Anet
18. *Chartres pp175–9*

## Tours

13. *Tour of the Loir Valley pp172–3*

For keys to symbols *see back flap*

# ❶ Musée Robert Tatin

**Road map** B2. La Frênouse. 🚆 Laval.
🚌 Cossé-le-Vivien. **Tel** 02 43 98 80
89. **Open** daily (Oct–Mar: pm only).
**Closed** Jan, 25 Dec. ♿ 📷 ♿
**W** musee-robert-tatin.fr

The multitalented artist Robert
Tatin (1902–83) devised an
extraordinary museum in
the little village of La
Frênouse, near Cossé-le-
Vivien. The building is
approached via the Allée
des Géants (Giants'
Avenue): lining the path
are huge, strange concrete
figures depicting
people who
impressed Tatin,
including Pablo
Picasso, Toulouse-
Lautrec, Joan of
Arc and the
Gallic warrior
Vercingetorix.
Beyond them, a statue of a
huge dragon with gaping jaws
stands guard. The grounds
also feature themed gardens
including a maze.

In the museum, awarded the
coveted *Maison des Illustres*
(Houses of the Famous) label in
2012, is a cross-section of Tatin's
work: paintings, sculpture,
frescoes and ceramics. Tatin
was also a cabinet-maker and
much else besides. He was
influenced by the megalithic
monuments in Brittany as well
as by Aztec art.

Tatin's statue of Picasso at
the Musée Robert Tatin

# ❷ Laval

**Road map** C2. 🏛 54,000. 🚆 🚌
ℹ 1 allée du Vieux St-Louis (02 43
49 46 46). 🛒 Tue, Sat.
**W** laval-tourisme.com

Laval straddles the River
Mayenne. On the west bank
is the **Vieux Château**. This
castle dates from the early
11th century, when the region
was under the sway of Foulques
Nerra, Count of Anjou – it
formed one link in his chain
of fortresses designed to keep
out the invading Bretons and
the Normans. The château has
a collection of the equipment
used by Laval native, Ambroise

Paré (1510–c.1592), known as
"the father of modern surgery".
It is best known, however, for
its **Musée d'Art Naïf** (Museum
of Naive Art) which was
inspired in part by Henri
Rousseau (*see p29*). He was
known as *Le Douanier*, his
nickname deriving from the
period when he worked
as a customs officer. His
Paris studio, complete
with piano, has been
well reconstructed here.
Although the museum
has only two works by
Rousseau, there are many
gems here, including a
painting of the ocean
liner *Normandie* by
the artist Jules
Lefranc (1887–1972).
Laval's old town
has attractive
houses as well as
the **Cathédrale
de la Ste-Trinité**,
with its Aubusson tapestries.
The city became famous for

producing elaborate *retables*
(altarpieces). **Notre-Dame-
des-Cordeliers**, on rue de
Bretagne, has several fine
examples. Laval and Mayenne
are also major cheese-making
areas. Discover how this
agricultural activity reached
industrial heights at the
**Lactopôle**. Laval also has a
couple of France's few surviving
**bateaux-lavoirs**, which now
form a museum of the same
name. Such floating laundries
first appeared in the mid-19th
century on the banks of rivers
in the western Loire Valley.

🏛 **Château & Musée du
Vieux Château**
pl de la Trémoille. **Tel** 02 43 53 39 89.
**Open** Mon–Sat, Sun pm. ♿ 📷

🏛 **Lactopôle**
**Tel** 02 43 59 51 90. **Open** Easter–Sep:
Sat & Sun (Jul & Aug: daily). 📷 by
reservation only. **W** lactopole.com

🏛 **Bateaux-Lavoirs**
quai Paul-Boudet. **Tel** 02 43 49 46 46
(tourist office). **Open** Jul & Aug. 📷

*Le lancement du Normandie* by Jules Lefranc, at the Musée d'Art Naïf

## ❸ Ste-Suzanne

**Road map** C2.  1,000. 🚉 Laval,
then bus. ℹ️ 1 rue du Bueil (02 43
01 43 60). 🇼 **ste-suzanne.fr**

This village, high on a hill, is
still partly surrounded by the
fortifications designed as a
defence against marauding
Normans in the 10th century –
it was sturdy enough to withstand an attack by William the
Conqueror, whose former
encampment site can be seen
just 3 km (2 miles) outside the
town. Although much of the
original castle was pulled down
by the English in the early 15th
century, a 10th-century keep
has withstood the ravages of
time. The **Château de
Ste-Suzanne** has
been restored, with
exhibitions focusing
on the area's heritage.
Village history is also
explored at the **Musée
de l'Auditoire**, with
reconstructions of
events and vignettes
of daily life.

🏛 **Château de
Ste-Suzanne**
1 rue Fouquet de la Varenne.
**Tel** 02 43 58 13 00. **Open** daily.
**Closed** mid-Dec–early Jan. 🚫 ✏️
🇼 **ciap.lamayenne.fr**

🏛 **Musée de l'Auditoire**
7 Grande Rue. **Tel** 02 43 01 42 65. **Open**
Apr–Sep: Sat & Sun (Jul & Aug: daily).
🚫 🇼 **museeauditoire.jimdo.com**

## ❹ Les Alpes Mancelles

**Road map** C2. 🚉 Alençon. 🚌
Fresnay-sur-Sarthe. ℹ️ 19 av du Dr
Riant, Fresnay-sur-Sarthe (02 43 33 28
04). 🇼 **tourisme-alpesmancelles.fr**

The name of this region of
wooded hills and green
meadows, between Fresnay-
sur-Sarthe and Alençon, means
"Alps of Le Mans". Although
certainly an exaggeration,
there is something faintly
alpine in the landscape, with
its streams winding through
gorges, fruit trees, and heather-
clad hillsides dotted with
sheep. A large part of the area
is incorporated into the

St-Céneri-le-Gérei's Romanesque church,
perched on a hill

regional natural park of
Normandie-Maine.

The enchanting village of
**St-Céneri-le-Gérei**
hides in a loop in the
Sarthe. It has a
wonderful Roman-
esque church
containing medieval
murals. In the 19th
and early 20th
centuries, artists,
such as Eugène
Boudin and Camille
Corot, were drawn to
this picturesque area.
They often stayed at the
**Auberge des Soeurs Moisy**,
now turned into a compact
museum. Exhibits focus on the
history and heritage of fine art
in the region. It is also worth
wandering through the themed
**Jardins de la Mansonière**,
which include a nuttery and a
perfume garden.

The neighbouring village of
**St-Léonard-des-Bois** lies south
down the Sarthe. The steep

Church doorway,
St-Léonard-des-Bois

slopes are appreciated by
mountain-bikers and walkers;
climb to the top for grand
views of the Sarthe plain
leading to Le Mans. Canoeists
also favour this section of the
river. Located on the outside of
St-Léonard-des-Bois **Domaine
du Gasseau** has an equestrian
centre, tree-top assault course
and an art centre. A restaurant,
hotel, café and a shop selling
local produce can be found
here too.

🏛 **Auberge des Soeurs Moisy**
rue du Dessous, St-Céneri-le-Gérei. **Tel**
02 33 27 84 47. **Open** Apr–Sep: Wed–
Sun, pm only. 🚫

🌳 **Jardins de la Mansonière**
rte d'Alençon. **Tel** 02 33 26 73 24.
**Open** mid-Apr–May & Sep: Fri–Sun
& public hols, pm only; Jun–Aug:
Wed–Sun, pm only. 🚫 📷
🇼 **mansoniere.fr**

🐎 **Domaine du Gasseau**
St-Léonard-des-Bois. **Tel** 02 43 34 34
44. **Open** Apr–Oct: Wed–Sun (Jul &
Aug: daily). 🇼 **legasseau.fr**

## ❺ Fresnay-sur-Sarthe

**Road map** C2.  2,400. 🚉 Alençon,
Sillé-le-Guillaume, La Hutte. 🚌
ℹ️ 19 av du Dr Riant (02 43 33 28 04).
🛒 Sat am.

From the 16th to the 19th
century, Fresnay-sur-Sarthe
was an important centre for
cloth weaving, and its outskirts
remain rather industrial. The
centre of Fresnay, however, still
retains a charming medieval
feel, with unusual church and
castle vestiges.

The River Sarthe from the town of Fresnay-sur-Sarthe

## ❻ Sablé-sur-Sarthe

**Road map** C2. 🏠 13,000. 🚂 🚌
ℹ️ rue du Château (02 43 95 00 60).
🏪 Mon, Fri & Sat. 🎭 Festival de la
Musique Baroque (late Aug).
🌐 **vallee-de-la-sarthe.com**

A good base from which to take
river cruises along the Sarthe,
Sablé is pleasant, although
fairly industrial. There is some
surprising modern sculpture
in this traditional setting: in
the cobbled place Raphaël Elizé
in the town centre stands
a contemporary sculpture
entitled *Hymne à l'amour*, by
local sculptor Louis Derbré,
and around the square are
several piles of "cannon balls",
a rather curious modern
installation that was inspired
by an 18th-century fashion.

Sablé has some attractive
shops in the pedestrian rue de
l'Île and in the nearby square,
where the Maison du Sablé
sells the famous shortbread-
like biscuits to which the
town has given its name.

The town's château, which
was built in the early 18th
century by a nephew of Louis
XIV's chief minister, Jean-
Baptiste Colbert, now houses
workshops for restorers of old
books and manuscripts of the
Bibliothèque Nationale, the
national library of France.
Although the château cannot

*The Entombment of Our Lord*, part of the "saints of Solesmes" group of stone carvings in the church of the Abbaye de Solesmes

be visited, the pleasant park
that surrounds it is open.

On the route de Solesmes,
opposite the summer swim-
ming pool, is the Jardin Public,
from which there are views of
the Abbaye de Solesmes.

## ❼ Abbaye de Solesmes

**Road map** C2. 🚂 Sablé-sur-Sarthe,
then taxi or walk 3 km (2 miles) along
the river. **Tel** 02 43 95 03 08. Abbey
Church: **Open** daily. 🕙 10am daily;
vespers: varies between 4 and 5pm.
🔊 🌐 **solesmes.com**

Services at the Benedictine
Abbaye de St-Pierre, part of the
Abbaye de Solesmes, attract
visitors who come from far and
wide to listen to the monks'
Gregorian chant. For over a

century, the abbey has been
working to preserve and
promote this ancient form of
prayer. Books and recordings
produced by the monks are
sold, outside church service
times, in the shop near the
entrance to the abbey.

Originally founded in 1010
as a priory, the abbey was
substantially rebuilt in the late
19th century in a somewhat
forbidding, fortress-like style.

The interior of the **abbey
church** has an austere beauty.
Its nave and transept are both
Romanesque, while the
19th-century choir imitates the
medieval style. Both arms of the
transept are adorned by groups
of stone carvings made in the
15th and 16th centuries and
known collectively as the "saints
of Solesmes". The chapel to the
left of the high altar contains
*The Entombment of Our Lord*,
with the haunting figure of
Mary Magdalene kneeling at
Christ's feet, deep in
prayer. In *The Dormition
of the Virgin*, which can
be seen in the chapel
on the right, the lower
scenes illustrate the
Virgin Mary's death
and burial, while the
scenes above depict
her Assumption and
heavenly Coronation.

The little **parish
church**, which is
located beside the
entrance to the abbey,
is worth visiting for its
interesting modern
stained-glass windows.

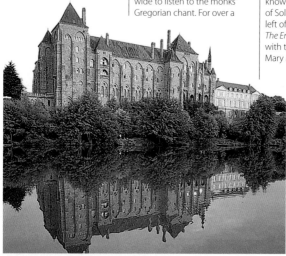

The imposing Abbaye de Solesmes, reflected in the River Sarthe

# ❽ Asnières-sur-Vègre

**Road map** C2. ⬚ 380.
🚉 Sablé-sur-Sarthe, then taxi.
ℹ️ Sablé-sur-Sarthe (02 43 95 00 60).
🌐 asnieres-sur-vegre.fr

This pretty village of old houses and watermills, with a 12th-century humpbacked bridge, is largely built in pinkish-yellow stone. Its church has lively wall paintings, dating from the 12th and 15th centuries, depicting scenes from medieval life and moral warnings in the shape of the damned being herded into hell by huge, slavering hounds. The 13th-century **Cour de Justice** is an impressive Gothic building, built as a meeting place for the canons of the Cathédrale St-Julien in Le Mans. The **Jardin Mosaïque** above the village is an ecological garden.

Nearby **Juigné** is on the old road from Le Mans to Sablé-sur-Sarthe. Its château was rebuilt in the early 17th century and the park, with its panoramic views of the river, is open to the public. It is possible to hire boats from Juigné's tiny harbour, from which one can see the church perched on the cliff above.

The 12th-century humpbacked bridge in Asnières-sur-Vègre

🏞️ **Jardin Mosaïque**
**Tel** 02 43 92 52 35.
**Open** late Apr–mid-Oct: Wed–Sun & public hols, pm only.
🅿️ 🌐 lejardinmosaique.com

Detail from the frescoes in Asnières' church

(pottery) just outside the town, also has a factory shop, while the **Malicorne Espace Faïence**, in the centre of town, boasts an extensive pottery museum.

Malicorne's small harbour is a popular spot for boaters, and both cruises and the hire of small motorboats are possible. The village also contains the pretty **Château de Malicorne**, dating from the 18th century, as well as a charming Romanesque church.

🏛️ **Faïenceries du Bourg-Joly**
16 rue Carnot. **Tel** 02 43 94 80 10.
Shop: **Open** Mon–Sat & Sun pm.
🌐 malicorne.com

🏛️ **Faïenceries d'Art de Malicorne**
18 rue Bernard Palissy. **Tel** 02 43 94 81 18. Workshop: **Open** Apr–Sep: Tue–Sat. Shop: **Open** Mon–Sat. 🅿️ ♿ 📷
🌐 faiencerie-malicorne.com

🏛️ **Malicorne Espace Faïence**
rue Victor Hugo. **Tel** 02 43 48 07 17.
**Open** mid-Feb–mid-Apr, Nov & Dec: Wed–Mon; mid-Apr–Oct: daily.
🅿️ ♿ 🌐 espacefaience.fr

🏰 **Château de Malicorne**
**Tel** 07 82 80 00 62. **Open** Jul & Aug: Wed–Sun. 🅿️ ♿ 📷 🌐 chateaudemalicornesursarthe.com

# ❾ Malicorne-sur-Sarthe

**Road map** C3. ⬚ 2,000. 🚉 Noyen-sur-Sarthe, La Suze-sur-Sarthe. 🚌
ℹ️ pl Désautels (02 43 94 74 45).
🛒 Fri. 🌐 ville-malicorne.fr

The chief claim to fame of this little town is its faïence (tin-glazed earthenware). Jean Loiseau, a potter, first set up here in 1747. At the **Faïenceries du Bourg-Joly** visitors can buy the open-work ware known as *Faïence de Malicorne*. The **Faïenceries d'Art de Malicorne**,

The harbour at Malicorne, surrounded by former watermills

# ⑩ Street-by-Street: Le Mans

The hilly, picturesque old town (La Cité Plantagenêt) is best explored on foot. Its narrow, cobbled streets are lined by 15th- and 16th-century half-timbered houses interspersed with Renaissance mansions. Several of the finest buildings served as temporary residences for France's kings and queens, although the one named after Richard the Lionheart's queen Bérengère, or Berengaria, was built two and a half centuries after her death. The quarter is bounded to the northwest by the old Roman walls, which run beside the River Sarthe.

**Maison d'Adam et Eve**
The carvings on this doctor's house illustrate the importance of astrology in 16th-century medicine.

**Hôtel d'Argouges**
Louis XI is said to have stayed in this 15th-century turreted mansion in 1467.

**The Roman walls** are among the best-preserved in Europe.

```
0 metres        50
0 yards         50
```

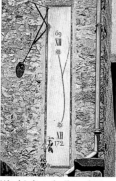

**Hôtel Aubert de Clairaulnay**
The sundial on the side of this late 16th-century mansion was placed there in 1789 by Claude Chappe, the inventor of semaphore.

QUAI LOUIS-BLANC

RUE DE VAUX

RUE DE LA VERRERIE

GRANDE RUE

RUE ST-FLACEAU

RUE DES FOSSÉS

RUE ST-BENOÎT

RUE DE LA VIEILLE PORTE

AVENUE DE ROSTOV-SUR-LE-DON

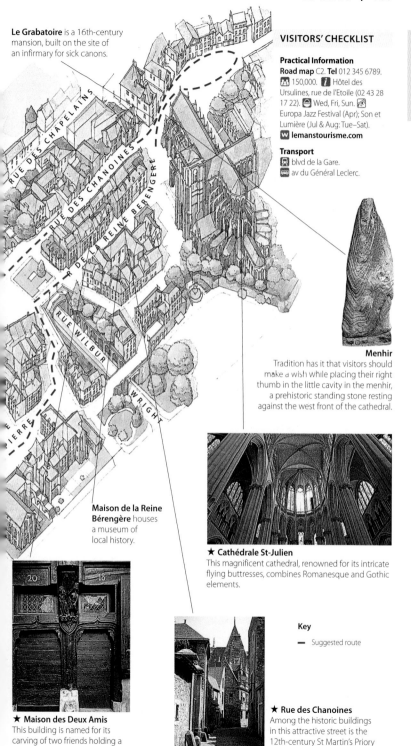

**Le Grabatoire** is a 16th-century mansion, built on the site of an infirmary for sick canons.

RUE DES CHAPELAINS

RUE DES CHANOINES

R DE LA REINE BÉRENGÈRE

RUE WILBUR

WRIGHT

IERRE

**Maison de la Reine Bérengère** houses a museum of local history.

**VISITORS' CHECKLIST**

**Practical Information**
Road map C2. **Tel** 012 345 6789.
150,000. Hôtel des Ursulines, rue de l'Etoile (02 43 28 17 22). Wed, Fri, Sun. Europa Jazz Festival (Apr); Son et Lumière (Jul & Aug: Tue–Sat).
**w** lemanstourisme.com

**Transport**
blvd de la Gare.
av du Général Leclerc.

**Menhir**
Tradition has it that visitors should make a wish while placing their right thumb in the little cavity in the menhir, a prehistoric standing stone resting against the west front of the cathedral.

★ **Cathédrale St-Julien**
This magnificent cathedral, renowned for its intricate flying buttresses, combines Romanesque and Gothic elements.

**Key**
— Suggested route

★ **Maison des Deux Amis**
This building is named for its carving of two friends holding a coat of arms.

★ **Rue des Chanoines**
Among the historic buildings in this attractive street is the 12th-century St Martin's Priory at No. 11.

# Exploring Le Mans

Although best known for its gruelling 24-hour motor race, Le Mans has many other attractions, not least of which is the magnificent Cathédrale St-Julien. The city's history stretches back to Roman times. The walls surrounding the old town, once the ancient city of Vindunum, date from the late 3rd and early 4th centuries. They originally stretched for some 1,300 m (1,400 yards). Eleven towers are still standing, and their massive walls are decorated with geometric patterns created by using courses of brick alternating with undressed stone in various colours. Outside the city walls, Le Mans has developed into a bustling, modern city with several memorable museums and a number of attractive churches.

The Plantagenet Enamel (1150) displayed in the Musée de Tessé

## 🏛 Cathédrale St-Julien

pl St Michel. **Tel** 02 43 28 28 98. **Open** daily. ♿

The best view of Cathédrale St-Julien's dramatic flying buttresses, unlike those of any other cathedral in their complex arrangement, is from the place des Jacobins. The cathedral is something of a hybrid: the 12th-century nave is essentially Romanesque, and the transepts were built a century later than the pure Gothic choir, one of the tallest in France, which dates from the 13th century. From the entrance via the Romanesque south portal, there is a striking view of the pillars in the choir. These used to be decorated with 16th-century tapestries that provided a splash of colour echoed in the medieval stained glass. These days, the tapestries are displayed only a few months a year.

*The Curate's Meal (1786), from the Musée de la Reine Bérengère*

## 🏛 Musée de la Reine Bérengère

rue de la Reine Bérengère. **Tel** 02 43 47 38 51. **Open** Tue–Sun (Oct–Apr: pm only). **Closed** 1 Jan, 24–26 Dec. ♿

This museum is set in three attractive half-timbered houses in the old town, their wooden façades lively with carved figures. Its collections of art and local history include faïence and pottery from many periods, with some examples of Malicorne ware (*see p167*). The museum also shows furniture made in the region. On the second floor, the 19th-century paintings by local artists show how relatively little the town of Le Mans has changed over the years. Also of note is Jean Sorieul's dramatic canvas, *The Battle of Le Mans of 13 December, 1793*.

## 🏛 Musée de Tessé

2 av de Paderborn. **Tel** 02 43 47 38 51. **Open** Tue–Sun. **Closed** 1 Jan, 24–26 Dec. ♿ ♿

In a pretty park a short walk from the cathedral, the bishop's palace was converted in 1927 into Le Mans' art museum, devoted to the fine and decorative arts, as well as archaeology. The permanent collection of paintings on the ground floor ranges from the late Middle Ages to the 19th century, and the archaeology section is mainly Egyptian and Greco-Roman, with two replica Pharaonic tombs. The Tessé's most famous exhibit is the vivid Plantagenet Enamel, a medieval enamelled panel depicting Geoffroy V, known as Le Bel (The Handsome).

## 🏛 Musée de 24 Heures

9 pl Luigi Chinetti. **Tel** 02 43 72 72 24. **Open** Wed–Mon (Jan: Fri–Sun; Apr–Sep: daily). ♿ ♿
Ⓦ musee24h.sarthe.com

Near Le Mans' famous racetrack is this museum, which displays a dazzling range of vintage, classic and modern racing cars and motorbikes. It includes some of the early designs of Amédée Bollée, an industrialist whose first pioneering car design dated from 1873. Bollée's family made the city famous for car design decades before the first 24-hour race (*see p61*).

16th-century tapestry hanging in the Cathédrale St-Julien

# ⓫ La Flèche

**Road map** C3. ⚲ 16,000. ☷
🛈 blvd de Montréal (02 43 94 02 53).
🏪 Wed & Sun. 🎭 Festival des
Affranchis (2nd weekend in Jul).
Ⓦ **tourisme-lafleche.fr**

La Flèche is an attractive town
on the Loir, with some restored
old mills in the middle of the
river. Its chief glory is the
**Prytanée Militaire**, the French
military academy. Founded as a
Jesuit college in 1604 by Henri
IV, it was assigned its present
function by Napoléon in 1808.
Of particular interest are the
church and the library.

On the opposite bank of
the river is Port Luneau, from
where Jérôme le Royer de la
Dauversière set off for the New
World. Nearby, the bustling
place Henri IV is lined with cafés.

At the heart of the town,
the 15th-century **Château
des Carmes**, the former town
hall, now hosts art exhibitions.
The charming Italian-style
**Théâtre de la Halle au Blé**
can be visited at weekends in
summer by arrangement with
the tourist office.

The **Parc Zoologique de la
Flèche**, just outside town, cares
for a wide range of animals and
stages shows with sea lions,
parrots and birds of prey.

🏛 **Prytanée Militaire**
rue du Collège. **Tel** 02 43 48 59 02.
**Open** Jul & Aug: daily. 🎨
Ⓦ **prytanee-national-militaire.fr**

🐾 **Parc Zoologique de la Flèche**
Le Tertre Rouge. **Tel** 0892 700 840.
**Open** daily. **Closed** 1 Jan, 25 Dec.
🎨 🌐 ♿ Ⓦ **zoo-la-fleche.com**

Place Henri IV in La Flèche, with the statue of the king in the centre

# ⓬ Le Lude

**Road map** C3. ⚲ 4,200. ☷
🛈 pl F-de-Nicolay (02 43 94 62 20).
🏪 Thu. 🎭 Marché Nocturne (night
market; 3rd weekend in Jul).
Ⓦ **tourisme-bassinludois.fr**

The oldest section of this
market town is the area
surrounding the **Château
du Lude**, where houses
dating from the 15th to 17th
centuries line the narrow streets.
The château's 15th-century
structure has been transformed
over the centuries into a more
elegant form. The interior is
beautifully furnished, largely
in the 19th-century style,
although there are some
pieces from the 17th and 18th
centuries, including French
and Flemish tapestries. The
Oratory is decorated with
16th-century frescoes, which
depict Old Testament scenes.
The formal gardens lead down
to the River Loir.

Cyclists and keen walkers
can follow the former railway
line northwest along the
Loir, from Le Lude to the
picturesque twin villages
of **Luché-Pringé**.

🏰 **Château du Lude**
**Tel** 02 43 94 60 09. **Open** Apr–Sep:
Thu–Tue, pm only; mid-Jun–Aug:
daily pm only. Park: Apr–Sep: daily.
🎨 🌐 ♿ ground floor. 🎭 Le
Weekend des Jardinières (1st
weekend in Jun). Ⓦ **lelude.com**

The imposing towers of the
Château du Lude

---

## Les 24 Heures du Mans

The name of Le Mans is known throughout the
world, thanks to its famous 24-hour car race. Since
it began on 26 May 1923, the event has attracted
huge crowds every June, both from France and
abroad – these days, more than 230,000 spectators
and 2,500 journalists watch the race. The circuit is
to the south of the city and is 13.6 km (8.5 miles)
long, including some stretches on ordinary roads.
Nowadays, drivers can cover some 5,300 km (3,300
miles) within the time limit. Within the course is the
Hunaudières track where, in 1908, Wilbur Wright
staged the first aeroplane flight in France.

One of the early races in Le Mans

# ⓭ Tour of the Loir Valley

Between Poncé-sur-le-Loir and La Flèche, the River Loir passes through peaceful, unspoiled countryside and picturesque villages. An unhurried tour of the valley takes two days and allows time to try some of the numerous riverside and forest walks. Families may enjoy the sailing, riding, angling and cycling facilities available in the area, while art lovers can seek out little-known churches adorned with delicately coloured Romanesque frescoes. Wine buffs will be interested in trying some of the area's wines, which can be sipped from locally blown glass – the Loir Valley also has an excellent reputation for its crafts.

The banks of the tranquil Loir, ideal for fishing and walking

### ① La Flèche
The home of the Prytanée Militaire (military academy, *see p171*), La Flèche is a charming town with wonderful views across the River Loir.

Entrance to the Prytanée Militaire

### ④ Vaas
The Moulin de Rotrou, on the edge of this pretty village, is a working flour mill and museum of breadmaking. In Vaas, the Eglise Notre-Dame de Vaas has fine 17th-century paintings.

### ② Parc Zoologique de la Flèche
Just outside the town, this zoo is one of the largest in France, with nearly 1,200 animals (*see p171*).

Loir

Thorée-les-Pins

Saumur

### ③ Le Lude
This market town is known mainly for its spectacular château (*see p171*).

## Tips for Drivers

**Tour length:** 103 km (64 miles).
**Stopping-off points:** The forests and riverbanks along the Loir are ideal for picnicking, and shops in the region sell delicacies to make a cold meal very special. This will be a doubly satisfying experience if you buy local produce from a market, such as that in Le Lude, first. If you prefer to eat in a restaurant, Le Moulin des 4 Saisons in La Flèche has local dishes on the menu. For those wishing to stay overnight, Le Relais Cicéro, also in La Flèche, is recommended.

The entrance to the Château du Lude

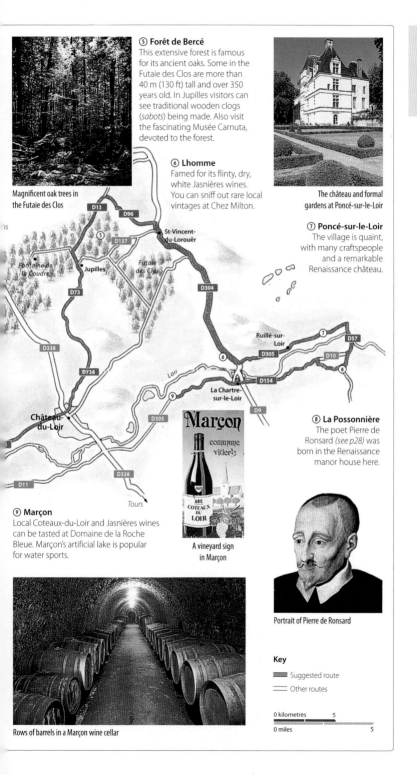

### ⑤ Forêt de Bercé

This extensive forest is famous for its ancient oaks. Some in the Futaie des Clos are more than 40 m (130 ft) tall and over 350 years old. In Jupilles visitors can see traditional wooden clogs (*sabots*) being made. Also visit the fascinating Musée Carnuta, devoted to the forest.

Magnificent oak trees in the Futaie des Clos

### ⑥ Lhomme

Famed for its flinty, dry, white Jasnières wines. You can sniff out rare local vintages at Chez Milton.

The château and formal gardens at Poncé-sur-le-Loir

### ⑦ Poncé-sur-le-Loir

The village is quaint, with many craftspeople and a remarkable Renaissance château.

### ⑧ La Possonnière

The poet Pierre de Ronsard (*see p28*) was born in the Renaissance manor house here.

### ⑨ Marçon

Local Coteaux-du-Loir and Jasnières wines can be tasted at Domaine de la Roche Bleue. Marçon's artificial lake is popular for water sports.

A vineyard sign in Marçon

Portrait of Pierre de Ronsard

Rows of barrels in a Marçon wine cellar

**Key**

Suggested route

Other routes

0 kilometres    5

0 miles    5

The Château de Courtanvaux with its towering walls

# ⑭ Château de Courtanvaux

Bessé-sur-Braye. **Road map** D3. **Tel** 02 43 35 34 43. **Open** Apr: Sat & Sun; May–Sep: Tue–Sun. **Closed** for private events. 🅿 🗗 Park: **Open** daily.
**W** chateaudecourtanvaux.com

Beyond Bessé-sur-Braye's outskirts, this Gothic and Renaissance château makes a romantic sight as it looms up at the end of a tree-lined drive. To see the château's carefully restored interior, book a place on a guided tour. The formal gardens are home to a tiny Gothic chapel; visitors are free to explore its 63 hectares (156 acres) of pools and woodland.

# ⑮ Châteaudun

**Road map** E2. 🗠 14,500. 🅿 🚐 🛈 1 rue de Luynes (02 37 45 22 46). 🛍 Thu. 🎪 Foire aux Laines (medieval fair, early Jul).
**W** tourisme-chateaudun.fr

Dominated by its fierce-looking **château**, the town of Châteaudun is situated above the River Loir where the Beauce plain meets the Perche district. Châteaudun was owned at one time by the aristocratic poet Charles d'Orléans (see p28), who then handed it on to his half-brother Jean Dunois, known as the bastard of Orléans and one of Joan of Arc's loyal companions-in-arms (see p141). It was Jean who began the château's south wing in 1460, and built the beautiful Late Gothic chapel, adorned with murals and life-size statues. The other wing was built half a century later.

Both wings are hung with wonderful tapestries, which date from the 16th and 17th centuries. Visitors can tour the château's living rooms, kitchens and massive keep.

Châteaudun's Old Town has a number of picturesque buildings, as well as several interesting churches: the Romanesque **Eglise de la Madeleine**, built in stages and now restored after damage sustained in 1940, and **St-Valérien**, with its tall square belfry. Situated on the far bank of the River Loir, the **Eglise St-Jean-de-la-Chaine** is also Romanesque. The **Grottes du Foulon** are located beneath the town. These large underground caves house remarkable crystallized sea creatures, preserved from the prehistoric era.

🏠 **Château**
pl Jehan de Dunoi. **Tel** 02 37 94 02 90. **Open** daily. **Closed** 1 Jan, 1 May, 25 Dec. 🅿 🗗 🅰 restricted.
**W** monuments-nationaux.fr

🏠 **Grottes du Foulon**
35 rue des Fouleries. **Tel** 02 37 45 19 60. **Open** Jan–mid-Apr: Wed–Sun; mid-Apr–Jun: Tue & Thu–Sun; Jul–mid-Sep: daily; mid-Sep–Dec: Sat & Sun.
🅰 **W** grottes-du-foulon.com

# ⑯ Illiers-Combray

**Road map** E2. 🗠 3,300. 🅿 🛈 5 rue Henri Germond (02 37 24 24 00). 🛍 Fri. 🎪 Journée des Aubépines (Proustian May Day, May).
**W** tourisme-illiers-combray.fr

The little market town of Illiers has added the word "Combray" to its name in honour of Marcel Proust's magnificent novel, *Remembrance of Things Past*, in which it is depicted as Combray (see p29). As a child, Proust spent many happy Easter holidays in the town, walking by the banks of the River Loir, which he later portrayed in his work as the "Vivonne". The author's admirers make pilgrimages to the places described in the novel, such as the big Gothic church, the Pré Catalan gardens and the house once owned by Proust's uncle Jules Amiot, **La Maison de Tante Léonie**. The house is now a touching museum about the famous writer's life, complete with the kitchen where the "Françoise" of the novel (who was actually Ernestine, the family cook) reigned supreme.

*Remembrance of Things Past* by Proust

🏛 **La Maison de Tante Léonie**
4 rue du Dr Proust. **Tel** 02 37 24 30 97. **Open** Tue–Sun. **Closed** 1 May, 1–11 Nov, mid-Dec–mid-Jan. 🅿 🗗 **W** marcelproust.pagesperso-orange.fr

A view of Châteaudun's castle from across the River Loir

Carved hounds and stag on the gateway of the Château d'Anet

## ⓱ Château d'Anet

**Road map** E1. 🚂 Dreux, then taxi.
**Tel** 02 37 41 90 07. **Open** Feb, Mar & Nov: Sat & Sun pm; Apr–Oct: Wed–Mon pm. **Closed** Dec & Jan. 📷 ♿ restricted. 🎥 🌐 chateaudanet.com

When the mistress of Henri II, Diane de Poitiers, was banished from Chenonceau after the king's accidental death in 1559, she retired to Anet, which she had inherited from her husband, and remained here until her death in 1566. It had been rebuilt for her by Philibert de l'Orme, who also designed the bridge over the Cher at Chenonceau (see pp110–11). The château was superbly decorated and furnished, as befitted the woman who reigned over a king's heart for nearly 30 years.

The château was sold after the Revolution and, in 1804, the new owner pulled down the central apartments and the right wing. However, you can still admire the magnificent entrance gate (the bronze relief of Diane by Benvenuto Cellini is a copy), the chapel, decorated with bas-reliefs by the Renaissance sculptor Jean Goujon (c.1510–68), and the richly furnished west wing. Just beside the château stands the mausoleum where Diane de Poitiers is buried.

## ⓲ Chartres

**Road map** E2. 🏙 42,000. 🚉 🚌
ℹ 8 rue de la Poissonerie (02 37 18 26 26). 🛒 Sat. 🎵 Festival d'Orgue (organ music; Jul & Aug).
🌐 chartres-tourisme.com

Surrounded by the wheat fields of the Beauce plain, Chartres was for many years a major market town. Visitors who come to see the Gothic cathedral (see pp176–7) should explore the town's old streets, particularly the rue Chantault, the rue des Ecuyers, the rue aux Herbes and, over the Eure, the rue de la Tannerie (which took its name from the tanneries that once lined the river). Some of the most remarkable buildings, including the town hall and historic churches, are lit up at night in extravagant manner from mid-April to mid-September. Pick up a leaflet on **Chartres en Lumières** to follow the trail after nightfall.

Beside the cathedral, the **Musée des Beaux-Arts** occupies the elegant 18th-century building that was once the bishop's palace. It has some fine Renaissance enamel plaques, a portrait of Erasmus in old age by Holbein and many 17th- and 18th-century paintings by French and

Half-timbered houses in the rue Chantault in Chartres

Flemish artists. There is also a collection of 17th- and 18th-century harpsichords and spinets.

Close by, the **Centre International du Vitrail**, a stained glass centre, is housed in the converted attics of the Cellier de Loëns, which was part of the cathedral's chapter house. Visitors can enjoy temporary exhibitions of old and new stained-glass, as well as changing exhibitions on the theme of stained glass. Beautiful stained glass can be seen in situ in some of the old churches around the historic town, notably the **Eglise St-Pierre** and the **Eglise St-Aignan**.

🏛 **Musée des Beaux-Arts**
29 cloître Notre-Dame. **Tel** 02 37 90 45 80. **Open** Wed–Mon. **Closed** Sun am & public hols. 📷

🏛 **Centre International du Vitrail**
5 rue du Cardinal Pie. **Tel** 02 37 21 65 72. **Open** daily. **Closed** 1 Jan, 25 Dec (and between exhibitions).
📷 ♿ 🌐 centre-vitrail.org

### In the Footsteps of Proust

No visit to Illiers-Combray is complete without retracing the hallowed walks of Marcel Proust's childhood holidays. When he stayed with his Aunt and Uncle Amiot, he would join in the family walks that became, in Remembrance of Things Past, "Swann's Way" and "Guermantes Way".

The first takes the walkers towards the village of Méréglise, crossing the Loire and passing through a park that was once Uncle Jules' Pré Catelan and appears in the novel as "Tansonville Park". The "Guermantes" walk covers a few kilometres towards St-Eman, following the river to its source, now trapped unromantically in a wash house in the village. The walks are signposted and guides are available at the local tourist office.

Illiers-Combray's "Tansonville Park"

# Chartres: Cathédrale Notre-Dame

According to art historian Emile Male, "Chartres is the mind of the Middle Ages manifest". The Romanesque cathedral, begun in 1020, was destroyed by fire in 1194; only the south tower, west front and crypt remained. Inside, the sacred Veil of the Virgin relic was the sole treasure to survive. Peasant and lord alike helped to rebuild the church in just 25 years. There were few alterations after 1250 and it was relatively unscathed by the French Revolution. The result is a Gothic cathedral of exceptional unity. Major restoration work has begun on the ochre coatings put on the internal walls in the 13th century.

**Elongated Statues**
These statues on the Royal Portal represent Old Testament figures.

**Gothic Nave**
As wide as the Romanesque crypt below it, the nave reaches a height of 37 m (121 ft).

**★ Royal Portal**
The central tympanum of the Royal Portal (1145–55) shows *Christ in Majesty*.

## KEY

① Labyrinth

② **The lower half** of the west front is a survivor of the earlier Romanesque church, dating from the 12th century.

③ **The taller** of the two spires dates from the 16th century. Flamboyant Gothic in style, it contrasts sharply with the solemnity of its Romanesque counterpart.

## The Labyrinth

The 13th-century labyrinth, inlaid in the floor of the nave, was a feature of most medieval cathedrals. Pilgrims interpret the labyrinth as a meditative journey through life, slowly making one's way towards God. The journey of 262 m (860 ft), around 11 bands of broken concentric circles, took at least an hour to complete.

### VISITORS' CHECKLIST

**Practical Information**
pl de la Cathédrale.
**Tel** 02 37 21 75 02.
**Open** 8:30am–7:30pm daily (Jun–Aug: to 10pm Tue, Fri & Sun). 🕐 11:45am Mon–Sat; 6:15pm Mon–Fri; 7pm Sun–Fri; also 9am Fri; 6pm Sat; 11am & 6pm Sun. ♿ 📷 check website for times. 📷 (tours).
🔤 **cathedrale-chartres.org**

**Vaulted Ceiling**
A network of ribs supports the vaulted ceiling.

**The Virgin Relic**
The Veil of the Virgin is said to have been worn by Mary when she was giving birth to Christ. Given to Chartres in 876 by Charles the Bald, it made the city a famous place of pilgrimage in the Middle Ages.

**★ Stained-Glass Windows**
The windows cover a surface area of more than 2,500 sq m (27,000 sq ft).

**★ South Porch**
Sculpture on the South Porch (1197–1209) reflects New Testament teaching.

**Crypt**
This is the largest crypt in France, most of it dating from the early 11th century. It comprises two parallel galleries and a series of chapels, plus the 9th-century St Lubin crypt.

# The Stained Glass of Chartres

Donated by the guilds between 1210 and 1240, this glorious collection of stained glass is world-renowned. Over 150 windows illustrate biblical stories and daily life in the 13th century (bring binoculars if you can). During both World Wars the windows were dismantled piece by piece and removed for safety. The windows have been restored and releaded thanks to generous donations.

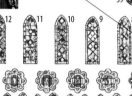

Stained glass above the apse

**Redemption Window**
Six scenes illustrate *Christ's Passion* and death on the Cross (c.1210).

**★ Tree of Jesse**
This 12th-century stained glass shows Christ's genealogy. The tree rises up from Jesse, father of David, at the bottom, to Christ enthroned at the top.

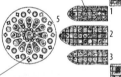

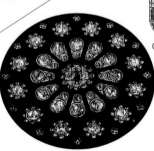

**★ West Rose Window**
This window (1215), with Christ seated in the centre, shows the *Last Judgement*.

## Key

| | | | |
|---|---|---|---|
| **1** Tree of Jesse | **12** Noah | **22** St Anthony and St Paul | **33** St Theodore and St Vincent |
| **2** Incarnation | **13** St John the Evangelist | **23** Blue Virgin | **34** St Stephen |
| **3** Passion and Resurrection | **14** Mary Magdalene | **24** Life of the Virgin | **35** St Cheron |
| **4** North Rose Window | **15** Good Samaritan and Adam and Eve | **25** Zodiac Window | **36** St Thomas |
| **5** West Rose Window | **16** Assumption | **26** St Martin | **37** Peace Window |
| **6** South Rose Window | **17** Vendôme Chapel Windows | **27** St Thomas à Becket | **38** Modern Window |
| **7** Redemption Window | **18** Miracles of Mary | **28** St Margaret and St Catherine | **39** Prodigal Son |
| **8** St. Nicholas | **19** St Apollinaris | **29** St Nicholas | **40** Ezekiel and David |
| **9** Joseph | **20** Modern Window | **30** St Remy | **41** Aaron |
| **10** St Eustache | **21** St Fulbert | **31** St James the Greater | **42** Virgin and Child |
| **11** St Lubin | | **32** Charlemagne | **43** Isaiah and Moses |
| | | | **44** Daniel and Jeremia |

**North Rose Window**
This depicts the *Glorification of the Virgin*, surrounded by the kings of Judah and the prophets (c.1230).

## Guide to Reading the Windows

Each window is divided into panels, which are usually read from left to right, bottom to top (earth to heaven). The number of figures or abstract shapes used is symbolic: three stands for the Church; squares and the number four symbolize the material world or the four elements; circles eternal life.

Mary and Child in the sacred mandorla (c.1150)

Two angels doing homage before the celestial throne

Christ's triumphal entry into Jerusalem

Upper panels of the Incarnation Window

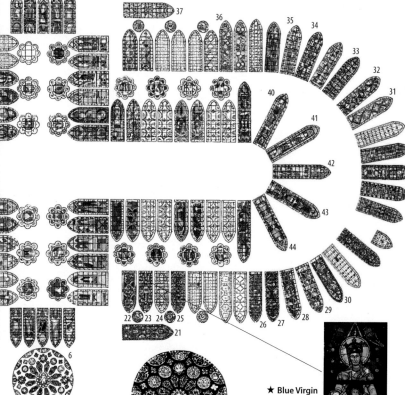

**South Rose Window**
This illustrates the *Apocalypse*, with *Christ in Majesty* (c.1225).

**★ Blue Virgin Window**
These panels, depicting the Virgin and Child in the famous Chartres blue cobalt, survived the 1194 fire and were inserted into a 13th-century window.

# LOIRE-ATLANTIQUE AND THE VENDEE

The region stretching from Guérande in the north to the Marais Poitevin in the south turns away from the Vallée des Rois, the land of châteaux, to face the sea. Pale limestone gives way to darker granite and, beyond the hilly, wooded areas to the east, plains stretch into marshlands and estuaries inhabited by clouds of birds.

Here, people have for centuries earned their living either from the land or the sea. Local communities were until quite recently isolated, conservative, religious and fiercely independent. Their loyalties were the basis of the Vendée Uprising *(see p191)* which, at the end of the 18th century, threatened the new French Republic and ended in the devastation of an entire region south of the Loire. Until the 1790s Nantes, the capital of the Loire-Atlantique, and its environs were part of Brittany, one of the last French duchies to be brought under the crown.

Nantes itself grew prosperous on the wealth generated by its maritime trade to become the seventh largest city of France in the 18th and 19th centuries. With its fine museums and elegant 18th-century *quartiers*, it remains a fascinating and likeable city.

The coast and islands of the Loire-Atlantique to the north, and the Vendée – as the region to the south is known – now draw thousands of summer visitors. Part of their charm is that most of the holiday-makers are French, since the rest of the world has barely begun to discover the beauty of the rocky headlands of Le Croisic or the beaches of golden sand that stretch from La Baule to Les Sables d'Olonne. In the south, dry summers and warm winters on the Ile de Noirmoutier have given it an almost Mediterranean look, with its whitewashed houses and Roman tiles.

In contrast, the Marais Poitevin, at the southern tip of the Vendée, is one of France's most fascinating natural environments. This land has been won back from rivers and the sea through the construction of dykes, canals and dams over hundreds of years.

An oyster gatherer in the Bay of Aiguillon

◀ The formidable bulk of the Château de Clisson, on the Sèvre Nantaise river

# Exploring Loire-Atlantique and the Vendée

The mighty River Loire finally reaches the sea at St-Nazaire, in the west of the Loire-Atlantique *département*. To the northwest lies the Guérandaise Peninsula, where long expanses of sandy, south-facing beaches give way to the dramatic, rocky Atlantic coastlines. The best Atlantic beaches stretch along the Vendée coastline, from the Ile de Noirmoutier to the Marais Poitevin in the south. The Marais Poitevin, 96,000 hectares (237,000 acres) of marshland, is networked with canals. To the east lie the Vendée Hills, where the roads wind gently through towns and along the hillsides, giving lovely views of the surrounding area.

A rocky inlet at L'Aubraie on the Atlantic coast

## Getting Around

Nantes, with its international airport and major train station, is the transportation hub for the region. The TGV takes only two hours to reach Nantes from Paris, and some trains continue to Le Croisic, only one hour further on. The fastest route by car to Nantes is *L'Océane* autoroute (A11) via Le Mans and Angers. While the D137 is the most direct route south to the Marais Poitevin, the coastal route, stopping off at the beautiful beaches along the way, is far more scenic. Inland towards the Vendée Hills, the D960, D752 and D755 around Pouzauges are scenic drives.

A canal in La Grande Brière

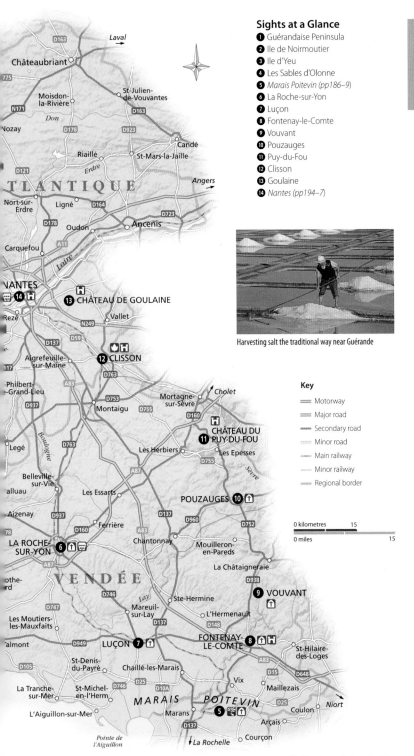

Harvesting salt the traditional way near Guérande

## Key

▬▬ Motorway
▬▬ Major road
▬▬ Secondary road
▬▬ Minor road
▬▬ Main railway
▬▬ Minor railway
▬▬ Regional border

```
0 kilometres        15
0 miles             15
```

# ● Guérandaise Peninsula

**Road map** A3. 🚇 Le Croisic, La Baule. 🚌 Le Croisic, La Baule, Guérande. 𝒊 Le Croisic (02 40 23 00 70); La Baule (02 40 24 34 44), 🅆 labaule.fr; Guérande (08 20 15 00 44), 🅆 ot.guerande.fr

La Baule, one of France's grandest seaside resorts of the late 19th century, has a superb 8-km (5-mile) sweep of golden sand, now dominated by apartment blocks. However, in the pines behind the modern buildings, there is a fascinating assortment of eccentric turn-of-the-century villas. The resort of Pornichet, which adjoins La Baule, also retains some older villas beyond a modern marina crammed with yachts.

Le Croisic, reaching into the Atlantic on the west, has a wilder charm. Beyond the lively main port are miles of salty headlands with small beaches, pounding surf and wind-sculpted pines. The **Océarium** near the port is one of France's largest aquariums.

The medieval walled town of Guérande grew rich on its *fleur de sel* – gourmet Breton salt "farmed" on extensive marshlands between here and Le Croisic. Exhibitions and a video in the **Musée des Marais Salants** at Batz-sur-Mer give an excellent idea of the painstaking techniques used to maintain its quality.

Guérande is protected by its ramparts, which are entered through four 15th-century gateways. The main gatehouse, St-Michel, houses a regional museum. In the centre of the town is the **Collégiale St-Aubin**, a medieval church with stained glass from the 14th and 16th centuries and Romanesque capitals depicting scenes from the lives of martyrs, mythology and arts.

Just 10 km (6 miles) to the east of Guérande is the **Parc Naturel Régional de Brière**, a park of 40,000 hectares (100,000 acres)

A traditional thatched house in the Brière regional park

of marshlands. Information about guided tours by flat-bottomed boat or on foot, bicycle or horseback is available from the tourist office in what was once a clog-maker's house in La Chapelle-des-Marais. Kerhinet, a village of 18 restored cottages, has displays on regional life.

**🄴 Océarium**
av de St-Goustan, Le Croisic. **Tel** 02 40 23 02 44. **Open** daily. **Closed** last 3 weeks Jan. 🈲 🅯 🅆 ocearium-croisic.fr

**🄼 Musée des Marais Salants**
Batz-sur-Mer. **Tel** 02 40 23 82 79. **Open** Tue–Sun (Jul & Aug: daily). **Closed** 1 Jan, 1 May, 25 Dec. 🈲 🅯

**🄴 Parc Naturel Régional de Brière**
**Road map** A3. 🚇 La Baule, Le Croisic, Pontchâteau, St Nazaire. 🚌 𝒊 Kerhinet (02 40 66 85 01). 🅆 parc-naturel-briere.fr

# ● Île de Noirmoutier

**Road map** A4. 🚌 Noirmoutier-en-l'Île. 𝒊 Noirmoutier-en-l'Île (02 51 39 12 42). 🅆 ile-noirmoutier.com

Whitewashed Midi-style beach villas on a long, low island of fertile polders (land reclaimed from the sea) give Noirmoutier a unique character. The adventurous visitor arrives along a bumpy causeway nearly 5 km (3 miles) long, which is above the sea for only three hours at low tide. Cockle-collecting locals park their cars in the mud, but those who flirt with the tides sometimes have to climb to safety on platforms (*balises*) along the causeway. Crossing periods are posted on the road at Beauvoir-sur-Mer. There is also a bridge from Fromentine.

The island's mild climate, fishing industry and salt marshes were the basis of its wealth. Now tourists come to visit its long dunes, pretty beaches and the neat main village of Noir-moutier-en-l'Île. The dry-moated **Château de Noirmoutier** dates from the 12th century. It has displays on aspects of local history, including the bullet-riddled chair in which the Duc d'Elbée was executed during the Vendée Uprising (*see p191*). There is also an **aquarium** and the

Porte St-Michel gatehouse, one of the entrances to Guérande

**Musée de la Construction Navale**, illustrating boat-making techniques and maritime traditions. **Parc Océanîle**, a water park that opened in 1994, makes for a fun family outing, with water chutes and slides, pools with artificial waves, torrents and hot geysers.

🏠 **Château de Noirmoutier**
pl d'Armes. **Tel** 02 51 39 10 42. **Open** Wed–Mon (Jul & Aug: daily). 🎫 🗂

🐟 **Aquarium-Sealand**
rue de l'Ecluse. **Tel** 02 51 39 08 11. **Open** mid-Feb–mid–Nov: daily. 🎫 ♿ 🖥 **aquariumdenoir moutier.com**

🏛 **Musée de la Construction Navale**
Rue de l'Ecluse. **Tel** 02 51 39 24 00. **Closed** for restoration. 🎫 ♿

🎡 **Parc Océanîle**
Site des Oudinières, rte de Noir Moutier. **Tel** 02 51 35 91 35. **Open** late Jun–Aug: daily. 🎫 ♿ 🏊 🖥 **oceanile.com**

*Polyprion americanas*, one of the fish in Noirmoutier's aquarium

## ❽ Ile d'Yeu

**Road map** A4. 🗺 5,000. 🚢 from Fromentine to Port–Joinville. 🛈 rue du Marché (02 51 58 32 58). 🖥 **ile-yeu.fr**

The sandy coves and rocky coastline of this island, only 10 by 4 km (6 by 2.5 miles), attract many visitors. Near the old fishing harbour of Port-de-la-Meule are a ruined 11th-century **castle** and the **Pierre Tremblante**, a giant Neolithic stone said to move when pressed at a critical spot.

The fishing village of La Chaume, near Les Sables d'Olonne

## ❾ Les Sables d'Olonne

**Road map** A4. 🗺 16,000. 🚌 🚍 🛈 1 promenade Marechal Joffre (02 51 96 85 85). 🛒 Tue–Sun. 🖥 **lessablesdolonne-tourisme.com**

The justifiable popularity of the fine, curving sands has helped to preserve the most elegant beach promenade in western France. Behind the 18th-century esplanade, hilly streets lead to a lively port on the sea channel. Opposite, the fishing village of La Chaume has a chic marina.

In Les Sables itself, attractions include the morning market at Les Halles (Tue–Sun; daily mid-Jun–mid-Sep), near the church of **Notre-Dame-de-Bon-Port**. Running between Les Halles and the rue de la Patrie lies France's narrowest street, rue de l'Enfer, which is only 53 cm (21 in) wide at the entrance on rue de la Patrie.

Masterly views of Les Sables in the 1920s by Albert Marquet are in the **Musée de l'Abbaye Ste-Croix**. Built as a convent in the 1600s, this now houses mainly modern paintings and Surrealist multimedia works.

🏛 **Musée de l'Abbaye Ste-Croix**
rue de Verdun. **Tel** 02 51 32 01 16. **Open** Tue–Sun (daily during school hols). **Closed** 1 Jan, 1 May, 25 Dec. 🎫 not first Sun of every month. 🖥 **lemasc.fr**

### The Best Atlantic Coast Beaches

Les Sables d'Olonne has hosted both the European surfing championship and the world windsurfing championship. It also offers family bathing at the Grande Plage. Surfers enjoy the bigger waves at Le Tanchet (Le Château d'Olonne) and L'Aubraie (La Chaume). Other good surfing beaches are Sauveterre and Les Granges (Olonne-sur-Mer) and, further north, La Sauzaie at Brétignolles-sur-Mer. Apart from Les Sables, major esplanades and beaches with fine sands and good facilities include the Grande Plage at La Baule and Les Demoiselles at St-Jean-de-Monts.

The wide, sandy beach of L'Aubraie at La Chaume

# ❺ Marais Poitevin

The vast regional park of the Marais Poitevin stretches 96,000 ha (237,000 acres) across the south of the Vendée. In Roman times, most of it was under water. One thousand years of dyke building and drainage, first started by medieval monks, have produced the agricultural plains of the western Marais Desséché (dry marsh), which are protected from river floods inland by a complex network of canals. The enchanting aquatic mosaic of the Marais Mouillé (wet marsh), also known as the Venise Verte (Green Venice), lies to the east. Here, summer visitors punt or paddle along quiet, jade-coloured waterways under a canopy of willow, alder, ash and poplar.

**White Charolais Cattle**
Prized for their meat, these cows are often transported by boat.

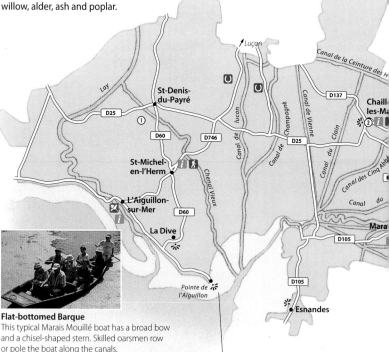

**Flat-bottomed Barque**
This typical Marais Mouillé boat has a broad bow and a chisel-shaped stern. Skilled oarsmen row or pole the boat along the canals.

**KEY**

① **The Réserve Naturelle Michel Brosselin** is a flourishing 200 ha (500 acre) nature reserve.

② **La Maison du Maître de Digues**, at Chaille-les-Marais, reveals the work of the dyke builders of the area.

③ **Abbaye de Nieul- sur-l'Autise**, Founded in the late 11th century, this abbey gained the patronage of Eleanor of Aquitaine in the 12th century. Remarkably, the church, cloister and monastic buildings have all survived the centuries.

**Mussel Farms**
Mussels are farmed on the coast around L'Aiguillon-sur-Mer. The larvae are placed on ropes strung between posts embedded in the silt, exposed to the tide's ebb and flow.

0 kilometres   5
0 miles        5

**Key**

☐ Marais Mouillé
☐ Marais Desséché
☐ Mud flats

### ★ Abbaye St-Pierre-de-Maillezais

The sombre vestiges of this once-influential Benedictine abbey are impressive. Many historical figures from western France are associated with the place. Find out more on a visit or, in summer, by watching the theatrical shows staged in period costume. Also visit the 12th-century Eglise St-Nicolas in the village.

## VISITORS' CHECKLIST

**Practical Information**
Road map B5.  Maillezais (02 51 87 23 01); Coulon (08 20 20 00 79). Good embarkation points for boating: Coulon, Maillezais, Arçais, Sansais, La Garette, St-Hilaire-la-Palud, Damvix; Tourist train: Coulon (05 49 35 02 29). Facilities for hiking tours, renting bicycles, caravans and horses.
**W** **parc-marais-poitevin.fr**

**Transport**
Niort.

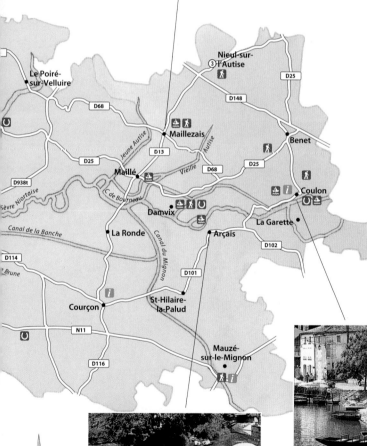

### ★ Arçais
This village in the Venise Verte has a small, stylish port and a 19th-century château.

### ★ Coulon
Coulon is the largest village in the Marais Poitevin. Its port is always crowded with the narrow, flat-bottomed boats that are traditional in this area.

For keys to symbols *see back flap*

# Exploring the Marais Poitevin

Early dykes, built to hold back the tide, did nothing to solve the problem of the rivers' annual flooding of the marshlands. So large canals were dug in the 12th and 13th centuries, under the supervision of monks who had acquired land rights to marshy areas. The Marais Mouillé (wet marsh) and the Marais Desséché (dry marsh) are still separated by one of these canals: the 13th-century Canal des Cinq Abbés, south of Chaillé-les-Marais, which was a joint effort by five abbeys. Peasants labouring for the monks were rewarded with common grazing rights, some of which are still in force. During the 17th century, Henri IV brought in Dutch engineers to improve the canals, hence the "Dutch Belt" (*La Ceinture des Hollandais*) southeast of Luçon. Current measures to control flooding on lands below high-tide level range from pressure-operated dam gates to bung holes that let water into the plains of the *marais* in summer.

## Eastern Marais

The best way to see this area is by boat. Guided tours are available from a number of villages in the region, while braver souls can hire their own boats from Arçais, Coulon, Damvix, La Garette or Maillezais.

## Coulon

**Road map** B5. 👥 2,300. 🚌 Niort. 🛈 31 rue Gabriel Auchier (08 20 20 00 79). 🛥 Fri & Sun. Ⓦ **niort maraispoitevin.com**

With its streets of whitewashed houses and its imposing 12th-century church, Coulon is the main entry point to the Marais

Mouillé. The quay on the Sèvre Niortaise river is lively in summer with punt tours and crews embarking on the maze of canals. **Coulontourisme** organizes accompanied or go-as-you-please boat trips and cycle hire. You can book online. Exhibits explaining local ways of life and the history of reclamation are displayed at the **Maison du Marais Poitevin**.

🗺 **Coulontourisme**
6 rue d'Eglise. **Tel** 05 49 35 14 14.
Ⓦ **coulontourisme.com**

🏛 **Maison du Marais Poitevin**
pl de la Coutume. **Tel** 05 49 35 81 04.
**Open** Apr–Oct: daily; Nov–Mar: groups by appt only. 🚗 Ⓦ **maison-marais-poitevin.fr**

## Maillezais

**Road map** B5. 👥 1,000. 🚌 Fontenay-le-Comte, then taxi. 🛈 rue du Dr-Daroux (02 51 87 23 01). Ⓦ **maraispoitevin-vendee.com**

Maillezais was one of the most important inhabited islands in the former Gulf of Poitou. Whether from a canal boat or from within the town, the great ruined **Abbaye St-Pierre**,

---

## Wildlife of the Marais Poitevin

An area of diverse natural habitats, including floodplains, copses, reclaimed agricultural land and estuaries, the Marais Poitevin supports a rich array of wildlife. It is a paradise for bird-watchers, featuring around 130 different species of nesting bird and more than 120 species of migrating and wintering birds. It also supports some 40 species of mammal, 20 species of snake, 30 species of fish and hundreds of insect species. The stands of elms, alders, willows and hawthorns supply herons with nest sites. Birds of prey such as the European kestrel and the common buzzard are present all year round, as well as breeding pairs of black kites, hobbys and, less commonly, honey buzzards in spring and summer. At night, long-eared and tawny owls scour the marshes for small rodents.
For bird-watchers, the real interest of the area lies in migratory waders and wildfowl. These can be seen on the water meadows of the Marais Mouillé, on the drier expanses of the Marais Desséché, especially, on the wide mud flats of the Bay of Aiguillon where the Sèvre Niortaise river reaches the sea.

The kestrel, one of the Marais' birds of prey

Birds to be seen here in autumn and winter include the common redshank, black-tailed godwit and whimbrel, and rare species such as the spotted crake. The Marais Desséché is also an ideal winter refuge for frogs, toads and grass snakes, and its wide canals, bordered by thick vegetation, are home to two rare species of warbler: the great reed warbler and savi's warbler. Small numbers of another rare species, Montagu's harrier, hunt field voles in the area's reclaimed agricultural land.

Reed warbler

The ruins of the 10th-century Abbaye St-Pierre at Maillezais

founded in the 10th century, is a dramatic sight. Much of the monastery was destroyed in 1587 by the Protestant armies. The church retains decorated capitals in the 11th-century narthex, the north wall of the nave and the Renaissance transept.

The abbey refectory is still standing, as is the kitchen, now a museum. From 1524 to 1526, Rabelais sought refuge with the monks here. To the right of the entrance is a small château, built in 1872 on the ruins of the bishop's palace.

### 🔼 Abbaye St-Pierre
**Tel** 02 51 87 22 80. **Open** Mar–mid-Nov: Wed–Mon (Apr–Sep: daily). 🎫 ♿ restricted. 🌐 abbayes.vendee.fr

### Chaillé-les-Marais
**Road map** B5. 🏘 1,800. 🚌 ℹ 7 rue de la Coupe de Rocher (02 51 56 77 30). 🛒 Thu. 🌐 ot-isles-marais poitevin.com

This village, beside cliffs once washed by the tide, was a centre for the reclamation works that established the fields of dark soil in the Marais Desséché. The techniques are explained at the **Maison du Maître de Digues**.

Long-haired Poitou donkey

### 🏛 Maison du Maître de Digues
In the tourist office. **Open** Apr, Jun & Sep: Sun–Fri; May: pub hols only; Jul & Aug: daily; Oct–Mar: Mon–Fri. 🎫 ♿ 🌐 mmd-maraispoitevin.fr

### Western Marais
Much of the early drainage work in the *marais* was led by the monks of **St-Michel-en-l'Herm**. The Benedictine abbey on this former island was originally founded in 682, but has been destroyed and rebuilt several times since then. Its 17th-century chapter house and refectory are the most important remnants.

A short drive to the south, on the River Lay estuary, are the ancient fishing port of **L'Aiguillon-sur-Mer** and the **Pointe d'Aiguillon**, with its 19th-century Dutch-built dyke. From here, there are marvellous views across the bay to the Ile de Ré and La Rochelle.

Shellfish farming, especially mussels and oysters, is a leading industry along this part of the coast as well as in the estuaries of the western *marais*. Mussels are grown on a forest of posts, which are visible at low tide, or on ropes hung from rafts in the Bay of Aiguillon.

## Habitats

*The Marais Mouillé's extensive network of canals provides an ideal refuge for otters, while its many trees provide an ample choice of nest sites for the purple heron. Migrating birds, such as garganey ducks, and waders, such as the lapwing, thrive in the Marais Desséché.*

Male garganey duck

Otter

A nesting purple heron

A lapwing wintering in the Marais Poitevin

Statue of Napoléon in the main square in La Roche-sur-Yon

## ❻ La Roche-sur-Yon

**Road map** B4. 🔼 54,000. 🚌 🚍
🛈 7 pl du Marché (02 51 36 00 85).
🔔 Tue–Sat. 🎪 Café de l'Eté, open-air free concerts (mid-Jul–mid-Aug).
🌐 ot-roche-sur-yon.fr

In 1804, La-Roche-sur-Yon was plucked from obscurity by Napoléon, who made it the administrative and military capital of the Vendée. The rectangular grid layout was centred on a large parade ground, now called **place Napoléon**.

The grandest 19th-century buildings include the **Eglise St-Louis** and the Classical theatre. The **Musée de la Roche-sur-Yon** covers the arts, while the older **La Maison Renaissance** is devoted to the town's history. The most popular attraction is the **Haras de la Vendée**, a smart national stud farm where you can watch equestrian shows.

🏛 **Musée de la Roche-sur-Yon**
**Tel** 02 51 47 48 35. **Open** Tue–Sat, pm. **Closed** public hols.

🏛 **La Maison Renaissance**
rue du Vieux-Marché. **Tel** 02 51 36 00 85. **Open** Jul & Aug: Mon–Sat, pm.

🔲 **Haras de la Vendée**
120 blvd des Etats-Unis. **Tel** 02 51 37 48 48. **Open** Apr–Jun & 1st half Sep: Wed, Sat & Sun; Jul & Aug: daily.
🐎 🌐 haras.vendee.fr

## ❼ Luçon

**Road map** B4. 🔼 10,000. 🚌 🚍
🛈 square Edouard Herriot (02 51 56 36 52). 🔔 Wed & Sat. 🎪 Les Nocturnes Océanes (every other year, mid-Jul). 🌐 **tourisme-lucon.com**

Luçon, once a marshland port, was described by its most famous inhabitant, Cardinal Richelieu (see p60) as the muddiest bishopric in France. Sent there as a 23-year-old bishop in 1608, he went on to reorganize first the town and then the kingdom. Richelieu's statue stands in the square south of the **Cathédrale Notre-Dame**.

The cathedral has an impressive Gothic nave with Renaissance side chapels. One of these contains a pulpit and two canvases painted by Richelieu's gifted successor as bishop, Pierre Nivelle, a naturalist painter. The beautiful cloisters date from the 16th century.

## ❽ Fontenay-le-Comte

**Road map** C4. 🔼 15,000. 🚌 Niort.
🚍 🛈 8 rue du Grimouard (02 51 69 44 99). 🔔 Sat. 🌐 tourisme-sudvendee.com

Fontenay, sloping down to the River Vendée, was the proud capital of Bas-Poitou until the French Revolution. Napoléon downgraded it in favour of a better-placed administrative centre, La Roche-sur-Yon, from which he could easily control the Royalist Vendée.

Although the city's castle and fortifications were destroyed in 1621, following repeated conflicts in the Wars of Religion, much of its Renaissance quarter survived, and a prosperous postwar town has sprung up around it.

The **Eglise Notre-Dame**, with its commanding spire, is a good place to begin threading through the old streets that lead

down from the place Viète. The building with the corner turret at No. 9 rue du Pont-aux-Chèvres was once the palace of the bishops of Maillezais. Many Renaissance luminaries, including the poet Nicolas Rapin and François Rabelais (see p104), lived in rue Guillemet, rue des Jacobins and the arcaded place Belliard. Rabelais was later to satirize soirées he attended here during his five years as an unruly young priest in the Franciscan friary (1519–24).

Painted pulpit in Luçon cathedral

Fontenay's motto "A fountainhead of fine spirits" is incised on the **Quatre-Tias** fountain in the rue de la Fontaine, which was built in the 16th century and embellished in 1899 by Octave de Rochebrune, a local artist and intellectual.

In the **Musée Vendéen**, displays range from Gallo-Roman archaeology to an excellent scale model of Fontenay during the Renaissance. Several 19th-century portraits convey the suffering of the Vendée in the wake of the 1793 insurrection. There are also displays on daily life in the *bocage*, the wooded region bordering the city.

Once a manor house, the **Château de Terre-Neuve** on the rue de Jarnigande, was converted into something more

The high Gothic nave of the Cathédrale Notre-Dame in Luçon

The medieval walls surrounding Vouvant, reflected in the River Mère

imposing for Nicolas Rapin, poet and grand provost, at the beginning of the 17th century. Two hundred years later, Octave de Rochebrune added decorative flourishes, including statues of the Muses.

The interior of the château has beautiful ceilings and two wonderful fireplaces together with a collection of fine art, furniture, panelling and a door brought from the royal study in the Château de Chambord.

### Musée Vendéen
pl du 137e Régiment d'Infanterie. **Tel** 02 51 53 40 04. **Open** Wed, Sat & Sun (May–Sep: Tue–Sun).

### Château de Terre-Neuve
rue de Jarnigande. **Tel** 02 51 69 99 41. **Open** May–Sep: daily; Oct–Apr: groups by appt.
**W** chateau-terreneuve.com

## ❾ Vouvant

**Road map** B4. 850. Fontenay-le-Comte. Luçon. 31 rue du Duc d'Aquitaine (02 51 00 86 80). Fête Folklorique (2nd Sun in Aug). **W** vendee-vouvant.com/tourisme.htm

The Romanesque **Eglise Notre-Dame** in the medieval village of Vouvant has a fantastically carved twin-portal doorway, from which rows of sculptures look down on an arch decorated with a Romanesque bestiary. On the tympanum, Samson wrestles a lion as Delilah advances with her shears.

Vouvant is home to many artists and a starting point for tours of the popular Mervant-Vouvant forest with its trails and folklore surrounding the serpent-fairy Mélusine: she tried to lead a life as a woman, but once a week her lower half would turn into a serpent's tail. The **Tour Mélusine** has splendid views of the River Mère.

The twin portals of Vouvant's Eglise Notre-Dame

## The Vendée Uprising

Portrait of Cathelineau (1824) by Anne-Louis Girodet-Trioson

Although it may at times seem a footnote to the French Revolution, the Vendée Uprising has never been forgotten in this region. The Revolution outraged the conservative, Royalist people here. Rising taxes, the persecution of Catholic priests and the execution of Louis XVI in January 1793 were then followed by attempts to conscript locals for the Republican army. This triggered a massacre of Republican sympathizers in the village of Machecoul on 11 March by a peasant mob. As the riots flared, peasant leaders, such as the wagoner Cathelineau and the gamekeeper Stofflet, took charge. They were joined by nobles including Charette, Bonchamps and La Rochejaquelain under the emblem of the sacred heart.

Using guerilla tactics, the Grand Royal and Catholic Army (Whites) took nearly all the Vendée plus Saumur and Angers by June 1793. They won several battles against Republican armies (Blues) but lost at Cholet on 17 October. Nearly 90,000 Whites fled, vainly hoping for reinforcements to join them. The Blues laid waste to the Vendée in 1794, massacring the populace. More than 250,000 people from the Vendée died.

Detail from the frieze in the church in Pouzauges

## ⑩ Pouzauges

**Road map** C4. 🏚 5,500. 🚉 La Roche. 🚌 ℹ️ 30 pl de l'Eglise (02 51 91 82 46). 🛒 Thu.
🌐 **tourisme-paysdepouzauges.fr**

This small town's ruined 12th-century castle was one of several in the Vendée owned by Gilles de Rais in the 15th century. Once Marshal of France and a companion-in-arms of Joan of Arc, de Rais' had a distinguished military career that ended in charges of abduction and murder; he came to be associated with the story of Bluebeard.

The little **Eglise Notre-Dame du Vieux-Pouzauges**, with its 13th-century frescoes uncovered in 1948, is one of the treasures of the Vendée. The frescoes depict charming scenes from the life of the Virgin Mary and her family.

## ⑪ Château du Puy-du-Fou

**Road map** B4. 🚉 Cholet, then taxi. **Tel** 08 20 09 10 10.
🌐 **puydufou.com**

The brick-and-granite Renaissance château of Puy-du-Fou is 2 km (1 mile) from the little village of Les Epesses. Partly restored after its destruction in the Vendée Uprising of 1793–4, it now houses an ambitious theme park, **Le Grand Parc**, which offers plenty of entertainment. It has two reconstructed villages, one medieval and one 18th-century, with costumed "villagers" and artisans, and a market town of 1900 along the same lines. Other features include wooded walks, lakes, aquatic organ pipes and a puppet theatre. Each day Le Grand Parc stages five big shows. These range from gladiatorial battles and a Viking assault to lively displays of jousting and falconry.

The château is also the backdrop to the **Cinéscénie**, a thrilling son et lumière show (*see pp46–47*). Note that the show requires a separate ticket.

### Environs
Northwest up the Sèvre Niortaise Valley, the 12th-century **Château de Tiffauges** is another great place for families. This castle serves as backdrop for lively re-enactments of the area's history. There is also a collection of reconstructed medieval war machines.

🎭 **Le Grand Parc**
**Open** mid-Apr–Sep: daily (but call ahead of your visit). 🅿️ ♿

🎬 **Cinéscénie**
**Tel** 08 20 09 10 10. **Open** mid-Jun–mid-Sep: Fri & Sat. Show: Jun & Jul: 10:30pm; Aug–early Sep: 10pm (arrive 1 hour earlier); book ahead. 🅿️ ♿

🏰 **Château de Tiffauges**
**Tel** 02 51 65 70 51. **Open** Apr–mid-Sep: daily. 🅿️ 🌐 **chateau-tiffauges.vendee.fr**

Château de Clisson, a feudal fortress now in ruins

## ⑫ Clisson

**Road map** B4. 🏚 7,000. 🚉 ℹ️ pl du Minage (02 40 54 02 95). 🛒 Tue, Wed, Fri. 🎉 Les Médiévales (last weekend Jul). 🌐 **levignobledenantes-tourisme.com**

Clisson, perched on two hills straddling the Sèvre Nantaise river, is notable for its Italianate beauty. After much of the town was destroyed in 1794 by punitive Republican forces following the collapse of the Vendée Uprising, Clisson was rebuilt by two brothers, Pierre and François Cacault, working with the sculptor Frédéric Lemot. Lemot's country home is now the **Parc de la Garenne Lemot**, which celebrates the style of ancient Rome with grottoes and tombs, including Lemot's own.

The evolution of defensive strategies can be followed in the massive, ruined **Château de Clisson**, dating from the 12th century and gradually

"Villagers" at work in Puy-du-Fou's Grand Parc

strengthened in stages up to the 16th century. This was a key feudal fortress for the dukes of Brittany. Peer into the dungeons, and into a well with a grisly story behind it: in the vengeful aftermath of the Vendée's defeat, Republican troops butchered and flung into it 18 people. Next to the château is a fine Renaissance covered market, it survived the destruction because it was used as Republican barracks.

The vineyards outside this town produce Muscadet white wines.

### 🔲 Parc de la Garenne Lemot & Villa Lemot

**Tel** 02 40 54 75 85. **Open** Park: daily. Villa Lemot: for exhibitions only. 🔲 restricted.

### 🔲 Château de Clisson

pl du Minage. **Tel** 02 40 54 02 22. **Open** May–Sep: Wed–Mon; Oct–Apr: Wed–Mon pm only. 🔲 🔲

## ⓭ Château de Goulaine

**Road map** B3. 🔲 Nantes, then taxi (15km/8 miles). 🔲 Bas Goulaine. **Tel** 02 40 54 91 42. **Open** Wed, Sat, Sun & hols (mid-Jun–mid-Sep: daily; mid-Nov–Mar: Sun). 🔲 🔲 🔲 grd floor château & butterfly park. 🔲 chateaudegoulaine.fr

Only a short distance southeast of Nantes, this is the most

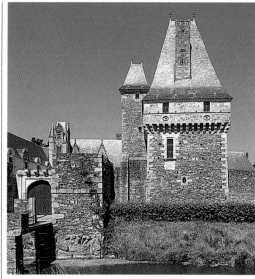

The machicolated entrance tower at the Château de Goulaine

westerly of all the limestone-and-slate Loire châteaux. The same family has made wine here for 1,000 years; the building dates from the 15th century with 17th-century wings. One tower survives from the 14th century. Towers rise from the central building: on one, there is a sculpture of Yolande de Goulaine, who is said to have spurred on her soldiers to repulse the besieging English by threatening to stab herself.

The château survived the Revolution because the family sold it to a Dutchman, only to recover it 70 years later. The present marquis, Robert de Goulaine, has restored the château and also opened a butterfly park where exotic species flutter about a large glasshouse. Butterflies also embellish the label of one of his *sur lie* Muscadets. At certain times of the year you can book a room for the night in this grand castle.

## Cinéscénie

Puy-du-Fou's late-night show is on a grand scale, with more than 1,100 performers and 14,000 seated spectators. It was conceived as a theatre of Vendée history using the full resources of contemporary open-air multimedia techniques. Laser lighting, music, water-jets and fireworks are all carefully orchestrated by computer.

Against the backdrop of the ruined château and its lake, hundreds of locally recruited actors form living tableaux to dance or grieve, joust or slaughter each other. Horses thunder about, fountains and fireworks soar, bells ring and the château bursts into "flames".

Although the spectacle can be enjoyed for itself, translations of the commentary are available in English, German, Italian, Spanish and Dutch to 150 of the seats on the huge stand. Warm clothing and advanced booking are advised.

A fire-eater in the Cinéscénie at Puy-du-Fou

# ⑭ Nantes

The ancient port of Nantes was the ducal capital of Brittany for 600 years, but is now capital of the Pays de la Loire region. Many of its fine 18th- and 19th-century buildings and houses were built on profits from maritime trade, especially in slaves, sugar, cotton and ship's supplies. The main port activities have shifted downstream towards St-Nazaire, where a modern bridge, one of the longest in France, crosses the Loire estuary *(see p38)*. Nantes is a vigorous modern city, with good museums, wide open spaces, chic restaurants, bars and shops and some amazing visitor attractions by the Loire.

The Neo-Classical theatre in the place Graslin

### Exploring Nantes
The most fashionable area of town is the **quartier Graslin**. Constructed between 1780 and 1900, the district's centrepiece is the place Graslin, with its Neo-Classical theatre

The dining room of Nantes' Art Nouveau brasserie, La Cigale

approached by a steep flight of monumental steps. The architect, Mathurin Crucy, designed the place Graslin as a rectangle within a semicircle with eight streets radiating from it. The theatre is fronted by eight Corinthian columns, and statues of eight Muses look down on the square. The wall behind the columns is made of glass, allowing light to stream into the foyer during the day.

Crucy's elegant architecture is seen again in the nearby cours Cambronne, a pedestrianized avenue with fine matching houses built in the early 1800s, and in the place Royale with its splendid fountain celebrating ocean and river spirits.

On the **Ile Feydeau**, the former island where Jules Verne *(see p197)* was born, 18th-century town

planning combined with middle-class trading wealth helped to produce beautiful Neo-Classical façades along streets such as allée Turenne, allée Duguay-Trouin and especially rue Kervégan where 18th-century architect Pierre Rousseau occupied No. 30. Wrought-iron balconies rise in pyramidal sequence supported by luxuriant carvings.

Just north of the Ile Feydeau is the place du Commerce and the ancient Bourse, an elegant 18th-century building, now the tourist office.

### 🖼 La Cigale
4 pl Graslin. **Tel** 02 51 84 94 94. **Open** daily. 🖼 🔲 lacigale.com

Facing the theatre, and in dazzling counterpoint to it, stands the famous brasserie-restaurant La Cigale, opened on 1 April 1895. This *fin-de-siècle* fantasy was conceived and largely executed by Emile Libaudière. The building is crammed with Art Nouveau motifs including the cicada from which it takes its name. The rich blues of its Italian tiling, its sinuous wrought-iron, bevelled windows and mirrors, sculptures and painted panels and ceilings have made this restaurant a favourite venue for aesthetes and food-lovers for a century.

### 🖼 Passage Pommeraye
**Open** daily.

To the east of place Graslin, rue Crébillon is the most elegant

The interior of the elegant passage Pommeraye

shopping street in Nantes. It is linked with the rue de la Fosse by a remarkable covered shopping arcade, the passage Pommeraye. Named after the lawyer who financed its construction, it opened in 1843 and must have astonished the bourgeoisie visiting its 66 shops.

The arcade's three galleries are on different levels, each linked by a handsome wooden staircase, lined with statues and lamps. The decoration is highly ornate. Charming sculpted figures look down on the galleries, lined with shops and rich with busts, bas-reliefs and other details in stone and metal, all beneath the original glass roof.

### 🏛 Musée Dobrée

18 rue Voltaire. **Tel** 02 40 71 03 50. **Closed** for renovations until end of 2016. 🗝 (except Sun).

Thomas Dobrée (1810–95), son of a rich shipowner and industrialist, spent most of his life building this collection of paintings, drawings, sculpture, tapestries, furniture, porcelain, armour, religious works of art, stamps, letters and manuscripts.

Part of the carved alabaster altarpiece in the Musée Dobrée

The impressive and palatial museum he built for them is based on a plan by the Gothic Revival architect Eugène-Emmanuel Viollet-le-Duc. One of the reliquaries stands out – it is a gold casket, surmounted

## VISITORS' CHECKLIST

### Practical Information
**Road map** B3.
**Tel** 08 92 46 40 44.
🏙 291,000. 🛈 rue des Etats.
🚆 Tue–Sun. 🎭 La Folle Journée (music, Jan); Printemps des Arts (Baroque music, painting exhibitions, May–Jun); Les Rendez-vous de l'Erdre (jazz, late Aug–early Sep); Festival des Trois Continents (cinema, Nov).
Ⓦ nantes-tourisme.com

### Transport
✈ 12 km (8 miles) Nantes-Atlantique. 🚌 blvd Stalingrad. 🚍 allée Baco.

by a crown, which contains the heart of Anne of Brittany, who asked for it to be buried in her parents' tomb in Nantes cathedral (*see p59*). A complete 15th-century altarpiece carved in alabaster statues from Nottingham, England, is another treasure.

In a second part of the complex, a modern museum houses an archaeological collection, with Egyptian, Greek and some locally found Gallo-Roman artifacts.

## Nantes Town Centre

① Musée Dobrée
② Place Graslin
③ Tour de Bretagne
④ Cathédrale St-Pierre et St-Paul
⑤ Château des Ducs de Bretagne
⑥ Musée des Beaux-Arts
⑦ Jardin des Plantes

# Around the Château

The Tour de Bretagne, the skyscraper built in 1976 that towers above Nantes, is a landmark dividing the city centre around place du Commerce and place Graslin to the west from the older district around the château and cathedral to the east. From the tower the cours des Cinquante Otages sweeps through the centre where the Erdre canal once flowed. This busy avenue has a memorial at the top, in place du Pont Morand, to the 50 hostages after which it is named. Their execution by the Nazis in reprisal for the assassination of the city's military commandant in 1941 turned many Nantais against the Vichy government.

The façade of the Cathédrale St-Pierre et St-Paul

### 🏠 Château des Ducs de Bretagne

4 pl Marc Elder. **Tel** 02 51 17 49 00. **Open** Jul & Aug: daily; Sep–Jun: Tue–Sun. **Closed** 1 Jan, 1 May, 1 Nov, 25 Dec. 🏠 château. 🎫 ♿ **W** chateaunantes.fr

The château, surrounded by a landscaped moat and strong curtain walls with round bastions, in the style of the Château d'Angers (see pp78–9), has been thoroughly restored. This was the birthplace of Anne of Brittany, who became duchess at 11 and then was coerced into marrying Charles VIII of France in 1491 at the age of 14. Charles died at Amboise in 1498 and, the following year, Anne married his successor, Louis XII, in the château chapel.

Anne's influence can be seen in the dormer windows and loggias of the **Grand Logis** to the right of the entrance, a graceful blend of Flamboyant and Renaissance styles. It was begun by her father,

Duc François II, who built most of the château. A smaller royal lodging lies to the west of it. It was here that Henri IV signed the 1598 Edict of Nantes, granting all Protestants permission to worship. The château now hosts a high-tech museum charting the history of Nantes from Gallo-Roman times to the present day.

### 🏠 Cathédrale St-Pierre et St-Paul

pl St-Pierre. **Open** daily.

Nantes has the most accident-prone cathedral on the Loire. The story of its construction and destruction over centuries is vividly told in the crypt. Most recently, on 28 January 1972, a workman's match caused an explosion that blew off the roof. Following the resulting fire, a major restoration programme was undertaken. The cathedral has been left with an unusual lightness and unity.

A notable feature of this spacious Flamboyant Gothic building is the splendid black-and-white marble tomb of Duc François II and his two wives, sculpted by Michel Colombe (see pp120–21).

### 🏛 Musée des Beaux-Arts

10 rue Georges Clemenceau. **Tel** 02 51 17 45 00. **Closed** for restoration until the end of 2016. 🎫 except 1st Sun of month. ♿ **W** museedesbeauxarts.nantes.fr

The grandeur of this museum and its collections is a good measure of Nantes' civic pride and wealth in the early 19th century. The galleries, under-going restoration, are on two levels and surround a huge, arched patio, whose clean lines are an appropriate setting for contemporary exhibitions. Although the museum has some sculptures, it is known for its large collection of paintings, especially those representing key movements from the 15th to the 20th centuries.

Gustave Courbet's *The Corn Sifters* (1854) in the Musée des Beaux-Arts

Nantes' lovely botanical garden, the Jardin des Plantes

### Le Lieu Unique

Quai Ferdinand-Favre. **Tel** 02 40 12 14 34. **Open** Tue–Sun, noon–late; check the events calendar on the website.
lelieuunique.com

This former LU biscuit factory, south of the castle, has been converted into a cutting-edge arts centre. It stages numerous theatrical events, from traditional theatre through to dance, music concerts and circus acts, plus cultural and philosophical debates. It also hosts art exhibitions. There's a restaurant (open Mon–Sat) and boutique on site, and even a spa. The building is signalled by an extravagant Art Nouveau tower which is a part of the factory and can be climbed for views of the city. At ground level, the café spills out onto a terrace beside the broad St-Félix canal, surrounded by modern buildings.

### Musée Jules Verne

3 rue de l'Hermitage. **Tel** 02 40 69 72 52. **Open** Wed–Sun pm & Mon. **Closed** Sun am, public hols.
julesverne.nantes.fr

A remarkably comprehensive display representing the life and work of Jules Verne (1828–1905) starts with a room of furnishings from the house in Amiens in which he wrote most of his books. The museum is packed with mementos, splendidly bound books, cartoons, maps, magic lanterns and models.

### Les Machines de l'Ile & Carrousel des Mondes Marins

Parc des Chantiers, blvd Léon Bureau. **Tel** 08 10 12 12 25. **Open** mid-Feb–Jun & Sep–Dec: Tue–Sun; Jul & Aug: daily. **Closed** 1 Jan, 5 Jan–mid-Feb, I May, 25 Dec.
lesmachines-nantes.fr

The enormous moving models created by Les Machines de l'Ile have helped make the western end of the Ile de Nantes a major tourist destination. These over-sized creations were dreamed up by two inventors from the region, François Delarozière and Pierre Orefice, inspired in part by that most famous of Nantais writers, Jules Verne, and his extravagant creations. You can board Le Grand Elephant, a massive mechanical elephant, for a leisurely, pleasureable tour of this corner of the island.

The Carrousel des Mondes Marins, likened to a "huge mechanical aquarium", is a giant 25 m- high (82 ft- high) carousel containing all manner of marine creatures. Visitors can explore three levels: the ocean floor, the depths and the ocean surface.

Also enter La Galerie des Machines, the ever-changing "workshop" space. Visitors are invited to get hands-on as they learn about the latest mechanical dreams on the drawing board that are turning, gradually, into reality.

### The World of Jules Verne

Just past the Pont Anne de Bretagne is a disused section of cobbled quay which, in 1839, was lined with boats. It was here that the 11-year-old Jules Verne slipped aboard a ship to see the world. He got as far as Paimbœuf, a short trip down river, before his father caught up with him. Later, while studying law, Verne started to publish plays and librettos. His science-fiction novels, including *A Journey to the Centre of the Earth* (1864), *Twenty Thousand Leagues Under the Sea* (1870) and *Around the World in Eighty Days* (1873), have been hugely successful, and he is among the most widely read and translated authors in the world.

**Bust of Jules Verne (1906) by Albert Roze**

# TRAVELLERS' NEEDS

# WHERE TO STAY

The Loire Valley has a wide variety of places to stay, many as charming as their surroundings. Family-style hotels predominate, with dining rooms that are also popular with locals, and comfortable, if sometimes old-fashioned, bedrooms. The region also boasts a selection of prestigious châteaux *(see pp204–5)*, mansions and manor houses converted into luxury hotels with elegant rooms, superb cuisine and prices to match.

Several smaller châteaux and refurbished farmhouses operate as atmospheric bed and breakfasts *(chambre d'hôtes)*, giving visitors the opportunity to stay as paying guests of the owners. *Gîtes*, the self-catering accommodation for which France is rightly famous, are also widely available in the Loire Valley, as are several well-equipped camp sites. The listings on pages 206–9 give details of establishments throughout the region, in every price category and style.

### City Hotels

All the major towns and cities in the Loire Valley offer at least one long-established hotel in the centre. Accommodation is liable to vary somewhat in quality, so it is advisable to ask to see the room offered if you have not made a booking in advance.

When you make a booking, be sure to specify that you want a room away from a main road or busy square (most of these city hotels have some quieter rooms overlooking a courtyard). City hotel bars are likely to be frequented by members of the local business community, who also entertain clients

in the hotel restaurants, where you can expect classic French cuisine as well as a range of regional dishes.

### Château Hotels

A number of châteaux and manor houses in the Loire Valley have been converted into expensive hotels. Often set in well-kept grounds and offering outstanding cuisine, they range from Renaissance manor houses to huge, turreted 19th-century piles. The **Relais & Châteaux** association, of which many are members, publishes an annual brochure.

Rooms in these beautiful establishments are usually

spacious and elegant, with some suites available. Some château hotels also offer more modest accommodation in outbuildings or even in bungalows or chalets in the grounds. If you prefer to stay in the main building, specify this when you make the reservation. Note that in many cases, booking in advance (weeks rather than days) is essential.

### Classic Family Hotels

These typically French small hotels, often run by the same family for several generations, are to be found throughout the Loire Valley. Most are basic roadside inns, with only a few listed in the main towns, but off the beaten track you can find charming farmhouses and inexpensive hotels. The atmosphere is usually friendly, with helpful staff able to provide leaflets and other information about local sightseeing and shopping.

Most of these hotels have only a small number of rooms, often reasonably spacious and pleasantly furnished with well-worn antiques and flowery wallpaper.

Many family hotels belong to the **Logis** association, which publishes an annual booklet listing more than 3,000 family-run hotels in France. Most of them have at least a dining room, while some have renowned restaurants in their own right. *Logis* hotels are proud

The Neo-Gothic, turretted Château de Vauloge *(see p208)*

◄ The impressive staircase at the Passage Pommeraye in Nantes

The sumptuous living area at Hotel Saint-Pierre in Saumur *(see p206)*

of their restaurants, which tend to specialize in regional cuisine. In the country districts, the bar and dining room are also likely to be widely used by locals, especially for Sunday lunch. Check the listings on pages 216–19 for restaurants that are also hotels.

## Modern Roadside Chain Hotels

A good alternative is to stay in one of the many modern chain hotels that are usually located in the outskirts near the motorways. Although they are generally not conveniently located for sightseeing, they are handy if all you want is an overnight stop when travelling from one town to the next.

The cheapest are the one-star, very basic **Formule 1** motels. Two-star chains that are widely used by French families on a low budget include **Ibis**, **Campanile** and **Inter Hôtel**.

More comfortable, but lacking in regional charm, are the **Kyriad**, **Novotel** and **Mercure** three-star chains. All the chain hotels offer some family rooms or connecting rooms, and in some hotels children can sleep in their parents' room without charge. These hotels may or may not have a restaurant; if not, there is always one within short walking distance.

## Meals and Facilities

Because most visitors to the Loire Valley choose to tour around the region, only a few hotels are willing to offer full-board rates to those who settle in one place for the duration of their holiday. However, some hotels do offer special prices for dinner, bed and breakfast, or *demi-pension* (half-board). Be aware that most quoted room rates do not include breakfast. If this is the case, you may prefer to have your breakfast in a nearby café.

Logo of the Logis association

Traditionally, family hotel rooms offer double beds, but twin beds is the more likely arrangement to be found in city and chain hotels. Prices are usually fixed per room, but single travellers may be allowed a small reduction. Bathrooms with a shower rather than a bath make the room less expensive. Those with only a *cabinet de toilette* (an alcove containing basin and bidet) are the cheapest.

It is perfectly acceptable to ask to view the room before making a decision.

## Gradings and Prices

French hotels are officially graded with one, two, three, four or five stars. These categories take account of facilities such as telephones, televisions and en suite bathrooms, but they do not necessarily indicate the quality of the decor or service. A few very modest hotels do not rate a star ranking.

Prices rise as the number of stars increases. Rooms may vary in quality within the same establishment, so it is not easy to classify hotels solely by price. Rates for a double room start at around €60 per night without breakfast in a basic rural hotel, although the average starting price across the region is around €95, with châteaux and other luxury establishments charging considerably more. A very small local tax (*taxe de séjour*) will be added to your bill, but service will already be included. It is customary to leave a small tip for the chambermaid.

## Booking

It is advisable to reserve your accommodation well in advance for hotels in popular tourist areas during the main holiday periods, especially in July and August. It may be necessary to give a credit card number or send confirmation via email. You may need to speak French to make a telephone booking for some hotels; however, letters in English are normally perfectly acceptable. Local tourist offices can supply listings of hotels and sometimes provide a reservation service.

Typical Loire Valley manor house hotel

Les Hautes Roches at Rochecorbon *(see p207)*

## Bed and Breakfast

French bed-and-breakfast accommodation, called *chambres d'hôtes*, can vary widely – from modest rooms above a hayloft, to elegant quarters in a manor house or château. Local tourist offices keep lists of those families willing to take in guests. Some hosts will cook dinner if given advance warning. Many such rooms are registered and inspected by the **Gîtes de France** organization – look out for its green-and-yellow logo.

## Self-Catering

Gîtes de France and **Clévacances** are the best-known organizations monitoring and booking self-catering accommodation. Run by the French government, Gîtes de France offers predominantly rural accommodation, ranging from a cottage to an entire wing of a château. Brochures are available from the *département* offices of Gîtes de France, from the Paris head office or via the Internet *(see Directory)*. Booking is essential.

Local tourist offices also have lists of properties for rent within the surrounding area, but it is important to book early.

The lower-priced *gîtes* have only very basic facilities. For more luxurious properties, the best way forward is to scour the major US and European newspapers, specialist magazines and the Internet, or to use a letting agency. Whatever the price, a holiday in a *gîte* is a great way to experience Loire Valley life.

## Camping

Camping is a cheap and fun way of seeing the Loire Valley. Information on camp sites can be obtained from *département* tourist offices. It can be useful to go armed with a Camping Card International (also known as a *carnet*), which doubles as an identity card at camp sites and entitles you to several discounts. It is available from the AA and RAC and from the addresses listed in the Directory.

# DIRECTORY

## Hotels

**Campanile, Kyriad**
Tel 08 25 02 80 38.
Ⓦ louvrehotels.com

**Formule 1**
Tel 08 92 68 56 85.
Ⓦ hotelformule1.com

**Ibis, Mercure, Novotel**
Tel 08 25 01 20 11.
Ⓦ accorhotels.com

**Inter Hôtel**
Tel 08 26 10 39 09.
Ⓦ inter-hotel.fr

**Logis**
83 av d'Italie, 75013 Paris.
Tel 01 45 84 83 84.
Ⓦ logishotels.com

**Relais & Châteaux**
UK: **Tel** (0800) 2000 0002.
US: **Tel** (800) 735 2478.
Ⓦ relaischateaux.com

## Bed and Breakfast

**Gîtes de France**
40 av Flandre,
75019 Paris.
Tel 0826 10 44 44.
Ⓦ gites-de-france.com

## Self-Catering

**Clévacances**
54 blvd de l'Embouchure,
31022 Toulouse. **Tel** 05 32
10 82 30.
Ⓦ clevacances.com

## Camping

**Les Castels**
Manoir de Terre Rouge,
35270 Bonnemain.
Tel 02 23 16 03 20.
Ⓦ les-castels.com

**French Federation of Camping and Caravanning**
78 rue de Rivoli, 75004
Paris. **Tel** 01 42 72 84 08.
Ⓦ ffcc.fr

## Camping Carnets

**The Camping and Caravanning Club (UK)**
Tel (0845) 130 7631.
Ⓦ campingand
caravanning.co.uk

**Family Campers & RVers (US)**
Tel (800) 245 9755.
Ⓦ fcrv.org

## Disabled Travellers

**Association des Paralysés de France**
Tel 01 40 78 69 00.
Ⓦ apf.asso.fr

**Mobility International USA**
Tel (541) 343 1284.
Ⓦ miusa.org

**Tourism for All**
Tel (0845) 124 9971.
Ⓦ tourismforall.org.uk

## Sources of Information

**French Government Tourist Office (UK)**
Tel 09068 244 123.
Ⓦ uk.franceguide.com

**French Government Tourist Office (US)**
Tel (514) 288 1904.
Ⓦ franceguide.com

**Hostelleries de France**
Ⓦ hostelleriesde
france.com

**Tables et Auberges de France**
Tel (514) 288 1904.
Ⓦ tables-auberges.
com

French camp sites are graded into five starred categories, but even one-star sites have lavatories, public telephones and running water (although this may only be cold). The top-ranked sites are remarkably well equipped. Always book ahead where possible. Most – but not all – camp sites are closed from sometime in September until April.

Gîtes de France has a guide to unpretentious sites on farm land (ask for *camping à la ferme*), and *camping sauvage* (camping outside official sites) is occasionally possible if you come to an agreement with the landowner. **Les Castels** is an upmarket association of sites within the grounds of châteaux and manor houses. Some camp sites also have cabins or other self-catering accommodation for rent. A good source of further information is the **French Federation of Camping and Caravanning**.

## Disabled Travellers

In the UK, **Tourism for All** publishes lists of accessible accommodation and sights in France and provides information on transportation and financial help available for taking holidays. In the US, **Mobility International USA** publishes several general guides to foreign exchange and travelling abroad with disabilities.

In France, information about accommodation with facilities for disabled travellers is available from the **Association des Paralysés de France**, which has also teamed up with Gîtes de France and Logis to recommend country *gîtes*, guesthouses and other places to stay that are suitable for people with physical disabilities. These places are listed on a national register that is available free of charge from its website or from the head office of Gîtes de France, and they also appear in listings for each *département*. The Association des Paralysés de France also has branches in each *département*.

## Sources of Information

The **French Government Tourist Office** is a good place to begin finding out about hotels, and every local tourist office has comprehensive lists of accommodation including *chambres d'hôtes*. Several organizations also select and classify hotels to make it easy to find the right place to stay in your price category.

Gîtes de France logo

The pretty Maison Fleurie in Bazaiges *(see p208)*

**Tables et Auberges de France** groups together hotels with highly rated restaurants, while **Hotelleries de France** specializes in "hotels-bureaux", establishments that offer breakfast but no other meals.

## Recommended Hotels

The various regions that make up the Loire Valley area have some of the most beautiful and stunning landscapes in France, ranging from tranquil countryside to the rocky outcrops of the coast, taking in historic towns, bustling cities and homely villages. We have chosen accommodations that reflect this wide range, including luxurious châteaux and manor houses, comfortable, family-run pensions, self-catering rural boltholes and well-equipped camp sites for all the family. Characteristic havens are highlighted as a DK Choice. The sumptuous Domaine des Hauts de Loire in Onzain is a stunningly located , ivy-clad hideaway which offers classic French elegance, while the modern wood cabins at Les Carres d'etoiles come equipped with telescopes, perfect for evenings spent stargazing. In Buzancais, relax in the beautiful gardens of Château de Boisrenault, a fairy-tale château in the heart of the Berry region; meanwhile, if you're in search of a bit of city life and spice, the former church Hotel Sozo is a tantalizing boutique hotel in Nantes with many fine design features.

Camping in a forest in the Loire Valley

# Staying in a Château

The establishments featured here have been
selected from our listings of recommended
places to stay on pages 206–9. They offer a
great opportunity to experience the style of
life in a private Loire Valley château, spending
a night within walls steeped in history, but
often with all the comforts of a modern hotel.
At many, you will be greeted like a house
guest, and efforts are made to make you feel
part of the owners' family, who may have lived
in the château for generations. They may also
create the atmosphere of a private party at
dinner, which can be booked and paid for
in advance.

**Château de Saint-Paterne**
This handsome family-owned château has
undergone a sympathetic renovation in
keeping with its 16th-century origins. The
gardens are ideal for lounging in, but there is
also a tennis court for the more athletically
inclined and play areas for children *(see p209)*.

**Château du
Plessis Anjou**
"Pastoral" is the best
word to describe the setting
of this 17th-century château,
with its English-style parkland.
There are eight bedrooms, all
featuring wooden beams and
Imperial-style decor *(see p206)*.

Mayenne

**NORTH OF
THE LOIRE**

Laval

Le Mans

Sergé

Blain

Angers

Loire

**ANJOU**

Nantes

Cholet

**LOIRE-ATLANTIQUE
AND THE VENDEE**

La Roche-
sur-Yon

| 0 kilometres | 50 |
| 0 miles | 50 |

**Château de l'Abbaye**
At this solid 19th-century château built
on the ruins of an old abbey, the decor
is a mixture of plush fabrics, gilt-edged
mirrors, comfortable furniture and deep
baths. The tree-fringed gardens are ideal
for relaxing outdoors *(see p209)*.

**Château de la Barre**
Twenty generations of the Counts of Vanssay have resided in this 15th-century château, set in peaceful grounds (see p208).

**Château de Colliers**
The rooms in this compact family-owned château are light and airy, decorated with antiques and comfortable furniture. The historic Château de Chambord is a short distance away (see p206).

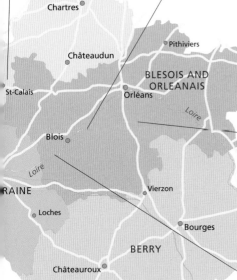

Chartres

Châteaudun

Pithiviers

**BLESOIS AND ORLEANAIS**

St-Calais

Orléans

Loire

Blois

Loire

RAINE

Vierzon

Loches

Bourges

**BERRY**

Châteauroux

**Château Les Muids**
This elegant 18th-century château with a quirky sense of decor mixes classical and bright colours. It is ideal for an overnight stopover since it is close to the motorway (see p207).

**Château de Boisrenault**
Beautiful gardens dotted with tree-shaded spots surround this fairy-tale château. Its turrets and towers suggest a compact Hogwarts, while inside, rooms are spacious and elegant (see p208).

**Château des Tertres**
Set within lush parkland, this good-value belle epoque château with cosy bedrooms once belonged to the mother of Marguerite Duras (see p207).

# Where to Stay

## Anjou

### ANGERS: Hotel D'Anjou €
Manor house     Map C3
*1 blvd du Maréchal Foch, 49100*
**Tel** *02 41 21 12 11*
W hoteldanjou.fr
City centre boutique hotel, part
of the Best Western chain. Room
decor is traditional, while the
lobby is an Art Deco riot of
stained glass and mosaics.

### BRISSAC QUINCE: L'Etang €
Camp site     Map C3
*rte de St Mathurin-sur-Loire, 49320*
**Tel** *02 41 91 70 61*
W campingetang.com
Go glamping at this luxury camp
site in the middle of Anjou wine
country. There are 125 pitches,
25 rental properties and plenty of
family facilities.

### CHAMPIGNE: Château des Briottières €€€
Château     Map C3
*rte de Marigné, 49330*
**Tel** *02 41 42 00 02*
W briottieres.com
Magnificent furnishings, comfortable bedrooms, lush parkland
and a candlelit dining room
make this 15th-century château
ideal for a special occasion stay.

### DOUE LA FONTAINE: Anjou (Les Fleurs) €€
Self-catering     Map C3
*21 rue du Château, Les Verchers sur Layon, 49700*
**Tel** *02 41 50 69 46*
W lesfleurs-loire.com/anjougite.htm
One of a trio of gîtes, this 19th-
century, three-bedroom former
farmhouse features exposed
stone walls, wooden beams and
– for that cosy winter stay – a
wood-burner. There is also a
secluded garden at the back.

### GENNES: Domaine De Joreau €€
Chambre d'hôtes     Map C3
*La Croix de Joreau, 49350*
**Tel** *06 18 35 17 21*
W domainedejoreau.fr
Home-made bread and jam
brighten up breakfast at this
comfortable rural hideaway. It
has two double rooms and a
family apartment.

### LA JAILLE-YVON: Château du Plessis Anjou €€
Château     Map C3
*Lieu-dit Le Plessis, 49220*
**Tel** *02 41 95 12 75*
W chateau-du-plessis.fr
Pastoral is the word for the
setting of this 17th-century
château with its English-style
parkland. There are eight
bedrooms featuring wooden
beams and Imperial-style decor.

### DK Choice

### LE PUY NOTRE DAME: Carrés d'étoiles €€
Self-catering     Map C4
*Chai de la Paleine, 10 pl Jules Raimbault, 49260*
**Tel** *02 41 38 28 25*
W carre-detoiles.com/lapaleine/uk
Unique quartet of modern,
two-person wooden cabins
set among the vineyards of
Saumur. Glass ceilings along
with a telescope and stellar
chart offer the chance to
spend evenings stargazing.
Perfect for getting away
from it all.

### SAUMUR: Hotel Saint-Pierre €€
Town hotel     Map C3
*8 Rue Haute Saint-Pierre, 49400*
**Tel** *02 41 50 33 00*
W saintpierresaumur.com
Family-run hotel situated at the
heart of the old town. The decor
is elegant and tasteful; ideal for a
romantic weekend.

The luxuriously appointed 15th-century Château des Briottières in Champigne

### Price Guide
Prices are based on one night's stay in
high season for a standard double room,
inclusive of service charges and taxes.

| | |
|---|---|
| € | under €90 |
| €€ | €90 to €160 |
| €€€ | over €160 |

## Touraine

### AMBOISE: Le Manoir Saint Thomas €€
Manor house     Map D3
*1 Mail Saint Thomas, 37400*
**Tel** *02 47 23 21 82*
W manoir-saint-thomas.com/
Large rooms, period fireplaces,
parquet floors and a sweeping
staircase all add to the luxury
of this Neo-Renaissance
manor house.

### CHINON: Hôtel Diderot €
Town hotel     Map D3
*4 rue Buffon, 37500*
**Tel** *02 47 93 18 87*
W hoteldiderot.com
Built in the 15th century and
renovated in the 1700s, this
friendly, family-owned hotel is
a comfortable resting place in
the centre of beautiful Chinon.

### LIGRE: La Closerie Saint Martin €/€€
Boutique hotel     Map D4
*6 rue du Prieuré, Les Roches Saint-Paul, 37500*
**Tel** *02 47 58 17 24*
W lacloseriesaintmartin.fr
Once part of the local monastery,
this stylish boutique hotel has a
quintet of rooms, each with a
different style. Home-cooked
dinner and a well-chosen wine
cellar add to the attraction.

### MUIDES-SUR-LOIRE: Château de Colliers €€
Château     Map E3
*rte de Blois, 41500*
**Tel** *02 54 87 50 75*
W chateau-colliers.com
The rooms in this compact
family-owned château are light
and airy and decorated with
antiques. The historic Château
de Chambord is a stone's
throw away.

### RILLE: Huttopia Rillé €
Camp site     Map C3
*Lac de Rillé, 37340*
**Tel** *02 47 24 62 97*
W france.huttopia.com
Comfortable camp site, part of
an environmentally friendly
company. As well as tent and
camper van pitches there are

cabins, huts, children's activities and a lake suitable for swimming.

## ROCHECORBON:
**Les Hautes Roches** €€€
Manor house     Map D3
*86 quai de la Loire, 37210*
**Tel** *02 47 52 88 88*
W leshautesroches.com
Intriguing "troglodyte" hotel, built into the side of a cliff overlooking the Loire. The rooms (former monks' cells) are tastefully decorated in warm colours.

## SAINT PATRICE:
**Château de Rochecotte** €€/€€€
Château     Map D3
*43 rue Dorothée de Dino, 37130*
**Tel** *02 47 96 16 16*
W en.chateau-de-rochecotte.fr
Elegant 18th-century château situated on a hillside terrace. The interior style is Baroque. Enjoy wine from the château's own vineyard.

## TOURS: Gîte du Vieux Tours €€
Self-catering     Map D3
*4 bis, rue de la Rôtisserie, 37000*
**Tel** *06 58 41 22 21*
W legiteduvieuxtours.fr
Four well-designed, modern gîtes located in a mansion in the centre of the old part of Tours. Ideal as a city base.

# Blésois and Orléanis

## BLOIS: Cote Loire
**Auberge Ligerienne** €
Town hotel     Map E3
*2 pl de la Grève, 41000*
**Tel** *02 54 78 07 86*
W coteloire.com
Located by the river in the historic heart of Blois, this charming 16th-century hotel is cosy, comfortable and decorated on a rural farmhouse theme.

## BOISMORAND:
**Auberge des Templiers** €€
Manor house     Map F3
*Les Bezards, 45290*
**Tel** *02 38 31 80 01*
W lestempliers.com
Half-timbered former coaching inn situated in lush parkland. Elegantly furnished rooms, *à la carte* restaurant, tennis courts and outdoor swimming are all on offer.

## BRACIEUX: Camping
**Indigo Les Châteaux** €
Camp site     Map E3
*11 rue Roger Brun, 41250*
**Tel** *02 54 46 41 84*
W camping-indigo.com/fr/
camping-indigo-les-chateaux.html
Large tree-shaded camp site close to many châteaux including

The Baroque-style interiors of the Château de Rochecotte

Chambord and Cheverny; featuring bike hire, swimming pool and a kids' playground.

## COMBREUX:
**Auberge de Combreux** €
Rural hotel     Map F2
*35 rte du Gâtinais, 45530*
**Tel** *02 38 46 89 89*
W auberge-de-combreux.fr/en/
Low ceilings and wooden beams add charm to this roadside country hotel (a former coaching inn) set in beguiling rural surroundings. The restaurant is popular with locals.

## LA FERTE-SAINT-AUBIN:
**Château Les Muids** €€
Château     Map E3
*RN20, 45240*
**Tel** *02 38 64 65 14*
W chateau-les-muids.com
Stunning 18th-century château set in lush woodland. The decor is quirky yet elegant, mixing up classical and bright colours. Ideal for an overnight stopover as it's not far from the motorway.

---

### DK Choice
**ONZAIN: Domaine des**
**Hauts de Loire** €€€
Manor house     Map D3
*rte d'Herbault, 41150*
**Tel** *02 54 20 72 57*
W domainehautsloire.com
This turreted, ivy-clad hunting lodge retains its yesteryear grandeur with lavishly furnished, elegantly decorated interiors. The rooms in the old coach house are the most opulent. The chef prepares cutting-edge food, served with superb local wines. The extensive, atmospheric forest surroundings offer plenty of chances to wander.

---

## ONZAIN: Château des Tertres €€
Château     Map D3
*11 Rue de Meuves, 41150*
**Tel** *02 54 20 83 88*
W www.chateau-tertres.com
Good-value *belle époque* château with cosy bedrooms and set within lush parkland. It once belonged to the mother of Maguerite Duras.

## ORLEANS: Hotel de l'Abeille €
Town hotel     Map E2
*64 rue Alsace Lorraine, 45000*
**Tel** *02 38 53 54 87*
W hoteldelabeille.com
Family-owned, Neo-Classical town house with elegantly-decorated rooms. Good value and centrally located; the rooms are spread over three floors. There is also a charming garden roof terrace with views of the cathedral.

## PIERREFITTE-SUR-SAULDRE:
**Les Allcourts Resort** €
Camp site     Map E3
*Domaine des Allcourts, 41300*
**Tel** *02 54 88 63 34*
W lesalicourts.com
As well as tent pitches, there are plenty of chalets and caravans at this lively woodland camp site. There is also a wave pool, aqua park and water slides. An ideal family stopover.

## PONTLEVOY:
**The Tower of Pontlevoy** €€
Self-catering     Map E3
*27 rue Colonel Fillous, 41400*
**Tel** *02 12 53 30 310*
W frenchconnections.co.uk/en/
accommodation/property/3606
Stone-built, 16th century town house located opposite the local abbey. The terrace, which has views of the town, is ideal for spending time with a book and a glass of wine. Three double rooms, one twin.

**For more information on types of hotels** *see pp200–203*

**SULLY-SUR-LOIRE:**
**Hotel La Closeraie** €
Boutique hotel **Map** F3
*14 rue Porte Berry, 45600*
**Tel** *02 38 05 10 90*
🔳 hotel-la-closeraie.com
Boutique hotel in a 19th-century
town house. The nine rooms
have neutral tones, bare beams
and comfortable beds. Close to
Sully-sur-Loire's famous château.

## Berry

**AUBIGNY-SUR-NERE:**
**Camping Les Etangs** €
Camp site **Map** F3
*rte d'Oizon, rte de Sancerre, 18700*
**Tel** *02 48 58 02 37*
🔳 camping-aubigny.com/en
Tents can be pitched amid
parkland and ponds, while there
is also the option of a chalet in
this family-friendly camp site.

**BAZAIGES: Maison Fleurie** €
Self-catering **Map** E4
*7 Le Petit Vavre, 36270*
**Tel** *02 54 25 39 79*
🔳 maisonfleurie.fr
Roses around the door and a
quiet shaded garden add lustre
to this cosy one-bedroom gîte in
the middle of the countryside.

**BOURGES: Ace Hotel** €
Chain hotel **Map** F4
*rue Joseph Aristide Auxenfans, 18000*
**Tel** *02 48 50 30 30*
🔳 ace-hotel-bourges.com
Value-for-money modern hotel
located a few minutes off the
motorway, ideal for stopovers en
route to or from Channel ports.

### DK Choice

**BUZANCAIS: Château**
**de Boisrenault** €€
Château **Map** E4
*Le Boisrenault, rte de Levroux,*
*36500*
**Tel** *02 54 84 03 01*
🔳 boisrenault.fr
Beautiful gardens dotted with
tree-shaded spots surround
this family-run château. Its
turrets and towers suggest a
compact Hogwarts, while
within rooms are spacious
and individually decorated.
A magnificent oak staircase
provides the wow factor.

**MAISONNAIS:**
**Notre-Dame d'Orsan** €€€
Manor house **Map** F4
*Prieuré Notre-Dame d'Orsan,18170*
**Tel** *02 48 56 27 50*
🔳 prieuredorsan.com

Luxury and restfulness are the
keywords at this former medieval
monastery. The beautifully
decorated rooms have views
of the Orsan gardens.

**SAINT-AMAND-MONTROND:**
**Hotel L'Amandois** €
Town hotel **Map** F4
*7–9 rue Henri Barbusse 18200*
**Tel** *02 48 63 72 00*
🔳 hotelamandois.fr/amandois
Comfortable and modern hotel
in the middle of the ancient
town of Saint-Amand-Montrond.
Good value; ideal for stopovers.

**SALBRIS: Camping De Sologne** €
Camp site **Map** E3
*8 allée de la Sauldre, 41300*
**Tel** *02 54 97 06 38*
🔳 campingdesologne.co
Lakeside camp site in the heart
of the beautiful Sologne region;
small bar, restaurant, children's
play area and 88 pitches, all with
electricity. Season April–Sept.

**VIERZON: Le Chalet de la Forêt** €
Rural hotel **Map** E3
*143 av Edouard Vaillant, 18100*
**Tel** *02 48 75 35 84*
🔳 www.lechaletdelaforet.com
Good-value inn-style hotel that
also has five wooden chalets.
Lush green setting, close to
motorway. It has a restaurant
specializing in regional cooking.

## North of the Loire

**CONFLANS SUR ANILLE:**
**Château de la Barre** €€€
Château **Map** D2
*Château de la Barre, 72120*
**Tel** *02 43 35 00 17*
🔳 chateaudelabarre.com
Splash out on a luxury stay at this
family-owned château. Gourmet
food and a great wine cellar
complete the experience.

**CROSMIÈRES: Hôtel**
**Haras de la Potardière** €€
Manor House **Map** C3
*Haras de la Potardière, Route de*
*Bazouges, 72200*
**Tel** *02 43 45 83 47*
🔳 potardiere.com
Horses wander about the leafy
parkland of this 18th century
family-run mansion; the rooms
are calm, stately and elegant.
Ideal for a romantic weekend.

**FERCÉ-SUR-SARTHE:**
**Château de Vauloge** €€
Château **Map** C3
*Vauloge, 72430*
**Tel** *02 43 77 32 81*
🔳 vauloge.com

Former monastery Notre-Dame d'Orsan

This Neo-Gothic, turreted
château is surrounded by a moat
in which swans swim. Rooms are
comfortable and classic, while a
walled garden offers tranquillity.

**LA FLECHE:**
**Hotel Le Gentleman** €€
Manor house **Map** C3
*17 rue de la Tour d'Auvergne, 72200*
**Tel** *02 43 45 89 36*
🔳 legentleman.fr
Centrally located town house
dating from the 18th century.
Rooms have tasteful yet quirky
decor. There is also a cosy
lounge and hidden garden.

**LE LUDE: 5 Grande Rue** €
Town house **Map** C3
*5 Grande Rue, 72800*
**Tel** *02 43 94 92 77*
🔳 5granderue.com
Starting life as a 17th-century
aristocratic town house, this is an
elegant hotel whose quintet of
rooms has a clean and stylish
simplicity. The shaded, walled
garden is a serene retreat.

**LHOMME: La Loge**
**de Courtoux** €€
Self-catering **Map** D3
*72340 Lhomme*
**Tel** *02 41 52 91 62*
🔳 demianville-jasnieres.fr
Compact, cosy cottage set in a
vineyard with a light and airy
bedroom that overlooks the
surrounding countryside. Rustic
style with a wood-burning stove.

**LOUE: Hôtel Ricordeau** €/€€
Town house **Map** C2
*13 rue de la Libération, 72540*
**Tel** *02 43 88 40 03*
🔳 hotel-ricordeau.fr
Former 19th-century coaching
inn in a pretty town. Rooms are
warmly decorated, some over-
look the leafy garden. The
restaurant uses local produce.

**SAINT-GEORGES-LE-GAULTIER:**
**Le Jarrier Gite** €€
Self-catering **Map** C2
*72130 Saint-Georges-le-Gaultier*
**Tel** *02 43 34 58 62*
**w** le-jarrier.com
Comfortable, recently converted
stable with two bedrooms and a
conservatory; rural location with
views of surrounding countryside.

**SAINT-MARS-D'OUTILLE:**
**Les Cheres Meres** €/€€
Chambre d'hôtes **Map** D2
*72220 Saint-Mars-d'Outillé*
**Tel** *02 43 39 40 05*
**w** loirebandb.com
The English owners have made
this farmhouse B&B into a
countryside retreat complete
with colourful gardens and
stunning views. Ideal for access
to Le Mans and its annual race.

**SAINT-PATERNE:**
**Château de Saint Paterne** €€€
Château **Map** C2
*rue de la Gaiete, 72610*
**Tel** *02 33 27 54 71*
**w** chateau-saintpaterne.com
Handsome family-owned
chateâu that has undergone a
renovation in keeping with its
16th-century origins. The gardens
are ideal for lounging in. There is
also a tennis court and play areas.

**SAINT-PIERRE-DU-LOROUER:**
**Le Chaton Rouge** €
Town house **Map** D3
*4 rue Calvaire, 72150*
**Tel** *02 43 46 21 37*
**w** lechatonrouge.com
Stylish town house set in an
attractive village. Furnishings are
simple but comfortable; breakfast
is served in the farmouse kitchen.

## Loire-Atlantique and the Vendée

**LA BAULE-ESCOUBLAC:**
**Hotel Villa Cap d'Ail** €€
Villa hotel **Map** A3
*145 av du Maréchal de Lattre
de Tassigny, 44500*
**Tel** *02 40 60 29 30*
**w** villacapdail.com
The golden sands of La Baule's
beach are a few minutes' stroll
from this former 1920s villa.
The balconied rooms are
decorated in bright colours.

**LE CLARAY:**
**La Maison de Ferme** €
Self-catering **Map** B3
*44110 Le Claray, Saint-Aubin-
des-Château*
**w** visitfrance.co.uk/
accommodation.cfm?i=7039
Farm workers used to call this

stone-built, wooden-beamed
cottage home; now it's an ideal
bolthole for families. Kids will
love the private garden and pool.

**CLISSON: Hotel**
**Villa Saint Antoine** €€
Boutique hotel **Map** B4
*8 rue Saint Antoine, 44190*
**Tel** *02 40 85 46 46*
**w** hotel-villa-saint-antoine.com
Eco-friendly, modern boutique
hotel set up in a former factory
with grand views of Clisson's
medieval castle.

**LE CROISIC: Hotel de L'Ocean** €€
Manor house **Map** A3
*Plage de Port Lin, 44490*
**Tel** *02 40 62 90 03*
**w** restaurantlocean.com
Recently refurbished, this hotel
stands on a rocky headland
overlooking the sea. Rooms are
contemporary and full of light.

**MISSILLAC: Domaine**
**de la Bretesche** €€€
Manor house **Map** A3
*44780 Missillac*
**Tel** *02 51 76 86 96*
**w** bretesche.fr
Guests are spoiled for choice
at this luxurious mansion with
rooms, suites, villas and cottages
with a blend of contemporary
and classic decor. Golfers will love
the 18-hole woodland course.

**MOREILLES:**
**Château de l'Abbaye** €€
Château **Map** B5
*Le Château de l'Abbaye, 85450
Moreilles*
**Tel** *02 51 56 17 56*
**w** chateau-moreilles.com
Solid 19th-century château built
on the ruins of an old abbey;
decor is a mixture of plush
fabrics, gilt-edged mirrors,
comfortable furniture and
deep baths.

**NANTES: Le Loft de l'Opera** €€
Self-catering **Map** B3
*16 blvd Gabriel Guist'hau, 44000*
**Tel** *06 72 77 43 85*
**w** welcomehome-nantes.fr/en/
our-lofts/loft-opera
Stylishly decorated loft
apartment; framed photos and
artworks dotted around add a
sense of creativity.

### DK Choice

**NANTES: Hotel Sozo** €€/€€€
Boutique hotel **Map** B3
*16 rue Frédéric Cailliaud, 44000*
**Tel** *02 51 82 40 00*
**w** sozohotel.fr
Formerly a 19th-century
chapel, this is now a modern
boutique hotel with 28 rooms.
Some of the past features, such
as stained-glass windows, have
been kept. Contemporary
decor; the vaulted stone lobby
features a grand piano and a
brace of acoustic guitars.
Unique setting.

**SAINTE-HERMINE:**
**Manoir du Moulin** €€
Manor house **Map** B4
*23 rue du Moulin, 85210*
**Tel** *06 26 97 24 12*
**w** manoirdumoulin.com
Recently renovated, stone-built
mill that is now a comfortable
rural retreat. Decor is a mixture of
modern and traditional ; stripped
stone walls, wooden floors and
high ceilings.

**SAINT-JEAN-DE-MONTS:**
**Camping La Forêt** €
Camp site **Map** A4
*190 chemin de la Rive, 85160*
**Tel** *02 51 58 84 63*
**w** hpa-laforet.com
Trees and hedges separate tent
pitches in this family-friendly
camp site on the edge of a forest.
It is just few minutes walk from
the beach.

A lavishly decorated bedroom at Château de la Barre

**For more information on types of hotels** *see page 200-3*

# WHERE TO EAT AND DRINK

In this generally prosperous region, with its excellent local produce, eating out is popular, and interest in cuisine is high even by the standards of this food-loving country. Lunch remains the main meal of the day: even in larger towns such as Tours, Orléans or Nantes, many office workers return home during their two-hour lunch break. Restaurants serve lunch from about noon, and it can be hard to find one willing to serve a meal if you arrive after 1pm, although cafés and brasseries in the towns are more flexible. Dinner is served from about 8pm onwards (sometimes earlier in the main tourist areas). Beware of last orders, which may be as early as 9pm, especially in country districts. The restaurants on pages 216–19 have been carefully selected for their excellence of food, decor and ambience, and cover all price ranges.

An outdoor café in the historic heart of Richelieu

## Types of Restaurant

In country districts and small towns, the most pleasant restaurants are often to be found in hotels, especially if they belong to the **Logis** association, which puts particular emphasis on good (and good value for money) regional cooking. Larger towns offer a broad range of places to eat, from basic pizzerias and *crêperies* to chic, gourmet establishments via cafés and brasseries. Unlike restaurants, brasseries and cafés generally serve a limited range of dishes outside regular mealtimes.

The Loire also has an ever-widening choice of restaurants specializing in foreign cuisines (most commonly Vietnamese, Japanese and North African).

## Vegetarian Food

True vegetarians do not fare well in France. It can be more convenient to head for a *crêperie* or a pizzeria, although in some of the university towns, the occasional vegetarian restaurant may be found. Some large cafés and brasseries in the tourist districts of major towns offer a small number of vegetarian dishes, and omelettes and other egg-based dishes are usually available. Alternatively, ask the chef for the meat or fish to be left out of a salad. In full-scale restaurants, it is essential to enquire in advance whether it is possible to have a vegetarian dish specially prepared.

## Reading the Menu

The vast majority of Loire Valley restaurants offer at least one fixed-price menu. You will often find a range of menus, culminating in an expensive *menu gastronomique* (gourmet meal), which may be available only if all members of your party choose it. Look out for a *menu régional* or *menu du terroir*, which will feature a selection of regional specialities.

In some restaurants, the most economical option is to eat either a starter and main course, or a main course and a dessert.

Many restaurants, especially in country districts, do not have a *carte* from which individual dishes may be selected. If they do, eating *à la carte* almost always works out to be more expensive than choosing from a fixed-price menu.

## Making Reservations

It is always advisable to book tables in advance at restaurants near the well-known châteaux, especially during the main tourist season (Easter to late September). If you enjoy eating alongside the residents at local restaurants in towns, which rarely take reservations over the telephone, make sure you arrive

A typical Loire Valley restaurant terrace

early. Restaurants in country districts are often closed on Sunday evenings as well as for at least one whole day during the week.

## Dress Code

Most French people take considerable trouble with their appearance but, with the exception of a few very chic and expensive places, formal dress is not required, and ties are rarely a necessity even in the top restaurants, providing you are neatly turned out.

The lavish restaurant at the Château de Rochecotte *(see p207)*

The sleek and modern dining room at L'U.Ni restaurant in Nantes *(see p219)*

## How Much to Pay

It is difficult to classify restaurants by price, since most establishments offer a range of fixed-price meals. Prices can be as low as €12 per head or as high as €100, but good, copious meals can be had everywhere for between €25 and €35.

A service charge of 15 per cent is usually included in the prices on menus, which are posted up outside for you to study before venturing in. It is usual to leave an extra euro or two as an additional tip. In more expensive restaurants, cloakroom attendants are given about €1 and lavatory attendants expect a small tip of about 30 cents.

Visa and MasterCard credit cards are widely accepted. Check first with the restaurant to find out whether American Express or Diners Club cards can be used.

## Children and Pets

Children are well received everywhere in the region, but they should be discouraged from wandering about during the meal. High chairs are sometimes available. Some restaurants offer special low-priced children's menus *(repas d'enfant)*.

Since the French are great dog lovers, well-behaved small dogs are usually accepted at all but the most elegant restaurants (but are often banned from food shops). Do not be surprised to see your neighbour's lapdog sitting on a *banquette.*

## Wheelchair Access

Few restaurants make special provision for wheelchairs, so it is wise when booking to mention that you or one of your party need space for a *fauteuil roulant*. This will ensure you get a conveniently located table and assistance, if needed, when you arrive. A list on page 202 gives names and addresses of various organizations that offer advice to disabled travellers to the Loire Valley region.

## Smoking

Under French law, smoking is banned in all public places including, somewhat controversially, *lieux de convivialité*, such as bars, cafés and restaurants. Smoking is permitted at outside tables and a few establishments have special enclosed indoor spaces for smokers, which are heavily ventilated in accordance with health regulations.

## Recommended Restaurants

All the restaurants in this guide, from the most magnificent establishment to the simplest brasserie, celebrate in various ways the produce of the Loire Valley. In every region there is one foodie favourite that is highlighted as a DK Choice. Sit in the shadow of the cathedral of Bourges, at La Gargouille, and lunch will be robust and hearty, starring such regional choices as steak tartare and rabbit. Or go modern at L'U.Ni, a hip Nantes restaurant, where the chef has devised dishes that include grilled scallops and puréed coconut, and foie gras with preserved lamb. For Michelin-starred fare, head to the village of Le Petit-Pressigny, where the family-owned La Promenade offers a fabulous selection of *amuse-bouches* and classic regional cuisine. Finally, there are several restaurants offering international cuisines as diverse as Japanese, Mexican and Indian.

Enjoy classic French cuisine with a twist at roadside inn La Promenade *(see p216)*

# The Flavours of the Loire Valley

This huge area can take pride in a truly diverse range of top-quality produce. The seafood from its Atlantic coastline, the freshwater fish from its rivers and lakes, the game birds from its forests, the bounty of fresh vegetables and the tiny white mushrooms that flourish in the darkness of its caves, have all helped to create a cuisine fit for kings. Many of the Loire's typical fish and meat dishes have become classics, now found all over France. Others remain very much local treats, using the region's finest and freshest produce, to be sought out and savoured in its many fine restaurants.

Young carrots

Fresh hake for sale, direct from the port, in the Loire-Atlantique

## Meat and Charcuterie

Free-range chickens are raised in the Sarthe, Touraine and Orléanais, and duck in the Vendée. Anjou and Mayenne are home to grass-fed cattle, and the Berry to hardy sheep. The forests of the Sologne are well known for deer, hare, wild boar, pheasant and partridge.

The main charcuterie is *rillettes* (shredded and potted slow-cooked pork), a speciality of Tours and the Sarthe. *Rillons* (large chunks of crunchy fried salted belly pork) are also popular. The Vendée produces some excellent cured ham. The Sologne is noted for its terrines, Chartres for its excellent game pies and the Berry for a pâté that comes baked in pastry with slices of hard-boiled egg.

## Fish

The ports of the Loire-Atlantique and the Vendée offer up a variety of fish and shellfish. La Turballe is the main sardine port on the Atlantic coast. The Ile de Noirmoutier is known for line-caught fish, lobster and oysters, as well as farmed turbot. But best of all is the region's freshwater fish, including pike-perch, shad, tench, eels and lampreys.

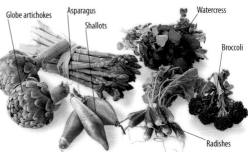

Globe artichokes   Asparagus   Shallots   Watercress   Broccoli   Radishes

A selection of the superb vegetables grown in the Loire Valley

## Local Dishes and Specialities

Meals often start with a terrine or pâté, spread thickly on crusty bread. Creamy vegetable soups, such as asparagus or pumpkin, are also popular, as are grilled sardines and shellfish along the coast. Main courses include fish baked in a salt crust or simply poached and served with a creamy *beurre blanc* sauce. Superb poultry may also be on offer, roasted or prepared as a fricassée with cream and butter. The region produces excellent beef and lamb: tender *gigot de sept heures* is a menu favourite. Game dominates the winter table in the Sologne, commonly served with the wild mushrooms that flourish in the area. Many desserts are based on fruit, often baked in a tart or poached in wine.

Ste-Maure cheese

**Gigot de Sept Heures** A leg of lamb is cooked slowly until tender with carrots, bacon, garlic, herbs and wine.

A cheese stall in the market at Loches in the Touraine

## Cheese

The Touraine and Berry produce some of France's finest goat's cheeses. The creamy, ash-covered Ste-Maure-de-Touraine is available both freshly made or matured in damp cellars. Selles-sur-Cher is a mild, flat, rounded, cindered cheese. Valençay, shaped into an ash-covered pyramid, is firmer with a stronger taste, and Pouligny-St-Pierre, a narrower pyramid, is mottled and blueish on the outside and white within. Most strongly flavoured are the small round Crottin de Chavignol cheeses.

Cow's milk cheeses of note include Feuille de Dreux, a flat, soft cheese with a chestnut leaf on the top, ash-covered Olivet and the washed-rinded Port-Salut.

## Fruit and Vegetables

Thanks to the mild climate, winter vegetables thrive in the Nantes area. Many of France's salad vegetables are grown here, as well as peas, radishes, turnips, early leeks and carrots. In damp caves along the banks of the Loire, tiny button

A busy vegetable stall in the market at Saumur

mushrooms are cultivated. Samphire is gathered from the salt marshes near Nantes, and the Ile de Noirmoutier is famous for its new potatoes. The Sologne produces fine asparagus and lentils are grown in the Berry.

Orchards across the Loire Valley are noted for their apples and pears; Comice pears originated near Angers. Other quality fruit includes the succulent plums of Touraine and sweet strawberries from Saumur.

### ON THE MENU

**Alose à l'oseille** Shad in a sorrel hollandaise sauce

**Canard nantais** Roast duck with Muscadet wine sauce

**Civet de marcassin** Hearty casserole of wild boar

**Géline à la lochoise** Géline hen in a cream sauce

**Porc aux pruneaux** Pork fillets cooked with prunes in a wine and cream sauce

**Potage d'asperges** Creamy puréed asparagus soup

**Prunes au Vouvray** Plums stewed in Vouvray wine

**Ragoût d'anguilles et cuisses de grenouille** A stew of eel and frogs' legs

**Tarte aux rillettes** Open savoury tart with a filling of potted pork, eggs and cream

**Lapin Chasseur** Rabbit is simmered with tomato and mushrooms to make this traditional hunters' stew.

**Sandre au Beurre Blanc** A poached pike-perch is served with a *beurre blanc* sauce of butter, cream and shallots.

**Tarte Tatin** This upside-down tart of caramelized apples on a puff-pastry base may be offered plain or with cream.

# What to Drink in the Loire

The Loire Valley is a major wine region (see pp34–5), so naturally the traditional tipple in cafés and bars is *un coup de rouge* or *un coup de blanc* (a small glass of red or white wine). The light rosés, such as Rosé d'Anjou or Rosé de Touraine, are drunk chilled, either in the afternoon with a slice of cake or as an apéritif. In November, bars and cafés serve *bernache*, the greenish, fermented juice left after the grapes have been pressed for winemaking. There is also a wide variety of other alcoholic drinks, including *eaux de vie* made with local fruits and light, lager-style beers, as well as non-alcoholic drinks such as coffees, teas and juices.

A waiter in a Loire Valley bar

White Sancerre

Red Bourgueil

Sparkling wine

## Wine

Wine usually accompanies meals in the Loire, as it does throughout France. Local wine is often served in carafes. Ordering a *demi* (50 cl, approximately ½ pint) or *quart* (25 cl) is an inexpensive way to try out a wide variety of the wines of the region before buying any to take home (see pp34–5).

French law divides domestic wines into four classes, in ascending order of quality: *vin de table, vin de pays, vin délimité de qualité supérieure* (VDQS) and finally *appellation d'origine contrôlée* (AOC). *Vin de table* wines are rarely found in good restaurants. If in doubt, order the house wine (*la réserve*). Very few restaurants will risk their reputation on an inferior house wine, and they often provide good value for money.

## Apéritifs and Digestifs

A glass of locally produced sparkling wine can be an excellent apéritif or a pleasant accompaniment to the dessert course. Slightly sparkling Vouvray *pétillant* is popular, and further west in Anjou you will find Saumur sparkling wine, made by the *méthode traditionnelle*. Keep an eye open, too, for Crémant de Loire, another good local sparkling wine.

## How to Read a Wine Label

Even the simplest label will provide a key to the wine's flavour and quality. It will bear the name of the wine and its producer, its vintage if there is one, and whether it comes from a strictly defined area (*appellation d'origine contrôlée* or AOC) or is a more general *vin de pays* or *vin de table*. The shape and colour of the bottle is also a guide. Most good-quality wine is bottled in green glass, which helps to protect it from light. The label's design may be appealing, but does not necessarily indicate a quality product.

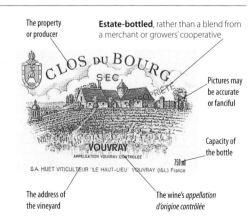

The property or producer

**Estate-bottled**, rather than a blend from a merchant or growers' cooperative

Pictures may be accurate or fanciful

Capacity of the bottle

The address of the vineyard

The wine's *appellation d'origine contrôlée*

A *kir* – white wine with a touch of *crème de cassis*, a blackcurrant liqueur – is a popular apéritif, and an appealing variation, often served as the house apéritif, combines sparkling wine with raspberry or peach liqueur. Bars, cafés and restaurants also stock the usual range of French apéritifs as well as international gins, sherries, ports and whiskies.

After dinner, a little glass of clear fruit brandy made from local raspberries, pears or plums may appeal. Cointreau, Combier and Giffard are also produced in the Loire Valley. Other traditional *digestifs*, such as cognac or calvados, are also drunk after meals in the region.

## Beer

The locals drink mostly lager-style draught beer in cafés – ask for *un demi*. A range of bottled beers can also be found, both French (which is considerably cheaper) and imported.

*Café crème*, often served at breakfast with a fresh croissant

## Coffee and Tea

Cafés, still the main focus of community life, serve good strong *express* (a tiny cup of black coffee). White coffees are prepared with hot milk and come in two sizes: small (*petit crème*) and large (*grand crème*). Together with fresh croissants, they make a good breakfast.

Tea served in cafés is often of the teabag variety (with a slice of lemon, it is *un thé citron*). Tearooms in towns, however, are more likely to use tea leaves. Many cafés also offer a range of exotic fruit and herb teas, which are caffeine-free. In restaurants an infusion of limeflower leaves (*tilleul*), mint (*menthe*) or camomile (*camomille*) is often drunk after dinner as an aid to digestion.

## Other Drinks

Children enjoy the colourful drinks served in tall glasses known as *menthe à l'eau* (green, minty syrup with tap water) and *grenadine* (a red fruit syrup), but these may be too sweet for adult tastes. Served with Vittel mineral water, for example, they become *Vittel menthe*, *Vittel grenadine*, and so on. *Vittel citron amer* (with bottled, still bitter lemon) is more refreshing than *Vittel citron* (with lemon syrup). Best of all for quenching the thirst – but also more expensive – is a *citron pressé*: freshly squeezed lemon juice served with a carafe of water and packets of sugar to mix to taste. *Orange pressée* is orange juice served in the same way. Bottled fruit juices (*jus de fruits*) are also available everywhere.

Tap water is safe to drink, but many people prefer mineral water (*eau minérale*), either sparkling (*gazeuse*) or still (*non-gazeuse*).

Locally-made apple juice

## Where to Drink

A café is the traditional place to pop in for a coffee or beer, to meet a friend or watch the world go by. City centres have bustling cafés on every corner, and many squares are crowded with outdoor tables when the weather is fine. However, the traditional café, with its long bar counter lined by regulars, is gradually being superseded, at least in towns, by more elaborate places.

Bars and *bars à vin* (old-style wine bars) are often the haunts of more hardened drinkers and of late-night revellers, although hotel bars can attract a more eclectic clientele. In larger towns, many

A wood-panelled hotel bar in Touraine

new-style wine bars, often with high-tech decor, serve wine by the glass, with light meals, plates of *charcuterie* or cheeses with crusty bread. Traditional *salons de thé* (tearooms), which serve coffee, tea and hot chocolate, are mainly frequented by women. They also serve *pâtisserie* and chocolates, which can be bought to take away. The newer version offers light lunches and a variety of sweets, cakes and tarts to a younger, mixed clientele.

People enjoying a break in a stylish café in Orléans

# Where to Eat and Drink

## Anjou

**ANGERS:**
**Les Sentiers du Dakar** €
International  Map C3
*3 rue Corneille, 49000*
**Tel** *02 41 20 39 96*
As the name suggests, French-African fusion is the draw at this compact restaurant hidden away down an alley, with dishes such as beef and okra and chicken yassa. Reservations are recommended.

**ANGERS: Ma Campagne** €€
Traditional French  Map C3
*14 promenade de la Reculée, 49000*
**Tel** *02 41 48 38 06* **Closed** *Sun, Mon & Tue eve*
Country-style *auberge* close to the town centre. Select the trilogy of frozen *macarons* for dessert.

**AVRILLE: Ciboule et Ciboulette** €
Modern French  Map C3
*60 av Pierre Mendes France, 49240*
**Tel** *02 41 72 00 77* **Closed** *Sun, Mon, & Tue*
Seasonal produce reigns supreme in this cosy restaurant where dishes are cooked with originality and verve. Try the hake with cider or the pig's cheek confit.

**DOUE LA FONTAINE:**
**Auberge Bienvenue** €
Traditional French  Map C3
*104 rte de Cholet, 49700*
**Tel** *02 41 59 22 44* **Closed** *Sun eve & Mon*
A charming inn offering hearty meals cooked from local produce, often doused in regional wines. Opt for roast duckling with ginger confit.

**DURTAL:**
**Restaurant des Plantes** €€
Modern French  Map C3
*54 av Angers, 49430*
**Tel** *02 41 76 41 57* **Closed** *Sun, Mon & Tue eve, Wed*
Modern restaurant in a small pretty town, where the menu offers intriguing contrasts such as marinated mackerel and black pudding or chicken supreme with crayfish sauce.

**GENNES: L'Aubergade** €€€
Fine dining  Map C3
*7 av des Cadets, 49350*
**Tel** *02 41 51 81 07* **Closed** *Tue, Wed*
Two elegant dining rooms serve a variety of imaginatively flavoured dishes influenced by what is in season. Classic French is fused with influences including Asian spices.

**LE LION-D'ANGERS:**
**L'Authentique** €€
Modern French  Map C3
*48 rue Général Leclerc, 49220*
**Tel** *02 41 27 32 46* **Closed** *Sun, Mon*
Whether it's the truffle salad or the perfectly cooked duck breast, there's a sense of joy and imagination about the dishes in this popular restaurant.

### DK Choice

**MONTSOREAU:**
**Diane de Méridor** €€
Fine dining  Map C3
*12 quai Philippe de Commines, 49730*
**Tel** *02 41 51 71 76* **Closed** *Tue, Wed*
Carved out of Tuffeau rock, this restaurant has exposed beams, an open fireplace and stunning views over the Loire. The chic, stylish decor matches the faultless presentation of the dishes. Specializes in freshwater fish. Good local wine selection.

**SAINT-MATHURIN-SUR-LOIRE:**
**La Promenade** €
Traditional French  Map C3
*138 levée Jeanne de Laval, 49250*
**Tel** *02 41 57 01 50* **Closed** *Tues eve, Wed*
Classic French cuisine is the draw at this roadside inn, with dishes such as caramelized roast quail and slow-cooked lamb shoulder.

One of the creative dishes served up at Le 36 in Amboise

**SAUMUR: L'Cancuna** €
International  Map C3
*15 rue Courcouronne, 49400*
**Tel** *02 41 51 38 24* **Closed** *Mon, Tue lunch, Sun*
Spicy Mexican dishes are the focus at this popular and lively cantina with fajitas, tortillas and quesadillas among the favourites.

**SAUMUR: L'Escargot** €€
Modern French  Map C3
*30 rue du Maréchal Leclerc, 49400*
**Tel** *02 41 51 20 88* **Closed** *Tues, Wed*
Unsurprisingly, snails are the speciality at this cosy restaurant just 10 minutes from the town centre; other choices include beef cheek and rack of lamb. The wine cellar majors in local vineyards.

**TURQUANT: L'Helianthe** €€
Traditional French  Map C3
*ruelle Antoine Cristal, 49730*
**Tel** *02 41 51 22 28* **Closed** *Wed April–Nov, Fri eve, Sat, Sun Nov–April*
Delightful restaurant in a limestone cave. Chef celebrates the use of "old-fashioned" vegetables in classic cuisine with the likes of rabbit, lamb and river fish.

## Touraine

**AMBOISE: Le 36** €€
Fine dining  Map D3
*36 quai C Guinot, 37400*
**Tel** *02 47 30 45 45* **Closed** *Tue, Wed (mid-Nov–mid-March)*
Lovely restaurant serving local, seasonal food creatively put together. One dining room opens out onto a pretty garden and another overlooks the Loire.

**BLERE: Cheval Blanc** €
Traditional French  Map D3
*5 pl Charles Bidault, 37150*
**Tel** *02 47 30 30 14* **Closed** *Mon, Tues*
Friendly, family-owned restaurant with an imaginative menu that marries classic French cuisine with a bold touch. Dishes include tuna Rossini and onion confit.

**BOURGUEIL: Le Moulin Bleu** €
Traditional French  Map C3
*7 rue du Moulin-Bleu, 37140*
**Tel** *02 47 97 73 13* **Closed** *Tue eve, Wed & Sun eve*

Farmhouse restaurant whose traditional dishes are served in two vaulted dining rooms. The semi-rural location is pleasing while service is friendly without being cloying.

### CHINON: Les Années 30 €€
Modern French — Map D3
*78 rue Haute St-Maurice, 37500*
**Tel** *02 47 93 37 18* **Closed** *Tue, Wed*
Elegant, understated restaurant offering interesting dishes such as pigeon and langoustine served with a truffle-flavoured vinaigrette. Staff are welcoming and the wine list exemplary.

### LANGEAIS:
**Au Coin des Halles** €€
Modern French — Map D3
*9 rue Gambetta, 37120*
**Tel** *02 47 96 37 25* **Closed** *Wed, Thu*
Top-notch bistro that combines chic interiors and a charming patio garden; the imaginative cuisine brings a hint of North African flavour to dishes that feature local produce.

### MONTBAZON: La Chancelière €€
Modern French — Map D3
*1 pl des Marronniers, 37250*
**Tel** *02 47 26 00 07* **Closed** *Sun, Mon*
Modern, sophisticated cuisine is prepared with precision and creativity at this chic and elegant restaurant. Standouts include the foie gras in wine broth and grilled lobster with broccoli and creamy satay.

---

### DK Choice

**LE PETIT-PRESSIGNY:**
**Restaurant la Promenade** €€
Traditional French — Map D4
*11 rue Savoureulx, 37350*
**Tel** *02 47 94 93 52* **Closed** *Sun eve & Mon, Tues*
Michelin-starred family restaurant whose reputation for boldly flavoured and finely textured dishes draws in both locals and visitors from near and afar. An amazing selection of *amuse-bouches*, a great wine list and fabulous dishes featuring the classic regional chicken *géline* Touraine and game (when in season) help to make this place unmissable.

---

### SACHE: Auberge du XIIéme Siècle €€
Traditional French — Map D3
*1 rue du Château, 37190*
**Tel** *02 47 26 88 77* **Closed** *Sun eve, Mon & Tue lunch*
Half-timbered and historic *auberge* with a good choice of fixed-price menus built around

The brightly coloured interior of L'Atelier Gourmand in Touraine

a classic selection of dishes such as sautéed lobster and game (when in season).

### SAVONNIÈRES:
**La Maison Tourangelle** €€
Traditional French — Map D3
*9 rte des Grottes Pétrifiantes, 37510*
**Tel** *02 47 50 30 05* **Closed** *Sun eve, Mon, Wed*
Beautifully located overlooking the river Cher, this impeccable inn is an elegant celebration of Touraine's regional cuisine as interpreted by masterful chef Frederic Arnault. The wine cellar is equally accomplished.

### SEMBLANCAY: Hostellerie de la Mere Hamard €€
Traditional French — Map D3
*2 rue de Petit Bercy, 37360*
**Tel** *02 47 56 62 04* **Closed** *Sun eve, Mon, Tue lunch*
You can both eat and stay in this charming village establishment. The kitchen serves a range of hearty regional dishes alongside a well-chosen wine list brimming with local heroes.

### TOURS: L'Atelier Gourmand €
Modern French — Map D3
*37 rue Étienne Marcel, 37000*
**Tel** *02 47 38 59 87* **Closed** *Sun, Mon*
With its vividly coloured interior and minimalist furniture, this restaurant contrasts wonderfully with the old part of Tours. The menu is bold with creations such as lamb and aubergine confit. Competitive prices.

### TOURS: L'Odéon €
Brasserie — Map D3
*10 pl du Général Leclerc, 37000*
**Tel** *02 47 20 12 65* **Closed** *Mon lunch, Sun*
Quality Art Deco-style restaurant close to the railway station. The kitchen team creatively re-invent French regional dishes using locally produced,

seasonally available ingredients. The seafood is particularly good.

### TOURS: BarJu €€
Modern French — Map D3
*15 rue du Changé, 37000*
**Tel** *02 47 64 91 12* **Closed** *Sun, Mon*
Lively restaurant with stylish decor in the old part of Tours. Careful use of spices brings out the best in fish dishes such as sesame-marinated pollock with avocado tartar or hand-dived scallops.

### TOURS: La Roche Le Roy €€
Fine dining — Map D3
*55 rte de St-Avertin, 37000*
**Tel** *02 47 27 22 00* **Closed** *Sun, Mon*
Michelin-starred restaurant located in a stunning 18th-century mansion. Loire and Bordeaux wines are carefully chosen to complement classic French dishes. Arrive early to admire the pretty garden. Staff are welcoming; atmosphere ambient.

## Blésois and Orléanis

### BEAUGENCY: Le Petit Bateau €
Modern French — Map E3
*54 rue du Pont, 45190*
**Tel** *02 38 44 56 38* **Closed** *Mon, Tue*
Located on a pretty, flower-lined road, this restaurant re-invents classic French dishes. Specialities include fresh fish and wild mushrooms. The cheese selection is impressive.

### BLOIS: Maison Tatami €
International — Map E3
*63 rue du Bourg Neuf, 41000*
**Tel** *02 54 78 18 05* **Closed** *Sun lunch*
Freshly made sushi, sashimi and tempura are the stars of the menu in this Japanese restaurant on the edge of the city centre.

**For more information on types of restaurants** *see pp210–11*

**CONTRES: La Botte d'Asperges** €
Traditional French        Map E3
*52 rue Pierre-Henri Mauger, 41700*
**Tel** *02 54 79 50 49* **Closed** *Sun eve &*
*Mon, Wed eve*
Delicious food served in a rustic
setting. Locally grown asparagus
features prominently on the
menu when in season.

**ONZAIN: Domaine
des Hauts de Loire** €€€
Fine dining        Map D3
*79 rue Gilbert Navard, 41150*
**Tel** *02 54 20 72 57* **Closed** *Mon, Tue*
Creative, Michelin-starred cuisine
featuring seasonal produce.
Served in an ivy-clad former
hunting lodge set within its
own park.

**ORLEANS: La Dariole** €
Traditional French        Map E2
*25 rue Etienne Dolet, 45000*
**Tel** *02 38 77 26 67* **Closed** *Sat, Sun,*
*Mon eve, Wed eve, Thu eve*
A 15th-century, half-timbered
building houses this charming
little restaurant and tearoom.

**ORLEANS: La Parenthese** €
Modern French        Map E2
*26 pl du Châtelet, 45000*
**Tel** *02 38 62 07 50* **Closed** *Sun, Mon*
Iced cream of asparagus soup
with smoked duck is just one
of the imaginative choices on
the menu in this 17th-century
building in the city centre.

**SAINT-BENOÎT-SUR-LOIRE:
Restaurant du Grand Saint
Benoît** €
Modern French        Map F3
*7 pl Saint-André, 45730*
**Tel** *02 38 35 11 92* **Closed** *Sun, Mon*
Popular restaurant in the heart
of a pretty village. The menu
focuses on intriguingly flavoured
dishes such as marinated
salmon with sesame seeds
in wasabi.

---

## DK Choice

**SAINT-OUEN: La Vallée** €€
Traditional French        Map D3
*34 rue à Barre de Saint-Venant,*
*41100*
**Tel** *02 54 77 29 93* **Closed** *Sun*
*eve, Mon, Tue*
Enjoy well-prepared, traditional
dishes in the rustic dining room
or on the sunny terrace of this
friendly restaurant located just
outside the city of Vendôme.
The cheese board is superb
and includes one cheese the
chef developed himself. The
quality of the food is matched
with a good selection of
regional wines.

---

# Berry

## DK Choice

**BOURGES: La Gargouille** €
Brasserie        Map F4
*108 rue Bourbonnoux, 18000*
**Tel** *02 48 24 23 59* **Closed** *Sun*
Friendly restaurant close to the
historic cathedral. Inside, the
bare stone walls, battered
wooden beams and comfort-
able courtyard add to the
amiable atmosphere. The
menu concentrates on hearty
helpings of robust local cuisine;
standouts include the steak
tartare and rabbit, and the fries
are excellent. Pudding fans rave
about the strawberry tart.

---

**BUZANCAIS: L'Hermitage** €
Traditional French        Map E4
*1 chemin de Villaine, 36500*
**Tel** *02 54 84 03 90* **Closed** *Mon*
*lunch; hotel closed Jan*
Traditional-looking hotel
restaurant set in beautiful
parkland. Popular with locals;
there is both a fixed and *à la
carte* menu. Food is imaginative,
perfectly presented and
desserts are delicious.

**CHAVIGNOL: Côte
des Monts Damnés** €
Modern French        Map F3
*pl de l'Orme, 18300*
**Tel** *02 48 54 01 72* **Closed** *Tue, Wed*
Regional cuisine restaurant in a
picturesque village surrounded
by vineyards and famous for its
goat's cheese. Service is attentive;
dishes are perfectly paired with
local wines.

**LA FERTE IMBAULT:
La Tête de Lard** €
Traditional French        Map E3
*13 rue Nationale, 41300*
**Tel** *02 54 96 22 32* **Closed** *Sun eve,*
*Mon & Tue lunch*
Housed in a refurbished country
hotel, this ambient and
affordable restaurant has a
traditional menu focussed on
seasonally sourced dishes.

**MOROGUES:
Au Gres des Ouches** €
Traditional French        Map F3
*2 Grande Rue, 18220*
**Tel** *02 48 64 17 51* **Closed** *Wed*
Remote village restaurant that
draws people from further afield
who come for the imaginative
remakes of classical regional
cuisine, served with fantastic
local wines and cheeses.

---

The charming, farmhouse-style interior of
La Petite Auberge

**SAINT-AMAND-MONTROND:
Auberge de l'Abbaye
de Noirlac** €/€€
Traditional French        Map F4
*Bruère-Allichamps, 18200*
**Tel** *02 48 96 22 58* **Closed** *Tue eve,*
*Wed*
Good portions, imaginative
dishes and great value make
this *auberge* opposite the abbey
worth a detour. Reservations
essential. Don't miss the
cheese trolley, stocked with
fresh, local varieties.

**SAINT-VALENTIN:
Au 14 Fevrier** €
Modern French        Map E4
*2 rue du Portail, 36100*
**Tel** *02 54 03 04 96* **Closed** *Mon, Tues,*
*Wed lunch, Sun eve; open Sun eve*
*April–Aug*
Japanese cuisine meets French
in canteen-like surroundings in
this small but romantically
named village. It is part of a trio
of similarly themed restaurants.

**SALBRIS: Le Dauphin** €
Traditional French        Map E3
*57 blvd de la République, 41300*
**Tel** *02 54 97 04 83* **Closed** *Mon*
*lunch, Wed, Sun eve*
Comfortable hotel restaurant
with an emphasis on regional
produce and stunning
presentation. Close enough
to the motorway to warrant
a lunchtime stop.

**SANCERRE:
Auberge La Pomme d'Or** €
Traditional French        Map F3
*pl de la Mairie, 18300*
**Tel** *02 48 54 13 30* **Closed** *Tue, Wed;*
*Oct–Mar: Sun eve*
Flavoursome cooking based
on seasonal produce from the
region. Enjoy the Chavignol
goat's cheese with a glass of
Sancerre wine.

**SANCERRE: La Tour** €/€€
Modern French **Map** F3
31 Nouvelle Place, 18300
**Tel** 02 48 54 00 81 **Closed** Sun eve, Mon
An elegant restaurant with views over the Sancerre vineyards. Serves good contemporary cuisine using the best local produce.

## North of the Loire

**ARNAGE:**
**Auberge des Matfeux** €€
Modern French **Map** C2
289 av Nationale 72230
**Tel** 02 43 21 10 71 **Closed** Sun eve, Mon, Tues
The langoustine ravioli is a favourite with regulars; elsewhere on the menus you will find many creative, beautifully presented dishes.

**CHARTRES: Le Georges,**
**Le Grand Monarque** €€€
Fine dining **Map** E2
22 pl des Epars, 28000
**Tel** 02 37 18 15 15 **Closed** Sun, Mon
The best of classic French cuisine can be enjoyed in this gourmet hotel restaurant. Dishes are accompanied by grand cru wine.

**LOUE: Ricordeau** €€
Modern French **Map** C2
11 rue de la Libération, 72540
**Tel** 02 43 88 40 03 **Closed** Mon, Tues, Sun eve
Classy hotel restaurant with a dining room overlooking a flag-stone garden where diners can sit in summer. Regional specialities with a contemporary twist.

**MALICORNE-SUR-SARTHE:**
**La Petite Auberge** €
Traditional French **Map** C3
5 pl du Guesclin, 72270
**Tel** 02 43 94 80 52 **Closed** Mon, Sun, Tue eve
Gourmet food in a charming riverside setting. In summer, dine on the terrace, and in winter, take refuge around the fireplace.

### DK Choice

**LE MANS: Auberge**
**des 7 Plats** €
Traditional French **Map** C2
79 Grande Rue 72000
**Tel** 02 43 24 57 77 **Closed** Sun eve, Mon
This unique, compact restaurant is located in the old city centre. As the name suggests, diners select from seven starters, seven mains and fourteen desserts on the menu, with an emphasis on local cuisine. Cosy and comfort-able; ideal for a romantic meal.

**RUAUDIN: Les Relais**
**d'Alsace Taverne Karlsbrau** €
Traditional French **Map** D2
zone des Hunaudières Antarès, Chemin de César, 72230
**Tel** 02 85 63 07 17
Parisian-style brasserie whose dishes display hearty Alsatian influences, particularly with sausages and sauerkraut. A wide-ranging menu make this suitable for all the family.

**SARGE-LES-LE-MANS:**
**Bombay** €
International **Map** D2
23 pl de l'Eperon, 72000
**Tel** 02 43 23 93 08
Authentic Indian cuisine is on the menu at this popular place on the edge of the city centre; there's no stinting on the spices and the chicken tandoori comes highly recommended.

## Loire-Atlantique and the Vendée

**CLISSON: Bonne Auberge** €/€€
Traditional French **Map** B4
1 rue Olivier de Clisson, 44190
**Tel** 02 40 54 01 90 **Closed** Sun eve, Mon, Tue & Wed eve
Comfortable auberge with three cool, high-ceilinged dining rooms plus a tree-shaded terrace for alfresco dining. Specialities include seafood, fish and game (when in season).

**LES CROISIC:**
**Le Fort Océan** €€/€€€
Fine dining **Map** A3
Pointe de Croisic, 44490
**Tel** 02 40 15 77 77 **Closed** Mon, Tue
Luxury hotel-restaurant with granite walls and stylish, bold cuisine with an emphasis on locally caught fish and seafood; the dining room has sea views.

**MESQUER-QUIMIAC:**
**La Vieille Forge** €
Modern French **Map** A3
rue d'Aha, 44420
**Tel** 02 40 42 62 68 **Closed** Tue eve, Wed
Charming family restaurant located in a former blacksmith's forge; creative dishes based on local produce. Oysters are a speciality.

### DK Choice

**NANTES: L'U.Ni** €€
Modern French **Map** B3
36 rue Fouré
**Tel** 02 40 75 53 05 **Closed** Mon, Tue & Sun lunch
This restaurant has made a name for itself in gourmet circles for serving creative food in a modern setting. Specialities include barely cooked brill with baby turnips and spinach, and desserts such as avocado and white chocolate millefeuille.

**LES SABLES D'OLONNE:**
**Affice** €
Seafood **Map** A4
21 quai Giné, 85100
**Tel** 02 51 95 34 74 **Closed** Mon
Intimate little fish restaurant in a pretty little seaside town with excellent food and great wine. Booking essential.

**SUCE-SUR-ERDRE:**
**L'Ecume des Jours** €
Traditional French **Map** B3
115 pl Charles de Gaulle, 44240
**Tel** 02 40 77 77 77 **Closed** Mon, Tue lunch, Sun
Convivial, modern restaurant run by two brothers. Inventive and original dishes makes the most of regional and seasonally sourced ingredients. The menu is accompanied by a well-planned wine list.

The ambient dining room at La Gargouille in Bourges

For more information on types of restaurants see pp210–11

# SHOPS AND MARKETS

Shopping for specialities of the Loire Valley is always a pleasure, and the region's towns and cities also offer many opportunities to purchase the goods that France is famous for – fashion accessories and clothes, kitchenware, porcelain and crystal, and particularly food. Specialist shops are everywhere, and visiting the

region's open-air and indoor food markets gives the visitor a wonderful opportunity to buy a vast range of local produce and culinary specialities. This section provides guidelines on shopping in the Loire Valley, and pages 222–3 show some of the best regional foods, wines and other specialist goods available.

The splendid interior of La Maison des Forestines, purveyors of boiled sweets in Bourges

## Opening Hours

Small food shops in the Loire region open early – around 7:30 or 8am – and close at around 12:30 for lunch, then reopen at about 3:30 or 4pm until 7 or 8pm. Other small shops are open from roughly 2 to 6:30 or 7pm on Monday (many remain closed all day), 9am to noon and 2 to 6:30 or 7pm Tuesday to Saturday. Small supermarkets generally take a long lunch break, but department stores and large supermarkets do not close for lunch. Sales are usually held in late June and January.

Open-air food markets take place one, two or three mornings a week, often including Sundays, while the large indoor food markets (*les halles*) are usually open from Tuesday to Saturday for the same hours as small food shops. This guide lists the market days for each town featured.

## Specialist Shops

Despite the mushrooming of supermarkets and large superstores, small specialist shops have continued to

thrive in France, and they add enormously to the pleasure of shopping trips. Food shops in particular often specialize in a single theme. *Boulangeries* sell fresh bread, but they may be *boulangeries-pâtisseries*, which means that tempting cakes and pastries will also be on offer. *Traiteurs* sell prepared dishes, while *épiceries* are small grocers. *Crémeries* specialize in dairy products, *fromageries* sell only cheese and *charcuteries* specialize in cooked and cured meats with a few prepared, cold dishes. An *épicerie fine* focuses on high-class groceries and is a good source of gifts to take home, such as local mustards or vinegars in attractive jars or bottles.

An *alimentation générale* (general food store) may have a self-service system. In small villages, this is sometimes the only shop, although fresh bread will always be available either there or from the local café. A travelling van

also supplies fresh bread in some regions. Cleaning products are bought in a *droguerie*, hardware from a *quincaillerie*, books from a *librairie* and stationery (much of which is particularly stylish in France) from a *papeterie*.

The area has some specialist shops that focus on a single product, such as umbrellas or walking sticks, chess sets or stamps, or in a single field such as militaria or natural history books. Their owners are usually extremely knowledgeable about their particular subject, and they enjoy sharing it if you show an interest. Antique shops (*magasins d'antiquités*) tend to be very pricey. Head instead for a *brocante* (bric-à-brac shop), or try hunting for bargains in local flea markets.

## Tasting and Buying Wine

The Loire Valley is famous for its wines and the region is scattered with producers. Signs beside the road saying *dégustation* mean that tastings are available at the winery. It is important to remember that the local *vigneron* will expect a modest purchase of a few bottles after you have drunk several experimental glasses. In Saumur it is possible to tour the wine growers' own cellars with the minimum of sales pressure. Best of all, visit the *Maisons des Vins de Loire* in most major towns, where the information and often free tastings are very helpful and interesting.

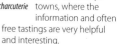

Sign for a *charcuterie*

## Hypermarkets and Chain Stores

Superstores and the larger hypermarkets (*hypermarchés*) are usually situated on the outskirts of towns, often as part of a *centre commercial* (shopping complex) that may also include small boutiques, a DIY outlet and a petrol station. Many of these big stores belong to the Auchan, Carrefour or Super U chains.

The old-style *grand magasin*, or department store, found in the region's towns has generally either been converted into a series of boutiques or taken over and modernized by the upmarket Nouvelles Galeries or Printemps national chains. These chic stores are good for clothes, accessories and perfumes. The popular Monoprix stores are worth visiting if you are looking for inexpensive stationery, lingerie and cosmetics. Many of them also have a reasonably priced food department.

A flower-seller and customer at the village market in Luynes

## Markets

Open-air food markets are one of the delights of the Loire Valley. Their offerings are mouthwatering: mounds of succulent vegetables, *charcuterie* specialities, goat's cheeses and plump poultry and game. Most of this excellent fare is produced locally, often in small-scale market gardens owned and worked by the stall-holder. Produce that has

Fresh local produce on sale in the market in Saumur's place St-Pierre

been grown locally is labelled *du pays*. Look out for unusual specialities, such as the strangely shaped squashes and pumpkins, wild mushrooms and flavoured honeys. Honey stalls often sell honey-flavoured confectionery and honey soap, too. Spice and herb stalls are also interesting, providing a wealth of gift ideas. Some markets have stalls selling clothes or shoes and leather goods. Look out also for local craft work.

Flea markets (*marchés aux puces*) are regular events in many towns and are often held in small towns and villages in countryside districts during the summer holiday season.

## VAT Rebates

If you are not a resident of the European Union, you are entitled to a rebate on value-added tax (*taxe à la valeur ajoutée* or *TVA*) for purchases totalling at least €175 in a single shop, on the same day, and taken out of the EU within three months. The export sales form you receive on purchase must be processed on your way out of France. Look for signs reading "Détaxe/Tax Refund" at the airport. Reimbursements usually go directly to your bank. Not all articles qualify for rebates. In stores frequented by foreign tourists, staff are familiar with the process. For more information, see p230.

Local goat's cheese for sale in Amboise market

see p230.

---

# DIRECTORY

## Regional Specialities

**Angers**
**La Petite Marquise**
22 rue des Lices.
Tel 02 41 87 43 01. **w** chocolat-lapetitemarquise.com
Quernons d'Ardoise and sweets.

**Bourges**
**La Maison des Forestines**
3 pl Cujas. Tel 02 48 24 00 24.
**w** forestines.fr
Forestines boiled sweets.

**Guérande**
**Terre de Sel**
Pradel. Tel 02 40 62 08 80.
**w** terredesel.fr
Guérande salt.

**Nantes**
**La Friande**
12 rue Paul Bellamy. Tel 02 40 20 14 68. **w** lafriande.fr
Nantaise biscuits.

**Orléans**
**Chocolaterie**
**La Duchesse Anne**
38 rue du Faubourg Bannier.
Tel 02 38 53 02 77. Chocolates.

## Arts and Crafts

**Chartres**
**La Galerie du Vitrail**
17 rue du Cloître Notre-Dame.
Tel 02 37 36 10 03. **w** galerie-du-vitrail.com Stained-glass panels and associated items.

**Gien**
**Faïencerie de Gien**
78 pl de la Victoire.
Tel 02 38 05 21 05.
**w** gien.com Porcelain.

**Malicorne**
**Faïenceries d'Art du Bourg-Joly**
16 rue Carnot. Tel 02 43 94 80 10.
**w** malicorne.com Pottery.

**Villaines-les-Rochers**
**Coopérative de Vannerie de Villaines**
1 rue de la Cheneillère.
Tel 02 47 45 43 03.
**w** vannerie.com
Wickerwork studio and shop.

# What to Buy in the Loire Valley

The best buys in the Loire tempt the eye as well as the stomach. A gourmet's paradise, the food shops and open-air markets of the region attract visitors with their delicious scents and sights. Local producers are justifiably proud of their goods and pack them with respect, in attractive crates or pottery jars. But gourmet treats are not the only local goods worth looking for. The region has long been famous for its china from Gien and for the fabric and lace of the Touraine, evocative of the remarkable history of the Loire.

A beautifully wrapped package of sweets

## Confectionery

Local confectionery specialities make good gifts to take home, especially when they are so prettily packaged. The region is well known for its wide range of sweets, which are available from tearooms and specialist confectioners, and many towns also have their own mouthwatering treats.

Macaron biscuits from Cormery

Forestines from Bourges

Pruneaux fourrés, prunes stuffed with marzipan

Chocolates resembling traditional slate tiles

Fruit-flavoured sweets

## Souvenirs

The châteaux and museums of the Loire Valley have well-stocked shops that sell an array of appealing souvenirs. In addition to the usual booklets and posters, many sell gifts with an historical theme, such as replica playing cards or tapestries. Wine bought direct from a local vineyard is another special souvenir (see pp34–5).

Playing cards with historical figures

Rosé wine

## Food and Drink

It is impossible to visit the Loire without being amazed by the abundance of delicious food. Much comes perfectly packaged for travelling. Near the game-filled forests of the Berry, you can buy jars and tins of pâtés and terrines. Goat's cheeses are moulded into a variety of shapes, and the firmer varieties travel successfully. Heather honey from Berry's heathland and wine vinegars from Orléans are also specialities of the region.

*Confiture de vin*, jelly made
from wine

Poulain chocolate made in Blois

Pickled samphire

Goat's cheese

Sea salt from Guérande

Crémant de Loire,
sparkling wine

*Cotignac*, quince jelly
from Orléans

## Local Crafts

Traditional crafts survive throughout the Loire Valley, and you can often visit craftsmen and women at work in their studios. Many towns in the region have long been renowned for their craft specialities, such as Malicorne for its lattice-work faïence, Villaines-les-Rochers for its baskets or Gien for its china.

Pottery from La Borne
in Berry

Gien china side plate

Wicker basket from Villaines

Dinner plate from Gien

# ACTIVITIES IN THE LOIRE VALLEY

A holiday in the Loire Valley can combine the cultural highlights of visits to the spectacular châteaux with enjoyment of the region's wealth of natural environments. The gentle terrain and beautiful forests are perfect for exploration on foot, horseback or mountain bike, and the clear waters of the lakes and rivers – not to mention the spectacular Atlantic coastline – are enticing spots for swimming or boating. Here is a selection of the activities on offer in the region. For more information, contact the relevant county or local tourist office *(see p227)*, which will be able to provide full details about the activities available in their area.

## Walking

The Loire Valley is renowned for its many accessible and scenic walks, which are called *Randonnées (see pp32–3)*. Although these routes are generally clearly signposted, it is a good idea to carry a large-scale map or a Topo-Guide. These are only available in French but do contain maps, a description of the itinerary, details of sites of architectural or natural interest to be found along the route, an estimate of the time it will take you to complete the walk and the addresses of local hotels, restaurants, hostels and camp sites. Most Topo-Guides cost around €15. A complete list is available from the **Fédération Française de la Randonnée Pédestre**.

You will never be more than a day's walk away from a town or village where you will be able to find food and accommodation, so it is not necessary to carry a large amount of equipment, but, as always, you should wear good, strong walking shoes. Remember that some paths can be damp and muddy during the spring and autumn.

## Cycling

The generally flat landscape of the Loire Valley makes it perfect for cyclists. Because many of the châteaux are so near to each other, it is easy to visit several by bicycle in only a few days. Mountain bike enthusiasts will enjoy riding the clearly signposted paths through the region's forests and nature reserves.

Motorways and some major roads are forbidden to cyclists; the sign has a white background with a red border and a cyclist in the middle. Cycle lanes, when they exist, are compulsory. Bicycles must have two working brakes, a bell, a red rear reflector and yellow reflectors on the pedals, as well as a white front light and a red rear light after dark.

It is also advisable to wear a helmet and to carry essential spare parts in case of break-down. While bicycle shops are common, foreign spare parts may not be available.

It is possible to hire touring bicycles and mountain bikes throughout the region. Local tourist offices will be able to provide you with a list of cycle hire centres.

Transporting your bicycle on local trains is free in most cases, although on major train routes the SNCF requires you to register your bicycle and will levy a small charge. The booklet *Train et Vélo*, available at most train stations, gives more information on carrying bikes on trains, and you can also visit the useful website, www.velo.sncf.com.

Among the many excellent itineraries for cyclists, the most ambitious is *Loire à Vélo*, a trail tracking the River Loire from Cuffy, near Nevers, to Saint-Nazaire. The route has a dedicated website, www.cycling-loire.com. There are numerous bike hire outlets along the trail, with the possibility of one-way rentals. Hotels, camp sites and *chambres d'hôtes* marked with the *Accueil Vélo* sign welcome cyclists and will forward luggage to the next stop if required. A handbook with maps and accommodation listings is available from local tourist offices or seek out specialist information via the regional and county *(département)* tourist boards *(see pp227 and 240)*.

Cycling, one of the most pleasant ways to see the Loire Valley

A riverside pony trek in the beautiful Vendée region

The **Fédération Française de Cyclisme** is the umbrella organization for more than 2,800 cycling clubs in France. They can provide advice and cycling itineraries if you contact them well in advance.

## Horse Riding and Pony Trekking

Horse lovers will enjoy a visit to the National Riding School in the equestrian town of Saumur, where the world-famous Cadre Noir riding team perform in regular displays *(see p87)*, or to the national stud farm, Le Haras de Vendée, in La Roche-sur-Yon.

The forests of the Loire Valley, with their well-maintained networks of trails and well-marked bridle paths, are ideal for riding. Topo-Guides are as useful for riders as they are for walkers.

Experienced riders can hire horses by the hour, half-day or day from numerous stables in the region. A sign reading *Loueur d'Equidés* means that horses are for hire without an instructor. If you prefer to be accompanied when riding, you should search out an *Ecole d'Equitation* or a *Centre Equestre* (riding school).

Many stables offer longer treks on horseback, called *randonnées*, which last between a weekend and a week. Small groups are accompanied on the trek by an experienced guide, and accommodation is usually in quite basic hotels or hostels, although some luxury tours are also available.

The rental of old-fashioned horse-drawn caravans is becoming increasingly popular in the Loire Valley. Travellers sleep in the carriage overnight and journey at a slow, leisurely pace during the day. Generally caravans come in two sizes: the smaller one carries four adults or two adults and three children; the other carries six to eight people. There are also larger, open wagons, driven by a guide, that are used for group excursions of up to 15 people.

Freshwater fish

## Fishing

The rivers of the Loire Valley are teeming with fresh-water fish, including bream, bullhead, carp, grey mullet, perch, pike, roach and zander. There are also trout in some of the faster-running tributaries of the Loire.

To fish in private waters, you must make arrangements with the owner. To fish in state-controlled waters, you must buy a permit, which is available from many tackle shops. Applicants must provide proof that they are a member of an angling association at home and pay a fishing tax.

There are two kinds of fishing tax: the basic tax covers fishing with worms in rivers that do not have trout runs; the special tax covers spinning, fly-fishing, and fish-bait fishing in all rivers, including those with trout. You cannot fish more than half an hour before sunrise or after sunset. There are set seasons for certain fish and limits on their size.

The **Fédération Nationale pour la Pêche en France**, which represents more than 4,000 local fishing associations, provides information on the regulations regarding fresh-water fishing and the starting dates of the different fishing seasons in France. Ocean fishing is free from any tax as long as you do not use nets, although there are restrictions on the equipment a boat can carry.

Fly-fishing on the tranquil River Loir

## Golf

Evidence of the growing popularity of golf in France can be seen throughout the Loire Valley, which has many beautiful and challenging courses. Some of the region's golf courses are set in the grounds of châteaux. Details of specific courses and regulations are available from the **Fédération Française de Golf**.

In the Loiret, many courses around Orléans have joined up to provide a golf pass that combines greens fees for the different courses and the added option of accommodation in nearby two- or three-star hotels (see the website www.golf tourismloiret.com). This is just one of such deals on the website catering to golfing tourists.

A similar deal is available in the Western Loire, where a pass offers reductions at golf courses near Nantes such as Golf Nantes Erdre (tel 02 40 59 21 21) and Golf Nantes Carquefou (tel 02 40 52 73 74). Contact the Nantes tourist office (see p231) or the participating golf courses for more information.

## Boating and Water Sports

Because the Loire Valley is crisscrossed with beautiful rivers, most visitors cannot resist the temptation to take at least one boat trip. A wide variety of short excursions are available from riverside ports de plaisance (marinas) throughout the Loire region, and in general they do not require advance booking.

The marshes of the Marais Poitevin (see pp186–9) are best viewed from its canal network in a barque (the traditional, flat-bottomed boat).

One option is to base your entire visit on the water by renting a houseboat or a cruiser for a period of a few days or for one or two weeks. Boats of different sizes and styles are available, from old-fashioned canal boats to sophisticated modern cruisers. Most prices are for round trips and include bedding, kitchen equipment and full training, and it may also be possible to rent bicycles or canoes, or to make a one-way (simple) trip. Further information is available from the main tourist offices.

If you are looking for a more adventurous way of enjoying the region's rivers, try canoeing or kayaking. It is best to take a guided tour. Although a river may look calm, there can be dangerous undercurrents and obstacles. **Fédération Française de Canoë-Kayak** can help to provide information. There are

Kayaking on the River Mayenne

good activity centres beside many of the rivers and lakes in the Loire Valley, and there may also be facilities for renting pedaloes, canoes and yachts – some centres even offer water-skiing. A good place to source information on sailing and surfing is the **Fédération Française de Voile.** There are also many Atlantic resorts where visitors are able to hire windsurfing equipment.

Swimmers should stay in the approved areas. While the sandbanks may look inviting, there are risks from strong currents and shifting sands. Further information on water safety is given on pages 234–5.

Windsurfing at La Tranche-sur-Mer on the Atlantic coast

## The Loire from the Air

One of the most luxurious ways to see the Loire Valley is from a hot-air balloon (*montgolfière* in French). There are daily flights in the summer, weather permitting, from Tours, Nantes and Amboise. **France Montgolfières** will put together custom-made excursions.

You can also take a tour in a helicopter or light aircraft. In addition to major airports at Tours and Nantes, there are many other airfields throughout the region. The tourist offices provide complete information. Flying lessons are also available at some of these centres. Learning to fly in France can be much cheaper than elsewhere. Details can be obtained from the **Fédération Française Aéronautique**. Visitors interested in gliding or hang-gliding should contact the **Fédération Française de Vol Libre**.

Ballooning over Le Plessis-Bourré in Anjou

# DIRECTORY

## Departmental Tourist Offices

**Cher**
11 rue Maurice Roy, 18023 Bourges.
**Tel** 02 48 48 00 18.
W berryprovince.com

**Eure-et-Loir**
10 rue Docteur Maunoury, 28000 Chartres.
**Tel** 02 37 84 01 01.
W tourisme28.com

**Indre**
pl Eugène Rolland Bat 1, 36003 Châteauroux.
**Tel** 02 54 07 36 36.
W berryprovince.com

**Loir-et-Cher**
W coeur-val-de-loire.com

**Loire-Atlantique**
W ohlaloireatlantique.com

**Loiret**
8 rue d'Escures, 45000 Orléans. **Tel** 02 38 78 04 04. W tourisme loiret.com

**Maine-et-Loire**
W anjou-tourisme.com

**Mayenne**
84 av Robert Buron, 53003 Laval. **Tel** 08 20 15 30 53. W mayenne-tourisme.com

**Sarthe**
31 rue Edgar Brandt, 72000 Le Mans. **Tel** 02 43 40 22 60. W tourisme-en-sarthe.com

**Vendée**
W vendee-tourisme.com

## Walking

**Fédération Française de la Randonnée Pédestre**
64 rue du Dessous des Berges, 75013 Paris.
**Tel** 01 44 89 93 93.
W ffrandonnee.fr

## Cycling

**Fédération Française de Cyclisme**
Vélodrome National de Saint-Quentin-en-Yvelines, 1 rue Laurent Fignon, 78069 Montigny le Bretonneux.
**Tel** 08 11 04 05 55.
W ffc.fr

## Horse Riding

**Fédération Française d'Equitation**
Parc Equestre, 41600 Lamotte. **Tel** 02 54 94 46 00. W ffe.com

## Fishing

**Fédération Nationale pour la Pêche en France**
17 rue Bergère, 75009 Paris. **Tel** 01 48 24 96 00.
W federationpeche.fr

## Golf

**Fédération Française de Golf**
68 rue Anatole France, 92309 Levallois Perret.
**Tel** 01 41 49 77 00.
W ffgolf.org

## Boating and Water Sports

**Fédération Française de Canoë-Kayak**
87 quai de la Marne, 94340 Joinville le Pont Cedex. **Tel** 01 45 11 08 50.
W ffcanoe.asso.fr

## Fédération Française de Voile
17 rue Henri-Bocquillon, 75015 Paris.
**Tel** 01 40 60 37 00.
W ffvoile.org

## The Loire from the Air

**Fédération Française Aéronautique (FFA)**
155 av de Wagram, 75017 Paris.
**Tel** 01 44 29 92 00.
W ff-aero.fr

**Fédération Française de Vol Libre**
4 rue de Suisse, 06000 Nice.
**Tel** 04 97 03 82 82.
W federation.ffvl.fr

**France Montgolfières**
4 bis rue du Saussis, 21140 Semur-en-Auxois.
**Tel** 03 80 97 38 61.
W france-montgolfieres.com

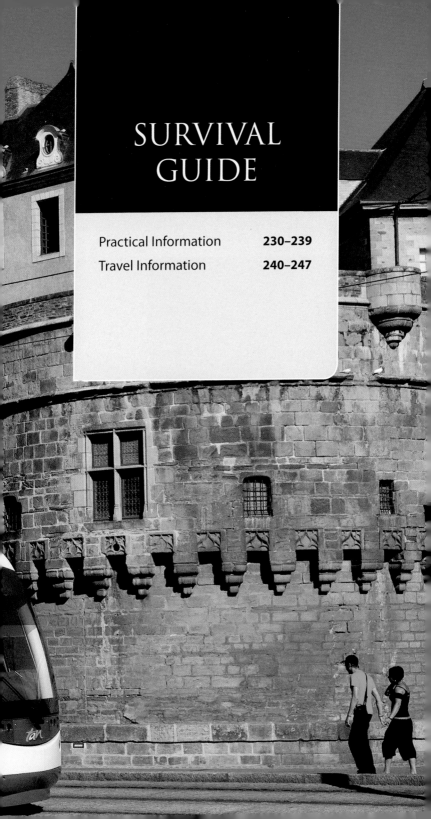

# SURVIVAL GUIDE

# PRACTICAL INFORMATION

The Loire Valley is very well prepared to meet the practical needs of its many visitors, providing accommodation ranging from five-star hotels and private châteaux to small camp sites, as well as a selection of excellent restaurants. Because of the profusion of places of great historical, aesthetic or natural interest, from stunning châteaux and cathedrals to windswept Atlantic beaches and wild marshlands, it is a good idea to draw up a list of priority sites you would like to visit and activities you want to experience before you travel. Also, check the entries in this guide of the places you plan to visit, or their websites, to make sure they won't be closed for seasonal breaks or for restoration work. With a wide variety of both outdoor and indoor pursuits available, the Loire Valley has something to offer all visitors. The following tips and suggestions will help you make the most of your visit.

Sunseekers enjoying the beach at La Baule

## When to Go

As elsewhere in France, the peak holiday period in the Loire Valley is from mid-June to the end of August, when the region's many festivals and *son et lumière* shows are in full swing (*see p46–47*). On the downside, main attractions may be crowded and inland temperatures can soar into an uncomfortable range – the maximum temperature can reach up to 38 °C (100 °F). In May, September and October, the weather is generally mild and sunny, although you may need an umbrella; November through to April are the rainiest months. When packing, think of layers of clothing you can easily add or remove during the day. While the winters are warmer than in Paris, they are still grey, cold and often wet. The advantage of this season, however, is having the famous châteaux that remain open practically to yourself.

## Visas and Passports

There are no visa requirements for citizens of the European Union. Visitors from the United States, Canada, Australia and New Zealand who are staying in France for less than 90 days need not apply for a visa. After 90 days, a *visa de long séjour* is required. Visitors from non-EU countries should request visa information from the French authorities in their own country before departure. Those intending to spend a good length of time in other European countries belonging to the Schengen agreement may want to apply for a 3-, 6- or 12-month Schengen visa, instead of obtaining individual visas for each country.

## Customs Information

There is no limit to the amount of money visitors may take in or out of France. However, if you are carrying cash worth more than €10,000 you should declare it to French customs. There are no longer restrictions on the quantities of duty-paid and VAT-paid goods you are allowed to take from one EU country to another, as long as you are over 18 and the goods are for your own use (not for resale). Customs officers may ask you to prove that the goods are for your personal use if they exceed 10 litres of spirits, 90 litres of wine, 110 litres of beer or 800 cigarettes.

If you are resident outside the EU, you can reclaim the TVA (VAT or sales tax) on certain goods, as long as you spend more than €175 (including tax) in the same shop in one day (exceptions are food and drink, medicines, tobacco, cars and motorbikes). When you make a purchase, show your passport, and the retailer will give you an export sales form. You should specify whether you want a cash refund or a payment into your bank account. When leaving France, scan this form at a PABLO barcode reader (located in airports and at ports). If you have asked for a refund in cash, go to the nearby reimbursement window. If in doubt about the system, check with customs.

French perfumes, available tax-free

◀ A modern tram on the historic streets of Nantes

Tourist information office in
Fontenay-le-Comte

## Tourist Information

Most towns have a tourist information office, known either as the *Syndicat d'Initiative* or the **Office de Tourisme**. This guide provides the address, telephone number and website of the tourist office in each town featured in its pages. Smaller villages often have inter-communal offices and websites. Tourist offices supply free maps, advice on accommodation (which can include booking hotels), and offer information on regional recreational and cultural activities, as well as details on upcoming concerts, festivals and other events. For a list of the main branches, see p233. You can also obtain details from French Government Tourist Offices before leaving your own country.

Local papers and magazines can provide details of festivals and sporting events as well as the regional weather forecast. They are available at news-agents (*maisons de la presse*) and some tobacconists' shops (*tabacs*).

## Admission Prices

Churches and cathedrals sometimes ask for a donation or charge a small admission fee to visit cloisters, bell towers and crypts. Museums, attractions and châteaux generally charge admission, from around €3 to €20. There are numerous special passes for museums and monuments, generally available from local tourist offices. In some cases, online discounts are offered if you book in advance. Some museums and monuments are free for one day a month, usually the first Sunday; some may also offer reductions on particular days. Call ahead or check the relevant website before you depart.

There are usually discounts available for students who have valid International Student Identity Cards (ISIC) *(see p232)*. Anyone under 18 years of age can also be eligible for a price reduction, and EU citizens under 25 are admitted free to French national monuments. A few sites offer discounts for seniors too.

## Opening Hours

Most shops, banks, museums and attractions are open from 8:30 or 9am until noon, and from 2 or 3pm until 4:30pm (shops usually stay open longer, until 6:30 or 7:30pm), Tuesday to Saturday. In larger towns, however, many shops, chain stores and supermarkets are open all day, as are the more popular museums and châteaux, especially in the summer. Restaurants may close for one day a week, so do check before setting off *(see pp216–19)*.

Off season, some seaside resorts, as well as many châteaux, smaller sites and museums, close down; telephone ahead or check the website for details.

Cathedrals and churches open daily but may shut for lunch or be closed to visitors during religious services. National museums and sights normally close on Tuesday, with a few exceptions that close on Monday. Opening times can also vary considerably by season, especially for country châteaux, estates and gardens. Most are closed on Christmas Day and New Year's Day, and many also close on the public holidays of 1 May and 1 and 11 November.

## Etiquette and Language

It is important to respect the French rituals of politeness. When you are introduced to someone, it is correct to shake hands with them. In shops, say *bonjour* to the assistant before asking for what you want, and then *merci* when you receive your change and finally *au revoir, bonne journée* (goodbye, have a nice day) when you depart. The usual greeting among friends of either gender is generally two or three "air'" kisses on the cheek.

Particularly in smaller communities, all efforts by English speakers to make enthusiastic use of their French, however limited, and to show a real interest in the area will be met with encouragement by the locals.

When visiting a church or religious institution, dress respectfully (avoid short skirts and shorts and bare shoulders).

Smoking in France is banned inside bars, restaurants, trains and stations, but still allowed in outdoor cafés. Many hotels are non-smoking or have non-smoking rooms. It's illegal for anyone under 18 to buy cigarettes or alcohol.

Friends greeting each other with two or three kisses

## Public Conveniences

Free public and wheelchair-accessible *toilettes publiques* (WCs) are most often found in town centres. They can be located by a *mairie* (town hall) or covered market, in train stations and in public parks. Larger cities have modern, self-cleaning toilets on street corners, which usually charge a small fee. Always carry a small packet of tissues with you.

Museums and shopping centres also have free public toilets, while cafés and bars often reserve their facilities for customers only.

## Taxes and Tipping

In France, sales (or value-added) taxes are incorporated into prices. For most goods the tax rate is about 20 per cent; food, books and restaurant meals are taxed at a reduced rate of 10 per cent. The city tax on accommodation (*taxe de séjour*) can be up to €1.50 per person per day. At cafés and restaurants, a 15 per cent service charge is included in the bill, but an extra few coins for good service is appreciated. Round up taxi fares and tip porters a couple of euros. It's customary to give a small tip to theatre ushers and tour guides.

## Travellers with Special Needs

Although the steep, narrow streets in the Loire Valley's medieval villages can be a problem, wheelchair access in the region is generally good. A number of châteaux and museums offer special services for disabled visitors; phone ahead and check before your visit. Access to and within hotels and restaurants has greatly improved, and well-marked disabled parking spaces are easy to find.

The **SNCF Accessibilité Service** and **Association des Paralysés de France (APF)** are good resources for practical help and information about facilites. **Les Compagnons du Voyage** provides companions to accompany disabled travellers on train journeys. **Handitec-Handroit**'s website (in French) provides information about the legal provisions in France for disabled travellers, and lists other useful websites.

## Travelling with Children

The Loire Valley is an ideal destination for families. Many châteaux and gardens have play areas and provide activities for children, as well as offering family discounts. There is a wide range of accommodation for families to choose from: camp sites, self-catering *gîtes*, hotels and B&Bs with family or connecting rooms.

Nearly all restaurants offer children's menus (*menus enfants*). Many families choose to eat their biggest meal at lunch because prices are lower, and most restaurants don't serve dinner until 7:30 or 8pm, which may be late for small children.

## Student and Senior Travellers

Students who hold a valid **International Student Identification Card** (ISIC card) can benefit from discounts of 50 per cent or more at museums, theatres, cinemas and many public monuments, as well as the same discounts available to anyone in France aged 25 or under.

Senior travellers are eligible for discounts on trains and buses throughout the region and occasionally at museums and monuments; carry identification just in case. For extensive travel, a senior rail pass (€60; valid for a year) is a worthwhile purchase as it offers savings of 25 to 50 per cent on train tickets. However, for a relatively short visit to the region the best way to save money is through the SNCF Prems tickets (*see p243*).

An ISIC international student card

## Time

The Loire Valley is one hour ahead of Greenwich Mean Time (GMT). France is in the same time zone as Germany, Italy, Spain and other Western European countries.

The French use the 24-hour clock (they do not use the am and pm system): after midday, just continue counting 13, 14 and so on to provide the 24-hour clock time. For example, 1pm = 13:00.

## Electricity

The voltage in France is 220 V. The plugs on French electrical appliances have two small round pins; the heavier-duty appliances have two large round pins. Some upmarket hotels offer built-in adaptors for shavers only.

Multi-adaptors, which are useful because they have both large and small pins, can be bought at most airports

A family rowing passed the embankment of Arcais harbour in Marais Poitevin

before departure. Standard adaptors can be purchased from most department stores.

## Conversions

**Imperial to metric**
1 inch = 2.54 centimetres
1 foot = 30 centimetres
1 mile = 1.6 kilometres
1 ounce = 28 grams
1 pound = 454 grams
1 pint = 0.6 litre
1 gallon = 4.6 litres

**Metric to imperial**
1 millimetre = 0.04 inch
1 centimetre = 0.4 inch
1 metre = 3 feet 3 inches
1 kilometre = 0.6 mile
1 gram = 0.04 ounce
1 kilogram = 2.2 pounds
1 litre = 1.8 pints

## Responsible Tourism

With its wide, green spaces and mild climate, the Loire Valley is known as the garden capital of France. As such, the region is dedicated to maintaining its beautiful landscape and is involved with conservation schemes including the Loire Nature scheme, which works to restore the region's river and nature reserves and conserve its biodiversity.

As well as the dozens of parks, formal gardens and vegetable gardens to visit, the region is also home to Europe's first horticultural theme park, **Terra Botanica**, designed to make botany fun and to provide education on the environment.

The area is also a leader in the *bio* (organic) movement. Two organizations, **Biocentre** and **Bio Pays de la Loire**, provide detailed lists of markets, farms and other suppliers of organic products. Many towns also have a **Biocoop**, which sell organic food.

The Loire Valley offers visitors the chance to stay and eat on local farms, where families prepare meals using their own produce. An easy way to locate farms that provide these services is through two umbrella organizations: **Accueil Paysan** and **Bienvenue à la Ferme**. Another way to support the local economy is to stay at locally owned B&Bs, *gîtes* or at one of the growing number of eco-lodges. **It's a Green Green World** is a great resource for visitors as it has a comprehensive catalogue of eco-friendly accommodation.

# DIRECTORY

## Customs Information

**Info Douane Service**
Tel 08 11 20 44 44.
w douane.gouv.fr

## Consulates and Embassies

**Australia**
4 rue Jean Rey, 75724 Paris. Tel 01 40 59 33 00.
w france.embassy.gov.au

**Canada**
35 av Montaigne, 75008 Paris. Tel 01 44 43 29 00.
w canada international.gc.ca

**Ireland (Eire)**
12 Ave Foch, 75116 Paris. Tel 01 44 17 67 00.
w embassyofireland.fr

**New Zealand**
103 rue de Grenelle, 75007 Paris. Tel 01 45 01 43 43. w nzembassy. com/france

**United Kingdom**
35 rue du Faubourg St-Honoré, 75383 Paris. Tel 01 44 51 31 00.
w ukinfrance.fco.gov.uk

**United States**
2 av Gabriel, 75382 Paris. Tel 01 43 12 22 22.
w france.usembassy.gov

## Tourist Offices

**Angers**
7 pl Kennedy.
Tel 02 41 23 50 00.
w angersloire tourisme.com

**Blois**
23 pl du Château.
Tel 02 54 90 41 41.
w bloispaysde chambord.com

**Bourges**
21 rue Victor–Hugo.
Tel 02 48 23 02 60.
w bourges-tourisme.com

**Chartres**
8 rue de la Poissonerie.
Tel 02 37 18 26 26.
w chartres-tourisme.com

**Le Mans**
Rue de l'Etoile.
Tel 02 43 28 17 22.
w lemanstourisme.com

**Nantes**
Rue des Etats.
Tel 08 92 46 40 44.
w nantes-tourisme.com

**Orléans**
2 pl de l'Etape. Tel 02 38 24 05 05. w tourisme-orleans.com

**Tours**
78 rue Bernard Palissy.
Tel 02 47 70 37 37.
w tours-tourisme.fr

## Tourist Websites

w us.rendezvousen france.com (US)

w int.rendezvousen france.com (Rest of the World)

## Travellers with Special Needs

**Association des Paralysés de France**
Tel 01 40 78 69 00.
Tel 02 41 34 81 34 (Angers)
Tel 02 38 43 28 53 (Orleans)
Tel 02 47 37 60 00 (Tours)
w apf.asso.fr

**Handitec-Handriot**
w handroit.com

**Les Compagnons du Voyage**
Tel 01 58 76 08 33.
w compagnons.com

**SNCF Accessibilité**
Tel 08 90 64 06 50.
w accessibilite.sncf.com

## Student Travellers

**International Student Identification Card**
w isic.org

## Responsible Tourism

**Accueil Paysan**
Tel 04 76 43 44 83.
w accueil-paysan.com

**Bienvenue à la Ferme**
Tel 01 53 57 11 50.
w bienvenue-a-la-ferme.com

**Biocoop**
w biocoop.fr

**Bio Pays de la Loire**
Tel 02 41 18 61 40.
w biopaysdelaloire.fr

**Biocentre**
Tel 02 38 71 90 52.
w bio-centre.org

**It's a Green Green World**
w itsagreengreen world.com

**Terra Botanica**
Rte de Cetenay-Epinard, 49106 Angers.
Tel 02 41 25 00 00.
w terrabotanica.fr

# Personal Security and Health

On the whole, the Loire Valley is a safe place for visitors, but it is always a good idea to take the normal precautions of keeping an eye on your possessions at all times, and avoid isolated and unlit urban areas at night. If you fall ill during your stay, pharmacies are an excellent source of advice, while the emergency services can be contacted for any serious medical problems. Consular offices can also offer help in an emergency.

French police officers

## Police

Violent crime is not a major problem in the Loire Valley, but as in any destination it is advisable to be on your guard against petty theft, especially in cities. If you are robbed, lose any property or are the victim of any other crime, you must report the incident as soon as possible at the nearest police station (*commissariat de police*). In an emergency, dialling 17 will also connect you to the police, but you will still have to go to a station to make a statement. In small towns and villages, crime is reported to the *gendarmerie*, the force responsible for rural policing.

At police stations you will be required to make a statement, called a *procès verbal* (PV), listing any lost or stolen items. You will need your passport and, if relevant, your vehicle papers. (Keep copies of your passport and papers in a different part of your luggage, in case the originals are lost or stolen.) Remember to keep a copy of your police statement for your insurance claim.

## What to be Aware of

As with elsewhere, if travelling late at night it is a good idea, especially for women, to remain within busy, well-lit areas and to be careful about talking to, or accompanying, strangers. If you are involved in a dispute or car accident, avoid confrontation, try to stay calm and speak French if you can to diffuse the situation.

Most of the beaches on the Atlantic coast are guarded in the summer by lifeguards (*sauveteurs*). There are a number of good family beaches where bathing is not generally dangerous. Look for the system of coloured flags: green flags mean that bathing is permitted and is safe; orange flags warn that bathing may be dangerous and usually that only part of the beach is guarded. The guarded area is marked out by flags, beyond which you should not swim. Dangerous conditions (high waves, shifting sands and strong under-currents) are denoted by red flags, which mean that bathing is strictly forbidden. Many of the region's beaches also display blue flags, used throughout the European Union to indicate cleanliness.

The River Loire and its tributaries may tempt summer bathers but, generally, avoid the temptation, as treacherous currents and shifting sands are associated with these rivers.

## In an Emergency

The phone number for all emergency services is 112, but in practice it is often quicker to call the relevant authority direct on their traditional two-digit numbers. In a medical emergency call the **Service d'Aide Médicale Urgente** (SAMU), who will send an ambulance. However, it can sometimes be faster to call the **Sapeurs Pompiers** (fire service) who also offer first aid and can take you to the nearest hospital. This is particularly true in rural areas, where the fire station is likely to be much closer than the ambulance service based in town. If you do call out an ambulance, the paramedics are called *secouristes*.

## Lost and Stolen Property

In big cities, try not to carry conspicuous valuables with you and only take as much cash as you will need. In major towns, most multistorey car parks are kept under surveillance by video cameras. Parking there will reduce the threat of anything being stolen from your car and avoids the risk of parking in an illegal space and being towed away to a police pound.

For lost or stolen property, it may be worth returning to the

Police car

Fire engine

Ambulance

police station where you reported the incident to check if they have retrieved anything. In addition, all French town halls have a *Bureau d'Objets Trouvés* (lost property office), although they are often inefficient. Lost property offices can also be found at larger train stations, which will be open during office hours. In all cases, leave a contact name and number in case the item is found.

If your passport is lost or stolen, notify your consulate immediately. The loss of credit or debit cards should also be reported as soon as possible to avoid fraudulent use.

## Hospitals and Pharmacies

All EU nationals holding a European Health Insurance Card (EHIC) are entitled to use the French national health service. Under the French system patients must pay for all treatments up front and then reclaim most of the cost from their health authorities. Therefore, non-French EU nationals who use health services in France will need to ensure they keep the statement of costs (*fiche*) that is provided by the doctor or hospital. The statement should include stickers for any prescription drugs, which must be affixed to the statement by the pharmacist once you have made your purchase. Around 80 per cent of the cost can be claimed back – follow the instructions provided with your EHIC card or by taking the paperwork to the nearest *Caisse Primaire d'Assurance Maladie* (CPAM; French National Health Service) office; there is one in each *département* (county) capital.

Non-EU nationals must have full private medical insurance and pay for services in the same way, claiming their costs back later on insurance.

All cities have hospitals with emergency departments (*urgences* or *service des urgences*). If your hotel cannot direct you to

one, call the ambulance or fire service. Your consulate should be able to recommend an English-speaking doctor if you need one; in Paris, there are both American and British private hospitals.

Pharmacies can be identified by an illuminated green cross, and there are many located throughout the region. French pharmacists are highly trained and can diagnose minor health problems and suggest treatments.

**Pharmacy sign**

## Minor Hazards

The summer sun in the Loire Valley is strong, so don't be caught out: use at least SPF 30 sunscreen and wear a hat.

Mosquitoes can be nuisances in the summer, especially in camp sites, so come prepared. In July and August, gardens, lawns and meadows can be infested with red harvest mites or chiggers (*aoûtats*), which are too tiny to see but attach themselves to the skin, causing red bumps and a terrible itch. Avoid them by wearing loose clothing and taking showers as soon as possible after walks in the country; if bitten, apply benzyl benzoate (available at pharmacies) to clean the area.

## Travel and Health Insurance

All travellers in France should have a comprehensive travel insurance policy providing adequate cover for any eventuality, including potential medical and legal expenses, theft, lost luggage, accidents, travel delays and the option of immediate repatriation by air in the event of a major medical emergency. Adventure sports are not covered by standard travel policies so if you are planning to undertake any extreme sports in the Loire Valley you will need to pay an additional premium to ensure you are protected. All insurance policies should come with a 24-hour emergency number.

# DIRECTORY

## Emergency Numbers

**All emergency services**
Tel 112.

**Ambulance (SAMU)**
Tel 15.

**Fire (Sapeurs Pompiers)**
Tel 18.

**Police (Gendarmerie)**
Tel 17.

## Lost & Stolen Property

**Blois**
51 rue Garenne. **Tel** 02 54 90 27 62.

**Nantes**
Mairie de Nantes (Town Hall).
**Tel** 02 40 41 90 00.

**Orléans**
Hôtel Groslot, pl de l'Étape.
**Tel** 02 38 79 27 23.

**Tours**
SNCF train station.
**Tel** 02 34 74 72 59.

## Hospitals and Pharmacies

**Angers Hospital**
4 rue Larrey. **Tel** 02 41 35 36 37.
W chu-angers.fr

**Bourges Hospital**
145 av François Mitterand.
**Tel** 02 48 48 48 48.
W ch-bourges.fr

**Le Mans Hospital**
194 av Rubillard.
**Tel** 02 43 43 43 43.
W ch-lemans.fr

**Nantes Hospital**
5 allée l'Île Gloriette.
**Tel** 02 40 08 33 33.
W chu-nantes.fr

**Orléans Hospital**
14 av Hôpital. **Tel** 02 38 51 44 44.
W chr-orleans.fr

**Pharmacie de garde**
**Tel** 3237 (or call the Gendarmie).

**Tours Hospital**
2 blvd Tonnellé. **Tel** 02 47 47 47 47.
W chu-tours.fr

## General

**French National Health Service (CPAM)**
Tel 36 46. W ameli.fr

**European Health Insurance Card (EHIC)**
W ehic.org.uk

# Banking and Local Currency

The easiest way to settle bills or convert money is by using credit or debit cards. Most French banks no longer exchange foreign currency or travellers' cheques, but be aware that withdrawing cash from an automated teller machine (ATM) may incur extra changes. It is possible to save on transaction fees by using Travel Money Cards, which provide a safe and convenient way to access your holiday savings.

## Banks and Bureaux de Change

Generally speaking, banks open from 9am to noon and from 2 to 4:30pm, Tuesday to Saturday. Most are closed on Monday. Over public holiday weekends, banks may be shut from noon Friday until Tuesday morning. Be aware that opening hours can be more limited in smaller towns.

If you need to exchange cash, look for *bureaux de change* offices in airports and busy tourist areas. Desks in central post offices will also exchange foreign currency into euros. Exchange rates can be quite variable.

In some banks, it is also possible to withdraw cash using debit and credit cards at the counter, although there may be charges from your bank. You will need your passport or some form of identification to make the transaction.

An automated teller machine (ATM)

## ATMs

The simplest and most convenient way to obtain cash in France is by using a credit or debit card in one of the many automated teller machines (ATMs) found at airports, train stations, banks and shopping malls, as well as other places. To withdraw money, you will need to enter your four-digit PIN (Personal Identification Number, or *code confidentiel*). ATM instructions are usually given in several languages, including English.

It's always a good idea to tell your bank that you are travelling overseas, and the country or countries you plan to visit, so your card isn't blocked for security reasons. Also ask if your bank has a partnership with a French bank, allowing you to withdraw cash from their ATMs without paying transaction fees.

## Credit and Debit Cards

In France, the most common credit cards are **Visa** and **MasterCard**, while **American Express** cards are not always accepted. Keep a spare credit card in a different place as an emergency backup and keep a record of your card's 16-digit number (found on the front of the card). If your card is lost or stolen, ring to cancel it as soon as possible; knowing the card number will make the replacement process much easier.

French credit and debit cards operate on a chip-and-PIN system so you will need to know your PIN (*code personnel*). If you have a North American card that does not use chip-and-PIN technology you must ask that your card be swiped. Most ATMs and retailers have machines that read both smart cards and older magnetic strips in a *bande magnétique* (magnetic reader).

Very few banks will cash travellers' cheques, and so, for the most part, they have now been replaced by prepaid Travel Cards (or Cash Passports). Available from Visa, MasterCard and other companies, these cards can be topped up online in the local currency. Like credit and debit cards, they come with PINs that allow users to access cash in ATMs and are protected if stolen or lost. Bear in mind, however, that ATMs may run out of notes during weekends.

## DIRECTORY

### Bureaux de Change

**Angers**
Office de Tourisme, 7 pl Président Kennedy. **Tel** 02 41 23 50 00.

**Blois**
La Poste, 2 rue Gallois.
**Tel** 36 31.

**Bourges**
La Poste Principale,
29 rue Moyenne. **Tel** 36 31.

**Chartres**
Ghislaine Laufray Brisson, 3 rue Bethlem. **Tel** 02 37 36 42 33.

**Nantes**
Le Change Graslin, 17 rue Jean-Jacques. **Tel** 02 40 69 24 64.

**Orléans**
La Poste, pl de Gaulle.
**Tel** 36 31.

**Tours**
La Gare (train station),
pl du Maréchal Leclerc.
**Tel** 02 47 66 78 89.

### Lost and Stolen Cards

**American Express**
**Tel** 01 47 77 70 00.

**MasterCard**
**Tel** 0800 90 13 87.

**Visa**
**Tel** 0800 90 11 79.

## The Euro

The euro (€) is the common currency of the European Union. It went into general circulation on 1 January 2002, initially for 12 participating countries. France was one of those countries, and the franc was phased out. EU members using the euro as sole official currency are collectively known as the Eurozone. Several EU members opted out of joining.

Euro notes are identical throughout the Eurozone countries, each one including designs of fictional architectural structures and monuments. The coins, however, have one side identical (the value side) and one side with an image unique to each country. Both the notes and coins are exchangeable in the participating countries.

## Bank Notes

*Euro bank notes have seven denominations. The €5 note (grey in colour) is the smallest, followed by the €10 note (pink), €20 note (blue), €50 note (orange), €100 note (green), €200 note (yellow) and €500 note (purple). All notes show the 12 stars of the European Union.*

5 euros

10 euros

20 euros

50 euros

100 euros

200 euros

500 euros

2 euros

1 euro

50 cents

20 cents

10 cents

5 cents

2 cents

1 cent

## Coins

*The euro has eight coin denominations: €1 and €2; 50 cents, 20 cents, 10 cents, 5 cents, 2 cents and 1 cent. The €2 and €1 coins are both silver and gold in colour. The 50-, 20- and 10-cent coins are gold. The 5-, 2- and 1-cent coins are bronze.*

# Communications and Media

French telecommunications are among the most advanced in the world, with high-speed internet available in most hotels, cafés and Wi-Fi hotspots. Although public telephones are rare, mobile networks are far-reaching and efficient. Post offices, or *bureaux de poste*, are identified by the blue-on-yellow La Poste sign. Foreign newspapers are available in most large town newsagencies, and some TV channels broadcast English-language programmes.

## International and Local Telephone Calls

All French public phone boxes take phone cards (*télécartes*) and most accept credit cards. Phone cards are sold in units of either 50 or 120 minutes, and have easy-to-use instructions. They can be purchased at post offices, tobacconists (*tabacs*) and some newsagents. With the advent of mobile phones, however, pay phones have become hard to find, apart from at airports and train stations, and most villages still have at least one phone box located centrally.

To call a number in France, simply dial the 10-digit number, always including the two-digit area code. Landline numbers in the Loire Valley begin with 02. Cheap rates operate from 7pm to 8am Monday to Friday, as well as all day Saturday, Sunday and public holidays. French mobile numbers begin with 06, and 08 indicates a special-rate number.

To make an international call from France, dial 00 and then the country code. Avoid making international calls from hotels, as they tend to add a hefty surcharge.

## Mobile Phones

French mobile phones use the European-standard 900 and 1900 MHz frequencies, so most European mobiles will work if they have a roaming facility enabled. North American mobile phones will only operate in France if they are tri- or quad-band; otherwise, another option is to buy a GSM phone and insert a French SIM card. Always check roaming charges with your service provider before

An Orange France mobile phone shop and Wi-Fi hotspot

travelling. Some companies offer "packages" for foreign calls, which can work out cheaper.

If you expect to use your phone frequently it can be more economical to get a pay-as-you-go French mobile from one of the local providers such as **Bouygues Télécom**, **SFR**, **Orange France** or **Free Mobile**, who have shops in most towns. You can topup your phone in post offices, supermarkets and at ATMs. It is possible to use a local SIM card in your own phone if it has not been blocked by your service provider.

## Internet

France has an extensive network of Wi-Fi internet hotspots (sometimes called *point Wi-Fi* or *borne Wi-Fi*), making it easy for visitors with laptop, notebook or tablet devices to get online and stay in touch through VoIP services such as **Skype** and **Viber**. Inevitably, Wi-Fi hotspots are concentrated in cities rather than the countryside. Most

### Useful Dialling Codes and Numbers

- To **call France**: from the UK and US: 00 33; from Australia: 00 11 33. Omit the first 0 of the French area code.
- Special numbers: 08 indicates a **special rate number**; all 0800 numbers are free to call. Most cannot be called from outside of France. 09 numbers are dedicated to **VoIP** (Voice-over-Internet Protocol), which are charged as local calls.
- For **operator service** and local directory enquiries, dial 118 218 or visit www.118218.fr.
- For **international directory enquiries**: 118 008.
- To make direct international calls, dial 00 first.
- The **country codes** are: Australia: 61; Canada and US: 1; Ireland: 353; New Zealand: 64; UK: 44.
- In the event of an **emergency**, dial 112.

hotels provide Wi-Fi access for the use of guests (check if there is a fee before use), while other hotspots can be found in airports, train stations, motorway service areas and libraries. Internet cafés are on the decline and are being replaced by conventional bars and cafés offering wireless internet access. If you need to find Wi-Fi access, check the online resources such as the **Wi-Fi Hotspot Directory** that can direct you to your closest hotspot. A fee may be charged for internet access; check the directory first for more information. **Orange WiFi** has a pay-as-you-go service, which is easy to use and widely available.

If you need to use a cable connection (which may be the case in a holiday home), note that the French modem socket is incompatible with US and UK plugs. Adaptors are available, but it is often cheaper and easier to buy a French modem lead.

Mailboxes throughout France are a distinctive yellow

## Postal Service

The postal system in France is fast and usually reliable. There are main offices in all cities, and branches in every town; in villages, however, there may just be a substation (*Relais Poste*) in a local shop, identified by a small **La Poste** sign. Postage stamps (*timbres*) are available at La Poste offices and tobacconists, sold either individually or in a *carnet* (book of 10 stamps). Letters are dropped into yellow mailboxes, which often have three slots – one for the town you are in; one for the surrounding *département* (the Loire Valley is divided into 11 *départements*, each with its own postcode) and one for other destinations (*autres destinations*).

La Poste sells useful parcel boxes (*colissimo*), including special wine bottle packaging. Also, large branches have internet terminals. To use them, buy a rechargeable prepaid card at the counter.

Post office hours vary. The minimum hours are from 9am to 5pm from Monday to Friday with a two-hour lunch break from noon to 2pm. On Saturday they are open from 9am until noon. Post offices in larger towns may open on weekdays from 8am until 7pm.

The postal service offers Chronopost courier services, guaranteeing next-day delivery for domestic mail and "as soon as possible" for international. For rapid worldwide delivery consider a private courier such as **DHL**, which has a wide presence in France and offices in Nantes and Orléans.

## Newspapers and Magazines

Newspapers and magazines can be bought at newsagents (*maisons de la presse*) or news-stands (*kiosques*). Regional newspapers such as *Ouest France* and *La Nouvelle République* tend to be more popular than Paris-based national papers such as the conservative *Le Figaro*, weighty *Le Monde* or leftist *Libération*.

English-language newspapers such as the *International Herald Tribune*, the *Guardian* and the *Financial Times* are often available for sale on the day of issue. Other English newspapers as well as Swiss, Italian, German and Spanish titles are sold on the day of publication in summer months and a day later out of season.

Many *départements* have listings magazines, usually in French and often free, which can be found at tourist offices. Websites listing local events include Culture Pays de la Loire (www.culture.pays delaloire.fr); also check the "What's On" listings on the AngloInfo websites (www.loire.angloinfo. com and www.centre.angloinfo. com). Les Inrocks (www.les inrocks.com) has information on music, film and arts events for the whole of France.

## Television and Radio

France has digital television rather than analogue, so there is a large range of free-to-air channels available. The most popular are commercial stations TF1 and M6, followed by the government channels France 2 and France 3, the latter offering daily regional programming. The Franco-German channel ARTE broadcasts programmes and films from all over the world, often in the original language with French subtitles. A film shown in its original language is listed as *VO* (*Version Originale*); a film dubbed into French is indicated as *VF* (*Version Française*). Most TVs allow you to switch from a dubbed version to a *VO* version.

*Canal Plus* (or *Canal+*) is a popular subscription-only channel that offers a broad mix of programmes, including live sports and a good range of films in English with French subtitles. Many hotels and holiday homes subscribe to *Canal+* and also pick up BBC World, CNN, Sky, MTV and other satellite channels.

UK radio stations available in France include *Radio 4* (198 long wave). Details for the BBC World Service can be found at www. bbc.co.uk/worldservice. *Voice of America* can be found at 90.5, 98.8 and 102.4 FM. *Radio France International* (738 AM) usually gives daily news in English from 3 to 4pm.

## DIRECTORY

### Mobile Phones

**Bouygues Télécom**
Tel 31 06.
W bouyguestelecom.fr

**Free Mobile**
Tel 1044.
W free.fr

**Orange France**
Tel 1014 or 09 69 36 39 00 (English speaking).
W orange.fr

**SFR**
Tel 1023.
W sfr.fr

### Internet

**Orange Wifi**
Tel 08 10 55 54 21 (24-hour assistance in English).
W orange-wifi.com

**Skype**
W skype.com

**Viber**
W viber.com

**Wi-Fi Hotspot Directory**
W hotspot-locations.com

### Postal Service

**DHL**
Nantes: Aéroport de Nantes Atlantique, rue de la Tour.
Orléans: 9 rue Henri Becquerel.
Tel 08 25 10 00 80.
W dhl.fr

**La Poste**
Blois: 2 rue Gallois.
Nantes: 10 bis rue Copernic.
Orléans: pl Général de Gaulle.
Tours: 67 rue Victoire.
Tel 36 31.
W laposte.com

# TRAVEL INFORMATION

Forming a broad band about 110 km (70 miles) south of Paris and stretching from the centre of France in the east to the Atlantic coast in the west, the Loire Valley is well served by international airports, motorways and rail links. The city of Nantes has a major international airport with flights operating to many major European cities; airlines from Britain and Ireland also serve Tours and Angers. For travelling across the region, the TGV rail service *(see pp242–4)* is a swift option; and the motorways are excellent, if a little crowded in summer. There are also many more green travel options to explore, such as cycling through the region.

## Green Travel

The Loire Valley offers a number of ways to lighten your carbon footprint. Rather than fly, travel by train or coach. It may take longer but there's no baggage surcharge and both coaches and trains go direct to city centres.

The regional train service is excellent, however bus services beyond main towns are patchy. An exception is the shuttle between the châteaux of Blois, Chambord, Cheverny and Beauregard run by **Transports du Loir-et-Cher** from April to September. Tourist boards also offer green initiatives such as the "Loire Valley Without a Car" package, organized by the **Tourist Office of Blois Pays de Chambord**, where tourists are taken on a three-day tour of the region, travelling by horse-drawn carriage, coach and a return train journey. Accommodation is included in the price.

The Loire is ideal for cycling. There are bike-rental schemes in Nantes and Orléans (**Bicloo** and **Vélo'+**), and excellent bike trails and **Voies Vertes** (paths along former railway lines) in rural areas. A network of lanes link Niort and the Marais Poitevin, while **La Loire à Vélo** follows the Loire River and is part of the **EuroVelo6** route that will one day link the Atlantic to the Black Sea. Along the way, bike-friendly hotels (*Velotels*), camp sites (*Velocamps*) and *gîtes* (*Velogite*) offer bike garages, repair kits and cycle hire. The **Châteaux à Velo** website has more information.

Among the many other self-guided cycling tours are Châteaux à Velo, **Loire Life Cycling Holidays** and **Randovelo**, which both arrange cycling tours in the region.

## Arriving by Air

The Loire Valley has three airports but Paris can be just as convenient an arrival point, particularly if you plan to start your visit in the east of the region. **Angers Airport** and **Tours Airport** receive flights from Ireland and the UK. However, the region's main gateway is **Nantes-Atlantique Airport**, which has flights from many European cities and Canada.

From Canada, **Air Canada** and **Air France** fly direct to Paris; while **Air Transat** flies from Montreal to Nantes (May to October). Several airlines fly direct to Paris from the US. **Qantas** provides connecting flights to Paris from Australia and New Zealand. If flying into London Heathrow to transfer onto a flight to the Loire Valley, be aware that connecting flights may leave from one of London's four other airports; check carefully before booking your tickets to allow yourself enough time.

**British Airways** operates from London Heathrow to Paris, and from London City to Angers. Air France flies to Paris from Dublin, Edinburgh and regional English airports; it also has transfers from Paris to Nantes. **easyJet** flies to **Paris Charles de Gaulle** from a number of British airports; and, in summer, from London Gatwick to Nantes.

**Ryanair** links Nantes to Shannon and Dublin; and also Tours to Dublin, London Stansted and other English city airports in peak season. **Flybe** connects Manchester and London Gatwick to Nantes, and Southampton to **Paris Orly**.

## Tickets and Fares

European budget airlines Ryanair, Flybe and easyJet offer the cheapest flights, especially if booked well in advance. Low-season promotional fares can cost next to nothing – at least until check-in and baggage fees are added. Fares on full-service airlines, such as British Airlines and Air France, can be reasonable too if booked early; prices are at their highest over the Easter period and in July and August. Long-haul prices tend to shoot up in July and August as well; save money by shopping around online well in advance.

Travellers check departure boards at Paris Orly Airport

## On Arrival

French airport formalities are usually straightforward. All arrivals must be in possession of a valid passport and, if necessary, a visa *(see p230)*. Non-EU citizens have to fill out a landing card to hand over at passport control. If you want to bring anything unusual into the country (especially large amounts of cash), check French embassy websites regarding prohibited items *(see p233)*. There is no departure tax.

Air France airbus 380

## Transport from Paris Airports

From Charles de Gaulle or Orly airports you can get to the Loire Valley by public transport, hire car or a domestic flight. If you hire a car, however, Orly is a better option as the airport is closer to the Loire Valley than Charles de Gaulle is.

Charles de Gaulle has its own TGV (high-speed train network) station in Terminal Two, linked to the other terminals by a free shuttle. From there, trains go directly to the Loire Valley. From Orly, take an Air France shuttle bus to Montparnasse station in Paris, then take a TGV train to your destination.

## Transport from Regional Airports

Buses leave every half hour from Nantes Airport to the main train station (€7.50). After each Ryanair flight lands at Tours, a coach take passengers to the city centre (€6.50). There is no public transport from Angers Airport. Taxi services to central Angers will cost about €45, to Nantes €40 and to Tours €35. Car rental companies have outlets at all airports.

## Package Deals

If you are flying with Air France into Paris's Charles de Gaulle Airport, save time and money by purchasing a combined flight-train TGVAir ticket to Angers, Le Mans, Nantes or Tours (for further details, visit the Air France website). Other companies, such as **Cresta Holidays**, offer tailor-made package holidays in the Loire Valley with flights, car hire and accommodation all included. **InnTravel** offer self-guided walking, cycling and skiing package deals.

---

# DIRECTORY

## Green Travel

**Bicloo**
Ⓦ bicloo.nantes
metropole.fr

**Châteaux à Velo**
Ⓦ chateauxavelo.com

**EuroVelo6**
Ⓦ eurovelo6.org

**La Loire à Vélo**
Ⓦ loireavelo.fr

**Loire Life Cycling Holidays**
Ⓦ loirelifecycling.com

**Randovelo**
Ⓦ randovelo.fr

**Tourist Office of Blois Pays de Chambord**
Ⓦ bloispaysde
chambord.com

**Transports du Loir-et-Cher**
Ⓦ tlcinfo.net

**Vélo'+**
Ⓦ agglo-veloplus.fr

**Voies Vertes**
Ⓦ voiesvertes.com

## Arriving by Air

**Air Canada**
France: **Tel** 0825 880 881.
UK: **Tel** 0871 220 1111.
Ⓦ aircanada.com

**Air France**
France: **Tel** 36 54.
UK: **Tel** 020 7660 0337.
Ⓦ airfrance.com

**Air Transat**
**Tel** 0825 120 248.
Ⓦ airtransat.com

**Angers Airport**
**Tel** 02 41 33 50 20.
Ⓦ angersloire
aeroport.fr

**British Airways**
France: **Tel** 0825 82 54 00.
UK: **Tel** 0844 493 787.
Ⓦ britishairways.com

**easyJet**
France: **Tel** 0820 420 315.
UK: **Tel** 0330 365 5000.
Ⓦ easyjet.com

**Flybe**
France: **Tel** 03 92 26 85 29.
UK: **Tel** 0871 700 2000.
Ⓦ flybe.com

**Nantes-Atlantique Airport**
**Tel** 08 92 56 88 00.
Ⓦ nantes.aeroport.fr

**Paris Charles de Gaulle**
**Tel** 33 1 70 36 39 50
(outside France).
France: **Tel** 39 50.
Ⓦ aeroportsdeparis.fr

**Paris Orly Airport**
**Tel** 33 1 70 36 39 50
(outside France).

France: **Tel** 39 50.
Ⓦ aeroportsdeparis.fr

**Qantas**
France: **Tel** 01 57 32 92 83.
UK: **Tel** 0800 964 432.
Ⓦ qantas.com

**Ryanair**
France: **Tel** 0892 562 150.
UK: **Tel** 0871 246 0000.
Ⓦ ryanair.com

**Tours Airport**
**Tel** 02 47 49 37 00.
Ⓦ tours.aeroport.fr

## Package Deals

**Cresta Holidays**
**Tel** 0844 800 720.
Ⓦ crestaholidays.co.uk

**InnTravel**
**Tel** 01653 617 001.
Ⓦ inntravel.co.uk

**Great Escapes**
**Tel** 0845 330 2084.
Ⓦ greatescapes.co.uk

# Travelling by Train

Travelling to the Loire Valley by train is fast and efficient. The French state railway, the *Société Nationale des Chemins de Fer Français* (SNCF), is one of Europe's best equipped and most punctual. The journey from Paris to Nantes or Tours is quick – *Trains à Grande Vitesse* (TGV) travel at up to 300 km/h (185 mph) and reach Nantes in 2 hours and 10 minutes, Tours in just 55 minutes. With the Eurostar high-speed service running through the Channel Tunnel, London to the Loire Valley by train takes around 4 to 5 hours.

Automatic ticket machine

### Railway Network

The main train routes to the Loire Valley from northern Europe pass through Paris. If arriving in Calais, the **TGV** network links the port with Paris Gare du Nord station. From there, passengers must transfer to Gare Montparnasse, before continuing their journey on the TGV Atlantique to the main towns in the Loire region. **Eurostar** passengers can change at Lille Europe station and transfer directly to a TGV for the Loire Valley. Check schedules online.

SNCF logo

**Intercité** express trains to Nantes also leave from Gare Montparnasse, while Intercité express trains to all other Loire Valley destinations leave from Gare d'Austerlitz. Tickets from London to towns within the Loire Valley, travelling via the Eurostar or ferry, are available online from the **SNCF** website or the SNCF office in London. From southern Europe, trains run to Nantes from Madrid (with a journey time of around 18 hours) and Milan (around 11 hours). SNCF's everyday trains are known as **TER** (Transport Express Régional).

Within the Loire Valley, the scenic route along the River Loire via Nantes, Angers and Orléans is popular, so reserve tickets in advance on this and other main rail lines *Grandes Lignes*.

### Main Stations

Located in the city centre, Nantes train station (*Gare de Nantes*) has two station exits: the Sortie Sud (south exit) brings you out in the Cité des Congrès district;

the Sortie Nord (north exit), in the Jardin des Plantes.

In Tours, most trains stop at the suburban station of St-Pierre-des-Corps, from which a *navette* (shuttle train) takes passengers into the town centre station in 10 minutes.

A similar shuttle service operates in Orléans, where many mainline trains arrive at Les Aubrais station, 3 km (2 miles) outside the town centre. In both cases, the price of the shuttle is included in the cost of the train ticket, and shuttles are timed so they coincide with mainline services. Before board-ing, check whether the departure time given on your ticket is for the shuttle or the mainline train.

### Reservations

Europe's main railways share a computer system, making it easy to check timetables and book Eurostar and French trains online through the SNCF website. If you

need to alter your return date, you may have to pay for another reservation unless you book a more expensive flexible ticket. When purchasing tickets, especially for travel outside the peak Easter or summer holiday seasons, check the Eurostar website for package deals that combine train travel with hotel stays and hire cars.

Besides ticket counters, there are also ticket and reservation machines (with English instructions) at main stations. A reservation differs from a ticket as it only reserves a seat, whereas you always need a valid ticket to travel. A ticket reservation is necessary when travelling on TGV, but this can be made as little as 5 minutes before the train leaves. Ticket prices for all trains rise at peak times, and reservations are compulsory during public holidays.

TGVs have two price levels for second class, normal and peak, and a single level for first class.

SNCF train arriving at Tours train station

The cost of the obligatory seat reservation is included in the ticket price. Tickets for other trains have just one price level for both first and second class. Seat reservations, where available, are included.

You can pick up reserved tickets from the counters or machines in the station, print them out at home or have them posted to you for free.

## Tickets

The best way to save money on TGV travel is by buying "Prems" (Saver) tickets, available 120 days to 14 days before travel. Those who book earliest get the biggest discounts; if you have to change plans, however, the cheapest tickets may not be refundable. Sometimes there are last-minute specials on certain destinations; check the rail websites *(see p244).*

If you intend to take several journeys while in France, you may be better off purchasing a discount travel card or a rail pass online. SNCF rail cards *(cartes)* give up to 50 per cent discount on fares for qualifying passengers. The *Carte Enfant+* is for children up to the age of 12; the *Carte 12–25* is for those between 12 and 25 years of age; the *Carte Escapades* for ages 26–59; and the *Carte Senior* is for anyone over 60. SNCF also caters for travellers with special needs *(see p232).*

Rail passes give unlimited travel within a specified period of time for a one-off fee but they must be purchased in your own country. There are two types: "global" cards cover several European countries, and "one country" passes are just for travel within one country. For European residents these passes are called Interrail and to non-European residents Eurail. For further details, visit the SNCF website (or the Rail Europe website if you are a North American resident).

## Bicycles

On TER trains, bicycles are carried free. On TGVs and Intercités, they should be dismantled, placed in a bag and stored in luggage spaces. If your train has a bicycle symbol next to its timetable listing, it will have designated areas for bikes, which you can book for €10. In Les Sables d'Olonne, Tours, Chinon, Amboise, Blois, Langeais, Beaugency and Onzain, it is possible to pre-book a bicycle *(Train + Vélo)* to await you at your destination.

## TGV Rail Service

*Trains à Grande Vitesse,* or high-speed trains, travel at up to 300 km/h (185 mph). Their speed and comfort make them relatively expensive. You must always reserve a seat in advance, the cost of which depends on your destination and the time and date of your journey.

### Key

—— High-speed lines

— Other lines

= = High-speed line under construction

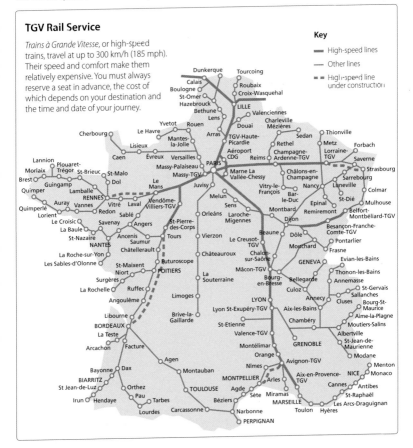

Eurostar train speeding through the French countryside

## Timetables

Timetables change twice a year, and leaflets for main routes are free at train stations.When reading French train timetables, pay particular attention to any footnotes, which may be indicated by a number or letter at the top of the column. *Circule tous des jours* means a train runs every day; *Sauf dimanche et jours fériés* translates not on Sundays or public holidays. Double-check the train time when you arrive at the station in case there is a delay. Coaches replace trains if lines are being repaired, or when not many passengers are expected (look for a bus symbol on the timetable). The status of the train will be displayed on a panel over the entrance to the platforms. If train workers have voted for strike action (*grève*) it will always be announced days in advance. If your TGV or Intercité train is more than 30 minutes late, and it's the fault of the SNCF, you are eligible for a 25 per cent refund; 50 per cent if the train is over 2 hours late or 75 per cent if over 3 hours late. Ask for an *enveloppe régularité*, or download the form online (aide.voyages-sncf.com).

Yellow validating machines (*composteur*) are located in station halls and on platforms. Before boarding, insert tickets and reservations separately, printed side up, and it will punch your ticket and print the time and date on the back. A penalty may be imposed by inspectors if you fail to do this.

## Eurostar

Eurostar currently runs about 15 services per day between London's St Pancras International Station and the Gare du Nord in Paris. Each train has two classes: Standard, and Standard Premier or Business Premier (both first class) which include Wi-Fi access and waiter-served meal. All passengers have access to a buffet car where refreshments can be bought. The journey takes 2 hours and 15 minutes. Tickets must be booked in advance and checked in at least 20 minutes before the departure time. For a variety of discount schemes check the Eurostar website.

Children under 4 travel for free (on your lap), and there are special rates for ages 4–11, 12–25 and over 60. To book, contact the Rail Europe office in London, ring the Eurostar bookings line or visit their website. You can also download a free mobile app for smart-phones that allows passengers to make bookings and check in using paperless mobile tickets.

## Eurotunnel

The **Eurotunnel** shuttle service carries cars and coaches and their passengers through the Channel Tunnel in 35 minutes. Tickets can be booked through travel agents, by calling the Eurotunnel Customer Service Centre or online. You can also purchase a ticket for the next train when you arrive at the terminals in Folkestone or Calais, but it is advisable to prebook your tickets. Fares are per car, with up to nine passengers allowed; special trains are reserved to carry large caravans (book in advance). Check online for discounted offers; the best fares will always be in the off-peak period (from Folkestone, 4pm to 5:59am; from Calais, midnight to 1:59pm). There are four trains an hour during peak times and every two hours during the night. All terminals have shops and restaurants. Before boarding you go through passport and customs controls for both countries.

## DIRECTORY

### Railway Network

**Eurostar**
France: **Tel** 08 92 35 35 39.
UK: **Tel** 08432 186 186.
ⓦ eurostar.com

**Eurotunnel**
France: **Tel** 08 10 63 03 04.
UK: **Tel** 08443 353 535.
ⓦ eurotunnel.com

### SNCF

**Intercité**
**Tel** 36 35.
ⓦ sncf.com/fr/trains/intercites

**Rail Europe USA**
44 South Broadway,
White Plains, NY 10601.
**Tel** 1 800 622 8600.
ⓦ raileurope.com

**SNCF**
**Tel** 36 35. ⓦ sncf.com;
ⓦ voyages-sncf.com

**TER**
**Tel** 0800 83 59 23 (Centre region);
**Tel** 08 10 32 43 24 (Pays de la Loire region).

**TGV**
**Tel** 36 35.
ⓦ tgv.co.uk

**Voyages SNCF Europe (for Eurostar and onward bookings)**
193 Piccadilly, London W1J 9EU.
**Tel** 0844 848 5848.
ⓦ uk.voyages-sncf.com

# Travelling Around by Road

France is a motorist's paradise, and the main routes to the Loire Valley are via an excellent, if expensive, tolled autoroute (motorway) network. There are many beautiful roads in the Loire region, particularly those running along the banks of the rivers. Popular routes, especially along the Atlantic coast and the roads leading between the châteaux, can be busy in high season. The minimum age for driving in France is 18 and for renting a car is 21.

## What to Take

If you are taking your own car, it is compulsory to take the original registration document, a current insurance certificate and a valid driving licence. You should also carry a passport or identification card. If your car is not fitted with number plates showing the country of registration, a sticker indicating this must be displayed on the rear of the vehicle. The headlights of right-hand-drive cars must be adjusted – kits for this are available at most ports. You must also have a red warning triangle and a reflective jacket (inside the car, not in the boot), as well as a breathalyzer kit. Other accessories you should take include spare headlight bulbs, a first-aid kit and a fire extinguisher.

The best general maps of the Loire Valley are the orange **Michelin** regional maps (No. 517 for the Pays de la Loire and No. 518 for Centre). **IGN** (*Institut Géographique National*) also produces two good touring maps covering this area: Central France (R08) and Pays de la Loire (R07).

Town plans are usually free at local tourist offices. More detailed town maps are published by Michelin or **Blay Foldex**. In the UK, **Stanfords** in London sells a range of maps and travel books. Those with tablet, smartphone or Android devices will find a wide choice of map apps online.

## Getting to the Loire Valley

Travellers from the UK arriving at Calais and Boulogne can avoid Paris by taking the A16 motorway south to Abbeville and then the A28 via Rouen to Le Mans. At Le Mans, take the A11 for Chartres, Angers and Nantes, or head across country to Tours, Blois and Orléans. Alternatively, brave Paris and take the A1 south, skirt around the city centre and connect with the A10 for Orléans and Tours, and the A11.

From western Spain, take the A8 from San Sebastian to the border, the A63 to Bordeaux and the A10 to Tours and Orléans. From the eastern Spanish coast you can reach Orléans on the A9, A62 and A20, via Narbonne and Toulouse. From Italy take the A8 and A7 or the A43 to Lyon, where the A72 and A71 head north to Bourges and Orléans. From anywhere in Germany, the quickest way to get to the Loire Valley is via Paris.

There are three main motorways in the Loire Valley: the A11 (*L'Océane*) from Nantes to Chartres via Angers; the A10 (*L'Aquitaine*) from Tours to Orléans via Blois; and the A71 from Orléans to Bourges. There are police stations located at motorway exits. In high season, the motorways get crowded and, if you have time, it may be worth taking more minor (and often more attractive) roads. Try not to travel over the first weekend in July and the last weekend in August when French holidays start and finish and hordes of holiday-makers are on the roads.

## Rules of the Road

Remember to drive on the right. Also be aware of *priorité à droite* in French towns, meaning traffic coming from streets to your right, unless halted by a white line and/or stop sign, has right of way. Seat belts are compulsory for both front and back seats. Overtaking when there is a single solid centre line is heavily penalized. Instant fines are issued for speeding, and driving with over 0.05 per cent of alchohol in the blood is illegal. There are many speed cameras along French roads. Signs warn drivers that they are coming up, but these signs may disappear soon. The police also carry out random speed checks.

Unless otherwise signposted, speed limits are as follows:
- **Toll motorways** 130 km/h (80 mph), 110 km/h (68 mph) in wet weather;
- **Dual carriageways and non-toll motorways** 110 km/h (68 mph), 100 km/h (60 mph) in wet weather;
- **Other roads** 90 km/h (56 mph), 80 km/h (50 mph) in wet weather;
- In **towns** and in **heavy fog** 50 km/h (30 mph).

No entry for any vehicles

One-way system

Give way at roundabouts

Right of way ends, give way to right

## Autoroute Toll

When you drive through a tollway to join an **autoroute**, take a ticket from the machine. This identifies your starting point on the tollway; you do not pay until you reach an exit tollbooth (*gare de péage*). Charges are made according to the distance travelled and the type of vehicle.

Major toll areas have two or three staffed booths, allowing you to pay with coins, notes and debit or credit cards. The majority of the area, however, is lined with automated machines that accept credit or debit cards and rarely coins as well. Insert your ticket into the machine and the price of your journey will be displayed in euros.

The scenic D751 route around Champtoceaux

## Great Drives

One of the pleasures of touring the Loire Valley is turning off the main routes onto the far more scenic country roads. The RN (*Route Nationale*) and D (*Départementale*) roads are marked in yellow or white on maps, and are often a good alternative to motorways. They are generally well signposted, however it is wise to carry a 1:250,000 map or a GPS. Popular drives include the riverside stretch of the D951, the D751 from Chambord to Tours and the 800 km (497 miles) of meandering wine roads, the *Routes Touristique du Vignoble* (see the **Vins Val de Loire** website for a map and guide).

**Bison futé** ("crafty bison") signs indicate alternative routes to avoid heavy traffic, and can be helpful during French school and public holiday periods, known as *grands départs*.

## Parking

Parking in large towns is strictly regulated. If you are illegally parked, your car may be towed, and you will have to pay a stiff fine to release it. For on-street parking, many towns in the Loire Valley have pay-and-display machines (*horodateurs*). Parking is usually free from noon to 2pm daily, overnight (7pm–9am), and on Sundays and public holidays, but it is always best to check.

Even if legally parked, you may find yourself hemmed in when you return to your car: the French usually honk their horn to attract the guilty party.

## Petrol

Petrol (*essence*) is relatively expensive in France, especially on autoroutes. Large supermarkets and hypermarkets tend to offer discounts so are more reasonable.

Many petrol stations in France are self-service (*libre service*). If otherwise, ask to the attendant to "*faire le plein*" (fill the tank).

Petrol stations sell two different qualities of unleaded petrol (*sans plomb*) as well as diesel (*gazole* or *gasoil*). Leaded petrol is no longer available, though some stations offer lead-replacement petrol (Super ARS) or a lead-substitute additive, if needed. LPG gas is also widely available.

Not all stations are open 24 hours, especially away from the big towns. Out of shopping hours, you can self-serve at supermarket petrol stations using a credit card at the pump.

## Breakdowns and Accidents

If you've had a breakdown, turn on your hazard lights, put on your reflective jacket and set up the red warning triangle 30 m (100 ft) behind the vehicle. On French motorways you are *not* expected to set out the triangle; get out of the right-hand side of the vehicle and onto the other side of the safety barrier as soon as possible. There are SOS phone boxes every 2 km (1 mile); walk to the nearest one, staying on the far side of the barrier. Pressing the button on the emergency phone will put you through to the emergency services. If you can't reach a box or have broken down off the motorway, dial 112 from a mobile phone to get help from the nearest *dépannage* (breakdown garage).

If your car is involved in a traffic accident with a French car, the driver should produce a form called a *constat à l'amiable* (European Accident Statement), which is used to record an agreed statement of events. If your French isn't up to filling this out, wait for a translator. Both drivers sign it and keep a copy. Post this to your insurer within five days of the accident.

Dial 17 for the police (*gendarmerie*) if someone is hurt or there is a dispute. You may have to accompany the other driver to the police station to make a statement (*procès-verbal* or *PV*). In case of a serious accident, dial 15 or 18 for an ambulance.

## Car Hire

Requirements for car hire vary, but in general you must be over 21 years old and have held a driving licence for at least a year. You will need to present your driving licence, passport and a credit card against a deposit. If you want automatic transmission, book well in advance.

**Europcar**, **Avis**, **Budget** and **Hertz** are the main companies in the region and all have offices in both Paris airports. It is worth contacting a number of firms before you leave for France, as there are often special offers if you prepay or book online. Price comparison websites, such as **Last Minute**, **Auto Europe** and **Car Rentals**, can also be useful for finding good deals. Other options include fly-drive packages, and train and car-hire deals from the SNCF, with collection from main train stations (*see p244*).

To hire a moped or motorbike, find the nearest **Holiday Bikes** outlet. Several companies rent out camper vans and motor homes, including **Avis Caraway** and **Hertz Trois Soleils**.

## Coach and Bus Travel

**Eurolines** operates coach services on Wednesday and Friday from London Victoria coach station to Tours, Angers and Nantes. The earlier you book, the cheaper the tickets. The rail operator **SNCF** often fills in gaps in its service with bus services. "Autocar" on a timetable indicates that a leg of the journey will be by bus.

Local buses operate from most towns' *gare routière* (bus station), often located near the main train station. Although bus services in the region are relatively good, timetables in rural areas tend to be geared towards the needs of local workers and schoolchildren. As a result, morning departures tend to be very early and services may not run on a daily basis. For more details on bus routes and timetables, contact local tourist information offices *(see p233)*.

## Taxis

Many taxis in rural areas are white and blue, and may double as an ambulance. In cities and large towns, vehicles can be various distinctive colours. Hailing a taxi is not customary in the Loire Valley; you must go to a taxi rank or book a car over the phone.

Prices for taxis tend to vary from one *département* to the next. The pick-up charge is usually around €2, followed by €1 or more for every kilometre (0.6 mile), depending on the time and day, and up to €30 per hour if stuck in traffic. There is an extra charge for luggage or for calling out a radio taxi. All taxis are required to carry wheelchair users for no extra charge and must use a meter (*compteur*). Most taxi drivers will accept four passengers.

**Taxis de France** is useful for ordering taxis, and lists the rates for each *département*.

## Hitchhiking

Hitchhiking in France is legal except on motorways, although it is possible to hitch from one service station to another. A modern internet-based alternative is *covoiturage*, or car-sharing. Via an organization such as **BlaBlaCar**, drivers can advertise for passengers to keep them company and share the costs of the journey. Pick-up and drop-off points are arranged between the two parties, and passengers give the driver a star-rating as a help to future users of the service.

A local bus driving through the streets of Nantes

# DIRECTORY

## What to Take

**Blay Foldex**
w blayfoldex.com

**IGN**
73 av de Paris,
94165 Saint-Mandé.
**Tel** 01 43 98 80 00.
w ign.fr

**Michelin**
w michelinonline.
co.uk/travel

**Stanfords**
12–14 Long Acre,
London WC2E 9LP.
**Tel** 020 7836 1321.
w stanfords.co.uk

## Autoroute Toll

**Autoroutes**
w autoroutes.fr

## Great Drives

**Bison Futé**
w bison-fute.
equipement.gouv.fr

**Vins Val de Loire**
w vinsvaldeloire.fr

## Car Hire

**Auto-Europe**
w auto-europe.co.uk

**Avis**
France: **Tel** 0821 230 760.
Nantes: **Tel** 0820 611 676.
Orléans: **Tel** 02 38 62 27 04.
UK: **Tel** 0808 284 0014.
w avis.fr

**Avis Caraway**
w aviscaraway.com

**Budget**
France: **Tel** 0825 00 35 64.
UK: **Tel** 808 284 4444.
w budget.fr

## Car Rentals

w carrentals.co.uk

**Europcar**
France: **Tel** 0825 358 358.
Nantes: **Tel** 02 40 84 01 39.
Orléans: **Tel** 02 38 63 88 00.
UK: **Tel** 0871 384 9900.
w europcar.fr

**Hertz**
France: **Tel** 0825 861 861.
UK: **Tel** 0843 309 3099.
w hertz.com

**Hertz Trois Soleils**
**Tel** 04 75 82 02 02.
w trois-soleils.com

**Holiday Bikes**
**Tel** 01 41 27 49 00.
w holiday-bikes.com

**Last Minute**
w car-hire.
lastminute.com

## Coach and Bus Travel

**Eurolines**
France: **Tel** 0892 899 091.
UK: **Tel** 0871 81 81 78.
w eurolines.com

**SNCF**
w voyages-sncf.com

## Taxis

**Taxis de France**
w taxis-de-france.com

## Hitchhiking

**BlaBlaCar**
w covoiturage.fr

# General Index

# Acknowledgments

Dorling Kindersley would like to thank the following people whose assistance contributed to the preparation of this book.

## Main Contributor
Jack Tresidder has been living and writing in France since 1992. A former newspaper journalist and theatre critic, he has edited and written books on art, cinema and photography as well as travel.

## Editorial Consultant
Vivienne Menkes-Ivry.

## Contributors and Consultants
Sara Black, Hannah Bolus, Patrick Delaforce, Thierry Guidet, Jane Tresidder.

## Additional Photography
Andy Crawford, Tony Gervis, Andrew Holligan, Paul Kenward, Jason Lowe, Ian O'Leary, John Parker, Jules Selmes, Clive Streeter.

## Additional Illustrators
Robert Ashby, Graham Bell, Stephen Conlin, Toni Hargreaves, The Maltings Partnership, Lee Peters, Kevin Robinson, Tristan Spaargaren, Ed Stuart, Mike Taylor.

## Cartography
Lovell Johns Ltd, Oxford.

## Technical Cartographic Assistance
David Murphy.

## Design and Editorial
Duncan Baird Publishers
*Managing Editor* Louise Bostock Lang
*Managing Art Editor* David Rowley
*Picture Research* Jill De Cet, Michèle Faram
*Researcher* Caroline Mackenzie
*DTP Designer* Alan McKee
Dorling Kindersley Limited
*Senior Editor* Fay Franklin
*Senior Managing Art Editor* Gillian Allan
*Deputy Editorial Director* Douglas Amrine
*Deputy Art Director* Gaye Allen
*Map Co-Ordinators* Michael Ellis, David Pugh
*Production* David Proffit
*Proof Reader* Sam Merrell
*Indexer* Brian Amos

## Revisions Team
Claire Baranowski, Sonal Bhatt, Tessa Bindloss, Poppy Body, Sophie Boyack, Samantha Cook, Imogen Corke, Dana Facaros, Anna Freiberger, Rhiannon Furbear, John Grain, Richard Hansell, Matt Harris, Julia Harris-Voss, Nicholas Inman, Lisa Jacobs, Gail Jones, Laura Jones, Nancy Jones, Maite Lantaron, Hayley Maher, Bhavika Mathur, Ciaran McIntyre, Rebecca Milner, Emma O'Kelly, Lyn Parry, Susie Peachey, Pollyanna Poulter, Erin Richards, Philippa Richmond, Ellen Root, Zoe Ross, Lokamata Sahoo, Alice Saggers, Sands Publishing Solutions, Susana Smith, Jill Stevens, Adrian Tierney-Jones, Conrad Van Dyk, Alison Verity, Dora Whitaker.

## Special Assistance
Mme Barthez, Château d'Angers; M Sylvain Bellenger, Château de Blois; Tiphanie Blot, Loire-Atlantique Tourisme; M Bertrand Bourdin, France Télécom; M Jean-Paul and Mme Caroline Chaslus, Abbaye de Fontevraud; M Joël Clavier, Conseil Général du Loiret; Mme Dominique Féquet, Office de Tourisme, Saumur; Katia Fôret, Nantes Tourisme; M Gaston Huet, Vouvray; Mme Pascale Humbert, Comité Départemental du Tourisme de l'Anjou; M Alain Irlandes and Mme Guylaine Fisher, Atelier Patrimoine, Tours; Mme Sylvie Lacroix and M Paul Lichtenberg, Comité Régional du Tourisme, Nantes; M André Margotin,

Comité Départemental du Tourisme du Cher; M Jean Méré, Champigny-sur-Veude, Touraine; Séverine Michau, Comité Régional du Tourisme Centre; Mme Marie-France de Peyronnet, Route Jacques-Cœur, Berry; M R Pinard, L'Ecole des Ponts et Chaussées, Paris; Virginie Priou, Comité Régional du Tourisme des Pays de la Loire; Véronique Richard, Vallée du Loir; Père Rocher, Abbaye de Solesmes; M Loïc Rousseau, Rédacteur, *Vallée du Loir*; M Pierre Saboureau, Lochois; Bertrand Sachet, Fédération Régionale de Randonnée Pédestre,Indre; M de Sauveboeuf, Le Plessis- Bourré; M Antoine Selosse and M Frank Artiges, Comité Départemental du Tourisme de Touraine; Mme Sabine Sévrin, Comité Régional du Tourisme, Orléans; Mme Tissier de Mallerais, Château de Talcy.

## Photography Permissions
Dorling Kindersley would like to thank the following for their assistance and kind permission to photograph at their establishments: M François Bonneau, Conservateur, Château de Valençay; M Nicolas de Brissac, Château de Brissac; Caisse Nationale des Monuments Historiques et des Sites; Conseil Général du Cher; Marquis and Marquise de Contades, Château de Montgeoffroy; M Robert de Goulaine, Château de Goulaine; Mme Jallier, Office de Tourisme, Puy-du-Fou; Château de Montsoreau, Propriété du Département de Maine-et-Loire; Musée Historique et Archéologique de l'Orléanais; M Jean-Pierre Ramboz, Sacristain, Cathédrale de Tours; M Bernard Voisin, Conservateur, Château de Chenonceau and all other churches, museums, hotels, restaurants, shops and sights too numerous to thank individually.

## Picture Credits
Key: a-above; b-below/bottom; c-centre; f-far; l-left; r-right; t-top.

Works of art have been reproduced with the permission of the following copyright holders: © ADAGP, Paris and DACS, London 2011: 81ca, 106tl, 154b; © DACS, London 2011: 52cla; © DACS, London and SPADEM, Paris: 108c

The publisher would like to thank the following individuals, companies and picture libraries for permission to reproduce their photographs:

**Air France:** 240br, 241tr; **Photo AKG, London:** 52br; Bibliothèque Nationale 54crb; *Catherine de Médicis* anon 16th-century 113tl; Stefan Diller 53bl; Galleria dell' Accademia *Saint Louis* Bartolomeo Vivarini 1477 54cl; Louvre, Paris *Charles VII* Jean Fouquet c.1450 51tl; Musée Carnavalet, Paris *George Sand* Auguste Charpentier 1839 28c; National Gallery, Prague *Self Portrait* Henri Rousseau 1890 29b; Samuel H Kress Collection, National Gallery of Art Washington *Diane de Poitiers in the Bath* François Clouet c.1571 112cla; **Alamy Images:** a la poste 239tl; Ni Anel 18c; Andrew Bargery 98br; Ian Dagnall 116bl; dgkphotography.com 24mt; Julian Elliott 242br; David R. Frazier Photolibrary, Brian Hartshorn 47cr; Hemis/CINTRACT Romain 228c; Hemis/GARDEL Bertrand 230cla; Hemis/RENAULT Philippe 146c, 232bl; Heritage Image Partnership Ltd / Fine Art Images 139bl; Inc 234cl; Jam World Images 36c; Neil Juggins 234crb, 242tr; Michael Juno 213 tl/c; Justin Kase zeightz 234cr; John Kellerman 134cr; Brigitte Merz 119tl; Minkimo 13br; Craig Roberts 204cl; Steve Vidler 79tl, 81tl; Didier Zylberyng 15tr. **Allsport:** Pascal Rondeau 63crb; **Ancient Art and Architecture Collection:** 28b, 54br, 55tl, 58tr, 59c; **Archives du Loiret:** 62clb; **AWL Images:** Hemis 2-3c; Karl Thomas 92c; Travel Pix Collection 122c.

**Y Berrier:** 81bl; **Bibliothèque Nationale, Dijon:** 153b; **Bibliothèque Nationale, Paris:** 56–7c; **Bridgeman Art Library:** Bibliothèque Nationale, Paris 51tc; British Library, London 50br, 56clb; Glasgow University Library 53bc; Kress Collection, Washington DC 51tr; Kunsthistorisches Museum, Vienna 58br; Louvre, Paris *François I* Jean Clouet 48; Musée Condé, Chantilly 50bl, 139b; Private Collection/Photo © Gavin Graham Gallery, London, UK 8-9; Scottish National Potrait Gallery, Edinburgh *Mary Queen of Scots in White Mourning* François Clouet 29c; State Collection, France 58bl; Victoria & Albert Museum, London 25tr; **Bridgeman Art Library/Giraudon:** 52ca; Château de

Versailles 60cla, *Louis XIV as Jupiter Conquering La Fronde* anon 17th century 138tr; Galleria degli Uffizi, Florence 58cla; Louvre, Paris *Henry IV Receiving the Portrait of Marie de Médicis* Peter Paul Rubens 59tl, 78b; Musée de Beaux-Arts, Nantes *The Corn Sifters* Gustave Colbert 196b; Tres Riches Heures du Duc de Berry, Limbourg Brothers (fl.1400-1416) Musée Condé, Chantilly 4br/29t; Musée Condé Chantilly 51bc/bl, 97b, *Gabrielle d'Estrées in her Bath* French School 17th century 100c; Musée d'Orsay, Paris *Marcel Proust* Jacques-Emile Blanche c.1891–2 28tc; Musée de la Venerie, Senlis *Diane de Poitiers as Diana the Hunter* Fontainebleau School 16th century 59crb; **British Museum:** 58–9.
**Cahiers Ciba:** 81crb; **Camera Press:** 81tr; **Cephas:** Stuart Boreham 67bl; Hervé Champollion 67cra, 156tr; Mick Rock 33crb; **Jean-Loup Charmet, Paris:** 49b, 55b, 61cra; **Château d'Angers:** Centre des Monuments Nationaux / Damien Perdriau 79bl; **Château d'Azay-le-Rideau:** Cadet-CMN 100cla; **Château Chambord:** Sophie Lloyd 136clb, 137cr/bl; **Château de Chamerolles:** 141cbl; **Château de Chenonceau:** Image de Marc 111crb; **Château de l'Abbaye:** Famille Renard 204bl; **Château de la Barre:** 205tl, 209br; **Château de Montgeoffroy:** 75cl; **Château de Rochecotte:** 207tr, 211tr; **Château de Vauloge:** 200bl; **Château des Briottieres:** 206bl; **Château des Tertres:** J. Ossorio-Castillo 205br; **Château du Boisrenault:** 205bl; **Château Les Muids:** Christian Jackson 205cr; **Chartres Cathedral:** 179fbr; **Christie's Images, London:** 57b; **Bruce Coleman:** NG Blake 75bc; Denis Green 189crb; Udo Hirsch 189bl; Hans Reinhard 188bl/br; Uwe Walz 75b/br, 189br; **Comité Départemental du Tourisme du Cher:** 31cra; **Comité Régional du Tourisme, Nantes:** 226tr/b; JP Guyonneau 227tr; J Lesage 225tr, 231tl; **Comité du Tourisme de L'anjou:** 88b; JP Guyonneau 88c; **Corbis:** Xinhua Press/Gao Jing 236clb.
**Diatotale:** Château de Chenonceau 110t; **Dreamstime.com:** Alxcrs 10br; Claudio Giovanni Colombo 64-3, 160c; Davidmartyn 11tc; Richard Gunion 15bc; Konstik 14tr; Machiavel 13tc; Neierfy 14bc; Ekaterina Pokrovsky 12bl; Jose I. Soto 12tl.
**C Errath:** 30br, 186tr/cbl; **ET Archive:** 54bl, 104br; **Eurostar:** 244tl; **Mary Evans Picture Library:** 57ca, 155tl; **Explorer:** F Jalain 60cl.
**Fédération Nationale de Logis de France:** 201c; **Fontenay-le-Comte Office de Tourisme:** 230cl; **Fontevraud Abbey:** 45bl, 90clb, 91b; **Fontqombault Abbey:** Frère Eric Chevreau 151clb.
**Getty Images:** AFP 240br; **Giraudon, Paris:** 52tr/bl, 80tr/c, 139c; Bibliothèque Municipale, Laon 54–5cr; Château de Versailles *Louis XIII – Roi de France et de Navarre* after Vouet 51br, 60bl; Musée Antoine Lécuyer 138b; Musée Carnavalet, Paris *Madame Dupin de Francueil* 113tr; Musée Condé, Chantilly 56br, 112b; Musée d'Histoire et des Guerres de Vendée, Cholet *Henri de la Rochejaquelein au Combat de Cholet le 17 Octobre 1793* Emile Boutigny 73cl; Musée de Tessé, Le Mans 170tr; Musée des Beaux-Arts, Blois 173crb; Musée du Vieux Château, Laval 164b (all rights reserved); Gérard Labriet 180c; Telarci 55ca; Victoria & Albert Museum, London 99tl; **Gîtes de France:** 203ct; **Glow Images:** Emilie Chaix 68c; La Goélette: JJ Derennes *The Three Graces* Charles-André Van Loo 110br.
**Sonia Halliday Photographs:** 57tl; **Robert Harding:** 41br; Stephan Gabriel 205tr; Paolo Koba 23br; Sheila Terry 106b; **D Hodges:** 171b; **Hotel Saint Pierre:** 201tl; **Kit Houghton:** 42c; **Hulton-Deutsch Collection:** 50tr, 115tc, 138cla.
**Image Bank:** 38cla; Image de Marc 20b, 94c, 107b, 121b; **Nicolas Inman:** 234br; **Inventaire Général:** Musée du Grand-Pressigny 52cla, 108c.
**L' Atelier Gourmand:** 217tr; **L'U.Ni:** Nicholas Guiet 211cla; **La Gargouille:** 219br; **La Maison des Forestines:** 220cla;

**La Petite Auberge:** 218tr; **Le 36, Amboise:** 216bc.
**Mairie de Blois:** J-Philippe Thibaut 46b; **Maison Fleurie:** 203tr **Mansell Collection:** 34b; T Mezerette: 32cla, 33tl; **Musées d'Angers:** 22t, 55clb, 61tl, 81cra; **Collection Musée d'Art Et D'histoire de Cholet:** 61b; Studio Golder, Cholet *Jacques Cathelineau* Anne-Louis Girodet-Trioson 1824 191b; **Musée d'Arts Décoratifs Et Musée du Cheval, Château de Saumur:** 86cr; **Musée des Beaux-arts de Rennes:** Louis Deschamps *Bal à la Cour des Valois* 113cbr; **Musée des Beaux-Arts, Tours:** P Boyer *Christ in the Olive Grove* Andrea Mantegna 118b; **Musée de Blois:** J Parker 130bl; **Musées de Bourges:** Musée des Arts Décoratifs, Hôtel Lallemant *Concert Champêtre Instrumental* French-Italian School 154cl; **Musée Dobrée, Nantes:** 59cl, 195c; **Collection Musée Estève** © ADAGP/DACS: Dubout *Samsâra* Maurice Estève oil on canvas 154b; **Courtesy, Museum of Fine Arts Boston:** *Valley of the Petite Creuse* Claude Monet 1889 oil on canvas Bequest of David P Kimball In Memory of his Wife, Clara Bertram Kimball (© 1995. All rights reserved) 151br; **Musée Historique d'Orléans:** 52clb; **Musées du Mans:** 170c; **Musée des Marais Salants, Batz-Loire-Atlantique:** G Buron 181cl; **Collection du Musée de La Marine de Loire, Châteauneuf-sur-Loire (Loiret):** 37bc.
**NHPA:** Manfred Danegger 189cl; M Garwod 83b; **National Motor Museum, Beaulieu:** 61clb; **Nortre-Dame d'Orsan:** François Berraldacci 208tr.
**Orange France Telecom:** Frederic Bukajlo - abacapress.com pour Orange 238ca.
**Parc Naturel Régional du Poitevin:** 189tr; **John Parker:** 24bc, 30bl, 31tl, 40crb, 41cla/cl, 42bl, 55cra, 58clb, 59cra, 67br, 77c, 91tc, 99bc, 110cla, 114bl, 115cr, 120tr, 121cr, 125br, 130cl, 131bl, 132tl, 134tl/bl, 135tl/bl, 136tr/cl/br, 137tl/cl, 148tr, 174br, 175br, 178-179 all; **Photographers' Library:** 163b; 203b; **By kind permission from Puy du Fou:** 47t.
**Rectorat de la Cathedrale de Chartres:** 177cra; **Restaurant La Promenade:** 211br; **Runion des Musées Nationaux, Paris:** Château de Versailles *Château de Chambord* PD Martin © (Photo RMN) 138crb; **Rex Features/Sipa Press:** Riclafe 63tl; Tall 62bl; **Route Historique Jacques Cœur:** 22bl; David Rowley: 87b.
**The Science Museum/Science & Society Picture Library, London:** 60br; **SNCF - Society National des Chemins de Fer:** 242c; Jean Marc Fabro 62ca; **Spectrum Colour Library:** 141ca; **Tony Stone worldwide:** 67tl/tr; Charlie Waite 158tl; **SuperStock:** Photononstop 247cl.
**Telegraph Colour Library:** Jean-Paul Nacivet 30cla; **TipsImages:** Photononstop 246tl; **trh Pictures:** 62tr.
**Ville d'Amboise:** Mairie de la Poste 37ca; **Vins de Loire:** 116clb; **Roger Viollet:** 56bc, 141tr, Musée d'Orléans *Entrée de Jeanne. d'Arc à Orléans* Jean-Jacques Sherrer 141br.
**J Warminski:** 83t; **C Watier:** 71t, 74b; **Wildlife Matters:** 98tr, 99c and br; **WYSE Travel Confederation:** 232cr.

Front end paper: **Alamy Images:** Philippe RENAULT / Hemis (br/R). **AWL Images:** Karl Thomas (bl/R); Travel Pix Collection (tr/R). **Dreamstime.com:** Claudio Giovanni Colombo (tr/L). **Getty Images:** Gérard LABRIET (bl/L). **Glowimages:** Emilie Chaix (tl/L).

Front Jacket and Spine: **Getty Images:** Gallo Images.

All other images © Dorling Kindersley.
For further information, see: www.dkimages.com

# Phrase Book

## In Emergency

| | | |
|---|---|---|
| Help! | **Au secours!** | oh se**koor** |
| Stop! | **Arrêtez!** | aret-**ay** |
| Call a doctor! | **Appelez un médecin!** | apuh-**lay** uñ med**sañ** |
| Call an ambulance! | **Appelez une ambulance!** | apuh-**lay** oon oñboo-**loñs** |
| Call the police! | **Appelez la police!** | apuh-**lay** lah poh-**lees** |
| Call the fire brigade! | **Appelez les pompiers!** | apuh-lay leh poñ-**peeay** |
| Where is the nearest telephone? | **Où est le téléphone le plus proche?** | oo ay luh tehleh**fon** luh ploo **prosh** |
| Where is the nearest hospital? | **Où est l'hôpital le plus proche?** | oo ay l'**opee**tal luh ploo **prosh** |

## Communication Essentials

| | | |
|---|---|---|
| Yes | **Oui** | wee |
| No | **Non** | noñ |
| Please | **S'il vous plaît** | seel voo **play** |
| Thank you | **Merci** | mer-**see** |
| Excuse me | **Excusez-moi** | exkoo-**zay** mwah |
| Hello | **Bonjour** | boñ**zhoor** |
| Goodbye | **Au revoir** | oh ruh-**vwar** |
| Good night | **Bonsoir** | boñ-**swar** |
| Morning | **Le matin** | matañ |
| Afternoon | **L'après-midi** | apreh-**meedee** |
| Evening | **Le soir** | swar |
| Yesterday | **Hier** | eey**ehr** |
| Today | **Aujourd'hui** | oh-zhoor-**dwee** |
| Tomorrow | **Demain** | duh**mañ** |
| Here | **Ici** | ee-**see** |
| There | **Là** | lah |
| What? | **Quel, quelle?** | kel, kel |
| When? | **Quand?** | koñ |
| Why? | **Pourquoi?** | poor-**kwah** |
| Where? | **Où?** | oo |

## Useful Phrases

| | | |
|---|---|---|
| How are you? | **Comment allez-vous?** | kom-moñ ta**lay voo** |
| Very well, thank you. | **Très bien, merci.** | treh byañ, mer-**see** |
| Pleased to meet you. | **Enchanté de faire votre connaissance.** | oñshoñ-**tay** duh fehr votr kon-ay-**sans** |
| See you soon. | **A bientôt.** | Ah byañ-**toh** |
| That's fine. | **C'est parfait.** | say parfay |
| Where is/are…? | **Où est/sont…?** | oo ay/soñ |
| How far is it to…? | **Combien de kilomètres d'ici à…?** | kom-**byañ** duh keelo-**metr** d'ee-**see** ah |
| Which way to…? | **Quelle est la direction pour…?** | kel ay lah **deer**-ek-**syoñ** poor |
| Do you speak English? | **Parlez-vous anglais?** | par-**lay** voo oñg-**lay** |
| I'm sorry. | **Excusez-moi.** | exkoo-**zay** mwah |
| I don't understand. | **Je ne comprends pas.** | zhuh nuh kom-**proñ** pah |
| Could you speak slowly please? | **Pouvez-vous parler moins vite s'il vous plaît?** | poo-**vay** voo par-**lay** mwañ veet seel voo play |

## Useful Words

| | | |
|---|---|---|
| big | **grand** | groñ |
| small | **petit** | puh-**tee** |
| hot | **chaud** | show |
| cold | **froid** | frwah |
| good | **bon** | boñ |
| bad | **mauvais** | moh-**veh** |
| enough | **assez** | as**say** |
| well | **bien** | byañ |
| open | **ouvert** | oo-**ver** |
| closed | **fermé** | fer-**meh** |
| left | **gauche** | gohsh |
| right | **droite** | drwaht |
| straight on | **tout droit** | too drwah |
| near | **près** | preh |
| far | **loin** | lwañ |
| up | **en haut** | oñ oh |

| | | |
|---|---|---|
| down | **en bas** | oñ **bah** |
| early | **de bonne heure** | duh bon **urr** |
| late | **en retard** | oñ ruh-**tar** |
| entrance | **l'entrée** | on-**tray** |
| exit | **la sortie** | sor-**tee** |
| toilet | **les toilettes, les WC** | twah-let, vay-**see** |
| free, unoccupied | **libre** | leebr |
| free, no charge | **gratuit** | grah-**twee** |

## Making a Telephone Call

| | | |
|---|---|---|
| I'd like to place a long-distance call. | **Je voudrais faire un appel interurbain.** | zhuh voo-dreh fehruñ apel añter-oorbañ |
| I'd like to make a reverse charge call. | **Je voudrais faire une communication PCV.** | zhuh voo**dreh** fehr oon syoñ komoonikah-peh-seh-veh |
| I'll try again later. | **Je rappelerai plus tard.** | zhuh rapel-**eray** ploo tar |
| Can I leave a message? | **Est-ce que je peux laisser un message?** | es-**keh** zhuh puh leh-**say** uñ mehs**azh** |
| Hold on please. | **Ne quittez pas, s'il vous plaît.** | nuh kee-**tay** pah seel voo play |
| Could you speak up a little? | **Pouvez-vous parler un peu plus fort?** | poo-**vay** voo par-**lay** uñ puh ploo for |
| local call | **l'appel local** | ap**pel** low-**kal** |

## Shopping

| | | |
|---|---|---|
| How much does this cost? | **C'est combien s'il vous plaît?** | say kom-**byañ** seel voo play |
| I would like … | **je voudrais …** | zhuh voo-**dray** |
| Do you have? | **Est-ce que vous avez?** | es-**kuh** voo zavay |
| I'm just looking. | **Je regarde seulement.** | zhuh ruh**gar** suhl**moñ** |
| Do you take credit cards? | **Est-ce que vous acceptez les cartes de crédit?** | es-**kuh** voo zaksept-**ay** leh kart duh kreh-**dee** |
| Do you take travellers' cheques? | **Est-ce que vous acceptez les chèques de voyage?** | es-**kuh** voo zaksept-**ay** leh shek duh vway**azh** |
| What time do you open? | **A quelle heure vous êtes ouvert?** | ah kel urr voo zet oo-**ver** |
| What time do you close? | **A quelle heure vous êtes fermé?** | ah kel urr voo zet fer-**may** |
| This one. | **Celui-ci.** | suhl-wee-**see** |
| That one. | **Celui-là.** | suhl-wee-**lah** |
| expensive | **cher** | shehr |
| cheap | **pas cher, bon marché** | pah shehr, boñ mar-**shay** |
| size, clothes | **la taille** | tye |
| size, shoes | **la pointure** | pwañ-**tur** |
| white | **blanc** | bloñ |
| black | **noir** | nwahr |
| red | **rouge** | roozh |
| yellow | **jaune** | zhohwn |
| green | **vert** | vehr |
| blue | **bleu** | bluh |

## Types of Shop

| | | |
|---|---|---|
| antique shop | **le magasin d'antiquités** | maga-**zañ** d'oñteekee-**tay** |
| bakery | **la boulangerie** | booloñ-**zhuree** |
| bank | **la banque** | boñk |
| bookshop | **la librairie** | lee-**brehree** |
| butcher | **la boucherie** | boo-**shehree** |
| cake shop | **la pâtisserie** | patee-**sree** |
| cheese shop | **la fromagerie** | fromazh-**ree** |
| chemist | **la pharmacie** | farmah-**see** |
| dairy | **la crémerie** | krem-**ree** |
| department store | **le grand magasin** | groñ maga-**zañ** |
| delicatessen | **la charcuterie** | sharkoot-**ree** |
| fishmonger | **la poissonnerie** | pwasson-**ree** |
| gift shop | **le magasin de cadeaux** | maga-**zañ** duh kadoh |

| greengrocer | le marchand | mar-**shoñ** duh |
|---|---|---|
|  | de légumes | lay-**goom** |
| grocery | l'alimentation | alee-moñta-**syoñ** |
| hairdresser | le coiffeur | kwa**fuhr** |
| market | le marché | marsh-**ay** |
| newsagent | le magasin de | maga-**zañ** duh |
|  | journaux | zhoor-**no** |
| post office | la poste, | pohst, |
|  | le bureau de poste, | boo**roh** duh pohst, |
|  | le PTT | peh-teh-teh |
| shoe shop | le magasin | maga-**zañ** |
|  | de chaussures | duh show-**soor** |
| supermarket | le supermarché | soo pehr-**marshay** |
| tobacconist | le tabac | tabah |
| travel agent | l'agence | l'azhoñs |
|  | de voyages | duh vwayazh |

## Sightseeing

| abbey | l'abbaye | abay-**ee** |
|---|---|---|
| art gallery | le galerie d'art | galer-**ree** dart |
| bus station | la gare routière | gahr roo-tee-**yehr** |
| cathedral | la cathédrale | katay-**dral** |
| church | l'église | ayg**leez** |
| garden | le jardin | zhar-**dañ** |
| library | la bibliothèque | beeb**leeo**-tek |
| museum | le musée | moo-**zay** |
| railway station | la gare (SNCF) | gahr (es-en-say-ef) |
| tourist | les renseignements | roñsayn-**moñ** too- |
| information | touristiques | rees-**teek**, sandee- |
| office | le syndicat | ka d'eenee-sya**teev** |
|  | d'initiative |  |
| town hall | l'hôtel de ville | oh**tel** duh veel |
| private mansion | l'hôtel | oh**tel** |
|  | particulier | partikoo-**lyay** |
| closed for | fermeture | fehrmeh-**tur** |
| public holiday | jour férié | zhoor fehree-**ay** |

## Staying in a Hotel

| Do you have | Est-ce que vous | es-kuh voo- |
|---|---|---|
| a vacant | avez une | **zavay** oon |
| room? | chambre? | shambr |
| double room | la chambre pour | shambr poor |
|  | deux personnes | duh pehr-**son** |
| with double | avec un | avek un |
| bed | grand lit | groñň lee |
| twin room | la chambre à | shambr ah |
|  | deux lits | duh lee |
| single room | la chambre pour | shambr poor |
|  | une personne | oon pehr-**son** |
| room with a | la chambre avec | shambr avek |
| bath, shower | salle de bains, | sal duh bañ, |
|  | une douche | oon doosh |
| porter | le garçon | gar-**soñ** |
| key | la clef | klay |
| I have a | J'ai fait une | zhay fay oon |
| reservation. | réservation. | rayzehrva-**syoñ** |

## Eating Out

| Have you | Avez-vous une | avay-**voo** oon |
|---|---|---|
| got a table? | table libre? | tahbl leebr |
| I want to | Je voudrais | zhuh voo-**dray** |
| reserve | réserver | rayzehr-**vay** |
| a table. | une table. | oon tahbl |
| The bill | L'addition s'il | l'adee-**syoñ** seel |
| please. | vous plaît. | voo **play** |
| I am a | Je suis | zhuh swee |
| vegetarian. | végétarien. | vezhay-**tehryañ** |
| Waitress/ | Madame, | mah-**dam**, |
| waiter | Mademoiselle/ | mah-demwahzel/ |
|  | Monsieur | muh-**syuh** |
| menu | le menu, la carte | men-**oo**, kart |
| fixed-price | le menu à | men-**oo** ah |
| menu | prix fixe | pree feeks |
| cover charge | le couvert | koo-**vehr** |
| wine list | la carte des vins | kart-deh vañ |
| glass | le verre | vehr |
| bottle | la bouteille | boo-**tay** |

| knife | le couteau | koo-**toh** |
|---|---|---|
| fork | la fourchette | for-**shet** |
| spoon | la cuillère | kwee-**yehr** |
| breakfast | le petit | puh-**tee** |
|  | déjeuner | deh-**zhuh-nay** |
| lunch | le déjeuner | deh-**zhuh-nay** |
| dinner | le dîner | dee-**nay** |
| main course | le plat principal | plah prañsee-**pal** |
| starter, first | l'entrée, le hors- | l'oñ-**tray**, or- |
| course | d'œuvre | duhvr |
| dish of the day | le plat du jour | plah doo zhoor |
| wine bar | le bar à vin | bar ah vañ |
| café | le café | ka-**fay** |
| rare | saignant | **say**-noñ |
| medium | à point | ah **pwañ** |
| well done | bien cuit | byañ **kwee** |

## Menu Decoder

| l'agneau | l'an**yoh** | lamb |
|---|---|---|
| l'ail | l'eye | garlic |
| la banane | ba**nan** | banana |
| le beurre | burr | butter |
| la bière | bee-**yehr** | beer |
| la bière | bee-**yehr** | draught beer |
| pression | pres-**syoñ** |  |
| le bifteck, | beef-**tek**, stek | steak |
| le steack |  |  |
| le bœuf | buhf | beef |
| bouilli | boo-**yee** | boiled |
| le café | kah-**fay** | coffee |
| le canard | kan**ar** | duck |
| le chocolat | shoko-**lah** | chocolate |
| le citron | see-**troñ** | lemon |
| le citron | see-**troñ** | fresh lemon juice |
| pressé | press-**eh** |  |
| les crevettes | kruh-**vet** | prawns |
| les crustacés | **kroos**-ta-say | shellfish |
| cuit au four | kweet oh foor | baked |
| le dessert | deh-**ser** | dessert |
| l'eau minérale | l'oh **meeney**-ral | mineral water |
| les escargots | leh zes-kar-**goh** | snails |
| les frites | freet | chips |
| le fromage | from-**azh** | cheese |
| le fruit frais | frwee freh | fresh fruit |
| les fruits de mer | frwee duh mer | seafood |
| le gâteau | gah-**toh** | cake |
| la glace | glas | ice, ice cream |
| grillé | gree-**yay** | grilled |
| le homard | om**ahr** | lobster |
| l'huile | l'weel | oil |
| le jambon | zhoñ-**boñ** | ham |
| le lait | leh | milk |
| les légumes | lay-**goom** | vegetables |
| la moutarde | moo-**tard** | mustard |
| l'œuf | l'uf | egg |
| les oignons | leh zon**yoñ** | onions |
| les olives | leh zo**leev** | olives |
| l'orange | l'oroñzh | orange |
| l'orange | l'oroñzh | fresh orange juice |
| pressée | press-**eh** |  |
| le pain | pan | bread |
| le petit pain | puh-**tee** pañ | roll |
| poché | posh-**ay** | poached |
| le poisson | pwah-**ssoñ** | fish |
| le poivre | pwavr | pepper |
| la pomme | pom | apple |
| les pommes | pom-duh | potatoes |
| de terre | tehr |  |
| le porc | por | pork |
| le potage | poh-**tazh** | soup |
| le poulet | poo-**lay** | chicken |
| le riz | ree | rice |
| rôti | row-**tee** | roast |
| la sauce | sohs | sauce |
| la saucisse | soh**sees** | sausage, fresh |
| sec | sek | dry |
| le sel | sel | salt |

| | | |
|---|---|---|
| **la soupe** | soop | soup |
| **le sucre** | sookr | sugar |
| **le thé** | tay | tea |
| **le toast** | toast | toast |
| **la viande** | vee-**yand** | meat |
| **le vin blanc** | vañ **bloñ** | white wine |
| **le vin rouge** | vañ **roozh** | red wine |
| **le vinaigre** | vee**naygr** | vinegar |

## Numbers

| | | |
|---|---|---|
| 0 | **zéro** | zeh-**roh** |
| 1 | **un, une** | uñ, oon |
| 2 | **deux** | duh |
| 3 | **trois** | trwah |
| 4 | **quatre** | katr |
| 5 | **cinq** | sañk |
| 6 | **six** | sees |
| 7 | **sept** | set |
| 8 | **huit** | weet |
| 9 | **neuf** | nerf |
| 10 | **dix** | dees |
| 11 | **onze** | oñz |
| 12 | **douze** | dooz |
| 13 | **treize** | trehz |
| 14 | **quatorze** | ka**torz** |
| 15 | **quinze** | kañz |
| 16 | **seize** | sehz |
| 17 | **dix-sept** | dees-**set** |
| 18 | **dix-huit** | dees-**weet** |
| 19 | **dix-neuf** | dees-**nerf** |
| 20 | **vingt** | vañ |
| 30 | **trente** | tront |
| 40 | **quarante** | karo**ñt** |
| 50 | **cinquante** | sañk**oñt** |
| 60 | **soixante** | swas**oñt** |
| 70 | **soixante-dix** | swasoñt-**dees** |
| 80 | **quatre-vingts** | katr-**vañ** |
| 90 | **quatre-vingts-dix** | katr-vañ-**dees** |
| 100 | **cent** | soñ |
| 1,000 | **mille** | meel |

## Time

| | | |
|---|---|---|
| one minute | **une minute** | oon mee-**noot** |
| one hour | **une heure** | oon urr |
| half an hour | **une demi-heure** | oon **duh-mee** urr |
| Monday | **lundi** | luñ-**dee** |
| Tuesday | **mardi** | mar-**dee** |
| Wednesday | **mercredi** | mehrkruh-**dee** |
| Thursday | **jeudi** | zhuh-**dee** |
| Friday | **vendredi** | voñdruh-**dee** |
| Saturday | **samedi** | sam-**dee** |
| Sunday | **dimanche** | dee-**moñsh** |

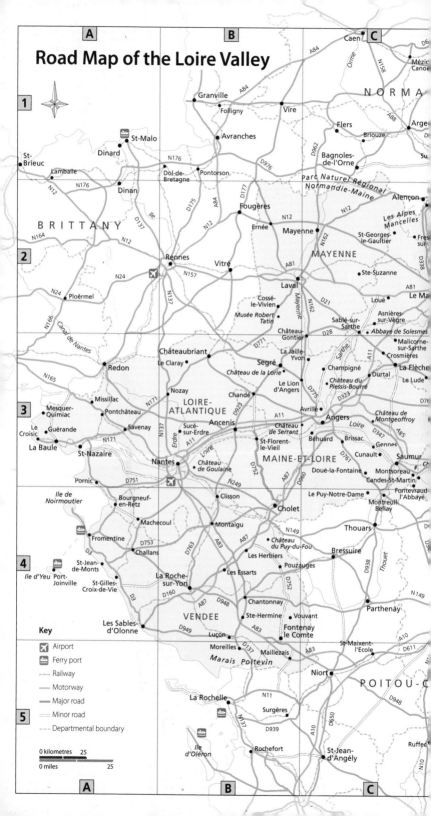